# WILLIAM SHAKESPEARE:

## A POPULAR LIFE

## Other Shakespeare Titles from Applause

ACTING SHAKESPEARE  John Gielgud

ACTING IN SHAKESPEAREAN COMEDY Janet Suzman

ACTING IN TRAGEDY Brian Cox

ACTING WITH SHAKESPEARE: THE COMEDIES
Janet Suzman

AN ACTOR AND HIS TIME John Gielgud

THE ACTOR AND THE TEXT Cicely Berry

APPLAUSE SHAKESPEARE LIBRARY

APPLAUSE FIRST FOLIO OF SHAKESPEARE

THE COMPLEAT WKS OF WILLM SHKSPR
(ABRIDGED)

FIRST FOLIO EDITIONS

FREE SHAKESPEARE John Russell Brown

RALPH RICHARDSON: AN ACTOR'S LIFE
Garry O'Connor

RECYCLING SHAKESPEARE Charles Marowitz

SHAKESPEARE'S PLAYS IN PERFORMANCE
John Russell Brown

SHAKESCENES John Russell Brown

SHAKESPEARE'S FIRST TEXTS Neil Freeman

SOLILOQUY: The Shakespeare Monologues
Men & Women

WORKING SHAKESPEARE Video Master Classes with
Cicely Berry

# WILLIAM SHAKESPEARE:

## A POPULAR LIFE

## Garry O'Connor

Grief fills the room up of my absent child,
Lies in his bed, walks up and down with me,
Puts on his pretty looks, repeats his words,
Remembers me of all his gracious parts
Staffs out his vacant garments with his form;
Then have I reason to be fond of grief.
— *King John*

**APPLAUSE**
**NEW YORK • LONDON**

William Shakespeare: A Popular Life,
Expanded Updated and Revised by Garry O'Connor
© 2000 by Garry O'Connor
ISBN 1-55783-401-6

### Library of Congress Cataloging-in-Publication Data

Library of Congress Catalogue Card Number: 99-068296


### British Cataloging in Publication Data

A catalogue record of this book is available from the British Library


APPLAUSE BOOKS
1841 Broadway
Suite 1100
New York, NY 10023
Phone (212)765-7880
Fax (212)765-7875

COMBINED BOOK SERVICES LTD.
Units I/K, Paddock Wood Dist. Centre
Paddock Wood,
Tonbridge, Kent TN12 6 UU
Phone (44) 01892 837171
Fax (44) 01892 837272


10    9    8    7    6    5    4    3    2    1


PRINTED IN CANADA

To Ion Trewin, and in memory of
his father, J. C. Trewin (1908-1990)

# CONTENTS

# A Note on Money

Estimates of money values between the years 1600 and 2000 are notoriously variable and undefinable. Multiply by 200, some say, but others suggest by at least 1000. The average wage of a manual worker is about 1200 times more; the price of the dearest seat in a London theatre around 800 times higher, the price of a chicken 500. To buy property in central London or land near Stratford would be at least several thousand times more expensive. A play could earn its author, in early Jacobean times, perhaps 500 respectable tavern lunches, average cost sixpence a meal; the £7 mentioned on page 69 would be £1400 to £7000 in modern purchasing power. Queen Elizabeth's £400,000 debt (page 213) would be £80 to £400 million.

Original drawing of William Shakespeare
by Nicholas Garland, 1991

# Introduction

What I have attempted to achieve in the pages that follow, is a popular, imaginatively told life of Shakespeare. My belief is that no such work, with its potential wide appeal exists, yet Shakespeare's influence and fame are greater now, with the success of the Oscar-winning film *Shakespeare in Love,* than at any time during history.

Shakespeare is universal, and in all definitions of the word, popular:

Popular,a. (sb)1490 [-Afr.populer,Ofr. Populier (later and mod. Populaire) or L. Popularis, f. Populus people].
1. Law. Affecting, concerning, or open to all or any of the people: public; esp. in *action p.* 2. Of, pertaining to, or consisting of the common people, or the people as a whole; constituted or carried by the people 1548. B. Plebeian – 1691. 3. Full of people; populous, crowded – 1911. 4. Adapted to the understanding, taste, or means of ordinary people 1573. 5. Studious of, or designed to gain, the favour of the common people; devoted to the cause of the people – 1771. 6. Finding favour with the people, or with many people; favourite, acceptable, pleasing 1608. 7. Prevalent among, or accepted by the people generally; common, general; (of sickness) epidemic 1603. S.O.E.D.

Many attempts have been made to deliver the whole man, in spite of the meagre historical record. I depict him as he has not been shown before, in a biography that is based on and rooted in the conception that Shakespeare is a contemporary figure – belonging as much to our age as to his own. Therefore we, in an epoch which began in the early 1960s at Stratford Upon Avon, his birthplace, with the productions of *The Wars of the Roses* and with *King Lear* with Paul Scofield in the title role in Peter Brook's production (and with the earlier publication of *Shakespeare Our Contemporary* by the Czech critic Jan Kott), hold in our hearts as many clues as to what the playwright was like, if not more, as can be found in history, or in the works themselves.

In researching this book therefore, first of all I have consulted and interviewed a selection of the best Shakespearian minds and interpreters of our own age. Most of those who have been deeply involved in making Shakespeare's plays live have formed insights, if only in their private thoughts, into what he was really like. In interviewing this whole range of people I have included the views and ideas of others such as doctors, philosophers, writers etc. who have had contact with Shakespeare's works, and I have drawn on their thoughts and feelings, however speculative. My aim has been to give Shakespeare a life, not only as a historical figure who can be brought to life, but the dimension of one who is still living. To do this I have dropped the usual tentative approach of scholars (the "might's", the "could have's" and "may have's"). Above all I have gone to the plays and poems to attempt to uncover the secret Shakespeare. By these various means I have attempted to bridge, in the words of that most reliable Shakespeare scholar, Samuel Schoenbaum, the "vertiginous expanse between the sublimity of the subject and the mundane inconsequence of the documentary record."

# FIRST PART

# CONSUMMATUM EST

# Blessed is the Womb

In the early summer of 1585, a short time after celebrating his twenty-first birthday, William Shakespeare left home. Forsaking his wife and young family – or so his wife Anne felt – Shakespeare was leaving the crowded provincial home in Henley Street where they had been living with his parents and brothers. He might never return.

But Anne would be well provided for by her mother-in-law, while not much more than a mile away, in Shottery, her brothers and half-brothers (her father had died four years before) were as concerned as ever for her safety and well-being. They had on a previous occasion, in 1582, pledged large sums – half the value of a fair-sized property – as surety when their twenty-six-year-old kinswoman was betrothed to the eighteen-year-old Stratford yeoman's son who had made her pregnant. Now, while he was away, they would guard her progeny as well as her honour.

The eldest son of Mary and John Shakespeare had a highly complicated nature. William had many feminine traits which had not, unusually at that time in a young man's upbringing, been suppressed. Having borne and lost two daughters before he was conceived, his mother Mary had in large part expected – dreaded as well as hoped – that her third child would be a girl. Like Henry VIII, John Shakespeare, a glover, having fathered two female offspring, was impatient for a male heir. William at his birth was acclaimed and embraced by his father, while his mother wished on him a residue of the guilt, grief and longing she felt for her lost daughters. These feelings became powerfully and unconsciously embedded in his nature: no wonder that later the poet will cry for lost children, at the very end for lost daughters. Each time his mother was pregnant again, on some five occasions at least after his own birth, the son had strongly identified with her, almost as if the child were his own.

His father, on the other hand, vigilant for signs of effeminacy in his son, had applauded every manifestation in William of aggressive, competitive behaviour; masculine drive, warlike vigour; cynicism and cruelty bred of the extremes of success and failure. Until he was twelve years old William did not experience directly any of the pain and woe of the decline in his family's fortunes, but he had seen and heard their effects; had seen his mother's modest inheritance whittled away by his father's prodigal behaviour and his reckless transactions, however often these stemmed from a good and helpful nature. Dwarfed by his father's overreaching, William had stood often in his shadow, observing his effect on others, especially on his mother.

The family was reduced to the status of outcasts, although not forced from the Henley Street home, and William, at twelve or thirteen the eldest son, had placed on him an even heavier burden of expectation than before: to recoup the family's wealth and restore its broken honour. So when, after a three or four years' absence from home, this warm-blooded and lusty "mother's glass" (in the words of Sonnet 3), who called back for his father the lovely April of his Mary's prime, had responded to that father's desperate need for help by getting big with child the daughter of their old friend and neighbour Richard Hathaway, John Shakespeare saw it as an act of betrayal. Once when he was in debt John Shakespeare had shored up that same Hathaway; now, considering Anne's advanced age, what William had done seemed a further and unnecessary deed of charity.

Crushed by the growth in his father of a dangerous, self-pitying invective, by his mother's silent reproaches, William's nature had become rawly exposed. A "sensual fault" had ambushed his young days, and he was suddenly and overwhelmingly "shamed by that which I bring forth". In the extreme sensitivity to guilt which had been awoken, he saw his mother's virtue "rudely strumpeted," for which he took the blame.

Guilt from this first pregnancy had stuck to William Shakespeare, although he tried later and unceasingly to detach it from him, or dissolve it. It was as well he did not manage this, even when, twenty years later, he wrote *Measure for Measure* , in which he was able to tackle the premature pregnancy head-on. Denied, or perhaps ultimately uninterested in, confession to a priest, he came over the years to turn his plays into secret and disguised confessionals, in which he could play both confessor and penitent. In *Measure for Measure* he could play the Duke, the "great member." whose phallic justice is shown at the end of the play as re-entering the female city of Vienna with the power of vaginal penetration. He could play the fornicator Claudio, encountering darkness as a bride, and the puritan hypocrite Angelo, unshaped and rendered "unpregnant" by the act of copulation. He could play Isabella, owner of herself, paragon of virtue, who will not compromise with Angelo's pent up lust even to save her brother's life.

But joy mingled with shame in Shakespeare's dual nature. He could live simultaneously at both ends of the same experience. Anne's first pregnancy and the birth of their daughter Susanna had been joyful, too: he had found self-approval in being a husband, with a wife and child. For Shakespeare, women were absolutes. It was men who changed. And best men were moulded out of faults. With Anne a nursing mother for the fist three years of their marriage Shakespeare felt secure, as the childhood feelings he had had about his mother's pregnancies were reawakened. Anne was nurtured and protected by both Shakespeare and his mother as few women were in Elizabethan times.

Even before he was aware of its creative implications, Shakespeare had absorbed the whole mythology, as well as practical aspects of child-bearing. He suffered from womb-envy to some degree, and in his future writing there was always, underlying his creative effort, a connection with the huge, physically creative act of which he would never be capable. When in his later self-projection as the Duke in *Measure for Measure* he proposes to Isabella that she join his plan to "frame" Mariana in bed with Angelo, he thinks instinctively, in terms of conception and child-bearing. Will she be able to "carry" this, he asks Isabella. At the end of the play the "motion" the Duke has towards Isabella which imports her good, so that "What's mine is yours, and what is yours is mine." is significantly sexual as well as matrimonial.

The medical terminology of the time linked the brain to the womb: cavities in the brain were little wombs or bellies – ventricles. For "teeming" Renaissance minds it was natural to relate the speculative enquiry as to man's nature to wider religious accounts, notably that of Genesis, but also to stories of the Hellenic gods, most speculatively to the birth of Athene, goddess of Wisdom, from the head of Zeus. Works of literature were likened to newborn children, but with the difference that they were born with the immediate power of speech. "My brain I'll prove the female to my soul", says Richard, son of the Black Prince, conceiving his brain as a woman ready to receive sperm in the act of coition.

Shakespeare had encountered, during the first weeks of Anne's pregnancy with firstborn Susanna, intimations of all the future black ink of shame and stress – as well as some relief at authorizing his trespass. But he had also felt resentment at being "hooked" by an older woman. With her second pregnancy the strong emotions he had felt were doubled; the creative ventricles of his brain had been stretched to bursting point. Yet as the belly of his spouse swelled abnormally large with visible evidence of twins, Shakespeare had also felt terror. Without modern medical knowledge as reassurance, his apprehension at the prodigality of nature deepened as the moment of birth approached.

For each pregnancy there had been compensations. They had then none of the puritan or later Victorian inhibitions about intercourse during pregnancy, and this was a time when Anne's sexuality had matched her procreative energy – although she also had a two-year-old tugging at her attention. In *The Winter's Tale* Hermione's pregnancy is to her a source of acute erotic sensation, into which Leontes' jealousy feeds. William had taken great delight in Anne big-bellied, like a sail with the wanton wind, both in bed and watching her "rich with my young squire", as she waddied about "pretty and with swimming gait." The seedbed of his fancy was by now thoroughly sown with wonder at the demesnes that lie adjacent to a woman's "white thighs." His adolescent feelings would be perpetuated in fancies, thick and swarming with sexual implication and ambiguity, when not with specific and concrete images. Not by any means the first man to be so fascinated, Shakespeare would never lose his near-obsession with woman's procreative equipment.

So besotted with creativity had he grown during Anne's second pregnancy that, had anything gone wrong, it might seriously have jeopardized, through shock, his whole future life. Even Mary Queen of Scots, surrounded with the care and panoply of majesty, had miscarried of twins when twenty-five. That the twins were not untimely ripped by miscarriage from their mother's womb is evidence both of Anne's strength and the security of the Stratford home. The safe delivery of their twins was Anne's greatest gift to Shakespeare's future fertility of wit: he came to impregnate his own characters so that, themselves duplicating cells, they grew autonomous in their power of augmentation, of hatching plots as well as extending themselves through their own progeny.

"My muse labours,/And thus she is delivered," says Iago. "'Tis very pregnant," says Angelo. "The jewel that we find, we stoop and take't." Shakespeare had not been disappointed. Childbirth was a rich pleasure. He called what he considered his first major literary effort, *Venus and Adonis,* the "heir of my invention". "New plays and maidenheads are near akin," was almost the last sentiment he uttered as a tired and worn-out writer. After his death, when describing their editorial function, his editors Heminges and Condell likened his plays to orphans which they were offering to the reader "cured and perfect of their limbs as he conceived them."

The safe delivery of the twins was a miracle. And perhaps even more extraordinary, on a par with the most unusual expression and oddity of the Renaissance spirit, was the rare, baroque differentiation in their sexuality. Similar though they were in appearance: "One face, one voice, one habit, and two persons, / A natural perspective, that is and is not," they bore different sexual organs. Here was the greatest paradox of all. Within the astonishing similarity resided an even more startling difference. "How have you made division of yourself?" asks Antonio of Sebastian in *Twelfth Night.* Close to his heart Shakespeare could nurture a living contradiction: his twins Hamnet and Judith made him aware both of the essential unity of nature, and yet how, with the addition or subtraction of one feature, the nature of being could be transformed into its opposite.

But now, the sweetest consummation of his marriage over, Shakespeare was called to the wars. "No man's too good to serve's Prince," says Feeble in *Henry IV Part Two:* "he that dies this year is quit for the next." Shakespeare was levied to fight, and perhaps might be looking to make as many holes in the enemy's "battle" as he had done "in a woman's petticoat."

# Rage and Swell

Desmond McCarthy said, in a memorable image, that trying to work out Shakespeare's personality was like looking at a very dark picture under glass. "At first you see nothing, then you begin to recognise features and then you recognise them as your own." To begin as I do with the assertion that Shakespeare left his true biography in his plays and poems, I have to be clear about separating Shakespeare from myself. While A.L. Rowse has temptingly said that all writers often speak through their characters, the truth is that sometimes they do, and sometimes they don't. Some of Shakespeare's characters are purely fictional, and have nothing to do with him.

Yet in each of his plays and poems there is a strong presence of the same man. There are continual trademarks of humour, character, thought or feeling which are individual and distinctive. Giovanni Morelli, the Italian art critic, applied himself mainly to the problem of attribution: his formula for the identification of a picture is that you do not look at the overall style. You do not apply yourself to the central exalted parts, but that an artist's methods were tantamount to a signature. The trivial details assume importance.

Shakespeare becomes therefore most identifiable to some, such as the director Jonathan Miller, in his off-duty wit: when Touchstone turns to Audrey in *As You Like It* he says to the Duke, "An ill-favoured thing, sir, but mine own;" when Lear says to the near –naked Edgar: "You, sir, I entertain for one of my hundred, only I do not like the fashion of your garments. You will say they are Persian," it is unmistakably the same recognisable voice.

For Iris Murdoch it was the supreme spiritual quality which belongs only to Shakespeare. "If you are looking for being," she said, "you will find it in the light, the reality and fundamental truth, which shines everywhere in Shakespeare."

This question of being, and the mysteries of Shakespeare's emotional and artistic identity are to be found, or at least implied and listened to, in what Peter Brook calls, in the context of directing Shakespeare, "the secret play... which is hidden and formless and resists analysis, but whose presence can be felt." This is what, through my own experience, I am trying to uncover: the secret play of Shakespeare's own being. "He divined the plan of his whole make-up," Ted Hughes has eloquently stated, "and projected it complete."

But uncovering the plan of this make-up, assuming it was there and that he was not an instinctive, inspired romantic genius, or an untutored, unlettered country bumpkin, (as some would have us believe), or that he was not himself but someone else, is a risky business. He, most of all, has issued the warnings: "I am that I am," he says in Sonnet 121, in a sequence that is surely an autobiography of a kind, although a most ambiguous and veiled one with most of the clues lost in time. "And they that level/At my abuses reckon up their own." Calling up his spirit from the vastly deep is fraught with danger. Hotspur's riposte to Mortimer, who claims he can raise spirits, might well prove the epitaph for an attempt to bring him to life: "Why so can I, or so can any man;/But will they come when you do call for them?"

So it is with these warnings and a sense of the awesomeness of the task I have set myself that I engage my imagination in the struggle to make Shakespeare live – and to make him convincing.

The contemporary aspect of my quest began in London, in the White Tower, a comfortable, Old World Greek restaurant on the corner of Percy Street, Soho. The distinguished actor sitting opposite me has, like Shakespeare, been described as anonymous and invisible. As Shakespeare did as a playwright, this man, has spent a lifetime putting a bit of himself, as well as not putting any of himself, into the parts he has played. It is with him, after months of reading and more formal research, that I have chosen to start my search for the Great Invisible.

My lunch companion has told me before we met that he really has "nothing imaginative, or even sensible to say about Shakespeare," and that he cannot even be described as a Shakespearian actor, having appeared in only three of his plays over the previous thirty-seven years. Of course, he added in an offhand way, "You might stimulate me to a new interest." This is off-puttingly Shakespearian.

Yet within moments of sitting down with him, I become transfixed by his description of what was for him authentically the face of Shakespeare: he had seen it some forty-odd years before, a portrait in an oldish gilt frame hanging on the wall of a smart West End flat. There was no doubt in his mind. The eyes were red-rimmed, as if the man read a lot – "not at all that austere thing on a plinth in Leicester Square" – the nose with dents left in it by spectacles. The subject was "grey-haired, advanced in years: autumnal. He breaks into a characteristic half-laugh, then quickly becomes serious again. "Perhaps you ought to track it down," he says. "Oh yes" – his eyes have conjured up a vivid memory – "and the right hand was raised, holding a quill pen"

At this point the actor, whose name is Alec Guinness, blows out smoke from a Silk Cut cigarette. "It was for me" – he stops again, then says very deliberately, "a convincing face…"

"I'm grateful for the fact that we know so little about his life," says Jonathan Miller, who likens knowing about Shakespeare to the situation of having the playwright present at rehearsal: "There is a certain sense where the presence of the author is inhibitory."

Yet I do see Shakespeare ever-present at his own rehearsals. "Secretly," writes Caryl Brahms and S.J. Simon in their 1941 *No Bed for Bacon*, which has recently come into prominence again, indeed under scrutiny for the many similarities between it and the screen play of the 1998 film *Shakespeare in Love,* Shakespeare was a little flattered at the way "his players took it for granted that he could supervise the rehearsals, rewrite the scenes, learn his own parts, alter everyone else's, be stool-shifter, prompter, and alarms heard off, keep an eye on the receipts, pay compliments to noble patrons, be available for any dinner-party in any part of the country, and on top of this, extract a masterpiece, virgin and complete, from under his ruff the moment it was called for."

The novelist Margaret Drabble calls the factual vacuum, the lack of documentation, a need of the poet's: "I feel he didn't want one to know about him." Barbara Everett, Shakespeare critic, endorses this: "You have to have the theory that had there been more to know about him, it would have been known."

It is hard to believe Shakespeare had much time for scholars. The pedant, the pedagogue, the dissector, the analyst, the critic, even the logician, is largely a figure of fun in his plays. Magicians (scientists) just about pass. He knew the nature of madness. He would probably, had he ever known of them, have been appalled at the thought of the many thousands of books about him.

I am sure he would never for a moment have collaborated in the writing of his life: he made this so elaborately ordinary he wanted it to pass unnoticed. We know more interesting things about Marlowe and Ben Jonson because they got into trouble with the authorities. Shakespeare, the quiet observer, kept his nose clean. He cultivated a stereotyped image of himself. He passed as Everyman. He covered his tracks so well it is not unreasonable to assume that his secrecy was deliberate and calculated. Perhaps he knew from the start that his need for invisibility and anonymity was a crucial, if not the saving quality of his gift.

The director John Barton, fierce protector of Shakespeare's ambiguity and anonymity, goes further: "It is impossible," he glowers from preposterously baggy eyes; "To begin with, in historical terms, it adds up to fuck-all." Judi Dench calls Barton "the Merlin of Shakespeare." Trevor Nunn, as well as one or two others, says he imagines Shakespeare to have been rather like John Barton. (These, and others like them, form the chorus of this book.)

William Shakespeare was born, at least according to tradition, on Friday 23 April, St George's Day, 1564; but it may have been another day in the same week, because this speculation is based on the record of his being christened, as "Gulielmus filius Johannes Shakspere." at Stratford parish church on 26 April of that year by the forty-year-old Christ Church graduate and vicar of Stratford, John Bretchgirdle. "Shakspere," "Shagspere," "Shaxspere," even "Shakeshafte", are but some of the spellings of his fluctuating name. Nicholas Rowe, who prefaced the first critical edition of Shakespeare's plays, published in 1709, with a short introductory life, states that John Shakespeare, William's father, was a wool dealer, and that he had ten children. The records, however, give the elder Shakespeare's trade as glover, although he did buy a "woolshop" in Henley Street, Stratford, in 1556. He and Mary Arden had eight children: their first, Joan (I), probably died at birth, but from other accounts she may have lived as long as ten years, until the year before the second Joan was born, in 1559. The Shakespeares' second child, Margaret, lived only five months and died almost exactly a year before William Shakespeare was born. Two years after William came Gilbert; then after Joan another sister, Anne, who lived seven and a half years; finally Richard (born 1574) and Edmund (born 1580).

The stones, the architectural layout, the spacious tree-lined streets and squares of Stratford, the river landscapes, became a permanent backcloth to the fifty-two years of Shakespeare's life. The town of Stratford had been built by the Bishop of Worcester as a housing speculation at an old ford on the river Avon in the early fourteenth century: it had high rents, but was exempt from feudal slavery, so an enterprising community of tradespeople and craftsmen had flourished, ranged in streets that focused on imposing central buildings: a chapel, a guildhall, an almshouse, a school (built at the beginning of the fifteenth century). The sumptuous new, mainly stone bridge across the Avon, downstream from the ford, had fourteen great arches in the middle and smaller ones at each end carrying a causeway; under the eighteenth arch and when in flood, the water has a distinctive motion:

> As through an arch the violent roaring tide
> Outruns the eye that doth behold his haste,
> Yet in the eddy boundeth in his pride
> Back to the strait that forced him on so fast,
> In rage sent out, recall'd in rage being past;
>    Even so his sighs, his sorrows, make a saw,
>    To push grief on, and back the same grief draw.

As in this passage describing Collatine's grief when he finds his wife Lucrece has been raped, the young Shakespeare interiorized the violence of the emotions he felt: he already looked for their alleviation and release in the phenomena of the natural world.

In Stratford well-to-do merchants, still an expanding class throughout Shakespeare's early life, made up the upper echelons of society, and some were as rich as the Cloptons and the Grevilles, the local grandees. Craftsmen, their apprentices and shopkeepers, merchants and artisans, even labourers filled the numerous small houses which, even then, were owned independently.

The landed aristocracy who hunted, ruled, made war or managed their estates, made up about two per cent of the population of England. When William was very small he would see these landowners ride into Stratford once or twice a week to conduct business in the Gild, or as local JPs to administer justice. Society was clear-cut in its divisions. Below the peerage and gentry were ranged the "yeomen" – substantial farmers; middling and smaller farmers were called husbandmen, while the main agricultural workers were the labourers or cottagers; but also there were milkmaids, poulterers, shepherds and many others. Unlike today, the countryside supported the great majority of the population, which included rural craftsmen of all kinds.

Shakespeare's Stratford, no less than the surrounding country-side, boasted its large numbers of beggars. One Mary Simpson, dubbed "blind wench", lived in and around Stratford for twenty-five years before a citizen paid for her admission to the almshouse next to the house in Henley Street. Throughout Shakespeare's childhood, begging children – although spared the branding and hanging of more serious offences – were whipped and stocked like adults and could be arrested by anyone of "higher calling".

Yet the better-off had to take care: the poor could retaliate with curses. Shakespeare believed early in the powerful and dramatic effect of a curse: John of Gaunt, Lear, the Witches in *Macbeth*, Caliban, among many other imprecators and denouncers, employ this everyday currency, the weapon God gave the weak. Curses could work if those who had resort to them had just cause: the beggar would turn his spite on you if you failed to drop a coin in his cap: hostile minds could cause physical harm. The Protestant authorities forbade such blasphemies: the popular superstitious mind rooted in more primitive Catholicism held fast to the power of malediction, or of the blessing. God could shorten the lives of your enemies.

Vagrants in Shakespeare's time also formed a whole closely knit society, held together by supernatural codes and alternative powers, of witchcraft, diabolism, crime and psychic abnormality. They often moved in a nether world of ghosts and painted visions, spectres, monsters. Remember, there was no street lighting. The day began with daylight and died as the light fell. The moon, in one of its phases, would guide you to dinner. The dark world, the world of alternative powers, seized control of that vast area of life denied the civilized: people of that world were dangerous. As Falstaff says in *The Merry Wives of Windsor*, "They are fairies. He that speaks to them shall die."

All the primitive forms of these people played on the early mind and imagination of Shakespeare. "The country gives me proof and precedent," says Edgar in *King Lear*,

> Of Bedlam beggars who with roaring voices
> Strike in their numbed and mortifièd arms
> Pins, wooden pricks, nails, sprigs of rosemary,
> And with this horrible object from low farms,
> Poor pelting villages, sheep-cotes and mills
> Sometime with lunatic bans, sometime with prayers
> Enforce their charity.

Edgar himself has to take on the disguise of an Abram man to fulfil the power of good within him. Many of these men were dispossessed former monks or servants of the dissolved monasteries, who could only enact their former security in grotesque parody.

Shakespeare's grandfather had borne arms for Henry VII and may have fought at Bosworth; his son John Shakespeare's view of life had been formed during the turbulent years of Henry VIII's breach with Rome – a time typified by the public brawl: arguments quickly became quarrels, with daggers always at hand. The England of that epoch was a rough, superstitious, excitable and volatile society, full of factions, mobs and group uprisings.

John Shakespeare, a powerful man, broad of character, sturdy if not burly in build, lived seventy-one years, an exceptionally long life. His wife, Mary Arden, who also survived till nearly seventy, was an accomplished and educated woman (we discount the cross with which she signed her name, as this did not signify illiteracy). "It is an undoubted fact that all remarkable men have had remarkable mothers, and have respected them in after life as their best friends," comments Charles Dickens's Mr Tetterby. Not always true by any means, but in Shakespeare's case, yes. This manifested itself particularly in Mary Arden's powers of observation, and her instinctive understanding of the working of the emotions.

Mary Arden married beneath her, but only to a slight degree. John Shakespeare, as a migrant husbandman, was one of the new commercial classes, a glove manufacturer and merchant who still farmed and who became a town official, one of the thirteen or fourteen aldermen who ran Stratford. But John Shakespeare – the prototype of the gentleman in Shakespeare's early mind and in his subsequent plays (culminating in Falstaff) – was bigger than his

Stratford boots (or gloves). Son of a farmer who lived in Snitterfield, a few miles outside Stratford, he had a happy-go-lucky nature; in the country he neglected his hedges, in the town he was fined for dumping rubbish in the street. As he dealt in hides of livestock a rumour grew later that he was a butcher, but he was not licensed as such.

An instinctive grasp of family chemistry belonged to Shakespeare from the very start, as he had been imbued with the smell of the compounds for drying, curing, tanning and dyeing used by his father. A Woodstock master glover tells me that making gloves is a process of taking one product and turning it into another. "Forget the craft aspect – basically it is a trade. Glovers come from the lowest of the low."

John Shakespeare became a physical pillar of Stratford, first in the function of ale-taster, an important civic post in a brewery town, then as one of four constables, a post to which he was appointed in 1558, the year of Elizabeth's accession. To be a constable he must have possessed forcefulness, size, and a sense of authority: he must have known how to use a sword and would have had to deal with dangerous malefactors. Large, convivial, wielding a "glover's paring knife" (as Mistress Quickly says of Master Slender in *The Merry Wives of Windsor*), he suited the quick-paced and handsome county town of Stratford and for half his life he thrived there.

In the convulsions of the realm in which his early years had passed, he had probably taken part in Henry VIII's military adventures, either against France or against Scotland, which debauched the wealth built up earlier in Henry's reign, as well as squandered the treasures and riches acquired from the dissolution of the monasteries. The elder Shakespeare may also have been involved in treasonable exercises against the boy King Edward VI, when for six years, before Edward succumbed to consumption, England had writhed in civil turbulence as rivals fought for power to protect his agonized existence. John Shakespeare filled William's ears early with tales of military activities and fired his imagination with every aspect of the conduct of war.

Although temperamentally a supporter of the old faith, it is unlikely that John Shakespeare was a Catholic recusant. Later, during the reign of Elizabeth, he was once so named in a Privy Council-inspired list of those who did not attend church monthly, as required by law, but no action was taken against him; one suspects that Stratford's rising clique of Puritans hated him, even tried to denounce him as a Catholic, in the hope of being rewarded with his land.

Neither John Shakespeare nor later his son William showed a passionate intensity of beliefs; moreover John possessed the qualities of a successful, well-rounded and well-liked politician to enable him to rise to such office. Moving on from constable, for which he wore a buff uniform, he spent his thirties heavily involved in town administration until 1556 when, as an alderman, he was addressed as "Master Shakespeare", and in 1567, as bailiff, he dispensed justice, dealt with civil matters, fixed the price of corn, and wore the much-cited alderman's thumb ring and a furred black gown.

# The kingdom of childhood

From the early years of his life, from the impact of the death of his siblings, as reflected later in the images and relationships of his writing, it becomes evident that Shakespeare never rejected the family, but held it central not only to his own dramatic method but to the values he cherished. His own family had undoubted strengths and qualities: it resolved its own internal disputes and difficulties within itself – rare in an age rife with family quarrels and legal disputes (and crime).

Over a span of twenty-two years, and discounting miscarriages of which there is no record, Shakespeare's mother, Mary Arden, had eight children. The regularity of the gaps between their births suggests that although Mary's origins were those of the minor aristocracy – able to trace back their ancestry to before the Norman conquest – she breast-fed them herself. She knew by so doing her children had a better chance of survival. "Better to be nourished by some brute beast than forced to sup the milk of a strange woman," commented a contemporary. Many years later, just after Mary Arden Shakespeare's death, memorative tactile images of breast-feeding seize prominence in *Coriolanus*: "thou sucked'st" valiantness from me, Volumnia says to her son.

Shakespeare was probably so fed for two years, or a little less, his mother protected during that time from further conception by the effects of her milk. He was a powerful energetic child, and he as eldest son, with his brother Gilbert and his sister Joan, the three born at similar intervals, had been closest to one another, and became the longest-living members of the family. In the year of his birth Shakespeare had survived possible contagion from bubonic plague, from which about 300 people in Stratford died. "The rich by flight into the country made shift for themselves," wrote Stow, although the Shakespeares stayed in town.

Having already lost two children Mary Shakespeare valued William exceptionally. He probably commanded more space in the household than was usual for the time. Children normally slept among parents who rowed, beat each other and expressed themselves without any awareness of what were later to be considered the susceptibilities of children. Children watched their parents engage in sexual intercourse. Innocence was not protected. Children would, without any shielding by their parents, witness strange sights, from the death of siblings, the violence of drunkards, to the unhygienic treatment of menstruation in sisters and mothers. They were present at the family gathering, with an experienced midwife, at the birth of each new child. Bed-sharing was common: the Bed of Ware, mentioned in *Twelfth Night*, was notorious for sleeping fifteen people. Two ground-floor parlours in the Angel Inn in Stratford's Henley Street had seven beds in each; above in chambers were another twelve.

One suspects that Shakespeare, through the protectiveness of his mother, was spared much of the coarse equalizing force of most children's early years. Yet, as eldest son, he suffered jealousy at having to share that love with his younger brothers: the vulnerability of separation, the pains of growing, are evident everywhere in his work. Centred in himself, not others, he probably did not relate deeply to siblings and friends, but was mindful of his sensitivity and theirs, nurtured in isolation but both threatened and self-sufficient as only those are who have been deeply loved by their parents.

Children were not, in a town such as Stratford, allowed out at night because of the curfews generally imposed. Apart from the feuds, the constant interventions of law (in Shakespeare's early days Stratford, once a largely Catholic town, was subject to anti-Catholic suppression ordered by the Duke of Leicester) and the remorseless toll of sickness, life was dangerous because of the normal adventurousness of children. John Baker, aged twelve, son of an Alveston husbandman, walked his horse into the Avon one day, suddenly sank in deep water and drowned; Edmund Nason fell thirty foot out of a tree looking for a heron's nest; so did Thomas Bate, seeking young jackdaws. Shakespeare as a child shared these experiences which underlined the sense of danger inherent in man and nature. "Demand that demi-devil / Why he hath thus ensnared my soul and body", calls out Othello in anguish, thus reducing his size of power and huge soul to that of a trembling trapped bird.

How could Shakespeare have revealed such sensitivity to nature when this was far from the norm? He could only have been deeply and unusually cared for by his mother. He had spent much time with her as an infant and child, so that in her absence he was able to recreate her and be alone with her while she, in some powerful and yet indefinable way, became the source not only of his strongest feelings of sympathy with nature, with animals in pain, and with the suffering side of humanity, but also of his extraordinary rich and attractive view of the feminine personality as embodied in his heroines. He never sought to humiliate woman nor did he make her disconnected in speech, feeble and frail, as Dickens so often did with his female re-creations. Likewise Shakespeare never sought, through his invention, revenge on the female sex as a whole. He never created maternal figures as imaginative compensation for his own lack of proper mothering. As Peggy Ashcroft says, "I think Shakespeare must have loved women very much ... he felt that even when women were capable of acts of cruelty or violence, there was a compulsion of emotion or frustration which forced them on."

Shakespeare's education was grounded more on self-development through intellectual learning than on experience: as his contemporary Roger Ascham noted in *The Schoolmaster*, "Learning teacheth more in one year than experience in twenty." Unworldly in a way curiously similar to that of English literature and drama faculties of the twentieth century, Elizabethan teachers found a means of imposing learning on the world and of forcing character and life to fit their own literary theories. The educated Elizabethan was often completely out of touch with reality or the demands of nature.

Shakespeare thus experienced at first hand the way in which Elizabethan Protestantism was imposed on society from above, enforced with endless rules and regulations, standards of conformity and punishments for aberration. To neglect disobedience and spare the rod, was considered as hatred towards the children: "To love them is to correct them betimes". Tolerant and easygoing by nature, Shakespeare found that rules and regulations circumscribed everything, but particularly his own education, when, as soft compliant wax (or so some of his teachers thought) he was ready to take on any impression stamped firmly on it – before the wax dried and hardened.

Paradoxically, one of Shakespeare's schoolmasters was Simon Hunt, a Catholic who later became a Jesuit and died in Rome. Another was a Welshman, Thomas Jenkins, a fellow of St John's College, Oxford, whom Shakespeare later caricatured as Sir Hugh Evans in *The Merry Wives of Windsor*; his last schoolmaster was probably a Brasenose College graduate, John Cotton, whose brother, a Jesuit, died alongside Edmund Campion, the Catholic martyr, in 1582. That two out of three of his teachers were Catholics showed the underlying religious identity and sympathies of Stratford, but not the public official face.

As he first experienced the more outward-looking life of school Shakespeare found that personal identity and integrity jostled uneasily against the external qualities of show, deceit, disguise and good timing that made the actual Elizabethan world so much larger than life. Everything was lived out publicly, and everyone knew one another's business; in spite of the time it took to travel from Stratford to London, what happened in the town was affected by what happened at court: a small provincial population like that of Stratford was unified by the powerful institutions that controlled so many aspects of national life.

Shakespeare was to make Shallow, Gloucestershire justice of the peace, come to London to make a Star Chamber case out of Falstaff beating his men and killing his deer. Adultery, fraud, disfigurement, drunkenness – nothing passed unnoticed, and no aspect of one man's life could be isolated from another. A man's religious convictions were mirrored in his public attendance at church; in the crowded streets of London or Stratford everyone looked into the halls or public meeting places of the houses of the well-to-do. "Miching mallecho", the devil, the spy, the usurper, was at work everywhere, and like the imagination, could take on any one of a thousand forms. The tender schoolboy was taught to hate the ubiquitous enemy.

Shakespeare, however, did not begin with such a heavy dose of suspicion in his nature. He lived roughly a quarter of a mile from the school room, which was over the Council Chamber in the Gild Chapel at Stratford, known as the King's New School. The teaching he received – in Latin, possibly a small quantity of Greek, in biblical studies and in history – gave him a basis on which to further his book learning. He worked his way through the easy classics with the aid of Lyly's Latin grammar and fell in love with Ovid, read Virgil, and possibly some of the comedies of Plautus and the tragedies of Seneca. He developed into an omnivorous autodidact.

The standard of teaching was very high. Emrys Jones emphasizes, in his *Origins of Shakespeare*, the importance of early academic rhetorical training, as taught in school, on Shakespeare. Elizabethans were instructed that to be fair every side of a question had to be considered: the comparative method operated in such a way "that both the audience and Shakespeare never became identified with one point of view". Each position was defended in turn, which led away "from the dogmatic method of a single cause, towards versatility of presentation". So Shakespeare, at an early age, submitted himself whole-heartedly to this principle – "his willingness to lend a voice of the utmost eloquence to every point of view ... is his dramatic secret".

Ben Jonson, eight years Shakespeare's junior, went through roughly the same curriculum – at Westminster School – although under the headship of William Camden the Westminster academic level was perhaps more intense. Jonson was required to parse, memorize, and translate a hundred lines of Latin a week; he committed large tracts of Latin authors to memory, and even some Greek. "Language most shows a man," he wrote later: "speak that I may see you."

Shakespeare had, however, an early experience that would prove seminal all his life. His sense of oneness with nature was not the evangelical sword of vision that it became to later poets such as Keats, Wordsworth and Coleridge, although for them Shakespeare, as a man of genius, became central to their vision as a godlike creator in touch with nature. Among actors the story is often told of two hedge-cutters working in the woods outside Stratford; asked what they were doing, one answers: "He rough-ends 'em and I shapes 'em". The countryside was Shakespeare's personal territory which he nurtured. He delighted in outdoor pursuits, good dietary habits which he acquired from his family background: Derek Jacobi thinks Shakespeare was "a countryman at heart – not at all rooted in the street life of London. He would go to the universal truth of something". If our environment is composed primarily of relationships by which a person's ego is threatened or fulfilled, not so Shakespeare's.

Although born in the same year as Galileo, who became the greatest advocate of the Copernican astronomical revolution, Shakespeare remained comparatively backward in scientific curiosity and medieval in outlook until he came to write *Hamlet*. He was a provincial. The revaluation of the natural world then happening, primarily in Italy, for many years left him cold. With his provincial upbringing, and without a university education, he was, as the mathematician and broadcaster J. Bronowski observes, "still dominated by the astrology and the superstition of the kind of medieval background in which he was brought up". Although he would adapt, he was never ultimately to stop dealing in images of providence.

He maintained throughout his life a child-like ability to tap the inner world of images and the imagination, which, as Salerio in *The Merchant of Venice*, he grasped in all the intricacies of its working:

> My wind cooling my broth
> Would blow me to an ague when I thought
> What harm a wind too great might do at sea.

Above all it was a spiritually charged universe that Shakespeare absorbed and later would reflect: dominated by the weather in all its diverse aspects, by the swift or slow succession of rain, wind and sun, fog and ice, this ever-changing world of forces became orchestrated in the lore of predictions, and read from signs or signals in a continuous living and dying. Between the outer and inner worlds the interchange never stopped. Man – or in Shakespeare's case a precocious, observant boy – was capable of absorbing in solitude this enormous range and diversity of signs and signals, finding in each an expression of something human. Shakespeare became able to register the most primitive subconscious impact of nature, while still allowing his mediating intelligence to reflect and comment on it.

# A father forgotten

Self was not "ego" in Elizabethan times. It was something more public and tangible, not one's sense of inner confidence, but more honour and reputation. Some of Shakespeare's most compelling characters are those who renounce conformity to these external values – lose face, but are determined to survive. Shylock, Falstaff, Malvolio, Paroles, Barnardine, all become reduced by humiliating circumstances, but survive their shame. In that very conspiratorial watching and self-scrutinizing world in which Shakespeare grew up – "paranoia", according to one social historian, "emerged fully armed from the head of the educational curriculum" – public disgrace was far more shattering than today. There was no flight possible, and above all you as a child bore the guilt of your father's crimes and misdemeanours as if you perpetrated them yourself. The disgrace in Shakespeare's family, which happened in or around 1576, when William was twelve, had great public significance, and became a cause of great private torment.

John Shakespeare was now thirty-six years old, powerful and in middle life. The disgrace was not occasioned by religious beliefs – there were even Catholics on the Council, and only a Puritan was expelled, and this not for his extreme convictions but for his bad behaviour. Nor did it forfeit John Shakespeare the support of his friends on the Council, who stalwartly refused to pass the statutory fines on him for non-attendance at meetings, as, over the next five years, he faded from the exercise of public office and civic responsibilities.

John Shakespeare's fall from grace centred on money. We have proof of how his complicated financial dealings and interests collapsed; documentary evidence exists of sums owed and not paid, of properties and land such as that of his wife Mary, conveyanced or mortgaged to raise ready cash, and of threats to his life, probably for non-payment of money owed. He had also engaged in illegal wool dealings and money lending, and had apparently been involved with a counterfeiter called Luther.

The Royal Courts in London, with information from a professional informer, James Langrake, fined John Shakespeare for lending one John Musshem, a sheep farmer, £80 and £100, large sums for those days. John Shakespeare charged £20 interest on both transactions, breaking the laws which forbade usury. In 1573 Musshem and John Shakespeare were sued jointly for debt by a certain Henry Higford. John Shakespeare was also accused of buying large stocks of wool from a recusant Catholic landowner in Snitterfield. By the standards of the day he was involved in shady business. Thus in 1576 he withdrew from public life. (Two of his associates who hid from the law and from creditors were William Fluellen and George Bardolphe, names which Shakespeare later revived in *Henry IV* and *Henry V*.)

This black disgrace hit the convivial and much-loved John Shakespeare in the prime of middle life: it darkened family life, turned him bitter as he valiantly, and without selling his main property in the town, fought to maintain his position in provincial society. Struggling to fend off his creditors, he drank more and more, injuring his growing family with frequent expressions of sharp-tongued malevolence which, in particular, filled his eldest son with melancholy and guilt, as well as with some feelings of resentment. Drink speeds up the routes taken in rages and jealousies and brutalities: it opens shame in those witnessing it who are emotionally dependent on the drinker. A responsible man and father who is at the same time an outcast, like John Shakespeare Lear carries all the worst traits of disappointment and failure: he cannot bear love, knowing he has no reason to be loved. William loved his father, but John Shakespeare pushed that love away from him, mistaking it for an emotional demand he could not satisfy. His father's disgrace made William instinctively "moralize" the world of nature, project on to it his own feeling of pain.

"I'll not love," cries out Lear in Act IV; even the presence of an old friend, Gloucester, appears an impossible demand. Here was the full cycle of guilt, alleviation, self-hatred, vituperation of those close to you, finally remorse: first initiated, this ritual burnt into William, so his father's words became Shakespeare's own. But as in the family of Charles Dickens – and here the two lives have a striking similarity – the story had an upbeat ending: recovery always superseded failure, optimism surged back. So John Shakespeare, in his drunken bouts, never ended up dead in the gutter. Shakespeare was definitely not Dostoevsky: there was always a buoyancy in him, always a resilience. Every play will re-enact the cycle of his own emotional problems in life: it will begin with an overthrow of order – it will go on to threaten a total overthrow of all rules and system, but it will end with the slow recovery of order. Goethe never stopped re-writing *Faust*; Shakespeare continued playing through that primal cycle of family life, which itself had a New Testament parallel: Birth, Crucifixion, Death, Resurrection. Here was the basic force field of his universality.

The sudden curtailment of early promise, thus indelibly imprinted on Shakespeare's life, led (as Aubrey Lewis, a consultant psychiatrist, has commented) "to a recurring emphasis on antagonism between father and son in the plays". The blow sharpened the significant discrepancy well observed by Shakespeare later, between the ideal of a gentleman and the reality of his father. It started him off on his obsession with rank. His sense of the rise and fall of ambition was particularly raw to the bitter defeat suffered by his father: "Robes and furred gowns hide all. Plate sin with gold, / And the strong lance of justice hurtless breaks."

The operative word is "hurtless". The Shakespeare family suffered some great hurt. It had more to do with gold, more with carelessness and improvidence, than with religious conviction. Much of Mary Arden's displaced social energy or frustration probably went into her son's later portrayal of kings and queens, just as her ambition and wounded feelings over the checks to her husband's ambition infused William's expressiveness with generative emotion. But she was no Mary Tyrone, Eugene O'Neill's portrait of the sensitive playwright's mother, driven to heroin addiction, originally from birth pains, but compounded by her husband's vanity and intransigence. Shakespeare's mother remained a strong and steady woman.

That Shakespeare stayed for the next three or more "lost" – that is, undocumented – years (1577–80) of his life at Hoghton Tower, the princely and comely Lancashire seat of Thomas Hoghton, called "a stately fabric environed with a most spacious park", six miles southeast of Preston, is not conclusively proven, as E. A. J. Honigmann forcefully argues. But if it was not to the Hoghton family he went, it was perhaps to one similarly placed.

Shakespeare had shown at school that he was gifted, and when the property troubles descended on the Henley Street family, his schoolmaster, by now John Cotton, probably suggested to John Shakespeare that his son should leave home for a year or two. If the suggestion to place William in a Lancashire household came from Cotton, John Shakespeare would have been pleased, for this "fostering" was the common way to advance a gentleman's son and widen his experience and education further. So during adolescence William was granted the chance to begin an autonomous intellectual and spiritual life, as a result of which he could start to see his parents more objectively. His mother wrote frequently: her feelings for her eldest son reflected the strong personal affinity and affection maintained between them.

During the dark period of his father's decline Shakespeare discovered literature. The golden age of Elizabethan literature was just beginning: the harbingers were Sir Thomas Wyatt, "present at the coronation of Anne Boleyn and the Earl of Surrey, present at her trial". John Lyly's romance *Euphues* was published in 1579, the same year as Edmund Spenser's *Shepherd's Calendar*, establishing Spenser as *primus inter pares*, and one of the greatest flowerings of any age was under way, irrepressibly exuberant and as adventurous as the expeditions which set out from Elizabethan England to explore every corner of the new globe. North translated Plutarch, Chapman Homer, Florio Montaigne, Sylvester Du Bartas – "O that ocean did not bound our style", wrote Michael Drayton,

> Within these strict and narrow limits so:
> But that the melody of our sweet isle
> Might now be heard to Tiber, Arne and Po:
> That they might know how far Thames doth outgo
> The music of declined Italy.

"The Elizabethan literary appetite grew by what it fed on," writes George Rylands.

Arthur Golding's translation of Ovid's *Metamorphoses* (1567), written in fourteen-foot lines, in particular appealed to Shakespeare's fluid, highly suggestible imagination: the constant surge of imagery, the rapid, condensed flow of love, erotic opulence, birth, death, blood, mystery, unexpected reversal, majesty, grandeur, cruelty, and absurdity developed his instinct for antithesis. The anthropomorphic gods of ancient Greece spawned legend after legend from their volatile passion, offering Shakespeare the constant dramatic principle of change. Ovid filled every blade of grass, wild flower, river, or green glade – or horrifying rock – with the presence of divine energy. He would draw on Ovid endlessly through his life: from *Titus Andronicus*, with its repetition of the tragic story of Philomel, through *Venus and Adonis*, and *A Midsummer Night's Dream* in which Ovid's account of Pyramus and Thisbe is dramatized, even to *The Tempest*, where Prospero's farewell to his magic is astonishingly close to Medea's great invocation before she ascends her heavenly chariot.

Catholicism, suppressed in outward religious observance, stimulated an inward need for a literature of startling range and diversity; which perversely and paradoxically gained its main thrust and vitality from the wonderful flexibility and subtlety of the national language. The English became chauvinistic, fierce proselytizers for the cause of their native tongue, as the country took on the lineaments and throbbing vitality of a nest of singing birds. Writer after writer lent his authority to his mother language. Epistles on orthography and pronunciation, manifestos, treatises proclaimed the merits of rhyme over classical metre and the need for purity in the use of English. The only genre of poetry conspicuously absent was the religious: except by Catholic recusants such as Robert Southwell, and self-tortured converts to the Anglican Church like John Donne, the soul was neglected in favour of the senses and the more wide-ranging fancy.

Some of the Hoghtons were practising and ardent Catholics. John Cotton, himself a recusant, would have been reluctant to advise his friends to take into their house a boy who was not from a similar background. Yet the master of this house was never at home. Thomas Hoghton lived in exile in Liège, having left England for his religion in 1569; Alexander, his brother, looked after his estate, outwardly conforming to Protestantism.

Shakespeare found himself absorbed in this complicated family's affairs, its divided loyalties and its fierce disputes over land and succession. The household was large – at least twenty gentlemen and several score of retainers: a court in miniature. Shakespeare had joined the family as an unlicensed schoolmaster in an area which the governing Protestant authorities had condemned both as full of unqualified schoolmasters and children trained up as papists. He was more likely than not to have been tutor to the young sons, and even the daughters, of Alexander Hoghton and a half-brother, also called Thomas. Shakespeare participated in frequent musical and dramatic entertainments, making contacts that provided openings for his talent later on, particularly with Ferdinando Stanley, Lord Strange, later fifth Earl of Derby, who became patron of a leading company of players.

Although the facts are scarce (a mention in Alexander Hoghton's will of 1581 of a "William Shakeshafte now dwelling with me" may well have been of a Lancashire Shakeshafte), support is strong in the expansion and development of Shakespeare's imagination. Had he remained at Stratford (as some claim, with plenty of textual evidence of Shakespeare's knowledge of the glover's trade), married at eighteen and joined a company which toured Stratford later, he would never have gained that insider's knowledge of a noble household that his early plays so powerfully demonstrate.

Not only did Shakespeare feel confused, betrayed, upset in expectations, when he thought (perhaps with a certain relief in his exile) of his own family. But he also discovered that the family's troubles still continued. When he went back to Stratford, he was shown fresh marks or wounds of ill-fortune. At the same time he still had terrible exhortations or guilt feelings placed on him to save his family's honour and rescue it financially. In Lancashire the web of tangled affairs, as well as the Catholic Lancashire warmth, the machinations and the atmosphere of suspicion, the sudden possibility of violence (Alexander's half-brother and heir, who inherited Hoghton in 1581, was killed eight years later in an armed mêlée over cattle rights) gave those confused and muddled thoughts and conflicts over his own family further space to expand and be identified, though not necessarily clarified.

On one side of Shakespeare's personality there dwelt all the richness and warmth of a family-minded man, his father's honoured eldest son, beloved and cherished of his mother. But the other side had, from the blow and its disgrace, and from being sent away, bred coldness and alienation. He guarded this watching and observing side, so that this early component of himself gradually becomes itself identified with stock theatrical types, with provisional selves, and then with connected or archetypal roles.

A murkiness of individual conscience, spiritual and political allegiance, existed in England during the crucial years of Shakespeare's late adolescence, when he was also affected by strong sexual stirrings. The threat to England from the counter-Reformation of Pope Gregory XIII was not directly political; but the Catholic seminary priests and Jesuits who landed in England from France and were hunted down were perceived as conspirators by the Protestant establishment. And the excommunication of Elizabeth by Pius V and rumoured plots against her life did no service to sincere and practising Catholics like the Hoghtons and prepared the way for the martyrdom of the Jesuits. The heroic growth of Catholic power in England during the 1580s, after Campion's death at Tyburn, came through those who loved the Jesuit martyr and spread his faith. Campion apparently led a charmed life, escaping death many times, arousing affection among a people who admired his spirituality and selfless bravery. "We are dead people to this world," he declared before his ultimate bestial punishment. "We travelled only for souls."

But Shakespeare, perpetrator of huge hills of flesh, wanton trollops as well as poetic kings, was not the stuff of martyrs. Flesh itself remained of paramount importance in its presence. Shylock, his first great comic personage, hinges his fate on a pound of flesh. Even as a boy Shakespeare was *l'homme moyen sensuel*; he was a burgher's son, surrounded by physical and material aspiration: he liked gossip, and dirty jokes. Part of him became the tabloid society columnist, part the best-selling novelist who supported the ruling establishment – of a more aristocratic and cultured outlook than our own – as well as mankind's future greatest protean poet. For him no martyr's death, or even the complication, or attraction, of its power or hold over his imagination, such as that struggled with by John Donne in later years.

The Catholic martyrdoms affected Shakespeare as they affected every thinking person of the times. The years 1580–2, when he was sixteen to eighteen, were impressionable years when Shakespeare aspired to becoming a poet. Fugitive Jesuits in disguise popped in and out of his imagination as vividly as images of woman's delight, and the sensual appeal of the courtly self-advancement of which he dreamed. The moral authority of the priests' heroism became a strand in his robustly patriotic nature, for this itself, specifically not directed against Elizabeth and her court, was representative of many of the best qualities of Englishmen. While in Roman Catholic Spain and Italy the whole of the English nation was denounced as ravening wolves, it was widely understood in England that those who hunted and persecuted holy men, from the highest in the land on down, suffered a corrosive moral stain.

Shakespeare, too, under an outwardly conformist respect for authority, with which he pleased his patrons and kept his audiences happy, always harboured an awareness of the evil possibilities latent in that authority. He learnt, early on, in the Hoghton household, how to keep his own counsel, and not to land himself in trouble. Like John Donne, he disguised his potential recusancy, but in a way utterly different from Donne's. He universalized it. In all of his plays he preserved the working out of a higher moral purpose, but he made it unspecific, what today would be called ecumenical. He was ahead of his times: he attacked racism; he deplored slavery; he toned down the anti-Catholicism of his sources; he gave the criminal, human sympathy (based on himself).

Much of Shakespeare's learning about life came in his first exposure to a rich and powerful household in Lancashire, or elsewhere. And once again, as with all the sights and sounds of nature, he stored and interiorized these experiences and observations.

What Shakespeare experienced at Hoghton was, in spite of what his father said in favour of the old loyalties, the fruits of change. England's easy-going majority, which did not consist of religious zealots of either the Puritan or Catholic persuasion, had never had it so good. Between them, William Cecil, later Lord Burghley, and Elizabeth had canalized the vast exuberance of the Renaissance: the purpose remained always a patriotic one: to make the courts secure, independent and insular, to foster competitive nationalism, industrialism, imperialism, the "looms and coal mines and counting houses, the joint-stock companies and the cantonments; the power and the weakness of great possessions".

Shakespeare's masters, the Hoghtons, although they would have preferred a Catholic regime, had seen the advantages of this change, and he had sympathized. He reinforced his own early book learning with the regime he himself had to participate in and pass on to the younger members of the Hoghton family. Each morning before leaving their rooms the boys had to kneel and say the Lord's Prayer and Creed. In the course of the year's teaching Shakespeare took his charges through the Psalms twelve times, the New Testament four times, and the Old Testament once. He learned the habit of work from his masters, rose at four, read widely in their well-stocked library and learned musical instruments; the great banqueting hall had a minstrel's gallery where he could sit and watch the visiting players perform their own adaptations of new secular plays – *Ralph Roister Doister, Cambyces, Gorboduc, Gammer Gurton's Needle.*

On Sunday after perhaps a secret Mass, with wax lights and Latin liturgy, the Hoghtons repaired to watch a bear-baiting in Preston, something that powerfully cut into Shakespeare's mind, from his earliest work, as when Richard Crookback describes his father York:

> Methought he bore him in the thickest troop
> ... as a bear encompassed round with dogs,
> Who having pinched a few and made them cry,
> The rest stand all aloof and bark at him.

To Gloucester in *Lear*: "I am tied to th' stake, and I must stand the course." Life presented weird contrasts.

On the one hand there was in Shakespeare a nervous pleasing nature; on the other he had little by way of an extrovert personality, and preferred to hide himself and remain anonymous; to some extent he was repressing his aggressive manly side, because he did not much care for what he saw in his father, especially his intemperate behaviour since the financial disgrace had fallen on the family.

Of all of them Shakespeare had been the one most affected by the downfall: and now living in the exile of his "fostering out" he felt loneliness and humiliation more keenly. The isolation he experienced heightened his fears about his own reliability: would disaster and shame – crime as well as madness – become his main inheritance? His sense of rise and fall – of the fickleness of fortune, the volatility of passion and ambition, above all the reversibility of all life – would become a symbol of the public world. He saw his own ugly sides, wanting to hide his visage from the forlorn world, "Stealing unseen to west with this disgrace".

His thoughts often found an outlet in imagining criminality. He knew early the meaning of suicide – he developed a terrifying awareness of self-damnation, of what it meant to commit spiritual suicide, to obliterate yourself in crime or guilt. In him was instilled a profound sense of guilt, a weight from which he would fly to the exhilarating comic heights of his early work. Yet however bad he felt, an inborn buoyancy would reassert a balance.

Life in the Hoghton family accentuated his shyness: outwardly he was anxious to please, he conformed, he could show off remarkable wit and learning, was an accomplished dancer and could play several instruments. He was clever, he knew. But at the same time he did not take the opportunities of advancement offered. He wanted instinctively to preserve something inside him, untainted. The master and others told him he could go far, offered to sponsor him, or patronize him, but he was too many-sided, too self-protective to venture further in the world of power. Something, even in this enlightened house, warned him off the deceptive and dangerous glories of this world: he could see into the heart of the court's darkness – "it glows and shines like rotten wood" – and did not want to end up sharing the doom. Shakespeare's antennae were alerted to his future: he cherished his roots and would remain essentially a middle-class businessman: this was the world he trusted. Upbringing in a nobleman's family was a training in suspicion and paranoia, as enforced in Cato's standard distichs: "Observe what's past and what may next ensue; / And Janus-like keep both ways under view."

So at this time was born the alienated side of Shakespeare's character, what Yeats in his epitaph called the "cold eye", the "antithetical self", the "thou art not what thou seem'st" aspect of human beings as well as the sense that any one human nature contains within his or her self the potential for all good and evil. Here was the seed not only of Richard Crookback, but of that gallery of characters who stand and observe and comment, culminating in Hamlet, the supreme existentialist outsider. While Shakespeare was more acutely tuned to family relationships than any writer had been, or has ever been since, a side of him, developed during adolescence, had remained watchful and distrustful of close bonds. Richard dislikes his brothers as a reflection of his parents:

> I had no father, I am like no father;
> I have no brother, I am like no brother;
> And this word, "love", which greybeards call divine,
> Be resident in men like one another
> And not in me – I am myself alone.

The 1580s had begun more chaotically than any other time during Elizabeth's reign, reminiscent of the violent, lawless and unstable days of Henry VIII's rule. There was a threat of a return to the gangster era that Shakespeare so colourfully renders in his early history plays. The atmosphere at the Hoghtons' house was becoming dangerous, there were family conflicts over religion, servants who might be informers – not a healthy place for one of Shakespeare's disposition. Misguided intellectuals with Catholic sympathies were considered "seedmen of sedition". Treason and its dreadful consequences were everywhere in the air, weaving a vast web: "Let these persons be termed as they list", warned Burghley, "scholars, school masters, bookmen, seminarists, priests, Jesuits, friars, beedmen, romanists, pardoners, or what else you will, neither their titles nor their apparel hath made them traitors, but their traitorous secret motions and practices; their persons have not made the war, but their directions and councils have set up the rebellions."

In 1582, aged eighteen, Shakespeare fled his gentry patrons and returned to Stratford. There was, as Gabriel Harvey termed it, a "queint mistery of mounting conceit" to attend to, someone there who had caught his "knack of dexterity".

# Fire in the blood

Most men of Shakespeare's time did not marry until they were twenty-five or more – when ready to support a wife and children of their own, and by the scale of their own life-expectancy well advanced into middle age. But Shakespeare had not joined the swollen ranks of university student apprentices, with their huge and overwhelming vices of lust and pride, living very much by the loyalties and standards of a group. He had been "pricked out" from the start to be an individual, his individuality and isolation heightened.

The cause was his marriage, for which a licence was issued in the Worcester Court on 28 November 1582, granting that "William Shagspere" and "Anne Hathaway of Stratford in the diocese of Worcester, maiden" may marry, with a surety of £40 posted by friends of the bride's father, a farmer. Aged twenty-six, eight years older than her husband, Anne was well known to Shakespeare's father, while her own family was of solid substantial yeoman stock. The Hathaway family farmhouse, Hewlands Farm, standing in Shottery on the very edge of the forest of Arden, in its time not only an enchanting setting but an inspiring picture used many times by the playwright, was a prosperous secure home of twelve rooms, which remained in the hands of family descendants until 1911.

Marital affection was not a normal expectation in 1582 and sometimes did not exist. Often husband and wife lived remote lives, but the closeness in Shakespeare's own family is evidenced in his plays, particularly the bond between brother and sister. Because Anne Hathaway remained unmarried at twenty-six, it has often been assumed that she was: first, an imaginative conflation of two women (the other Anne Whateley, whose name was recorded probably in error in the Bishop of Worcester's registry on 27 November); second, a sexually forward and experienced single woman who saw the educated and talented Shakespeare as a good catch; or third, a dull, half-backward country wench whom the playwright had the misfortune to impregnate in a Stratford stubble field.

Anne Whateley's name has generated romantic speculation (notably in this century by Ivor Brown) that Shakespeare ran away with an upper-class girl, but was forced to marry the pregnant Anne Hathaway. John Barton describes Anne Whateley as a black-eyed, black-haired daughter of great estate who so frustrated Shakespeare that he tumbled her serving girl (Anne Hathaway) in a barn, then left immediately for London.

Certainly Anne was pregnant when they married, and their first child, a daughter whom they named Susanna, was christened on 26 May 1583, so Anne must have conceived in August 1582, three months or more prior to the marriage. James Joyce's *Ulysses* began the twentieth-century global warming of the sexual imagination, especially with regard to Shakespeare: there, in Stephen Dedalus's vivid mosaic of his life, the playwright is overborne in a cornfield by Anne Hathaway; no later undoing will undo the first undoing, so he goes through life being both ravisher and ravished. In Anthony Burgess's fictional account, *Brighter than the Sun*, Shakespeare has fantasies of bedding noble ladies; prematurely wedded to Anne, he is lured into outlandish sexual practices with a dildo.

But was not William in love with Anne? I believe she was a much more complex, better educated and more many-sided woman than has generally been depicted. Biographers of Shakespeare have for the most part formed her in a stereotyped provincial image. She was competent, practical, literal and sensual. It is not too fanciful to see her as dark-eyed and dark-haired, features common enough with yeomen's daughters. In any case, the young poet's imagination, protean as it was, rooted itself in her, and transformed her into a thousand different forms. It was not for nothing that the penultimate line of Sonnet 145 contains, in Shakespeare's characteristic fashion, a pun on Hathaway: "hate-away":

Those lips that love's own hand did make
Breathed forth the sound that said "I hate"
To me that languished for her sake;
But when she saw my woeful state,
Straight in her heart did mercy come . . .
"I hate" she altered with an end
That followed it as gentle day
Doth follow night who, like a fiend,
From heaven to hell is flown away.
        "I hate" from hate away she threw,
        And saved my life, saying "not you."

There is no reason why Sonnet 144, "Two loves I have, of comfort and despair, / Which like two spirits do suggest me still", and the two great sonnets, 146 and 147,

> Poor soul, the centre of my sinful earth
> [My sinful earth] these rebel powers that thee array . . .

> My love is as a fever, longing still
> For that which longer nurseth the disease . . .

should not originally have come of his feelings for Anne, either directly, or recaptured some years on. He may often have felt, culminating in his later expressions of horror, regret, and condemnation of pre-nuptial sex, great and continuing remorse over the expression of the sexual side of his being. But celebrative enjoyment as well.

Susanna – who as a first child strongly mirrored her mother's own background, as well as her physical and mental makeup – clearly was a success from the start, prototype of those wonderfully rich and lively girls advancing to marriage age and maturity that Shakespeare so perfectly depicted later. Like her mother, Susanna married late, not until she was twenty-five, and then to John Hall, a distinguished Stratford physician whose fame, practice and importance (as a diarist) spread far beyond the county's border. Mother and daughter shared between them an important power: the gift of discernment.

The same gap – or almost – existed between the birth of Susanna and the twins as that between Shakespeare's own siblings. Anne breast-fed Susanna until nearly a year old and became pregnant again only in the early summer of 1584. She was a healthy young woman still, her procreative powers at their height, for the twins she conceived were a spontaneous expression of fertility – a non-identical boy and girl, and therefore two eggs, as opposed to the split single egg of identical twins. The carrying of twins is gynaecologically infinitely more fraught than that of single children, and that she carried and bore three healthy babies in less than three years is a tribute to the prudence and good management of both the Shakespeare and Hathaway families. Hamnet and Judith were so named after a happily married pair, Hamnet, Stratford's High Street baker, and Judith Sadler, old family friends who became the twins' godparents.

Anne's relationship with William's mother was sound. The Henley Street home was full of children. Susanna, Hamnet and Judith Shakespeare had two uncles who were under ten and an aunt, Joan, who was in her early teens. John Shakespeare had stood at the font for the last time on 5 May 1580, with his son Edmund, possibly an unwanted child, only three years before the birth of Susanna. William was then sixteen, Gilbert fourteen, Joan eleven, Richard six. Edmund was named after his uncle Edmund Lambert, to whom Mary Arden's Wilmcote property had first been mortgaged.

It may have been in many ways a failed marriage, but it was never a dead marriage. Often the pain and the failures outweighed the advantages, at least during the early part of his career, until Shakespeare grew to emotional maturity and could confront himself fully and reflect, and then develop that personal confrontation and insight about himself in his writing. Many have suspected that Anne Hathaway led Shakespeare a dance: "You only have your own family to draw on," says Jonathan Miller, remarking on Shakespeare's curious sense of rage about women. Stephen Dedalus speculates in *Ulysses* that Anne "was hot in the blood. Once a wooer twice a wooer", and that she later betrayed William with his brothers, while the playwright used the names of Richard and Edmund for evil characters not just because they were in the chronicles: "Why is the underplot of *King Lear* lifted out of Sidney's *Arcadia* and spatchcocked on to a Celtic legend older than history?"

Asked about Shakespeare's unhappiness in marriage, in Hugh Kingsmill's *The Return of William Shakespeare*, the playwright answers, "Nor must you think that Shakespeare was insensible to Anne's unhappiness and to the love for him beneath her shrewishness." As Adriana says, in *The Comedy of Errors*, "My heart prays for him, though my tongue do curse". In *Twelfth Night* Orsino holds that a man's fancies are more giddy and unfirm than a woman's, so his wife should be younger than himself, "or thy affection cannot hold the bent". Kingsmill maintains that Shakespeare's marriage was a mistake from every standpoint, and that he was right to see it so quickly as a failure – nor could he have managed the failure better than "by building on it a comfortable home for his wife and children". Late twentieth-century opinion largely corroborates this: Trevor Nunn sums it up, "Anne was always the second-best bed".

Yet possibly we betray our own short-sighted and cynical view of marriage. If Shakespeare's marriage was unhappy some of the time, it may well not have been unhappy all the time. Shakespeare, says Barbara Everett, was not only "one of the most intelligent men who was ever born", but he "possessed a peculiar openness which made him suffer". The advantages he gained from marriage to Anne Hathaway were considerable and he must soon have become aware of them. His marriage at eighteen to a twenty-six-year-old woman opened in him a window into the intimacies of the female heart: his perceptions of her, often learnt or experienced in pain, in quarrels and misunderstandings, and in blindness on his part, were an extraordinary educative process. He experienced, close to, this rich but disturbing power that had drawn them together in the first place: the "onlie begetter" of his three children, Anne was at once at the centre of his ceaseless thinking and feeling. She became the furnace, the generator of emotional powers which his clanking fancy and quick shuttering production line shaped unceasingly.

> Variable passions throng her constant woe,
> As striving who should best become her grief.
> All entertained, each passion labours so
> That every present sorrow seemeth chief,
>     But none is best. Then join they all together,
>     Like many clouds consulting for foul weather.

Anne was wilful, individual, guarded her middle-class "heiress" status, later refused to become an actor's wife, or a camp-follower in any way, fought ferociously to preserve this dual nature, her first allegiance being to that truth of feeling and to family values, not to art. She became, as a mother of twins, outwardly a primal force of nature, and however much the often variable emotional nature of Shakespeare wanted to run away, he knew always that he must remain rooted in that dark and eternal female nature. Mother, wife, daughter, they began, grew and separated in Anne, back to Mary, forward to Susanna and Judith: "Grief hath two tongues, and never woman yet / Could rule them both, without ten women's wit."

It is most unlikely that, some eighteen months to two years after the birth of the twins, Anne and William Shakespeare did not try to have more children. Twins are exhausting, and breast-feeding them both was taxing for Anne, but twins are such a biologically spectacular phenomenon, revelatory of human feeling and family bonding in a way quite unexpected to parents who have never experienced it, that the twenty-year-old father could not but have delighted in these permutations of feeling and response, and insights into sexual differentiation, that paternity of twins presents. It may well be, for instance, that the boy Hamnet had more feminine characteristics than the girl, Judith: Shakespeare could not have failed to notice, and be moved by, that unique closeness that exists between twins and makes them a loving unit independent of their parents. Twins certainly – in the experience of this writer who is also the father of non-identical twins – do not suffer the same vulnerability and exposure as non-twins in their development. They are in some inexplicably strong way socially connected; they seem extraordinarily at home on the earth, and they are also accommodating and adaptable in the way single children are not. They may seem a deep burden, and are, physically at first, especially in a household affected by debt as was the Shakespeares', yet they turn out more often than not to be a blessing. They duplicate the marriage bond within a family.

# A great profession

Shakespeare had now, as the signs indicate, joined the military in some or other unknown capacity. He may have been drafted, or he may have been seeking military adventure and reputation even, as Jaques says, in the cannon's mouth. He may only have been among a nobleman's retinue – among, as Fluellen says in *Henry V*, the "poys and the luggage". But it was a reluctantly mounted campaign that he found himself drawn into; every man in England from sixteen to sixty was liable for military duty at that time, and it was well-nigh impossible that he should have escaped, and even more unlikely, although a common enough occurrence, that once press-ganged he deserted. "You've got", says Richard Eyre, the director of the Royal National Theatre, "an awful lot of his characters who are military men; if not fighters, then conspicuously not fighters." The disgrace of Anne's first pregnancy had been enough: like Ben Jonson, who escaped the humiliation of failure to win a scholarship to Cambridge, the only alternative being bricklaying, Shakespeare embraced the military spirit, reacting to form himself along conventional, manly lines.

A war started, conveniently enough, just when Shakespeare was looking for some gainful activity. Ten years later when John Donne, at a comparable age, sought foreign service and joined the Earl of Essex on his Cadiz expedition, the idea of booty was a positive enticement – the nobility formed themselves into limited companies to share the spoils. But plunder was never much of a motive for the defence of the United Provinces of the Netherlands. Elizabeth, to check the tyranny of Catholic Spain and pre-empt the threat to England, in late 1584 ordered 6,000 foot soldiers and 1,000 horsemen, under the command of her former long-standing suitor, the Earl of Leicester, to occupy three towns in the Netherlands and assume military responsibility for the protection of the whole area.

Leicester, however, and his "brave fleet with silken streamers", did not leave England until the end of 1585; the expedition swelled to enormous proportions, transforming itself in the process into a personal military cavalcade:

> behold the threaden sails,
> Borne with th'invisible and creeping wind,
> Draw the huge bottoms through the furrowed sea,
> Breasting the lofty surge.

Leicester established himself regally in Amsterdam as Governor and Captain-General with a display of aquatic monsters, mostly whales, which towed his ship to the shore. The Protestant Dutch greeted the English force with triumphal arches, banquets, and varied forms of classical pageantry whose images and emblems became embedded in the mind of Shakespeare – together with their realistic opposite, the miseries of military campaigning, the graft, the corruption, the failed promises of reward. Elizabeth quickly grew furious at the way Leicester bathed in undeserved glory, and railed against the embezzlement rife in his army, dubbed by one of her aides the "conduit along which English treasure passed into the abyss of Dutch Bankruptcy". But the worn-out and aging Earl, himself only a few years short of death, harboured no treasonable designs: his main idea, lamentably unrealizable, was military honour, which Shakespeare's great invention Falstaff later, when attached to honour's invariable companion, a corpse, calls "grinning".

Leicester's army, though it gained one or two minor successes, rapidly dwindled: many of his followers took to their heels. They had been conscripted into an old-fashioned army still largely weaponed with the long bow – muskets at two pounds each were too expensive; with their captains siphoning off their pay, the men could afford only bad pork and cheese. The punishment for petty misdemeanours was draconian – a five-shilling fine for being caught swearing, a whole day's pay for failing to attend church (the average craftsman's wage was a shilling a day, a labourer's, eightpence). As Sir William Pelham, their Marshall, wrote, "I know not how to turn to satisfy them, for some wanting wherewith to feed them, others almost naked, many falling sick daily, and all in general barefoot wanting hose or shoes, do by hundreds flock about me if I stir abroad amongst them, crying to relief of their troubles."

Shakespeare later in *All's Well That Ends Well* colours both the glory and pageantry into toylike and childish bravura – and shows in Paroles the cynical retainer reduced to beggary. But in 1585 the zest for glory was real. One of Leicester's subordinates, his nephew Sir Philip Sidney, soldier, poet, courtier, had joined in the purest spirit of chivalry, abandoning his dream of establishing an American colony in the New World to upset Spanish rule there. His privately circulated pastoral romance, *Arcadia*, written in 1579–81 for his sister, the Countess of Pembroke, had already created his reputation. A friend tried to persuade him of the absurdity of the chivalric ideal: "You and your fellows, I mean men of noble birth, consider that nothing brings you more honour than wholesale slaughter." Sidney's presence in the Netherlands became inspiring to Shakespeare, who later took up themes for his Sonnets from the posthumously published *Astrophel and Stella* (and even in *Coriolanus* competed with themes from Sidney's *Defense of Poetry*). In his sonnet sequence Sidney, addressing Penelope Devereux ("Stella"), captured the contradictoriness of passion,

> Oh heavenly fool, thy most kiss-worthy face
> Anger invests with such a lovely grace,
> That Anger's self I needs must kiss again

which Shakespeare later came supremely to capture and embody.

Sidney mentions, as a messenger bearing a letter to his wife from the Netherlands, a Will "the jesting player" which some have taken to mean Shakespeare. More likely it was the clown Will Kempe, known to have been a member of the Earl of Leicester's company, and who later became a fellow player of Shakespeare's in Lord Strange's company. Though it is unlikely that Shakespeare was part of Leicester's immediate entourage, he may well have been numbered in the retinue of a subordinate officer: certainly his experience of this campaign, however short a time he stayed, was two-sided. His view of military action was on the one hand wildly fanciful and baroquely expressive of the spirit of chivalry – on the other, realistic and brutal. The Dutch winter was damp and so cold that Robert Cecil could write to a friend, "Your nose would drop off." Wolves roamed at large in once prosperous areas, and attacked sentries. Later Shakespeare would view his battles and campaigns from the particular vantage point of the non-commissioned officer, a corporal or sergeant; his moral position was that of the ordinary people – he had the gut reaction of the crowd, although he hated the mob.

He witnessed and recorded at first hand troops investing and defending positions, building up fortifications and towns changing hands. He acquired a comprehensive grasp of the logistics of war: an awareness of supply lines, the dangerous uncertainty of stores arriving by sea, the crucial importance of morale and leadership. At times he felt the claims of war strongly over those of peace, and often in the plays the soldiers outnumber the civilians: "Let me have war," remarks a common serving man in *Coriolanus*, to which his friend agrees – "It exceeds peace as far as day does night. It's sprightly walking, audible and full of vent ... peace is a great maker of cuckolds."

Elizabeth's anger at Leicester's presumptuous vice-regal behaviour duly humbled her commander in chief. His wife resented not being allowed to share the triumphs and proud titles bestowed on her husband; Lady Leicester's plan to join him "with such a train of ladies and gentlewomen, and such rich coaches, litters and side-saddles as her Majesty had none such" was flattened summarily. Leicester, in fear of losing his commission, grovelled before Elizabeth in remorse and contrition, and when he pleaded that all he hoped for was to be employed in the Queen's stables to "rub her horses' heels" Elizabeth relented and let him retain his command.

The Earl of Essex, then aged eighteen, distinguished himself in the cavalry charge at Zutphen and was knighted by Leicester. Philip Sidney won lasting reputation at Zutphen – he became another thread in Shakespeare's life, representing an absolute: glory. "Thou are not conquered," Shakespeare's lover Romeo says of Juliet, invoking the power of military honour to express his love:

> Beauty's ensign yet
> Is crimson in thy lips and in thy cheeks,
> And death's pale flag is not advancèd there.

"Death's pale flag" captures the impact on Shakespeare of such a figure as Sidney, who, as he lay wounded on the field, passed his water bottle to a dying soldier – "Thy necessity is yet greater than mine." Nursed by his wife Frances, the exquisite daughter of Sir Francis Walsingham, who had travelled over at once on hearing he was wounded, Sidney died three weeks after the battle, to become the first great English Protestant military hero, a direct ancestor of Nelson at Trafalgar.

The fledgling England had as yet little experience of running a military machine: it improvised as best it could. For Shakespeare, as for everyone else, war was an exciting if terrifying constituent of the new patriotic consciousness, and he would depict it in every aspect. But although exalting military glory and serving well the pomp and ceremony of great leaders, he was never to show a direct, insider's view of the conduct of a campaign, or even detail gained at first hand of the lives of great commanders. His military leaders are pitched, in character and outlook, firmly in the middle strata of army life. Brutus and Cassius quarrel at the level of warrant officers: "I said an elder soldier, not a better," Cassius rebukes his leader. Enobarbus, Antony's supreme warrior, speaks like a man not so much risen through the ranks as having remained an old ranker: when he chats to Admiral Menas on board the galley they swap courtesies as if they were downing pints in a sergeants' mess. Othello too has an extremely vulgar, barrack-room image of his wife's unfaithfulness:

> I had been happy if the general camp,
> Pioneers and all, had tasted her sweet body,
> So I had nothing known.

Shakespeare simplifies military leaders, emphasizing their headline appeal, playing down what is remote, inaccessible, or highly gifted in them. Endowing them with his wit, his popular easy power, his gift of imagery, he makes them versions or copies of himself, reflecting his own observation and experience of war.

Shakespeare's first history plays are filled with realistic detail, with small sieges, gunnery methods, but especially with the peculiar atmosphere of a military campaign. "Sirs," says a French Sergeant in *Henry VI* Part One to his sentinels,

> take your places and be vigilant.
> If any noise or soldier you perceive
> Near to the walls, by some apparent sign
> Let us have knowledge at the court of guard.

The Sentinel reflects when the Sergeant has departed:

> Thus are poor servitors,
> When others sleep upon their quiet beds
> Constrained to watch in darkness, rain, and cold.

When Talbot speaks contemptuously of "*Pucelle* or puzzle, Dauphin or dog-fish" he is, one historian has remarked, the true ancestor of the British tommy who called Ypres "Wipers" or Ploegstraat "Plugstreet". After love, the next great excitement in life, totally obliterating all else, was war; as Mercutio puts it, "then dreams he of cutting foreign throats, / Of breaches, ambuscados, Spanish blades".

It is not surprising that Shakespeare, from first-hand experience of both – although he, unlike Ben Jonson, did not kill anyone in single combat – should come so quickly, when he first begins writing, to employ sexual metaphors for the sieges of small fortified towns. Witnessing rape and looting at first hand, his disgust at war's dirtier sides did not stimulate reformist or radical social attitudes. Like most men who served in the army, he resorted to an extensive and metaphoric vocabulary for the female anatomy to compensate for the misery of enforced chastity. Not only are there the round turrets, destitute and bare, of Lucrece's lovely breasts, but sexually explicit geographical references to the female genitals. Having crossed the Channel and had experience of male cynicism in the forward lines, with the pickets, he could share their invocation of those secret parts as the "low countries" or the "Netherlands".

# Factions and fictions

In the 1580s, turbulent times in England, anyone might be accused or denounced. Shakespeare absorbed the insecurity – the guilt and precariousness of England's sovereign state – that made him later the advocate of and mouthpiece for more settled times. Plots in those years succeeded plots with almost comic-opera density: their absurdity sometimes matched the deviousness and paranoia of those trying to uncover them. England was a land of factions, spies and counterspies. Richard Topcliffe, whom the Jesuit John Gerard later called "the cruellest tyrant of all England, a man most infamous hateful to all the realm for his bloody and butcherly mind", was given a free hand to persecute and torture Catholics. He had devised a special rack, which he kept at home in Westminster, with authority to use it. He boasted he had been allowed to put his hand into the Queen's bosom and had seen her above the knee.

Mary Queen of Scots – the Scottish "Clytemnestra" so dubbed by the Bishops in Parliament, and "the most notorious whore in the whole world" – was incarcerated first at Sheffield, where she continually intrigued for her half-sister's downfall. Elizabeth, who saw Mary as "the bird that had flown to her for safety from the hawk", refused her counsellors' clamourings that she shed her kinswoman's blood. But privileged and comfortable as was the life she led in captivity, Mary would not stop plotting, with Anthony Babington and others, while publicly maintaining a distance from conspiracy, saying "I would never make shipwreck of my soul by compassing the death of my dearest sister".

Mary was moved from Sheffield to Tutbury, then Chartley in south Derbyshire. Sir Francis Walsingham, the Secretary of State, a master-manipulator of Elizabethan paranoia, had begun organizing a secret service; his efforts had gathered momentum from his first-hand experience of horror at the massacre in Paris, on St Bartholomew's Eve in 1572 when he was serving at the British Embassy there, of 4,000 Huguenots. Elizabeth disliked Walsingham's Puritan tendency and the lack of esteem was mutual. Whereas he put a higher value on creed than on popular nationalism, Elizabeth, for her part, was tolerant and non-committal towards the forms of religion, a fanatic only when it came to defending her country's safety.

Walsingham tightened a net of surveillance and informers around Mary, leaving open loopholes in order to gather proof of her treachery. With a naïve openness Mary went on communicating with subversives in ways which made her seem an Othello of trust in the face of Walsingham's Iago-like tactics. He set up an elaborate secret mechanism, as well as the usual formal censorship, so that he could keep her under surveillance: "He was", wrote William Camden, "a most subtle searcher of secrets, nothing being contrived anywhere that he knew not by intelligence".

Walsingham did not have long to wait. Soon he was writing to the Earl of Leicester that he knew of murderous plots afoot: "if the matter be well-handled, it will break the neck of all dangerous practices during Her Majesty's Reign."

The gentlemen plotters played easily into the hands of the authorities: their plan to assassinate Elizabeth – well publicized beforehand, even boasted of – was rapidly foiled and they themselves barbarically disposed of; but a big question mark hovered over Mary's guilt and complicity, though well attested. Rumours spread wildly: Elizabeth had been murdered; civil war had broken out. "The musters were called out for the defence of the coast," runs one account. "The fleet was ordered to sea. The hunt for priests increased in vigour." Would Elizabeth authorize the arrest and trial of her Scottish "sister", granddaughter of her father's elder sister?

She did, but then, with her capacity for procrastination and inconsistency, her strange combination of delicacy and brutality, she delayed, offering possibilities of compromise. Mary goaded her on with the prospect of her own glorious martyrdom for the cause of the restoration of Catholicism in England. New fears swept England in early 1587: of invasion, of Mary's escape, of fresh plots and fires ravaging the country. In this atmosphere Elizabeth signed her "sister's" death warrant; but then dropped it to the floor with a sarcastic word. She would not release it for execution, but it was carried by William Davison, Walsingham's under-secretary, to the Chancellor, as she further delayed.

Her courtiers acted for her. Braving both temporary and, in one case, long-term disgrace, the Privy Council, unknown to the Queen, saw the warrant put to immediate effect. At Fotheringay Castle in Northamptonshire Mary was brought to the block. General rejoicing, as of a deliverance from some great calamity, greeted the beheading: bonfires, banquets, ringing of church bells, the whole public paraphernalia of celebration hardly stopped for a week, although many deemed it sacrilegious murder. Elizabeth was furious; she pined and she wept, as her courtiers scattered wildly to avoid her fury: Walsingham pretended to be ill; Leicester and Burghley were snubbed. Davison, who had let slip the warrant, came near to being hanged, and spent eighteen months in the Tower.

Where was Shakespeare during all this turbulence and confusion? We do not know, but he was close to the pulse of events. Leaving the Netherlands, now demobbed, he was issued with a pass which gave him just enough time to reach London or Stratford, but no more. The Elizabethans felt safer with everyone settled into their little niche, and the government was particularly anxious about discharged soldiers: without papers, Shakespeare would have been arrested at once as an unemployed vagrant. In his middle years he would picture that countryside of the 1580s roamed by masterless men: not only do *King Lear, Macbeth* and *Cymbeline* draw on that time, but also *As You Like It* and *The Winter's Tale*.

Shakespeare heard about the arrest and execution of John Somerville, a Warwickshire papist, who had sought to kill Elizabeth with a pistol. In London, a capital of less than 200,000 souls, about the size of present-day Oxford, he wandered the streets, like Restif de la Bretonne during the nights of the French Revolution, forming impressions of life, talking to bystanders and participants, gathering the materials of his future work. He attended public trials and executions. The comic interrogations which would form the basis of his humour, the clever answering back, the reversals by which the victim overturns his persecutor, these had their source in the darkness of what he saw, the rigged trials and the endless torment-ing and self-justifying of the prosecutors: above all such sights stimulated "gallows" humour. Comedy became the means to purge the underlying sense of terror and hysteria: it was only the despised Puritans who wanted laughter savagely repressed.

There can be little doubt, now, that William Shakespeare was intel-lectually ambitious and, for his time, well read. He had absorbed much Latin, which for him was like the study of Gaelic for writers of the Irish literary renaissance: it gave him a whole world of source literature, and different, more rudimentary, social attitudes and emo-tions to draw on. It provided him with primitive household from gods with which to enliven the dark conflicts of contemporary Christianity. It set up in him that crucial sense of men separating from gods and finding their own individuality and responsibility, which he himself would transform and interiorize into a new Renais-sance consciousness. This and his profound familiarity with the Bible – in the popular 1560 Geneva version, translated into English by Protestant exiles there – especially with the New Testament, the Psalms and the Book of Job, deepened his sense of spirituality. He awakened to a responsibility and to an awareness that men are only capable of real good when they first become capable of evil, and aware of their own capacity for it.

Although the Bible had always been read, if not always in a Renaissance English translation, in the 1570s and 1580s the classical literary worlds of Greece and Rome were brand-new discoveries for the Elizabethans – similar to the uncovering of ancient legends and folk-tales by the Irish literary élite from 1890 to 1910. This revelation of antique literature took on a hectic, accelerated pace as new versions, new texts, were prepared and published, or acted out on the stage. Dealing in treasures of the mind became highly competitive.

This adoption by the aristocracy and by the enlightened middle class of Roman and Greek classicism as a bulwark against the threat of foreign and papal intervention and influence also assumed a peculiarly English character, and it spread through commercial and cultural life. It rationalized medieval Christianity by means of a thorough absorption and implementation of Roman law in the conduct of the state. It substituted for the pious and miraculous aspects of continental Catholicism, a secular celebration of pagan deities which neutralized, or kept at arm's length, the most important religious issues, above all separating the well-being of the state, its ruler, and its people, from any holy mission in life. Religious fundamentalism was anathema to Elizabeth, and the Elizabethan citizen and citizeness – learned, virtuous, hard-working, but desirous of having a good time – modelled their lives on their sovereign's. Her influence permeated every aspect of everyday life.

But along with classical learning, a more vivid and racy streak of informative power captured Shakespeare's imagination. The Elizabethans had fashioned to an extraordinary degree another capacity that links them to their late-twentieth-century counterparts: a thirst for news. The passion for recording local events was insatiable: and as today they wanted their stories pre-digested: they were impatient; they pursued short-cuts to knowledge, which was considered the Open Sesame to everything: books and manuals of potted instruction proliferated. There were fewer than 4,000,000 Elizabethans, but their literary activity, both in density and diversity, was quite out of proportion to their number. Sidney's death at Zutphen, for example, inspired between 200 and 300 elegies.

The desire for information was rooted in political need: this was a fiercely individualistic people who felt connected, through the peculiarly populist instincts of the Queen and government, with events: Elizabeth knew what her people were thinking. To Shakespeare, who had a keen eye, a ready verbal wit, an alienated, underdog streak but no deep social animus, the information was also highly entertaining. However gory, sad, extreme, or trivial it was, the public lapped up this new popular entertainment: "Scarce a cat can look out of a gutter but out starts a half-penny chronicler."

For the heart and fancy of the developing dramatist there was even better to come. Irish writers such as W. B. Yeats and Sean O'Casey found in their Easter Rebellion of 1916 the melting-pot for national passion, disillusionment and aspiration. Shakespeare was a very different kind of national genius: in the new and devastating shadow cast over his country he discovered rich material. He saw England as a great potential subject. And nothing focused his attention on it so firmly as the threat posed to the country by Elizabeth's former half-brother-in-law, Philip of Spain, six years her senior, who had once – he cursed himself for it in later life – entertained a passion for her.

From popular versions of Greek and Roman tragedies and comedies he saw presented with increasing frequency in places of public entertainment, Shakespeare noticed how the family relationships of the protagonists were echoed in the extraordinary and tangled dynasty of the English royal family. Family passion, revenge, envy, all the local, domestic springs of popular and entertaining plays, were the generative forces of world politics. The new writers like Christopher Marlowe and those fellow university graduates he dominated were just beginning to perceive and transform these disturbing ingredients into their classical models with some slight degree of realism. It would take someone greater to see that, dressed up and disguised, the realism of political events could be transplanted almost without further adaptation on to the public stages.

The great epic of the Armada invasion of 1588 was a bit too spectacular, demanding too much of scant theatre resources, to be a subject for Shakespeare's art. But its menace, the preparations to meet it, the insecurity and heroism it called up remained with him, and would emerge in a hundred different guises. England became, as in 1940, centre stage in world history: it was a moment for death or survival.

Philip II of Spain, Elizabeth's "brother", decided to move against England at the time Elizabeth was mounting her, militarily speaking, amateur Netherlands expedition. He formed a plan for a combined military and naval operation, relying heavily – as it turned out, unwisely – on the support he would receive from English Catholics: one intelligence report spoke of the likelihood of the whole of Yorkshire rising in arms. But English Catholics, with some notably unpleasant exceptions, were intensely patriotic: they would not submit their land to the yoke of foreign conquest, and from July 1586 onwards the whole of England was on fire with preparations to repel a foreign invasion. Footbands, such as those parodied in *Henry IV* Part Two, were mustered in the shires, compulsory harquebus training imposed on able-bodied men; in the towns, watches (how many realistic watches would Shakespeare echo later, notably in *Hamlet* and *Othello*) were set up nightly, and primitive signalling – beacons, messengers – was organized nationally.

As in 1940–1, when England lay at the apparent mercy of the Nazi invaders, the English possessed two supreme advantages. The first was that of intelligence (as would be true 350 years later): the excellent spy service that Walsingham had set up on the Continent "listened in" to every stage of the Spanish preparations, and reported back what it heard. But the second factor, the advantage of British naval gunnery methods,

> the nimble gunner
> With linstock now the devilish cannon touches,
> And down goes all before them,

– as with the superiority of the English fighter command over the Luftwaffe in English skies in the later summer of 1940 – was the more crucial.

Shakespeare did not see any of the deciding conflict at first hand: but the experience already gained was reinforced by the ferment during Armada year. For Spain was intent in 1588 not just on a naval victory over the English fleet, but on all-out military conquest. And if John Shakespeare had not sold a piece of pasture to buy him a horse, his eldest son went on foot, armed with his sword, to Kent to meet the Duke of Parma's expected invasion with 30,000 men from the Netherlands.

Ten days' struggle at sea decided the outcome: Spanish ships named after saints – *San Felipe, San Mateo* – met their more secular counterparts, *Lion, Tiger, Revenge, Dreadnought*. Philip, surrounded by priests, monks and relics, prayed in his chapel in the Escorial: but Elizabeth had been among her troops at Tilbury. Bare-headed, mounted on a white horse with dappled grey hindquarters, corseted in steel and with a page behind her bearing a plumed helmet, she rode through the English lines, with Leicester leading her horse: "I know I have the body of a weak feeble woman," she said; "but I have the heart and stomach of a king, and a king of England too."

There is no doubt that the outcome was a triumph of popular nationalism, uniting every shade of religious opinion in England, over an intense, almost fanatically backward continental spirituality and sense of superiority. Conciliatory, peaceful in spirit, the new outlook of middle-class capitalism was on the side of the English, who had done everything they could to avoid war. At news of the great victory some of the English students in the Jesuit College at

Rome burst out cheering, and even Pope Sixtus V, who had shown no great enthusiasm for the outdated crusade against England, uttered admiration for the English Queen's courage and bravery. The Spanish withdrew to lick their wounds, and contemplate their calamity as a judgement of God.

But the English, in true Elizabethan spirit, failed to follow up their victory or take revenge: "Sufficient unto the day is the evil thereof" was the Queen's motto. Shortly afterwards Leicester died: in his will he left Elizabeth a magnificent pendant – a huge diamond embedded in emeralds with a rope of 600 "fair white pearls". Elizabeth, reacting with hysterical distress, withdrew to her Whitehall Palace bedchamber and barred the door. Only the national rejoicing, and a spectacular service at St Paul's, tempered her grief.

In spite of their cruelties to practising Catholics the English response to the Armada excited general admiration, not only at home but abroad. By depicting retrospectively, in other historical contexts – even in one as far-flung as ancient Rome – those patriotic emotions, and the great ferment of a populace harnessed to a cause in which it believed passionately, under a leader it worshipped (a ferment which he himself had seen and experienced at first hand), Shakespeare would define for all time, both individually and collectively, the whole range and mood of a country suffering its gravest peril.

The defeat of the Spanish Armada confirmed the particular power and qualities of the new English nation. England had proved its inward greatness: "Like little body with a mighty heart".

In the plays he was to write over the next twelve years Shakespeare would hold up the mirror to that emergent power.

# The wonder of our stage

The unknown actor could walk in a jig, make water in a cinque pace, entune a song through his nose, extemporize a melody on the viol-de-gamboys. His eyes scoured dance manuals, he hummed from popular song sheets, he culled jokes from everything – simple and crude, or highly sophisticated, the level did not matter much – and invented puns from basic body functions to the most sophisticated use of foreign tongues. "For what says Quinapalus," teases Feste in *Twelfth Night*, "Better a witty fool than a foolish wit." Who was Quinapalus, the learned Greek or Roman authority? "Qui-n'a-pas-lu" – pronounced as French – makes it clear: "Mr No-one-has-read".

Apart from the straightforward version: bit-part player rises to leading roles, there are various mildly damnifying accounts of how Shakespeare joined the theatrical profession. The idea of poaching was popular, so one report has him stealing a deer from Charlecote Park, estate of the local landowner Sir Thomas Lucy, and forced to flee his home-town. This picturesque legend has him whipped for his crime, but wobbles in probability when confronted with evidence that the Lucys had no deer park until later. It is usually supported by one of many local references to people or places: Shallow's conversation with Master Slender and with the Welsh parson Evans in *The Merry Wives of Windsor* propels the device of the "luce", a freshwater fish punningly assumed by the Lucy family, into further paranomaniac waters. Referring to a lawsuit against Falstaff, Slender invokes a "gentleman born", who adopts the customs of gentlefolk: they may, says Slender, "give the dozen white luces in their coat". But Shallow objects that it is an old coat.

> EVANS:  The dozen white louses do become an old coad well. It agrees well passant: it is a familiar beast to man, and signifies love.
> SHALLOW:  The luce is the fresh fish; the salt fish is an old cod.

The game becomes, to our ears, tedious. Supporters of this legend have claimed this was Shakespeare's revenge for the whipping: good-humouredly calling his former castigator a "louse".

Other apocryphal accounts of Shakespeare during the mid- and late 1580s have him variously employed: one as apprentice in his father's glove-maker's shop, cutting and shaping the felt and buckram, trimming the fur and goatskins, sewing on lace, or glueing feathers, handling satin, camlet and silk, ribbons and cotton: "Gloves as sweet as damask roses, / Masks for faces, and for noses" – as the servant says of Autolycus in *The Winter's Tale*, "He hath songs for man or woman, of all sizes. No milliner can so fit his customers with gloves." He may also have travelled to buy raw materials for his father.

As from 1573 to 1587 no fewer than twenty-three travelling theatrical companies visited Stratford, another possibility is that Shakespeare joined one of these. In one year, 1587, when Shakespeare was twenty-three, five companies, including the Queen's, the Earl of Essex's and the Earl of Leicester's, played this thespian stronghold: one of these companies, under strength, could well have recruited a new member on the spot, thus providing a specific year for the commencement of Shakespeare's career in the theatre.

Whatever he did, he certainly did not remain bound by the "small experience" of staying at home, as Petruchio calls it in *The Taming of the Shrew*; some wind "as scatters young men through the world" had swept him away from Stratford. He was about to embark on "the career of an exile", the director Trevor Nunn describes it: "somebody who has already forfeited the notion of being acceptable in all parts of society." James Joyce wrote that the note of banishment – "banishment from the heart, banishment from home" – sounds uninterruptedly "from *The Two Gentlemen of Verona* onward till Prospero breaks his staff".

Dr Johnson, in the Preface to his 1765 edition of Shakespeare's plays, provides a colourful explanation of what Shakespeare first did: when he fled to London from the "terror of criminal prosecution" (over the theft of the deer), writes Johnson, his first expedient was to wait at the door of the playhouse, and "hold the horses of those that had no servants, that they might be ready again after the performance". Shakespeare became so good at this, that "in a short time every man as he alighted called for Will. Shakespear, and scarcely any other waiter was trusted with a horse while Will. Shakespear could be had."

This was the beginning of better fortune. Finding more horses put into his hands than he could hold, Shakespeare hired boys to wait under his inspection, who, "when Will. Shakespear was summoned, were immediately to present themselves, I am Shakespear's boy, Sir."

This creates an unduly humble picture of the young poet-playwright: he may not have had noble lineage, and while his father's application for a coat of arms, with its falcon crest and spear, first made in 1568 when he was bailiff of Stratford, had slipped back into an anonymous file in the College of Heralds – yet Shakespeare was not the forelock-tugging type, and not unconnected. A later acquaintance of his, whose epitaph he supposedly wrote, was Elias James, who managed a brewery in Blackfriars. A supplier of inns could easily have helped an aspiring actor on to the stage. Shakespeare was notably and proudly middle-class.

An Elizabethan theatre manager, such as Philip Henslowe, proprietor of the Rose Theatre in Southwark, who left a valuable record of his activities in a folio volume of accounts, would put on, or have in repertory, some seventy plays a year, of which as many as fifteen might be new. It needed but a few days to stage a play, so production values, such as we have today, were rudimentary. Rehearsal was minimal. Scenery – which was fixed – and properties were functional or symbolic. Actors would "dry", fluff their lines, transpose whole speeches from one part of the play to another, or even miss their entrance cues. The quick-witted would often be called on to invent, the dullard would be booed or hissed off the stage.

"Character" was not an Elizabethan idea at all, so no actor could say, "Who is the character I am playing . . . ?" He played a "part", not a "character". We apply our terminology backward. Fortunately Shakespeare resists. The past is another country – different customs, different values and expectations weave and militate among its people. Motivation is a nineteenth-century idea, while the tangled web of what we now call "relationships" was also an outcome of that century's leisured times, and the huge development and growth of the novel.

Elizabethans had rudimentary and childlike needs when they went to the theatre: they wanted to be gripped. They were familiar with basic, well-known plots. More often than not they would be asking themselves, "What will they make of the story this time?" To become a devilishly clever manipulator of well-known tales, to weave and blend together two or three of them at a time, this was the height of mastery for an aspiring playwright. "We will do it in action," says Peter Quince, the bookkeeper in *A Midsummer Night's Dream*, although more often than not the words were the action.

Scenery and production existed largely within the language, at least until the affluent playhouses of James I's reign could supply more special effects. "This green plot shall be our stage, this hawthorn brake our tiring house," says Quince. The playwright would "block out" the actions of his fiction with directions constantly incorporated in the verse or prose. "Pray you, undo this button," instructs Lear; "He is about it," says Lady Macbeth of her husband's evil deed, "The doors are open, and the surfeited grooms / Do mock their charge with snores." In Act V of *Hamlet*, most spectacularly of all, the dialogue crackles with stage action: every stab and cut of the three-and-a-half-round duel between Hamlet and Laertes is completely realized in the verse dialogue. Claudius at first manages the fight by telling Osric to supply the foils, sets out the poisoned stoup of wine, directs the martial flourishes. As the pace quickens towards the final bursting of the impostume of rottenness, each participant turns excited commentator on the motives and effects of his or her actions. Laertes, woodcock to his own spring, is "justly killed with mine own treachery". Claudius's foul practice turns itself on him. Gertrude's penultimate concern is to wipe her son's face. Hamlet, himself, drains off the poison cup. The director merely has to follow instructions.

Acting was serious, heavy work: an actor played a different part every night. Staggering as it might seem, Shakespeare could have acted in 1,000 different productions or revivals, although many of the parts would have been very small. Any performer so engaged must have had an intricate and flexible memory, a talent for improvisation and an extremely cool nervous system. The bookkeeper or prompter had most of his work cut out making sure the actors came on in the proper order.

Acting was extremely popular work: the rolls were overcrowded then, as now. Actors of standing owned their own costumes, properties and playbooks, yet might easily find themselves out of work and on the road. English actors were considered the best in the known world – one, only mediocre, touring company became the hit of the Frankfurt Fair in Germany where "both men and women flocked wonderfully" to see them.

A major company such as that to which Shakespeare belonged seldom had more than ten or twelve permanent members, known as "sharers" or "fellows", as they invested in the stock and shared receipts and expenses. They employed "hired" actors for about six shillings a week and supported and housed boy apprentices who played the women's roles. Sometimes, for an important performance, there would be as many as thirty, or even forty, in a cast; sometimes, as when on tour, perhaps as few as twelve, so that many parts would be "doubled". The first necessity for an actor was to possess a good voice, but the demands on his physical prowess were no less great: the fashion was for violent, spectacular dances like the galliard, an exaggerated leap known as the "capriole", and the convulsive raising of a partner high in the air – the "volte". Shakespeare, proficient at these, might also have graduated in "tumbling", for some companies began as little more than a group of circus acrobats.

Battles and sieges were compulsory, spectacular leaps such as Laurence Olivier's in the film of *Hamlet,* or his death fall on the stage in *Coriolanus,* were the order of the day. Above all the actor had to fight: the average Londoner was a connoisseur of fencing: fights were not so much arranged, as they are today, as improvised between two expert swordsmen. Young actors such as Shakespeare in his early twenties spent many hot and exhausting hours in practice with the sword, wielding a long heavy rapier in the right hand; in the left a quillon dagger for parrying, and for savage thrusts at close quarters.

Exact training, with perfect physical coordination, was needed to achieve the brutal realism without injury. Richard Tarleton, the great popular comedian of the Elizabethan stage, had conferred on him the honorary title of Master of Fence. Not all were so adept: on one occasion at the Swan Theatre a fencer was accidentally stabbed through the eye. A proficient swordsman, Ben Jonson not only killed an enemy in personal combat in the Netherlands, he later murdered a fellow actor in what may have been a duel, and was branded with a "T" for Tyburn, escaping execution by pleading benefit of clergy. He had been proud of being a soldier.

Actors performed in the glare of the afternoon sun without the hard or soft illusions of twentieth-century stage lighting. Lodging in a single room in a Shoreditch suburban house, probably a mile or two out of the City centre, Shakespeare rose early: *profecto enim vita vigilia est* – Pliny the Elder's motto, "to live is to be awake", was widely adopted among rich and poor. There was virtually no interval between leaping from bed and leaving the house. Shakespeare slept in a simple bedchamber, with as few trappings as there would be today on the starkest of his stage sets. A bed, a chest, a desk, a window heavy with shutters, a few books, a chamber pot. He would have gone to bed naked – just thrown aside his clothes on the back of the chair but kept a "night-" or dressing-gown to hand. Clothes were expensive. The impecunious Don Armado in *Love's Labour's Lost* confesses to having no shirt under his doublet.

Shakespeare rehearsed in the morning, while in the evening, the time he mostly devoted to writing in his lodgings, the acting company, often reduced in number, gave special performances at embassies or noblemen's houses. He had always kept a commonplace book, in which to copy down jests and fine phrases from the latest play. It was general practice to amass such social information.

In *Hamlet* (Bad Quarto, 1603) there is a warning against using old jokes: "And Gentlemen quote his jests down in their tables, before they come to the play, as thus: 'Cannot you stay . . . 'till I eat my porridge?' . . ."

The formation of an Elizabethan actor was as hard an acting school as there has ever been, or ever could be. Shakespeare had a powerful body and a strong voice; his physical, emotional and vocal stamina was exceptional, his quick committal to memory of new parts was prodigious. Not only were Elizabethan actors infinitely more dextrous with words than actors today: they memorized swiftly, and speaking and listening were more potent and subtle. Shakespeare started acting five or six years before he became known as a playwright, and he continued up to performances of *The Tempest*, although he acted less and less after 1600. He trod the boards for twenty-five years, if not more. This is, as a feat of sustained professional survival, quite extraordinary, when you consider the arduous conditions of touring, the appalling diet, the exposure to the plague and every other infection, as well as the sheer physical and emotional wear and tear of being an actor.

Shakespeare reached his peak as an actor by the age of twenty-eight. Henry Chettle, the publisher, in an epistle to *Kind-Heart's Dream* (1592), called Shakespeare "excellent" – his demeanour, he said, is no less civil "than he excellent in the quality he professes". This is echoed some years later by John Davies of Hereford, who wrote in *Microcosmos* (1603) that he loved players and their "quality": next to the line, "And some I love for painting, poesy", he printed in the margin the initials, "W.S.R.B." – intending Shakespeare and Richard Burbage. Shakespeare may even have played the king in Peele's *Edward I*, as hazarded by E. K. Chambers: "Shake thy speares in honour of his name / Under whose royalty thou wearst the same."

It is evident from *Hamlet* that Shakespeare disliked overacting, hated over-demonstrative, ad-libbing clowns, and applauded a restraint which kept within "the modesty of nature". The purpose of playing, Hamlet says, is to hold "the mirror up to nature, to show virtue her own feature, scorn her own image, and the very age and body of the time his form and pressure".

Later traditional gossip as handed down does not rate Shakespeare's acting so highly: James Wright says he had heard he was "a much better poet, than Player", while Edward Capell recalls that he played Adam, "was no extraordinary actor", and that he might even have been, accidentally, lame. Present-day speculation finds him competent. Alec Guinness says, "I don't see why he shouldn't have been a good actor – he knew what he was talking about"; "I think he was all right, but no great shakes," avers Derek Jacobi; "a much better actor than you are given to understand," claimed J. C. Trewin.

John Barton believes that Shakespeare probably did not want to play big parts; "no one says he was a major actor, so we mustn't assume he played the big roles". George Rylands sees him discreetly submerged in a company of perhaps thirty or forty, directing his work himself, similar in style to John Gielgud. "He would dart hither and thither, fire off dozens of different ideas and suggestions – not at all an authoritarian director like Peter Brook."

# Outer and inner worlds

The Theatre in Holywell Lane, off the Shoreditch Road, where the Burbage company played *The Two Gentlemen of Verona* possibly as early as 1589, was the oldest surviving playhouse in England. Here, outside the Puritan jurisdiction of the City of London yet felicitously placed near enough to draw on its population for audiences, James, father of Richard Burbage, had built his first theatre when Shakespeare was just twelve. Up to then companies had acted in the London innyards as they had on scaffolding erected all over England in the inner courts of the victualling houses. The staging had sometimes been quite elaborate, with better-off spectators ranged round the upstairs rooms and galleries, but freight, mail, and carters interfered with smooth theatrical presentation more than a few days a week. Without the special "tiring house" from which they could be properly administered, the costumes, props and the collection of admission fees must have posed their own headaches.

Burbage, a lucky combination of actor and "joiner", like Snug in *A Midsummer Night's Dream*, imaginatively expanded the innyard space in the first purpose-built playhouse which he erected in the marshy grounds of the sacked and "dissolved" Priory of Holywell, just outside Moorgate postern. He drew architecturally on Southwark's two bear-baiting and bull-baiting arenas, circular in arrangement like the old Roman circuses, with upstairs seats arranged in curving tiers; it gave a visibility much improved on that of inn courts. The ordinary public who formerly had stood in the innyard in front of the scaffolding, now had their special "promenade", still open to the elements; but a sophisticated inner stage, for interior scenes such as bedroom or cave, and where hand properties could be hidden and used, together with backstage dressing rooms and storage sheds, were significant innovations. With capacity audiences of more than 2,000, and with privileged spectators in the galleries paying higher prices, the takings from a packed performance represented, relative to the times, an immense fortune, soon making actors into successful *arrivistes* – as rich as the burghers of London's explosive market economy.

Language was more important than visual illusion: in the Irish literary renaissance from 1900 to 1920, when the Abbey Theatre, Dublin, made its reputation out of the newly forged literary styles and the attitudes of Irish nationalism, people went to hear plays, not to see them. "I will hear that play," says Theseus of the "tedious brief scene" presented by Quince and his players. "Will the King hear this piece of work?" asks Hamlet. In Dublin listening to a play was also more important than watching it: the word "shift", used in a play of largely poetic invention based on rhythms of folk speech, caused a riot at the first performance of J. M. Synge's *Playboy of the Western World*. The representation of a prostitute with outspoken affirmation of her human qualities led to equal commotion at the first performances of O'Casey's *The Plough and the Stars*.

Three hundred years before, Ben Jonson had been sent to prison for satirizing the government in *The Isle of Dogs*, which he partly wrote and acted in. Plays were dangerous. They could have their authors hung for treason or stabbed on a dark night. Plays whose rich, bawdy and inventive language could shock, and whose rhetoric could move – when audiences went along primarily to hear – disappeared more or less completely in England in 1968 with the abolition of the office of the Lord Chamberlain. In Shakespeare's day only a sermon or a royal procession could gather together a comparable number of people.

Burbage created a space primarily to enable every word to be clearly heard. Texts, even in the case of the earliest plays staged at the Theatre by Lord Strange's men, such as Robert Greene's *Friar Bacon and Friar Bungay*, appealed primarily as what Paul Claudel many centuries later called "intelligible mouthfuls". With beard waxed to a spike and red hair, silk-stockinged, cloaked in green, a brother as bodyguard and a demi-monde tart in tow, Greene had a high profile for drinking and other disreputable antics. As volatile as the times that produced them, such texts as have come down to us are in different forms, answering the needs of different production conditions or reflecting the variable vanities of their authors, the inaccurate exploitation of printers or pirates, or the love of perfection of the true devotees. As John Barton says, "You can see from Henslowe's diary that he paid five dramatists each to write one act of a play. With these texts any hypothesis will work: when you have ... no copyright, where there is plague, where you run out of copyright, then the idea of an authoritative text is crazy. All you can say is that a given text represents a text at some point in its history." George Peele's play *The Battle of Alcazar*, for instance, mysteriously known as "mulumurco", gathered the enormous sum of twenty-nine shillings one night in February 1592; its text survives only in a cut version for a small cast on tour.

Blank verse, a heightened yet everyday rhythm organized in the most predictable falling of stresses and chopping up of syllables, helped actors to act with power and authority out of doors; it aided them in controlling their breathing: it also facilitated learning. It gradually became beautifully modulated, and had all kinds of contrapuntal systems with breaks, checks and subtleties of flow.

Fluency was paramount: the poet Ted Hughes describes the innate trick of this, as far as Shakespeare was concerned, as a pincer movement, "a latinate word on one wing and an Anglo-Saxon on the other". Meaning was overwhelmingly suggested by inspired signalling and hinting of "verbal heads and tails above and below precision", a kind of "primitive, unconscious but highly accurate punning". The sound of words had an incantatory presence, and became meaningful in a magic way that it is hard to imagine: "a weirdly expressive underswell, like a jostling of spirits", says Hughes.

The 30,000 different words Shakespeare would eventually come to employ were first and foremost enjoyed by his mixed audiences of the highly literate and totally illiterate as a profane and entertaining, but also sacred, distribution of words. Breath sustained the whole intricate span of Shakespeare's creation. A vowel is a breath, and a consonant is a muscular contraction: respiration, breathing out, carries the vowel sound which is then censured, or sculpted, by muscular contractions. Words are modelled like sculptures and sent travelling through the air.

The text filled out the parts and gave each his or her own individual life. They are inconceivable without the particular mixture of rhythms and images with which they express themselves. Shakespeare, very soon after he started writing, evolved stage figures to which his own vision and use of language were indispensable. Above all he had the knack of urgency: all the parts are spurred on to improvise from the seat of their passions, to express themselves with a sense of crisis, to give identity to themselves by a flash of instant verbal energy. Shakespeare knew all about crisis.

He learned by writing: his early, anonymous contributions to works either lost or not attributed to him served a public apprenticeship – before their audiences. Every play reflected the public for which it was tailored. For his first known comedy, which even in its buoyant self-assurance is patently an experimental and apprentice play, Shakespeare planted the story in three different Italian locations, and described how passion makes men forget the duties of friendship. The only source known for the plot of this play is the Portuguese Jorge de Montemayor's story *Diana*.

In elaborating every Italian device he could seize on Shakespeare tried out comic schemes and complications which he would later take up again. The girl from *Two Gentlemen of Verona* he later incorporated into *Twelfth Night*, where she is disguised as her lover's page and obliged to plead his suit with her rival; several other strands, like a friar, a ladder of cords, and exile from court, turned up again in *Romeo and Juliet*. The spirited band of outlaws in the forest became the *sine qua non* of *As You Like It*. The more sophisticated switch of rings and the girl dressed as a man recurred triumphantly in *The Merchant of Venice*; so would a scene where a noblewoman discusses her suitors with her maidservant.

Shakespeare had absolutely no qualms about adopting hackneyed or shopworn material. Even at the start he showed no great aspiration to become an innovator. Yet he originated a practice, by use of cheap plot materials, and of conventional clowns such as Launce and his trick dog, and Speed, of creating plot precedents and character ancestors which became to him almost second nature to follow. He set up conditions by which, in plagiarizing old stock material from the work of others, he could begin to plagiarize and improve on himself. He was quite happy to make concessions to an audience which he wanted to please. He experimented in order to go deeper, not to become newer. The one criterion for use of the materials he took up was, "Are they vital to me?"

Some were, and some were not. Some would become self-feeding and self-reinforcing; some would remain dull and wooden. Some could be used again – and some could not. But a personal note was at once audible in *Two Gentlemen* which grew more markedly identifiable later in the Sonnets. The mood of admiration of Valentine, the wronged friend, for Proteus had a parallel in the friendship Shakespeare had started a year or so before with the Earl of Southampton, who was nine years his junior. Valentine has himself been an idle truant, failing to clothe himself "with angel-like perfection". Yet Proteus has

> Made use and fair advantage of his days:
> ... And in a word – for far behind his worth
> Comes all the praises that I now bestow –
> He is complete, in feature and in mind.

That passion makes men forget the duties of friendship is also a theme of the Sonnets. The two gentlemen love Silvia. Proteus, rejected by her, betrays his friend finally by trying to force Silvia to yield to his desire. Proteus repents, so Valentine forgives his friend in the terms of Sonnet 40 ("I do forgive thy robb'ry, gentle thief"). He receives him "honest" once more, and avouches

> Who by repentance is not satisfied
> Is nor of heaven nor earth. For these are pleased;
> By penitence th' Eternal's wrath's appeased.
> And that my love may appear plain and free,
> All that was mine in Silvia I give thee.

This withdrawal is not convincing, merely a feeble and sputtering extinction of any motivating flame. Shakespeare, perhaps wrestling with a problem too near to some source of pain to be comfortable, seemed unable yet to control all its latent possibilities.

Shakespeare was grappling also with a disillusioning awareness, which fortunately he seems never finally to have become discouraged by – either in person or in his art – namely that while a man or woman seeks naturally, in the loved one, a mirror-image of him or herself, the very boundlessness of his own nature would lead, in his own case already had led, to unhappiness. As he could only find small fragments of himself in others, any passion he worked up for another would lead to frustration – unless he accepted the discrepancy between his own fertile nature and power, and the rest of the world. Here, too, was an as yet unrecognized but highly productive strain in his continually developing character: as Proteus says, caught between Julia, his first love, and Silvia, his friend's catch,

> ... e'en that power which gave me first my oath
> Provokes me to this threefold perjury.
> Love bade me swear, and love bids me forswear ...
> At first I did adore a twinkling star,
> But now I worship a celestial sun.
> Unheedful vows may heedfully be broken.

London's seething life was only thinly disguised in the props and accoutrements of the delightful world conjured up by *Two Gentlemen of Verona*. Shakespeare followed the popular prose, and the Arcadian court dramas of John Lyly, but, writing also for the new commercial theatre, he gave back his own audience its own problems in an enhanced reflection. "Thy master is shipped," says Panthino to Proteus' body servant, Launce, "and thou art to post after with oars" – in other words he must bloody well hurry: "You'll lose the tide if you tarry any longer." Hardly a Veronese waterway. Launce replies,

> It is no matter if the tied were lost [he refers to his dog, the scripted incarnation of the timeless funny man's appendage], for it is the unkindest tied that ever any man tied.

Panthino then asks what is the unkindest "tide", meaning Thames's tide.

LAUNCE:  Why, he that's tied here, Crab my dog.
PANTHINO:  Tut, man, I mean thou'lt lose the flood, and in losing the flood, lose thy voyage ...
LAUNCE:  Lose the tide, and the voyage, and the master, and the service, and the tied? Why, man, if the river were dry, I am able to fill it with my tears.

Thus Shakespeare homed in on the massive arterial waterway of the Thames. In easy comic, sentimental, or simply journalistic references to popular circumstances the playwright set the standard of his own accessibility and appeal.

Late in 1592 or early in 1593, Henry Chettle published post-humously the last pamphlet of Robert Greene. Terminally ill, and overwhelmed with repentance, Greene had written the *Groatsworth of Wit* in which he tried to atone for his debts, his plays, for deserting his wife and for having a mistress. In this violent, semi-legible diatribe, which Chettle toned down especially not to give offence to one object of Greene's attack (Marlowe, whom he berated for atheism), Greene inveighs against actors, calling them "apes", "peasants", "painted monsters", and puppets "that speak from our mouths" and are "garnished in our colours". While he lay starving and impecunious the actors grew fat with prosperity from the new playhouses, and one in particular had achieved a dubious eminence: "There is an upstart crow" runs the well-known passage from the *Groatsworth of Wit*, "beautified with our feathers, that, with his tiger's heart wrapped in a player's hide, supposes he is as well able to bombast out a blank verse as the best of you; and being an absolute Johannes fac totum, is in his own conceit the only Shake-scene in a country."

This punning reference to Shakespeare singled out, also, a famous line from the third part of that playwright's *Henry VI*, which attracted large audiences in the early 1590s: "O tiger's heart wrapped in a woman's hide". No doubt Shakespeare's facility of invention, combined with his success, galled the failing pedantic wit; Chettle later regretted not modifying the attack, and wrote: "That I did not, I am as sorry as if the original fault had been my fault".

Shakespeare did not, at least publicly, take offence. Nor did he appear to rate the attack seriously, although by now his friend and patron the Earl of Southampton was prepared to stand up for him, as the poet reported in Sonnet 112, where he also coined a word and punned on his detractor's name:

> Your love and pity doth th' impression fill
> Which vulgar scandal stamped upon my brow;
> For what care I who calls me well or ill,
> So you o'er-green my bad, my good allow?

How hard did the members of this new breed of playwrights work at the beginning of the 1590s? Greene, just turned thirty, had written six or eight plays. That Shakespeare wrote, or almost wholly wrote, fewer than forty was not unusual, nor was the labour of their creation heavily time-consuming, although their consistently high quality fell into a different category from hard work. Thomas Heywood, the Catholic recusant playwright and descendant of Thomas More, also like Shakespeare a full-time player, had "either an entire hand, or at least a main finger" in writing 220 plays. Shakespeare, unlike Ben Jonson who also began as an actor, never supported himself entirely by his pen; yet as an outright payment a playwright could expect £7 from a play, roughly one third of a schoolmaster's annual salary.

The age despised revisers, who expected to "lie in child-bed one and thirty weeks and eight days of three bad lines and afterward spend a whole twelve-month" making them run better. Jonson was pilloried for taking five weeks over a play. Like the Hollywood film-makers of the 1930s, the Elizabethan playwrights were intoxicated by working in a completely new industry. Like the latter-day script-writers, who were often also the best wits of the age, these playwrights cannibalized and patched up each other's work. No one revived old plays, they wrote new ones. The pace of creation was hectic.

And the battle-lines were drawn. Professional scholars and actors were at war. Although Greene in his shrill condemnation may appear a lone voice, he was a spokesman for the university school of playwriting – notably himself, Lodge, Peele, Nashe and Kyd, all of them overtowered by Marlowe. Gifted, learned, but often ill-regulated, insanely bombastic, deficient, as pedants are, in humour, this group was more and more coming up against a harder and more popular, less literary form of theatre, produced by the collaborative efforts of playwrights and actors: "the public means which public manners breed". The most individual wielder of these means was himself ready to tap a richer source.

# The ground-plan of imagination

In the late 1580s and early 1590s religion was politics and politics was religion. All Shakespeare's work became political in the specific sense that Mrs Thatcher, in the 1980s, viewed politics: "I am in politics because of the conflict between good and evil, and I believe that in the end good will triumph." The Protestant virgin Queen was steering a successful middle course between Catholic ardour and Puritan extremism: she loved her people steadfastly, was attuned to their needs and wants. England was not withering under the papal curse of Pius V, and she sought ways of accommodating loyal and patriotic Catholics as her reign went on and the physical threat of Spain receded. Although the new literary culture was unrecognized beyond its shores, England became a land of enhanced prestige: even the exiled Cardinal Allen in Rome protected Protestant travellers from the Inquisition: two of Elizabeth's ministers, Lord Burghley and Francis Bacon, wrote books proclaiming the material virtues of England's individual Protestantism. Elizabeth herself became her land's chief propagandist, writing in April 1591 to the Duke of Florence, to repudiate attacks on England, that "It is clear as daylight that God's blessing rests upon us, upon our people and realm, with all the plainest signs of prosperity, peace, obedience, riches, power and increase of our subjects". This was the moral of England's prosperity.

Like Shakespeare, although with greater idealism and sanctifying force, Edmund Spenser beat the drum of political concord, and castigated the dragon of civil strife, seen as the old religion. Spenser promoted the idea of national discipline in a more single-minded way, and with allegiances different from Shakespeare's, but his allegorical method had a profound influence on the younger playwright. Shakespeare borrowed, and would continue to borrow, from other writers, adapting their innovations, through his acute understanding of them, to his own particular needs and personal flair.

The Renaissance gave everyone an experience of emergence, a definition of what his or her new discovery of civilization actually was: it portrayed in many forms – and this is where it became fused with Protestant individualism, which was immediately recognized as potent and adopted by the Catholic counter-Reformation – the story of the individual emerging from the tribe's clan, or anonymity. It illuminated a new differentiation between mythology and man. At what point did man cease to be a god and take responsibility for himself? The *Odyssey*, the *Aeneid* were definitions of man's new-found attributes in the ancient world. Orestes had to shoulder the burden of his own crimes: his fate was arbitrary and unkind, but it had come under his own control.

Spenser attempted the same kind of definition, but wrapped up in a peculiarly Elizabethan invention, the "dark conceit", as he called it, of allegory, which appealed in its ambiguities and clusters of meaning to the self-contradictory and paradoxical Elizabethan nature. The notion was that as the poet told a story a deeper, more profound meaning emerged from a parallel progression in that story which the reader had to unravel for himself.

Shakespeare, a lifelong admirer of Spenser yet sensibly divergent from him both in subject-matter and direct allegorical style, drew on *The Faerie Queene* to build up complex personages. Spenser's Archimago, the arch-magician, master of disguise whether as hermit or Red Cross Knight, and Iago, the dominating evil figure of *Othello*, both have the same false and delusive creativity. Archimago's black art defines Spenser's valuation of truth: quick in answer he drives the virtuous to despair, as when he tells Una her knight is slain, picking up the tones to weave a convincing duplicity: "Ah dearest dame (quoth he) how might I see / The king, that might not be, and yet was donne", with a wit and plausibility that is typical of Iago, whose name even has the ring of Archimago. Likewise Spenser's Arthur is England, an embodiment of the very special qualities Shakespeare would depict in *Henry V*.

*The Faerie Queene* was published in 1590. Crucial to Shakespeare's development, it gave a significant push to his growing powers, as well as leading him to focus on England and royal personages, such as Elizabeth, as "polyvalent" beings – attaching to themselves, that is, a number of different meanings, challenging exploration and interpretation in a way similar to a biblical text. The absorption of the allegorical method was an important stage in developing his universality, which transcended method and became a quality of his own nature. As Coleridge wrote two and a half centuries later, "in all his various characters, we still feel ourselves communicating with the same nature, which is everywhere present as the vegetable sap in the branches, sprays, leaves, buds, blossoms, and fruits, their shapes, tastes and odours". Twentieth-century figures who have spent their lives working in Shakespeare agree: "You recognize the same voice," says John Tydeman, head of the BBC Sound Drama department, whose computer is called Will. "I've always felt comfortable with the man," affirms Barbara Jefford, who has acted many of his female roles. "I grew up with him."

Bloody deaths and mutilations provided the main drawing power in *Titus Andronicus*, which became, to Ben Jonson's chagrin, one of Shakespeare's most popular and most often performed plays. Audiences liked seeing swords run through actors' heads or entrails torn out. Sheep's blood was used – ox blood was too thick to run well. In *Titus* several of the cast wore bladders of blood inside white leather jerkins, daubed with paint to look like skin. In Peele's *Battle of Alcazar* there had been a disembowelling scene for which the property department supplied three vials of blood, and the liver, heart and lungs of a sheep. Nothing like it was seen again on the European stage until the 1960s when the Paris-based director Jérôme Savary, reviving the Theatre of Cruelty theories of Antonin Artaud, produced *The Raft of the "Medusa"*, a dramatized version of Géricault's painting, with animal lights as human internal organs hanging on a washing line.

Like the first half-dozen plays Shakespeare wrote, or mainly wrote, *Titus* can be dated roughly 1590–3. There are tantalizing parallels between it and Thomas Kyd's equally popular *The Spanish Tragedy*: both are Senecan-type revenge plays. Shamelessly peddling rape, tongue and hand mutilation, murder and cannibalism, Shakespeare made *Titus* remarkable by turning it into a feast of prototypical scenes, while the shades of pathos and the compass of violent emotions on offer gradually come to temper, if not actually – and finally – to dwarf the gory gratuities.

Character motifs of the future also lie unpolished, but brightly visible, in *Titus*'s maelstrom of revenge. In Aaron's flamboyant unrepentent harmony, again, there is fermenting the elemental and motiveless evil of Iago. In Titus and his sons Shakespeare aired for the first time the problems of disobedience of Lear with his daughters. Tamora unites the seductive playfulness of Cleopatra with Lady Macbeth's murderous intent; the ridiculous dispute over who will offer, literally, his hand in barter for the lives of Quintus and Martius foreshadows the competitive daring of the conspirators in *Julius Caesar*. Demetrius and Chiron profess great love for their prey, like Richard Crookback or Richard III.

But Shakespeare also gave *Titus* its own beauties. He began with what was virtually an innovation in the theatre of the early 1590s: a decision and an action from which the whole disturbing tale unfolds. Tamora pleads for her son's life: "Thrice-noble Titus, spare my first-born son". Titus rejects her plea and brings down calamity and vengeance. When Titus later tricks Tamora and her sons into believing that he has parted from his wits, this creates an eerie mixture of irony and exultancy. Titus' merciful and self-questioning son, Lucius, and his brother, Marcus, add a redemptive quality.

Shakespeare had extracted the plot of *Titus* from a lost source, but also drew on Ovid's tale of Philomela, from Seneca's *Thyestes* and *Hippolytus* and from Plutarch's *Lives*; he wrote this play rather as a schoolboy who has learnt Latin and retained some of it. Closer to his audience's church-going habits, he scattered echoes of Job, the Psalms, Ecclesiastes and Lamentations. "Till all these mischiefs be returned again / Even in their throats that hath committed them", says Titus in Act III: this is a resounding recasting of Psalms 7:16 in the Geneva translation. He entwined a Christian vision of hell in Act V with Titus' primitive classicism, while Tamora's end is a paraphrase of the Old Testament Jezebel's "But throw her forth to beasts and birds to prey".

*Titus* was probably not first performed at Henslowe's theatre, the Rose, but was certainly revived there by the Earl of Sussex's men on 24 January 1594, by which time it had been played by three companies. To fit the urban audience's taste Shakespeare included few country images or metaphors. A sketch by Henry Peachum, drawn at the time, reveals an unmistakably Negro Aaron, Titus wearing Roman cuirass, laurel wreath buskins, with spear and patriarchal beard, while Tamora bears a spiky crown. *Titus* was so popular that had Shakespeare been surrounded by today's backers and film moguls they would probably have done their best to stop him developing into the creator of *King Lear*.

# Half a god

Shakespeare had probably finished a cycle of histories by the time he turned thirty, in 1594, adding a third genre to his writing art, that of the chronicle play. *Henry VI*, written in three Parts, forcibly demonstrated that he had little feeling for revolution, and even less respect for the mob. He left no doubt about the confidence of his creative ambition: here was an undertaking grander and more expansive in design even than the two parts of Marlowe's *Tamburlaine the Great*, a cumbrously dramatized epic which contained uncut diamonds of wondrous size and splendour. Shakespeare could steal and imitate ruthlessly, and some of *Henry VI* sounds as if it had passed through the hands of other playwrights, or had been skilfully imitated. Dating the parts exactly John Barton, adapter of all three, calls "an impenetrable problem". There are a lot of layers, says Barton: "All writers around 1590 aped each other. They also picked from each other. Part Two is better than Part Three as a play. Shakespeare shook up some earlier play. Certain bits, like the death of York in Part Two, scream out, 'Hey, I'm Shakespeare'."

Plays based on English history were highly popular: although Shakespeare was not worried about historical accuracy, his version betrays the intractability of the material. He made Talbot's death precede the capture of Joan of Arc: but Joan actually died twenty-two years before Talbot. The portrait of Joan as a crafty peasant who overturned the brave English because she was in league with devils was highly Protestant. But Shakespeare may not have written the Joan of Arc scenes in Part One. The effective Temple Garden scene, in which the supporters of York and Somerset pick their emblems of white and red roses, he wholly invented:

> VERNON: Then for the truth and plainness of the case
> I pluck this pale and maiden blossom here,
> Giving my verdict on the white rose' side.
> SOMERSET: Prick not your finger as you pluck it off,
> Lest, bleeding, you do paint the white rose red,
> And fall on my side so against your will.

Shakespeare's first-hand experience of campaigning abroad filled each part of *Henry VI* with realistic, almost brutal, urgency. The battlefield had become part of an individual, personal experience which had matured inside him. The technology of battle fascinated him: the French Master Gunner advises his assistant on how the English, who have entered the suburbs of Orleans, have set up an advanced post:

> The Prince's spials have informèd me
> How the English, in the suburbs close entrenched,
> Wont, through a secret grate of iron bars
> In yonder tower, to overpeer the city,
> And thence discover how with most advantage
> They may vex us with shot or with assault.
> To intercept this inconvenience,
> A piece of ordnance 'gainst it I have placed –

*Henry VI* reeks of cordite, the feel of the earth, of ramparts, of stones torn out with desperate bleeding nails, of guns, of drums, of wounds. Above all it has a frantic, almost farcical intensity of towns and positions changing hands, as happened in the Netherlands.

At a deeper level the strength of the three Parts, considered as a trilogy – and apart from what Barton calls their "most volatile of all texts" – resides in their piling up example upon example of the blood–ambition tie between father and son, which perpetuates blood and pain; of men growing up to fulfil other men's fates, to face revenge or suffer betrayal. Shakespeare found villainy attractive at this time. He provided in *Henry VI* the equivalent of the Hollywood gangster story, a series of crime narratives, with double-crossing and detection, jealousy and tear-jerking passion. He was determined to conquer the emotions of his audience by any means he could muster, including crude jingoism. The characters are savage and grasping superstitious and sentimental by turn. The pathetic figure who carries the crown through this whirligig of blood and daring is gently iconoclastic and high-minded, likeable and laid back – if not Shakespeare himself, then most likely a part he played. Shakespeare/Henry reflects on the fickleness of the mob:

> Look as I blow this feather from my face,
> And as the air blows it to me again,
> Obeying with my wind when I do blow,
> And yielding to another when it blows,
> Commanded always by the greater gust –
> Such is the lightness of you common men.

Shakespeare supplied in Part Two four property severed heads: Lord Saye's and his son-in-law's, Jack Cade's, and that of Suffolk, for which Queen Margaret has a special stage direction – "Queen Margaret carrying Suffolk's head". The property men carved these dummy heads using the actors as models, and added dough kneaded with bullock's blood to them to make them bleed.

The best of the three *Henry VI* plays, Part Two – or, as it was known before the folio edition, *The First Part of the Contention* – has nearly fifty characters. Shakespeare was as hazy about chronology here as in Part One: but he gave the ironic and comic presentation of the Jack Cade rebellion a coherent structure, while Henry's powerlessness has poignant appeal, especially when he is repelled by battlefield horror, and told by his Queen and Clifford they are better off without him. In Part Three he sits down on a molehill and meditates on the quiet life:

O God! Methinks it were a happy life
To be no better than a homely swain.
To sit upon a hill, as I do now;
To carve out dials quaintly, point by point,
Thereby to see the minutes how they run . . .

But, certain passages apart, in the comparative absence of vital imagery, Shakespeare betrayed the lack of a more profound engagement of personality. He conveyed the overriding impression of ambition in these exploitative chronicles. Keats later accuses them of a journalistic lifelessness, as if the facts kept the playwright "to the high road", and would not allow him down "leafy and winding lanes, or to break wildly and at once into the breathing fields". Because it is "ironed and manacled with a chain of facts", Keats complains, the poetry cannot escape the prison of history, "nor often move with the clanking of its fetters".

Yet Shakespeare created, in Queen Margaret, the "she-devil of France", the first realistic *femme fatale* of dramatic entertainment, and, as Peggy Ashcroft, an indomitable interpreter of the role, calls her, "this powerful, rather monstrous character, a fighting mother figure, the woman of vengeance". With Cade himself Shakespeare showed humour, as well as prose, as his natural medium for revealing character. Audiences loved the Cade scenes, which brought back memories of the rise of Tamburlaine. Such popularity did *Henry VI* achieve in performance, especially the figure of Lord Talbot, that the playwright and pamphleteer Thomas Nashe wrote: "How much would it have joyed brave Talbot to think . . . he should triumph again on the stage, and have his (two hundred years old) bones new embalmed with the tears of ten thousand spectators (at several times)."

In Deptford, three miles from London, on 30 May 1593, one of four men who drank all day in a low-class tavern, the house of Eleanor Bull, widow and potwoman, was a shadowy individual called Robert Poley. He had, some seven or more years before, been involved in the Babington Plot as a Walsingham *agent provocateur*, a courier if not the instigator of a crucial faked letter, and as such had aided the doom of Mary Queen of Scots, contrived as we know by Sir Francis Walsingham with diabolical ingenuity.

Now a new but no less pernicious enemy of the Elizabethan state was at large: not a public enemy armed with sword or pistol pointing at the leader, but the spreader of a dangerously corrosive, immoral influence, who himself had a great power to please and was held to be one of the rising glories of English culture. Had Christopher Marlowe just kept his private thoughts deeply embedded in rebellious heroes like his Faustus and Edward II he would have posed no threat. But he had taken to pamphleteering, specifically to declare the virtues of atheism. Rapidly, in the manner of an Italian Renaissance figure, his own life began uncannily to ape the *terribilità*, the grandeur and simplicity of the destruction of a tragic villain–hero. Finely draped in "sombre velvet, with gold lace and a glittering ear-ring and buttons far beyond his station", the sensual-faced Marlowe, with dangerous smile, seemed to be seeking trouble.

The grisly skeleton of facts purporting to Marlowe's end (unravelled in 1925 in some inspired detective work by the Shakespearian scholar Leslie Hotson) begins with Poley, Walsingham's man, sitting in a room with Marlowe. The latter had himself been – if not still was – in Walsingham's employ, for Marlowe was a violent anti-Catholic. Two others – Nick Skeres, a servant of the Earl of Essex, and Ingram Frizer, possibly Marlowe's lover and servant, and like Marlowe a dependent of Sir Thomas Walsingham, the nephew of Francis – were with them.

The day was hot and sunny, the kind with which Shakespeare later began his *Romeo and Juliet*. The men drank, dined and walked in the garden, filling in the time agreeably with much joke-telling and roistering behaviour until 6 p.m., when a serious quarrel developed.

Later, various causes were advanced for the quarrel: that Marlowe, unlikely though it seems, had been in love with a woman who played him false ("comme Shakespeare, comme Molière, et comme tant d'autres", says Victor Hugo of this theory), and that his rival was Ingram Frizer; that Marlowe was double-spying for leading Catholic recusants, reporting back to them the deliberations of the Council; more simply Mistress Bull's "le reckoning", or what in Italian slang is called *la dolorosa*, was advanced as the tinder-box of dispute (Shakespeare wrote this up later in *As You Like It*, which became a reinforcement for the evidence Hotson uncovered). Marlowe already had a reputation for violence, having in 1589 been charged with, but found not guilty of, the murder of one William Brady.

The events, even as documented, are murky: subsequently, when Frizer was cleared of culpable homicide and granted pardon on the grounds of self-defence, it was claimed that Marlowe, helped by the other pair, had trapped Frizer at the table so that he could not get away. He then drew Frizer's dagger, attacked him from behind and inflicted a severe cut on his head, whereupon Frizer is supposed (unaided, which seems unlikely) to have turned his own dagger back upon Marlowe and stabbed him in the head with the death blow. It was not reported that Marlowe died swearing, although this became part of the apocryphal account. In our own time the novelist and QC John Mortimer has visualized the whole event as a simple plot to kill Marlowe.

The leap is easy and justified. The subtlety with which plots could be initiated by the Secretary of State, Sir Francis Walsingham, the isolation that writers, as opposed to noblemen, suffered in daily life, added to which the way Marlowe, already perceived as drunken and belligerent, had laid himself open to provocation, so that it would have been easy to impute him as the cause of his own demise, makes suspicion of foul play convincing. Thomas Kyd, who had shared a chamber with Marlowe two years earlier and who for six years served Lord Strange, alleges that he left Marlowe's company "in hatred of his life and thoughts". Tortured on the rack, Kyd accused Marlowe of reporting that St John was "our saviour Christ's Alexis", that he esteemed St Paul "a juggler", and that he wanted James VI as King of England.

Marlowe had been summoned that May to appear before the Privy Council. The connection between that summons and his death was crudely cemented in a Walsingham-inspired pamphlet sold on the streets later in June. The purpose of his death emerged with shocking clarity. By setting out the claim that it was the will of God that brought Marlowe to such an abominable end, the pamphlet exhorted all atheists in the realm, "by remembrance and consideration of this example", either to

> forsake their horrible impietie, or that they might in like manner come to destruction: and so that abominable sin which so flourisheth amongst men of greatest name, might either be quite extinguished and rooted out or at least smothered and kept under.

The threat to similar offenders could hardly have been more clear: cleverer members of Elizabeth's government were masters at stage-managing the acts of God. But Marlowe did, undeniably, contribute to his own fall: his increasing obsession with fomenting propaganda suggests that his work had already reached, and even passed, its zenith. Certainly he bowed out at his peak.

What the coroner's record did not disclose was that the twenty-nine-year-old Shakespeare called, later that evening, at the house of Eleanor Bull, widow, to seek out his friend Marlowe, and there found him dead, laid out in the garden. This murder had significant consequences for Shakespeare. It shocked him profoundly, but as he benefited so enormously from it himself, he felt a certain guilt. Now there was no one to rival him.

To Marlowe Shakespeare owed everything. Although they had started out almost at opposite ends, one as the poor scholar who spent seven years at Cambridge, the other as the unlettered high-flying burgher's son, their paths had quickly merged in Shakespeare's apprenticeship, so that there were times when the latter's voice was virtually indistinguishable from that of his mentor. Marlowe's own literary formation during his years at Corpus Christi had been through the classics – he had access to more books and was much more widely read than Shakespeare, and more profoundly an innovator: he had virtually invented the dramatic use of blank verse, chucking out wooden versification and regular rhythm, as well as creating prototypes of three or more different genres: the history play based on character (*Edward II*); the sprawling epic (*Tamburlaine the Great*); the black comedy (*The Jew of Malta*); and, for Shakespeare the most important model of all, the spiritual tragedy (*Doctor Faustus*). There were many unemployed graduates in Shakespeare's day and the classics or the study of literature hardly fitted out young men for the thrust and pace of business life. Marlowe had also invented a new career for the ambitious, over-educated graduate, that of dramatist.

What Marlowe achieved in his short life – he was born in the same year as Shakespeare – was inordinate: homosexual, atheistic, he was extremely provocative and unorthodox. He lived and died violently, like another great master, Caravaggio, but he never acquired the popular, easy accessibility of the non-university mind. His images, his metaphors and similes, came from thought rather than feeling: rebellious as he was, he over-reached himself, carrying the questioning spirit of Protestant defiance and individualism to an unacceptable extreme. The moderate, non-hedonistic consolidators of English nationalism, using, when it suited them, Puritanism as their cutting edge, had their revenge.

Shakespeare, who had not studied widely, had more of an instinctive artist's make-up. He noted potentiality, the humanly suggestive, and made it his own. By acting in Marlowe he had learned to speak and think in blank verse; Marlowe, as the more experienced playwright, had acted as story editor and co-ordinator of his early efforts: he may even have ordered him to rewrite sections. Much of *Henry VI* appeared to be a reworking, under Marlowe's instruction, from Shakespeare's earlier texts. We might imagine the more experienced playwright's reactions to Shakespeare's first efforts at a history play: "Where are you in your play?" Marlowe would certainly have asked.

Marlowe had always planted himself firmly at the centre of his work: he had made himself Tamburlaine, ecstatically bathing in self-glory: he had been Barabas, wrestling with his own early destiny of entering the Church, taking his revenge by depicting – as no author dared in those days – Christianity as a relative, not an absolute form of belief. Above all, although he probably wrote only some 700 or 800 lines out of the 2,000 in the first text of *Doctor Faustus*, he explored as Faust a personal and individual relationship with God. *Dido, Queen of Carthage*, too, was a text of considerable importance to Marlowe (and to Shakespeare, who tackled the same kind of challenge with Queen Margaret), because in it he wrote, uniquely, a great tragic role for a boy player. In that age of extremes, more than anyone else, Marlowe pushed beyond the limits.

Whereas Marlowe was provocative and unorthodox, Shakespeare was completely different: out to please his patrons, whether they were the aristocracy or the ordinary playgoer, he completely reversed Marlowe's instinctive rebelliousness: he had the common touch. In *Henry VI* he assumed a Marlovian mode and depicted emotions without being specific, just as in *Two Gentlemen* he had adopted the Lylean mode; as he developed further, he stumbled upon and strengthened the specificity of his art, and did not just reflect mere autobiographical concerns; his creation, as time went by, grew personal in an entirely unexpected way. It became a vision.

Adopting Marlowe's style, Shakespeare reversed his insidious, rebellious drift; even though he relished the gangster-like antics of the insurgent lords in what we call popularly the Wars of the Roses, the *Henry VI* trilogy was the start of a continuous tableau of the catastrophic effects of revolt and rebellion. Shakespeare believed these were not only unwise but tragic. Marlowe's plays pictured men, ultimately, as depraved and vicious – Shakespeare's, as everything opposite to this. Also, pragmatist that he was, Shakespeare absorbed Marlowe's brutal end as a warning – more forceful than anything so far encountered – of the appalling consequences of meddling in politics.

# The body is his book

Responsibilities lay heavy upon Shakespeare as he rode, in troubled, plague-ridden times, back and forth between London and Stratford, stopping off on the way at Oxford, or Banbury, or Daventry, from whose watering places or customs he retained some detail for future use. "The beast that bears me", he wrote (Sonnet 50), carries me away from my friend, but it is not the specific nature of the friend that matters – whether a man or a woman is not so important – as that the poet is on the move, driving himself in the direction of duty and responsibility:

> The bloody spur cannot provoke him on
> That sometimes anger thrusts into his hide,
> Which heavily he answers with a groan
> More sharp to me than spurring to his side;
>     For that same groan doth put this in my mind:
>     My grief lies onward and my joy behind.

The responsibility of love meant a great deal to the conscience of the educated Elizabethan: his or her thinking was rooted in medieval theology. The Church was the bride of Christ. Fidelity in marriage was a law, to love was a commandment.

Yet, whatever his burden of care, Shakespeare found, certainly at first, possibly throughout his life, his marriage to an older but attractive woman an "occupation" in the sense that Othello mentions it as part of his lost career at the end of the play, meaning his sexual possession of Desdemona. Yet the jealousy of Othello contains also a blind projecting of his own lack of trust in himself, a muddled fear of his own promiscuity, as well as sexual insecurity and guilt. Shakespeare was recollecting his own unsureness as a young man, sometimes, at least, in fear of being sexually overwhelmed by the older woman. As Ted Hughes says, poetry "has its taproot in a sexual dilemma of a peculiarly blank and ugly sort". Shakespeare's choice of subject for his first poem, that of the myth of Venus and Adonis, indicated the depth of that dilemma, and also the whole range of erotic sensation and aspiration he experienced as a young married man both in and out of marriage. Like many a sensitive man and lover, he derived part of the pleasure of sex from participating, both imaginatively and with great empathy, in the woman's role and self-expression. Shakespeare captured this perfectly, and realistically, in *Venus and Adonis*, which was first published ten years after the birth of Susanna.

Although the poem draws on the *Metamorphoses* for story and theme, though not exclusively, Shakespeare heightens the sexual voracity displayed by Venus, transferring to it Echo's importunate pursuit of Narcissus, her tormented need for satisfaction, as if he believed, like Ovid, that women receive more sexual pleasure from love than men. Tiresias, in the *Metamorphoses*, confirms this judgement, for which he was rewarded by Juno with blindness. Part of the erotic fascination of Shakespeare's poem – amatory exploits recollected not only in tranquillity but even in ongoing repetition – resides in his instinctive grasp of the nature of active female sexuality. From the very start Shakespeare tantalizes and plays with this knowledge – "Backward she pushed him, as she would be thrust, / And governed him in strength, though not in lust" – and quite teasingly he places in Venus' mouth her justification of her lust: for she wants a child. He acted therefore as advocate for the mature Anne's seizure of him (which he played on in a hundred different ways) and for the birth of his own child, although she was conceived out of wedlock. "Torches are made to light, jewels to wear," he says. "Dainties to taste", and that as Adonis was once begot: "to get it is thy duty." By the law of nature he is bound to breed "That thine may live when thou thyself art dead".

Shakespeare displays his Venus subject to lust, just like a man; although he makes a certain allowance he captures the physical effect vividly.

> And, having felt the sweetness of the spoil,
> With blindfold fury she begins to forage.
> Her face doth reek and smoke, her blood doth boil,
> And careless lust stirs up a desperate courage,
> > Planting oblivion, beating reason back,
> > Forgetting shame's pure blush and honour's wrack.

He then builds the poem up to a complex form of female rape, in which, through Adonis' impotence, the phallic goddess Venus is denied what she most wants:

> She sinketh down, still hanging by his neck.
> He on her belly falls, she on her back.
>
> Now is she in the very lists of love,
> Her champion mounted for the hot encounter.
> All is imaginary she doth prove.
> He will not manage her, although he mount her,
> That worse than Tantalus' is her annoy,
> To clip Elysium, and to lack her joy.

As well as being graphically precise in amatory detail – for instance in failure of penetration being described as "to clip Elysium" – Shakespeare expresses with awesome succinctness the paradoxical and fleeting nature of desire. By now he knew intimately and could show the emotional changes that early marriage had held for him: "The colt that's backed and burdened being young, / Loseth his pride, and never waxeth strong". He entertained a wistful tenderness towards his earlier, more immature state, shocked at thus being so overwhelmed: "'Fair Queen,' quoth he, 'if any love you owe me, / Measure my strangeness with my unripe years'."

But he could still explore and exult in that richer awareness, and experience an imaginative knowledge of the interchangeability of sexuality, which is one of the keys to his growth as an artist. Adonis, who has grown hot and saturated with Venus' "hard embracing", or rough sexual handling, becomes rapidly in turn like a wild bird, a fleet-foot roe, a fractious infant, willed into submission by a domineering power: "He now obeys, and now no more resisteth, / While she takes all she can, not all she listeth".

*Venus and Adonis* was printed in 1593 by Richard Field, a fellow Stratfordian who was three years older than Shakespeare; it was entered in the Register at Stationers' Hall on 18 April 1593, a few days before Shakespeare's twenty-ninth birthday. Impeccably printed for a work of that time, it bears evidence of Shakespeare's conscientious concern that it should do well. He had either written it at Stratford, or drawn on his instant recall of many rural details for the delicately drawn, naturalistic background to the poem. He dedicated it, in courteous but not unduly sycophantic terms, calling his lines "unpolished" – they are far from that – to Henry Wriothesley, Earl of Southampton. Shakespeare promised Southampton in the future some "graver labour". His tone, as a much older man addressing a younger, is confident, as if he is well aware of his powers: it is impersonal yet not cold; personal yet not vulnerable. If the first "heir of my invention prove deformed, I shall be sorry it had so noble a godfather, and never after ear so barren a land for fear it yield me still so bad a harvest".

*Venus and Adonis* quickly established itself as a popular work and was many times reprinted, as well as constantly being mentioned in adulatory terms by other writers, notably by John Weever in an epigrammatical sonnet (1599), *Ad Gulielmum Shakespeare*, listing his "issue" which the honey-tongued poet begot upon some heaven-born goddess, which includes "Rose-cheeked Adonis with his amber tresses, / Fair, fire-hot Venus charming him to love her". Weever concluded that Shakespeare's children "burn in love".

A series of Christmas plays performed at St John's College, Cambridge, around the turn of the century affectionately parody "sweet Mr Shakespeare": to honour him, says the character Gullio, he will "lay his Venus and Adonis under my pillow, as we read of one (I do not well remember his name, but I am sure he was a king) slept with Homer under his bed's head".

*Venus and Adonis* enjoyed no less *réclame* at court, for an easily discernible parallel. (A mad soldier, William Renolds, thought it had been published to persuade him that Elizabeth loved him.) As he amiably, and with no apparent effort, rose in his profession, Shakespeare was fortunate in so many ways, but in no way more supremely lucky than in the unique occurrence that his monarch, whose ultimate patronage he aspired to, was, like Venus, an older woman. Her dangerous reign had stabilized her, had intensified and inwardly strengthened her character. Even though she was now sixty, less prone to hysterical collapse, her virginity was the very opposite of that of an old spinster: vain as she was, covering her greying hair with a reddish wig, daubing her cheeks with make-up, with sunken eyes, face "wasted like the waning moon's" in the 1592 Ditchley portrait, her long, exquisite Italian hands still vibrated with command. She dressed and bejewelled herself even more as the magical Gloriana.

Above everything this ageing Venus still made sure that her court hummed with her unfulfilled sexual nature, so that it was not, in the slightest, unexpressed. Of all the extreme paradoxes of the day, with its cruel and abruptly juxtaposed opposites, this romantic urgency of behaviour in the ruling power was by far the most theatrical. Much of her restlessness, her rapid changes of mood, her extreme spiritual versatility – she could project herself with incredible rapidity into every sinuous shape of belief, or into any emotional posture – lay close and intimately allied to a thinly crusted volcano of sexual feeling.

For Elizabeth vanity was not only the supreme game, but almost a conscious alternative to sexual climax: that vanity would be nurtured, flattered, caressed, gradually or dramatically built up – to prove, finally, either satisfying or disastrous.

Her father had beheaded her mother before Elizabeth reached the age of three. He accused Anne Boleyn of having slept with five men, one of them her brother; yet who knows if Henry's sudden impetuous act of revenge – her miscarried saviour of a boy child apart – had not had its origin in the six years of violent frustration Anne caused him, refusing to gratify his lust before making sure of possessing his hand. Manhood spelt betrayal to Elizabeth: it had first come upon her "concealed in yellow magnificence in her father's lap", as Lytton Strachey couches it in the vivid Bloomsbury *Elizabeth and Essex*. And if it threatened her too much the Queen would be tempted to act as her father had acted – to revenge herself on her father. It was above all by insulting her vanity that Essex finally brought about his own downfall.

Elizabeth had always been passionately tempted by brave and good-looking men. Attractive as a girl, she was worshipped as a woman and continually wooed. She would never give in: "I hate the idea of marriage," she told Lord Sussex, "for reasons that I would not divulge to a twin soul." Another time she said, "I am already bound to a husband, which is the Kingdom of England." On a third occasion she told Sir James Melville that she would not marry unless driven to it. Melville replied, "If you were married you would be but Queen of England, and now you are both King and Queen. I know your spirit cannot endure a commander."

She had taken herself to the brink of marriage many times, most notably with the Earl of Leicester. In his younger days, tall, with well-shaped legs, gypsy-like in complexion, with round, hard, glittering eyes and a short, bird-of-prey nose, his looks had typified an aggressive manly ideal which, later and after his death, faded before the rash and volatile moodiness of younger men. Up to the point of giving in, Elizabeth relished being made love to: her abnormality of appetite stemmed, apparently, from a deranged sexual instinct. In spite of constant rumours that she had done so, she would never have been unchaste enough to commit the sexual act with Leicester; but to display herself to him naked was not a sin. She liked to inflame the worship of a suitor to beyond its limit: this fanned an exquisite sense of torture: the "incense of her vanity".

Was Elizabeth physically capable of the sexual act? Much later, when he could speak freely of such matters, Ben Jonson told the royalist dilettante, William Drummond of Hawthornden, that "she had a membrana on her, which made her incapable of men, though for her delight she tried many". Trying them was first and foremost a diversion: "To talk of love, to talk of marriage", writes one of the Queen's biographers, "above all, to listen while someone talked, or was talked of, as wanting to marry her, gave her an exhilaration that was the keener because such feelings had to do duty for others that had been put to death."

Knowing all this, from what he observed and had heard, Shakespeare became close to Elizabeth; with no more than the most minimal of formal contacts – a compliment perhaps, or the expression of a wish – he assumed the mantle, through his plays, of her most intimate biographer, because she above all others gave form and pressure to the time. She was, almost in a physical, sexual sense, the form and body of that time. Shakespeare has Hamlet say later, of the Player King, that had he the cue for passion that this actor had, he would drown the stage with tears, "Make mad the guilty and appal the free". Elizabeth might have been able to say something similar about her own feelings. Indeed the protean Shakespeare found his perfect element in such emotional undercurrents; he swam and luxuriated in the moods of his sovereign, her unsatisfied impulses and her deeper, unconscious life. He became her most secret biographer – but afterwards, as with himself, he burned the code.

In comedy after comedy, in particular, in which the harsh and often cruel ritual of wooing was turned inside-out, or on its head, or romantically pursued in Arcadian unreality where an amorous ruse was suddenly stripped to the naked ambition at its core, or a warped passion uncorked, Shakespeare appealed, by his common sense and wit, over everyone else's head directly to the Queen. His comedies, while entertaining the court, became much more than entertainment, they became "physic" to their patroness's moods. They operated as counselling: they addressed themselves directly to the health of the nation, which meant the moral well-being of those close to the Queen as well as to the Queen herself. A sick, moody or unhappy monarch meant a disordered and ailing kingdom, which threatened the security of everyone. Shakespeare unlocked memory, pleasure and desire, and released a sense of well-being.

The looking-glass of his time was completely dominated by the virginity, the heightened moods and emotions, the vacillation and inconstancy of this vain and ageing, yet extraordinarily strong-minded woman. Everyone was a servant of the Queen.

# Drops of water

Shakespeare, as he began to stand out as a distinctive dramatic writer, abandoning styles interchangeable with those of other play-wrights, recognized that his great power was that of loving his characters. Richard, Duke of Gloucester had already awakened in him that Hollywood-type identification with evil when writing *Henry VI* Parts Two and Three: the "Al Capone of his imagination", Crookback, also has something strikingly similar in his character to the Disney Big Bad Wolf. Vivien Leigh describes him as "the most sexually compelling villain ever to have disgraced the stage". Part Three of the trilogy, earlier known as *Richard Duke of York*, had ended with the King-to-be, Richard of Gloucester, promising him-self that he would "snarl and bite and play the dog". Shakespeare already had in mind the sequel, and also entertained the ambition to make Richard into the central commanding figure.

In its conception Richard's character remains extremely juvenile, which suggests that, ten years on from his own adolescence, Shake-speare was still shaping adolescent attitudes and fantasies about power and sex. Richard is an amplification of the boar of blackness which emerges at the end of *Venus and Adonis* to gore Adonis. Many of the scenes of the play, such as Richard's wooing of Anne, are witty and realistically-rendered nightmares. Yet by stretching the scope and breadth of such a central character so that Richard domi-nates monolithically all aspects of the play, Shakespeare arrived at something entirely new. *Richard* foreshadows the great tragedies. Marlowe had built most of his great plays around one towering villain; Shakespeare, slipping more easily into Marlowe's shoes, now had the confidence also to do this.

*Richard III*, in one quite crucial way, is not an original play, but a stage version of the well-known *Chronicle* of 1542 by Edward Hall. It draws, too, on Holinshed as well as on Sir Thomas More. Shakespeare's version follows Hall's narrative closely, even including scenes from the original which carry little dramatic point. One such is the account of Jane Shore, a goldsmith's wife who had been the mistress of Edward IV, which he used to drive home the message that "all is vanity". In the totally fanciful inclusion of Queen Margaret as a choric figure of grief (she had in fact returned to France and died *before* Richard came to the throne), Shakespeare revived, with shape-shifting sleight of hand, the French "she-wolf" entirely on the basis of Hall's description of Jane Shore. How can one guess the beauty of one so long departed, runs the passage, from her scalp in the charnel-house: "for now is she old, leane, withered, and dryed up, nothing left but riveld skinne and hard bone".

Richard Burbage, neutral and impressive in mien, steady in temperament, began the line of famous interpretations of the title-role. It was not many years before someone showing guests around the Bosworth Field, where Richard lost his crown, pointed out that this was where "Richard Burbage" had shouted "A horse! a horse! My kingdom for a horse!" Such a great part was not only written for a great actor, who created the role first at the Theatre, but by an actor who composed at full tilt a dramatic role which caught exactly and with consummate excitement the compelling rhythms of evil ambition. The man behind the naked ambition swaggers like a caricature – what could be more patently make-believe than the rudimentary motive Richard gives for his maniac behaviour? "Since I cannot prove a lover", he said,

> To entertain these fair well-spoken days,
> I am determinèd to prove a villain
> And hate the idle pleasures of these days.

But the vitality spreads in a dozen different directions – deceiver, wit, overpowering suitor – all beating with an electric, creative rhythm of thought. Shakespeare allowed Richard to invent himself, and he fed him with an artist's unlimited love for a rich artefact. The character never runs away with the playwright, never takes over, as he might in a more subjective age. Richard could not have been created by a modern solipsistic author such as James Joyce or

Vladimir Nabokov (Nabokov once described his audience as a roomful of people just like himself). Shakespeare confined Richard within the bounds not only of theatrical convention, but of the imagination of his audience and the well-defined limits of Anglican morality. He knew that he was creating a completely objective character: it was love that allowed the characters of fiction to grow to their full independent stature, just as the love of parents for their children enables those children to reach their fullest potential and power to separate. Paradoxically, Shakespeare lets us know everything there is to know about himself – in the dynamics of the character he creates, showing how his own histrionic wit and spirit work – but also hides himself in such a way that he reveals how life itself works.

No one has ever been so evil, and so reasonable and witty about it: ultimately Richard is fiction. He is an actor, glorying in self-presentation. But this lovable element is finally what we most enjoy: Shakespeare lent his eternal spirit to illuminate an evil character's destructive path, but that eternal creative spirit was only on loan. Shakespeare picked up the impersonal, destructive quality of ambition, of power-seeking, at the very beginning, and gradually but ultimately revealed it as being in control. Thus the play, apparently relishing the wickedness, condemns a great moral evil: Richard, laying himself open to the appetite of absolute power, loses those good qualities of wit and perception, and degenerates into just an animal fighting for survival, aware, with horror, that "There is no creature loves me / And if I die no soul will pity me". His creator, to elevate his status to a tragic one, progressively torments him with violent devices from the Roman dramatist Seneca, such as the ghosts of his victims, until the inevitable outcome arrives, of personality overcome by impersonality: as Henry Earl of Richmond remarks, "The bloody dog is dead."

In the first act of *The Comedy of Errors*, Shakespeare describes actors' conditions during their annual provincial tours in the early 1590s:

> Within this hour it will be dinner-time.
> Till that I'll view the manners of the town,
> Peruse the traders, gaze upon the buildings,
> And then return and sleep within mine inn;
> For with long travel I am stiff and weary.

Basing this play on not one but two of the Roman Plautus' improbable plots, he supplied few such realistic touches. One plot deals with twin brothers, the other with a wife denying her husband entrance to his own home while entertaining his brother. Shakespeare with his usual prodigality furnished two lots of twins, more shadowy than their originals, and demonstrated, in what is his shortest play, that he could manipulate comically different strands of a story with more reversals and unforeseen revelations, more obstructions and comic opposites, than any of his rivals. He structured *Comedy of Errors* as a classical, almost academic, counterpart to the excesses of *Titus Andronicus*: here we have, he is saying, a correct Roman play, with a fixed set of three doors opening off a market-place – one leads to an abbey, one to Antipholus' house, one to a courtesan's house: "Especially there must not want a brothel," admonished an Italian architect.

Shakespeare hammered out some remarkably condensed narrative in Aegeon's long opening speech; yet otherwise he let the comedy tiresomely run its course of puns, dupes, doggerel and lame obscenity: with its intricate and well-turned japes, he may have offered it to the Alleyn company: it cries out to be sacrificed to comic business, and as a whole adds up to one of his most untypical and anonymous products.

Even the mention of twins carries a curious comic defence against, or distance from, anything personal. Although in the second scene Antipholus of Syracuse hints at the family quest or relationship Shakespeare would explore at another time:

> I to the world am like a drop of water
> That in the ocean seeks another drop,
> Who, failing there to find his fellow forth,
> Unseen, inquisitive, confounds himself.
> So I, to find a mother and a brother,
> In quest of them, unhappy, lose myself –

Shakespeare quickly allowed the dramatic connotations of "unhappy" to disappear. Determined to prove himself the professional, he excluded any hint of his own family circumstances. Unaware of the disaster and grief that was later to overcome his own twins, he eschewed realism of feeling. Confronting the two sets of twins, the Duke of Ephesus exclaims,

> One of these men is *genius* to the other:
> And so of these, which is the natural man,
> And which the spirit? Who deciphers them?

The play was cleverly designed for a boisterous night out at Gray's Inn. The whole of *Comedy of Errors* is contained within what Coleridge would later call "shape as super-induced". Virtually stripped of poetic imagery, *Comedy* acts supremely well, has great vigour, while its construction can hardly be faulted.

# Queint mistery of Ovid

In 1594 Shakespeare quickly followed the success of the publication of *Venus and Adonis* with a second long poem, *The Rape of Lucrece*, also published with unusual typographical accuracy by Richard Field, and again dedicated to Southampton, who this time is addressed in more affectionate terms. But Shakespeare still carefully adhered to convention; for instance the "unpolished" lines of *Venus* become "untutored" in *The Rape*, which he dismissed as a "superfluous moiety" compared to his "love ... without end" for Southampton, which is standard hyperbole for the time. Shakespeare felt sure of the friendship, or so "the warrant I have of your honourable disposition" conveys; the central assertion carries an air of exact sincerity: "What I have done is yours; what I have to do is yours, being part in all I have, devoted yours".

In *The Rape of Lucrece* Shakespeare provided an account of the perfect victim, as much as, if not even more than, the unrepentent sexual activist. He could show how he had benefited from writing *Venus and Adonis* just over a year before. The balance, the matching of criminal and prey, is exactly right, while the advancement of the action is more economical. Shakespeare understood how lust, a vice of intemperance like excessive anger, was just as much a burden to the perpetrator of evil as to the person fated to suffer it: he set two crucial lines, like the bejewelled eyes in a toad's head, at the poem's centre: "She bears the load of lust he left behind, / And he the burden of a guilty mind."

In *Lucrece* Shakespeare recorded, as in a personal literary notebook, what he would do in the next few years. In his treatment of the rape and the emotions it generates, the action before it and that consequent upon it, he outlined, with uncanny foresight, the way he would examine crime and punishment in the great tragedies. He forcefully painted the adulterous desire of Tarquin, bereft of love but filled with amorous images to inflame his sensuality. He did not deny himself titillation: to say Lucrece's breasts were "unconquered" except by her lawful husband was to cast a glow of heroic approval over the ravishment. Those "ivory globes circled with blue" had "known" – again a sexually loaded word – "save of their lord no bearing yoke": him lying on top of them, as well as making them naked. But their sight bred new ambition in Tarquin, "Who like a foul usurper went about / From this fair throne to heave the owner out". The detailed anatomy of Lucrece's distress, the turmoil of passion in which her abuse pours out, is seminal to Shakespeare's future, both in its understanding and in its dramatic orchestration.

Grief makes people regress: Lucrece "cavils" with everything she sees like a testy child who "wayward once, his mood with naught agrees". Like an unpractised swimmer she plunges and drowns by making "too much labour". Drenched in care, she compares all sorrow to her own, while every object serves to renew the shock of wounded feeling, so that "as one shifts, another straight ensues".

Shakespeare touches perfectly on her refusal of help – "Grief best is pleased with grief's society" – the ungovernable projection of her grief on to that which would stop it or do it good, again with images of overflowing or flooding: "Grief dallied with nor law nor limit knows".

But nothing can quite compare with the essence of Lucrece's tragedy as revealed in her lament at the loss of her chastity:

> Ay me, the bark peeled from the lofty pine
> His leaves will wither and his sap decay;
> So must my soul, her bark being peeled away.

This drives her to death. Here, in blueprint, was Shakespeare's future tragic power, that ability to individualize the soul's grief in a sympathetic character. *The Rape of Lucrece* provided an early prototype for the hunting of the violent vanities, the emotions of the tragedies: Shakespeare was in training to corner them or catch them on the wing.

This and *Venus and Adonis* are the centre of Shakespeare's own personal poetic fable, what Ted Hughes calls "beautifully intact and precisely analysed", caused by the conflict between the new puritanism, "the newly throned God", and the traditional power of

Venus, the feminine principle of all love including the erotic. Both these opposites assume dozens of different forms, even sometimes combining with or containing each other. The puritan mind is "Perjured, murderous, bloody, full of blame, / Savage, extreme, rude, cruel, not to trust –", and therefore de-sensitized to the true condition of nature.

The goddess Venus is gradually and progressively defeated until the feminine spirit is cast, as Hughes says, "into the bottom of the hell of the Puritans, as their secretary Milton faithfully recorded". Shakespeare's perjured murderers, men of chaos, stalk round the rim of the pit. Yet he was never to let go of his own sense of normality which he deliberately placed in the mouths of certain characters, to reassure his public that a tragic outcome was only a temporary distortion of the order of the world.

"Why, Collatine," asks Junius Brutus at the end of *Lucrece*, making the profoundly commonsensical observation,

> is woe the cure for woe?
> Do wounds help wounds, or grief help grievous deeds?
> Is it revenge to give thyself a blow
> For his foul act by whom thy fair wife bleeds?
> Such childish humour from weak minds proceeds;
> Thy wretched wife mistook the matter so
> To slay herself, that should have slain her foe.

*The Rape of Lucrece* had hardly less rapturous a reception than *Venus and Adonis*, while the two poems, together with *Love's Labour's Lost*, established the reputation of Shakespeare as "Venus' ownë sonne" – pre-eminently a love poet. Nicholas Rowe reported that the two poems earned Shakespeare a magnificent "purse" of a thousand pounds, a gift from Southampton: "to enable him to go through with a Purchase which he heard he had had a mind to". The sum named, if not the gift itself, was probably a gross exaggeration. In the early autumn of 1594 Shakespeare is mentioned, for the first time in print, as a poet, and as author of *The Rape of Lucrece*:

> Though Collatine have dearly bought,
> To high renown, a lasting life,
> And found, that most in vain have sought,
> To have a fair, and constant wife,
> Yet Tarquin plucked his glistering grape,
> And Shake-speare, paints poor Lucrece' rape.

The source was *Willobie his Avisa*, an eccentric collection of verse and prose by an Oxford student, Henry Willobie. His poem, more satire than panegyric, was subtitled "The True Picture of a Modest maid, and of a Chaste and Constant Wife"; it apparently testified to an unsuccessful love affair conducted by one "W.S.". Among the importunate wooers the chaste Avis inflames with a fantastical fit of passion is "H.W." or Henrico Willobego, who betrays the secret of his disease to his close friend, the "old player", W.S.; the latter had himself, not long before, tried the "courtesy of the like passion" and had now recovered. W.S. cannot offer much by way of consolation, but enlarges the wound – like Berowne, "conceit's expositor" – and proves a miserable comforter.

H.W., still failing to "obtain . . . his purpose", finds no release from his malady, and sinks into "divers and sundry changes of affections or temptations which Will, set loose from reason, can devise". Although Willobie punned on the "old player's" name, apparently enjoying a joke at the expense of his writing, it may be going a bit far to suggest that "H.W." had also to serve for Henry Wriothesley, and that he and Shakespeare had "let blood in the same vein", while Shakespeare secretly laughed at the young Earl's discomfort.

Henry Wriothesley, Earl of Southampton, a ward of Lord Burghley, the Lord Treasurer, had turned sixteen on 6 October 1589: later, he and two scions of other old families, Bedford and Rutland, then aged fifteen and thirteen respectively, by supporting the Earl of Essex turned against their mentor Burghley. But for the moment Southampton was a dutiful protégé; his precocious wit had ridden out St John's, Cambridge, achieved an M.A. and he had been introduced into Gray's Inn. He wrote to Burghley daily in Latin, but refused to enter into an advantageous marriage with Burghley's grand-daughter, his mind bent on the glories of war and of literature – he even disdained advice from his Catholic grandfather, Lord Montagu.

His beauty, even when so young, was renowned. "A woman's face, with Nature's own hand painted", wrote Shakespeare in Sonnet 20, "a woman's gentle heart, but not acquainted / With shifting change" – "as is false woman's passion", he added hurriedly; and this description is borne out by Hilliard's celebrated miniature. "Refined, aristocratic face", as Southampton's biographer records, "the long oval he got from his mother; rather a feminine face, with its regularity of feature, the sensitive curve of lip and nostril, the fine arched eyebrows. Above all there are the long curling tresses brought forward over his left shoulder." But, with all, "a cock-sure stare of the eye, an obstinacy of expression".

The cynosure of a brilliant circle, which also included the somewhat unbalanced Edward de Vere, Earl of Oxford, and Ferdinando Strange, Shakespeare's early acquaintance and now an important theatre patron, Southampton came, in no way passively, to be to some degree in collusion with those who flattered him: "You to your beauteous blessings add a curse, / Being fond on praise, which makes your praises worse."

Southampton played up to his admirers, one suspects, with a dark and neurotic mixture of arrogance and bashfulness, although he was altogether a much more reasonable character than Essex, whose touchiness and self-obsession, exaggerated sense of self-worth, and boundless fantasy later cost him his head (and almost cost Southampton his). But life on the pinnacle of social glory was preposterously vain as well as insecure, and while Shakespeare and others may have detected an underlying soundness and goodness in the young Earl's character – and this is what humanizes him in the sonnets that Shakespeare addresses to him – Southampton continued to offer himself imaginatively, for the potential reward of patronage and protection, to at least three poets.

In Marlowe, who was working on *Hero and Leander* when he was killed, the romantic ardour so passionately first explored in *Dido, Queen of Carthage* had been growing, especially in *Edward II*, more overtly homoerotic. Marlowe carried the Protestant love of the pagan world of Rome to the outer limit of extravagance. Who else should be his target now but the young Earl, perhaps for Marlowe's dark taste even more delectable on account of his Italianate papist connections? He identified Leander as Southampton, with the uncut dangling tresses seen in the portraits, and the fair-skinned, aristocratic straightness. To touch his neck, Marlowe wrote, was delicious meat, and he indulged in concrete sexual fantasy: smooth breast, white belly – while, he asks,

> whose immortal fingers did imprint
> That heavenly path with many a curious dint
> That runs along his back?

As with Gaveston's passion for Edward II, this great poetry stems from unrealized lust for a noble erotic image: Marlowe consorted with fellow spies, serving boys or wenches, indeed with anyone in his twilight bohemian world, but his passion for Southampton was pure wish-fulfilment.

Even Marlowe had to bow to poetic convention, however, and in spite of his Leander–Southampton being a maid in man's attire, with looks that "were all that men desire", he made him plead with Hero to give up her virginity to him, just as Venus argues with Adonis in Shakespeare's poem. With the two great wordsmiths of the age fighting to bestow on him a sexual identity, it is hardly surprising that Southampton, far from being tempted to turn inward and concentrate the whole romance of his nature on himself, should have sought plunder and booty in foreign expeditions. His nature may have been intensely feminized, but it would not find much room for self-expression in the mighty images of Marlowe and Shakespeare.

Lesser lights were also eager to press their claims for Southampton's attention: in May 1593 Barnabe Barnes beseeched the right virtuous lord to give the monstrously octosyllabic pair of which his muse had been delivered, *Parthenophil and Parthenope* (their names sound to our ears like pain-killers or surgical probes), the once-over with those "heavenly lamps which give the Muses light". Thomas Nashe too had tried – it appears unsuccessfully – to harness Southampton to his muse, declaring him, in the fulsome dedication of his *The Unfortunate Traveller*, to be both lover and cherisher, as "well as the lover of poets, as of poets themselves". Nashe positively whinged with envy at the Earl's reception of *Venus and Adonis*; "Ovid's wanton muse did not offend", he said, so why should I?

But how far did young men go, beyond wild talk, in "loose unchastity"? Of all aspects of human life sexual behaviour is the most prone to exaggeration, and while complete licentiousness between young men – or even between young men and women – may be imagined, it is unlikely to have been practised except in certain circles, and never in quite the self-knowing, cold and extreme way we now consider as sexual freedom. Puritanism, which saw the deed of darkness as met with physical retribution, had bred great superstition among ordinary people. Even among non-Puritans, in whom there was a residue of the old faith, or who conformed to the new middle-class aspirations, there was widespread belief in the strong link between moral behaviour, health and worldly success. Yet with beds being shared by boys and young men; with whole families, even middle-class families, sleeping together in one room;

with the communal life at court, where interconnecting doors meant that people walked through one another's rooms and had little privacy – and with a heavy incidence of pre-nuptial pregnancy (more frequent in England than in France), there must have been plenty of peremptory (and even semi-conscious) sexual activity going on. Much, one suspects, was the result of animal need, stirred by the drunkenness that accompanied virtually every social occasion.

Most sex at the time would, by our standards, have been low-grade, almost animal-grunting and sweating in an enseamèd bed – the act probably performed hastily in stinking, crowded conditions, without hygiene, or space for the growth of affection or feeling, generally clothed, and thus bereft of classical, sensual nakedness – above all devoid of sexual intimacy. It was one thing for poets like Marlowe and Shakespeare to dream of multiple coition and indescribable erotic rapture; naked, except in the years of adolescence and early maturity, the Elizabethans must have been on the whole a pretty horrific-looking and evil-smelling bunch. Nowhere was the contrast more stark between the absurd rose-tints of fantasy and its opposite, the cold and brutish coupling, over only too rapidly: the will is infinite, the desire boundless, says Troilus in *Troilus and Cressida*, the act "a slave to limit". Dr Alex Comfort had not yet appeared on the scene.

Language was a compensation: poetry was both an escape and a consolation. "Before, a joy proposed; behind, a dream", wrote Shakespeare of the sexual act in Sonnet 129: "Enjoyed no sooner but despisèd straight". Where sexual passion became dangerous, as Marlowe showed in *Edward II*, was not so much in its exercise as when it threatened to corrupt the moral being of a king, when that king actually proclaimed its virtues. Thus the nobles in Edward's court object, not so much to what he does, as to the way in which he presents himself. The extreme of sexual licence was not in what was done but in the public avowal of it. Edward flaunts himself with sex in the head, in the playwright's mighty line which is itself redirected sexual aggression. Here Marlowe pierced to the very roots of the Anglican dual morality which took such a hold on the British national character: it operated in spiritual matters, and in sexual morality: as long as neither challenged the hegemony of the state, it was, the Puritan backlash permitting, tolerated.

But beauty *was* brief in Elizabethan times: summer's lease had a very short span. Disease was mostly untreatable. Eyes, teeth, skin, hair, all rapidly deteriorated or vanished. Sanitation was hopeless, and the nobility travelled like nomads from one dwelling to another to allow the filth to decompose, the smell of ordure to be washed away by wind and rain – the "wind and the rain" of Feste's song probably the only reliable cleansing agents they knew. Infection was rife and spread rapidly, unchecked by proper diet or any knowledge of how germs or immunities functioned. The body – not without some basis in reality – was believed to be constituted along the lines of man's emotional make-up, and the elements as observed in the climate and the natural world. Aristotle had viewed nature as trying to restore itself to a state of balance. According to Hippocrates and Galen, from whom the Elizabethans took their ideas of medicine, when a man or woman fell ill something similar to a storm, a drought or a flood took place. "Correspondences" existed everywhere. At the simplest, most absurd level the viola tricolor, or pansy, with its heart-shaped lower petal, was used to treat heart disease, the lungwart lungs, because – or so it was believed – its white-spotted leaves resembled lungs with diseased spots. The four humours of man – blood, phlegm, yellow bile and black bile – had to be purged, dosed or otherwise adjusted to restore them to their correct ratios. Thus Queen Elizabeth, who menstruated infrequently if at all, was often bled. The rich who, like certain breeds of dog, ate only meat, were chronically constipated, while Third World diseases of malnutrition were common in every class.

The most dramatic killer was bubonic plague, but other epidemics of dysentery, typhus, influenza and, from Queen Elizabeth's time onwards, smallpox, periodically swept through the land, accounting together for a third of all deaths. The life-expectancy of a boy born into the nobility in the late Tudor or Stuart period, when his chances and living conditions were far superior to those of other classes, was less than thirty years.

Two years before Shakespeare's birth Queen Elizabeth caught smallpox, but was cured by a skilful German doctor who saved her from permanent disfigurement. The Earl of Leicester's sister, Lady Mary Sidney, mother of Sir Philip Sidney, who nursed the Queen in her bedchamber, suffered the full virulence of deformity: "I left her a full fair lady," wrote her husband Sir Henry, "in mine eyes at least, the fairest, and when I returned I found her as foul a lady as the smallpox could make her." Elizabeth cherished those who served her, and when Lady Mary later visited her at Hampton Court, but shunned appearing in public, the Queen visited her every day in her room. Who knows if Shakespeare was not foredoomed in his youth by some epidemic or fever which in later life weakened his liver, his kidneys, lungs or arteries? Nearly everyone, Jonathan Miller says, "trailed behind them the long-term infections of child-hood – such as diphtheria". Everyone, more or less, suffered pain of one kind or another; Shakespeare was certainly no exception.

The plague was the most spectacular killer of all: 20,000 Lon-doners died in the year before Shakespeare's birth; now, in 1592 and 1593, it tightened its grip. The court dispersed. The thirty-eight Fellows of the Royal College of Physicians left for their country retreats. The hundred or so apothecary shops did a spectacular business, but the theatres quickly emptied.

# The lure of foreign parts

To write his next play Shakespeare returned to Stratford to stay with Anne, Susanna and his twins, now nearly in their teens. He also visited Southampton at Titchfield, his Hampshire home near Fareham. Elizabeth had stayed there in 1591; the hospitality extended to the playwright was not quite so munificent, although the new play became the Earl's favourite, acted in its earliest version either at Titchfield or at his London house in the plague winter of 1593–4.

*Love's Labour's Lost* was a more subtle and complex experiment than any Shakespeare had tried out before, a long, extended joke under the shadow of death, in which he proved conclusively that he could turn his literary art to any fashion. Ten years before *Love's Labour's Lost*, in *Euphues*, John Lyly had written a novel which, Thomas Nashe said, even he had devoured when "a little ape at Cambridge". In a sequel, *Euphues His England*, Lyly used the gynae-cological imagery of literary parenthood which affected Shake-speare strongly. The pain he sustained for *Euphues* "in travaile", Lyly wrote, "hath made me past teeming". "Teem", as "time", is a word Shakespeare put to use even in the first speech of *Love's Labour's Lost*.

Bringing the euphuistic mode – rhetorical flourishes and highly mannered and ornamental style – into mainstream London theatre may have been slightly old hat by now, but Shakespeare wanted to cut a dash before a private audience: *Love's Labour's Lost* was written fastidiously to delight Southampton and his circle now based on Gray's Inn. The subject was a variation on the Southampton theme of the renunciation of women. "They have been at a great feast of languages and stolen the scraps," Moth sums up the talk of a large proportion of the characters. Holophernes, the comic schoolmaster, comments similarly: "He draweth out the thread of his verbosity finer than the staple of his argument."

Although prepared to satirize himself while doing it – and Shakespeare's writing always carries an in-dwelling, self-aware streak, even in extreme and self-oblivious moments of passion – he became in *Love's Labour's Lost* unrepentantly besotted with technical problems connected with craft. Egged on by his patrons, he was not prepared to spare anyone the full treatment: the question of inspiration, use of rhetoric, the exercise of vocabulary, orthography, oddities and linguistic innovations, "excesses of the aureate style" – he explored them all. Berowne declares:

> Taffeta phrases, silken terms precise,
> Three-piled hyperboles, spruce affectation.
> Figures pedantical – these summer flies
> Have blown me full of maggot ostentation.

The chief characters write sonnets to their loves: even Don Armado, the stage Spaniard – "Assist me, some extemporal god of rhyme, for I am sure I shall turn sonnet. Devise wit, write, pen, for I am for whole volumes, in folio." The portrait of Don Armado, the refined traveller from Spain who haunts the court, was based on the figure of Don Antonio Pérez, an exile from Philip's court, a guest of the Earl of Essex and his director of intelligence, Shakespeare's friend Anthony Bacon.

Shakespeare fashioned *Love's Labour's Lost* in a peculiarly contemporary way that he never repeated. He had it follow, although absurd in general design, certain historical facts more closely even than parts of *Henry VI*. The real King of Navarre received two embassies from France, either of which might have served as model. Shakespeare filched the names of Berowne, Longaville and Dumain from news pamphlets about the war in France. The royal envoy from France to Navarre was accompanied by a famous bevy of ladies-in-waiting – known as "L'escadron volant". Navarre, in real life, also became royal patron of a Plato-inspired debating society. In making a continual comic butt of Don Adriano de Armado, Shakespeare, as well as conjuring up a local figure, reminded his jingoist audience of the threat of mighty Spain – and that England had beaten her. The comedy was contrived to reawaken and purge deep national fears.

Shakespeare made his text gather puns and double meanings like a snowball racing down a slope. Navarre's first speech,

> Let fame, that all hunt after in their lives,
> Live registered upon our brazen tombs,
> And then grace us in the disgrace of death
> When, spite of cormorant devouring time,
> Th'endeavour of this present breath may buy
> That honour which shall bate his scythe's keen edge
> And make us heirs of all eternity

contains a complicated running joke. In the pronunciation of the day "fame", before this young and sophisticated male audience, attuned to ribald or erotic *double-entendre*, becomes "femme"; in other words not only woman, but more basically "queint" or centric part – hence "brazen" holds the boast of sexual conquest. "Death" in the third line achieves, as a result, its common Shakespearian usage of sexual intercourse, while time, pronounced "teem", means to tup, or couple. "Keen edge" is the male sex organ, while "make us heirs" also means "beget us children". With such a lubricious secondary meaning the whole following part of the speech, encouraging the young men to stand against the "huge army of the world's desires", gathers a two-sided, comic complexity. Even Navarre, as then pronounced in "Navarre shall be the wonder of the world", becomes "*Never* shall be the wonder of the world" – as, of course, total sexual abstinence would, to an audience of privileged young bloods. This was essentially the same Inns of Court audience as that of approximately 1,500 young men who were circulating among them John Donne's unpublished satires and love poems. Women in these poems and in this circle were male gifts, and the main if not the only sexual rapture experienced was that of the exploring male. Shakespeare, by making the joke turn upon abstinence, was bearding the lion in its den.

Shakespeare directed *Love's Labour's Lost* specifically at the needs and preoccupations of a particular audience. The wonder is that he had an audience capable of meeting such ostentation and responding at the same sophisticated level. He reversed expectation by doing the opposite of what would provide easy gratification of taste or passion. So in the minds of his basically male audience, instead of celebrating women as objects for male gratification, to be paraded, stripped naked and enjoyed sexually, he covered over the basic sexual need and impulse with a high and hypocritically absurd pretension – which he would then reveal as inevitably crumbling in the face of the real world; a place he liked and could then demonstrate as being sound in its romantic feelings, as opposed to reductive. To do this he catacombed *Love's Labour's Lost* with hidden meanings, purposes and intentions most of which elude us today. Parts of the text appear senseless: one edition has a list of at least ten passages which embody jokes now lost, most of them puns.

Shakespeare also dramatized himself. He had taken Marlowe's advice and put himself on the stage with his own personal voice. Not to reveal much, of course. But the confident Berowne expatiates in self-projection and spills out of the play as Shakespeare the well-known poet of *Venus and Adonis* and *The Rape of Lucrece*, as well as of privately circulated, unpublished sonnets; wanders at will among his coinages of wit with Mozartian bravura. It was not immodest of Shakespeare to describe himself as Berowne, this lit-up figure whose sense of mirth knows no bounds, ravishing young ears and causing old ears to "play truant" at his outrageous stories.

> His eye begets occasion for his wit,
> For every object that the one doth catch
> The other turns to a mirth-moving jest,
> Which his fair tongue, conceit's expositor . . .

This convincingly reinforces later direct or hearsay accounts of the sweet and voluble Shakespeare. Berowne's scorn of scholarship, not by any means limited to this play: "Small have continual plodders ever won / Save base authority from others' books" and "Why, universal plodding poisons up / The nimble spirits in the arteries . . ." reflects not only Shakespeare's feeling and new-found awareness of his advantages over university wits. In his own research and reading, which was voracious and wide-ranging, he worked unsystematically, upon instinct, and swiftly. Although by basing his plays on published texts and his ready assimilation of other works, Shakespeare was in some ways academic and literary, his opportunist scholarship was geared to popular needs.

If Shakespeare's black-eyed mistress of the Sonnets was more than a literary creation, then she too flaunts herself in maggot ostentation in Rosaline's person, who is described as "velvet-browed" and as a "whitely wanton" with "two pitch-balls stuck in her face for eyes". She has the appeal, for the sexually clamorous audience, of being "one that will do the deed / Though Argus were her eunuch and her guard". The dark eyes that haunted Shakespeare were also those generalized organs of seduction that even manifest themselves in such late-twentieth-century works as *Black Eyes*, by Dennis Potter, which explores an elderly writer's fixation on a young woman. Berowne even scorns the red hair of his sovereign in their favour, saying that to imitate her brow, red "paints itself black". Black had not always been equated with beauty, as the whole of Sonnet 127, beginning that in the old age black was "not counted fair", testifies. Berowne also roundly condemns sonnets, especially their profanity: "This is the liver vein, which makes flesh a deity, / A green goose a goddess, pure, pure idolatry – " But while he forswears the writing of them, the playwright reserved the right to continue.

Apart from the more perfect *A Midsummer Night's Dream*, *Love's Labour's Lost* is nearer to a Mozart opera than anything else Shakespeare wrote: "Never very far from the actual formality of song and dance," attests Harley Granville-Barker: "The long last act is half mask and half play, and in song and dance the play ends." The crepuscular and solemn ending, with its stirring *coup de théâtre* of Mercadé's entrance and his message that the king is dead – "The words of Mercury are harsh after the songs of Apollo" – re-establishes that "cormorant time", as well as "teem", was a dominating preoccupation. *Love's Labour's Lost* was written for a private performance behind closed doors, while the plague stalked at large in the streets of London.

The acting companies were dispersed in January 1593, because, following the outbreak the previous summer which had not been brought under control, public congregations – plays, bear-baitings, bowlings and other like assemblies for sports – were forbidden within a seven-mile radius of London. All through 1593 the infection spread virulently; by the end of the epidemic some 15,000 people had died.

The summer of 1593 was long and hot; the actors and playwrights came and went, touring, giving private performances. Marlowe was killed in May. Robert Browne, the actor, playing at Frankfurt Fair, left wife and family behind him in Shoreditch, where they were locked up in their infected house and died. People fled the worst areas, to be met by violence from country folk when they tried to settle as refugees; looting was rife, and armed violence often greeted the stringent quarantine regulations. Householders killed their cats and dogs, which spread the plague further by enabling the flea-bearing rats to breed. The price of tobacco soared; so did that of arsenic, quicksilver and dried toads, quack cures "past reason hunted". No one knew where the plague came from, why it was sent, and how to cure it.

Shakespeare was forced to adopt a *mouvementé* life: if he had been a Queen's player, earlier on, he was now probably still attached to the Earl of Pembroke's company, and as such had been an associate of Marlowe. Though he may have been involved with the production of *Edward II*, allegiances at this time were invariably temporary, and Shakespeare free-lanced, as did Jonson later, for several companies. Edward Alleyn had already parted company with the Burbage Theatre and the Curtain and had set up with Henslowe at the Rose. It took guts, a strong constitution, and huge entrepreneurial skill to survive professionally. It required an acute sense of smell, an instinct for avoiding trouble, and an exact grasp of the lie of the land, such as that possessed by a campaigning soldier – and a good horse as well – to avoid plague spots and mob unrest. Shakespeare had all of these.

Many did not survive. It was in September 1592 that Robert Greene had died, having aggravated his disease by drinking Rhenish wine and eating pickled herrings; his miserable end was spitefully distorted by his enemy Gabriel Harvey, contentious coxcomb and friend of Edmund Spenser. An identifiable "R. B. Gent." wrote in 1594 an ironically elegiac farewell:

> Greene, is the pleasing object of an eye:
> Greene, pleased the eyes of all that looked upon him.
> Greene, is the ground of every painter's dye:
> Greene, gave the ground, to all that wrote upon him.
> Nay more the men, that so eclipsed his fame:
> Purloined his plumes, can they deny the same?

As chief purloiner, Shakespeare lives in these lines.

"Sporting" Thomas Kyd, so dubbed by Jonson with macabre wit, as author of *The Spanish Tragedy* and *Jeronimo*, grisly, bloody plays filled with extravagant ranting and an extraordinary jumble of ghosts, murders, thunder, treachery and horrors, disappeared after informing on Marlowe and was never heard of again. George Peele, author of the sycophantic *The Arraignment of Paris* (1584) which had sugaringly commended him to his sovereign, faded into obscurity or death not much later. Lyly, once influential, now forty, a ghost who haunted court and wrote plays for the choristers of St Paul's, apparently met his end, too, at this time. Closer to Shakespeare, and especially to Marlowe, Thomas Watson, London-born, Oxford-educated, who composed in Latin and English, died also in 1593. The sonnets in his *Passionate Century*, published in 1582, Watson himself foolishly devalued, claiming they were elaborate literary pastiche; pastiche or not, they share themes with some of Shakespeare's better-known sonnets.

Living in such perilous times, Shakespeare was sorely tempted to take refuge in a haven of protection, such as the household of Southampton, or that of the Pembrokes. He had the highest gifts of flattering sincerity and literary affection known even in that flowery age. But to profit from their use he would have had to continue to write in voluptuous Italian vein, in luscious imitation of the many popular models on sale in the bookshops, or filled his work with images gathered from visiting Italians he met at inns or restaurants. Two such places have been named which he might have frequented, the Oliphant on Bankside, and a lodging house in Hart Street, St Olave's, run by Marco Lucchese, whose name, or its approximation, turns up later in *Othello*, when the Duke asks, in the council chamber, "Marcus Lucchesa, is not he in town?"

Italy beckoned. What easier means could Shakespeare have found to make his way there, than secure in the entourage of a nobleman?

# THIRD PART

# THE TRUE PATRON

# A friend's infirmities

In the Sonnets Shakespeare appears often as victim in his relationship with two figures to whom many of the poems are thought to
be addressed, the Earl of Southampton and the Dark Lady. But
there are compelling reasons to form the opposite conclusion about
what actually happened: that it was Shakespeare who gave up both
of them. In love poetry the lover is generally the victim of his
feelings, his loved one's behaviour, his poor circumstances, the
erratic behaviour of gods or chance. Simon Callow sees Shakespeare
as ontologically unstable, like an actor who, talking to someone,
takes on the face, tone and even the vocabulary of that person.
(Callow, further to this, picks out Maggie Smith as a present-day
performer who has this immense power of transmission of imagination to whatever she describes: she is taken over, lives inside the
experience she creates.)

Shakespeare was – or so the received idea runs – enamoured of
becoming a gentleman. This has often been held against him, most
passionately by Hesketh Pearson who says bluntly that, as a genius,
such an aspiration warped his sense of values: "everything that is
weak and paltry in his works springs from that defect: his false
rhetoric, his pomposity, his affectations, his cheap sallies of wit,
some of his later bitterness, his self-humiliating dedications and
sonnets." Pearson goes on that while his worldly thoughts were
caught up so demeaningly, his imagination redressed the balance:
"Falstaff is the comment of the genius on the coat-armour of the
gentleman." This denies the possibility that Shakespeare consciously enjoyed paradox and knew what he was doing.

Nothing was more paradoxical than his attachment to Southampton. Both men died at the age of fifty-two, but Southampton
never quite lived up to the promise that Shakespeare so lovingly
depicted in his early years. While Southampton became, after a
shaky start, the man of action *par excellence* (he shone in his last

campaign in the Netherlands in 1624), the able politician and Privy Councillor, the noble patron of letters, he certainly never achieved maturity in the complete way that Shakespeare did. He diminished into the moon to Shakespeare's sun, the reflector of a light more powerful than his own.

Shakespeare presented his persona – or the poet's persona, which may not necessarily be that of Shakespeare himself – as deferential, over-awed, devoted, and even both passionately and platonically in love, although never sexually so. Sonnet 20 is emphatic on the score that the penis added to Southampton's anatomy by doting Nature made all the difference –

> And by addition me of thee defeated
> By adding one thing to my purpose nothing.
>> But since she pricked thee out for women's pleasure,
>> Mine be thy love and thy love's use their treasure.

He surrendered the sexual "use" of Southampton to women. Their love was not physical, but a marriage of true minds, which existed at its strongest in the years 1591–3.

Southampton, attractive to everyone, was an especially seductive figure for Shakespeare, not primarily, then, for erotic reasons – or even vicariously erotic reasons – but for the many provocative ambiguities he presented. The central ambiguity, which gave Shakespeare such delight to investigate, consisted of his own attitude towards the nobility, for what he had discovered in his relationship with the young Earl was the limits of the value of patronage to himself. He perceived the frightening extent to which such a noble figure was completely trapped by his position.

In Shakespeare's time everyone fed off the nobility. The shows they put on, the spectacle they offered in their own carriage of rank and deportment, the coats of armour they commissioned from France, the horses they rode, even the stone they used for decorating their houses made them as visible as the most sensational female film stars. That they were men did not matter: women today are more the focus of glamour and intrigue, but men in that time identified and worshipped themselves and each other as great male pin-ups at court. Men were sex objects because the supreme arbiter of all was a woman, and an unmarried virgin who, while apparently never acting on her sexual preferences, never hid them either.

Sir Walter Scott in *Kenilworth* catches this male sensuality of appeal to other men as well as women in showing the wily and murderous Leicester offering himself to the Supreme Sovereign like a vestal virgin:

> The favourite Earl was now apparelled all in white, his shoes being of white velvet; his understocks (or stockings) of knit silk; his upper stocks of white velvet, lined with cloth of silver, which was shown at the slashed part of the middle thigh; his doublet of cloth of silver, the close jerkin of white velvet, embroidered with silver and seed-pearl, his girdle and the scabbard of his sword of white velvet with golden buckles; his poniard and sword hilted and mounted with gold . . .

– even Leicester's sword, symbol of his virility, is "sheathed" in white velvet, while what could be more explicitly sexual, for the early nineteenth century, than the "slashed part of the middle thigh"?

Shakespeare quite shamelessly exploited in his Sonnets the nature of the nobility as "love object", and even *Venus and Adonis* contained a fantasy projection of Southampton as part of the vision of Adonis. But Shakespeare also progressively defined the image of nobility as useless to his own development in life. And by the time the Sonnets were published in 1609, they had become, in so far as Southampton was their focus, biographically prophetic.

Southampton, whether as a prototype for Adonis or Leander, or as the beautiful but bashful young man who withholds himself from women, had, in addition to his lordly attributes, something that made him especially attractive to Shakespeare: an experience of life utterly different from his own. At the time that Shakespeare was exploring seriously the idea of becoming more closely identified with a great nobleman's entourage and way of life – as opposed to being a playwright dependent on market forces – he was enumerating in the Sonnets, with great care, the self-hugging, or hoarding, qualities that such a path entailed. His own experience had been so different: married at eighteen, three children, a background of struggle and family humiliation, a gruelling apprenticeship leading to recognition in middle age, or even late middle age (for such was twenty-eight in those times): he was confronting the marks of time indelibly scored on himself, with – again, his instinct for dramatic contrast – their opposite: the gilded and charmed perfection that Southampton, with his St John's College education, his untold wealth and power of patronage, possessed.

Naturally Shakespeare had to present the world of his patron, the subject of the Sonnets, as being in every way superior to his own thought-goring and cheap professional world of actor and playwright. But this was not how the contrary, paradoxical mind of the poet really thought of that world: in fact he was progressively revealing it as sterile. As, in the Sonnets, he besought Southampton to breed, to perpetuate himself, to take notice of him, he was defining what Southampton – because of his high-born circumstances, but also because of certain ambiguities and deficiencies in his character – would never be able to do: namely, to fulfil his promise.

While Shakespeare recognized, nurtured and explored in Southampton the side of himself that would like to have been born a gentleman, at the same time he was bristling with painful awareness – despite (or even because of) his abashed feelings about his own more modest circumstances – that it would never have suited him. For all his youth, Southampton was sensitive and many-sided in a way strikingly similar to Shakespeare. "If you want to develop," Shakespeare almost shouted at him in sonnet after sonnet, "you have to throw yourself away in the same fashion that I threw myself away. But, paradoxically, if you do so, you will lose your star quality. You will not be Marilyn Monroe" (to adopt W.S.'s own style of anachronism). "You will become plain Will in over-plus."

That is the meaning of the key sonnet, 94, in which Shakespeare makes such apparently completely contradictory assertions:

> They that have power to hurt and will do none,
> That do not do the thing they most do show,
> Who moving others are themselves as stone,
> Unmovèd, cold, and to temptation slow –
> They rightly do inherit heaven's graces,
> And husband nature's riches from expense;
> They are the lords and owners of their faces,
> Others but stewards of their excellence.
> The summer's flower is to the summer sweet
> Though to itself it only live and die,
> But if that flower with base infection meet
> The basest weed outbraves his dignity;
>    For sweetest things turn sourest by their deeds:
>    Lilies that fester smell far worse than weeds.

Shakespeare would have liked to believe in a Platonic ideal of nobility – the perfect gentleman, the divine ruler, the lord and owner of his fate as well as the permanent storehouse of beauty and the aristocratic ideal. But ultimately he was not convinced of it. The sudden shift in thought and mood in the final six lines, beginning "The summer's flower...", prefigures his dark judgement on Southampton's kind. For the "sweet thing" was to turn sour in his deeds, culminating in his support of Essex. Sentenced to a spell in the Tower, he became, at least for some years, a festering lily.

In time Shakespeare came to discount the values of aristocratic breeding. "The property by what it is should go," says the King of France in *All's Well That Ends Well*, summarizing Shakespeare's later feelings about the nobility, "not by the title". If you poured all our bloods together, they would "confound distinction". Wealth and honour could be conferred, but not virtue.

Sonnet 94 was also ambiguous. Southampton was good at concealing his feelings. His father had died when he was very young. He had papist connections. Precocious in wit, his behaviour was that of a delayed adolescent even as late as 1599, when as Essex's General of Horse he took Piers Edmunds, a professional cavalryman promoted by Essex to Corporal-General, to drink with him at his table and lie in his tent. Here he would, according to a witness at his trial, "cull" Edmunds, and "hug him in his arms and play wantonly with him". Until he settled down with his loving wife Elizabeth Vernon, Southampton thought all women were as false as his exquisitely attractive mother, Mary Browne, who had been unfaithful to his father.

Shakespeare fed off him emotionally: he was a perfect subject, whose unfulfilled suggestiveness could be rounded out by Shakespeare's rapid-fire imagination, reviving and yet goading, then castigating, his own virility, pretending to be dominated by Southampton's youth and glamour – indeed rejuvenating himself at his fire – yet at the same time setting the young Earl to work hard for the attention he was given. Shakespeare transformed him, turned him inside out, in dozens of different ways.

The early sonnets addressed to the young man, flattering his beauty and exhorting him to bring children into the world before it is too late, are therefore, as well as being about what they purport to be about, supremely narcissistic. Shakespeare is telling himself not to waste his own time, but to impregnate, conceive, and produce all he can. Conscious, from his balding, middle-aged looks, that he was past the first flush of youth, he was experiencing prematurely, as many writers have (Samuel Beckett is another example), a sense of his powers dwindling. He saw in the younger man, whose life was ahead of him, a reflection of himself ten years before: in an ideal state, with the importance and the future he himself had never had, and the opportunities he would have liked but which had been denied him.

As with his dramatic parts, Shakespeare was in the Sonnets both the poet in a relatively older persona, addressing the subject, and the subject himself. He put himself into everybody: in the simulated gesture of a poem he placed himself in Southampton's shoes, living out the other's beauty, his attraction, his vast range of qualities (many of them more imaginary than real). The ambiguous sexuality of Southampton's appearance, borne out by his occasional behaviour, attracted Shakespeare because it reflected Shakespeare, not Southampton, mesmerized him with its literary appeal; the male/female interpenetration offered wisdom, got at the heart of life's mystery, like the hermaphrodite being of Plato's *Symposium*, who in the Greek creation myth is split into two, with one half forever doomed to seek its twin in order again to become whole. Shakespeare had experienced this creation myth directly, in the fathering of his own twins, the girl and boy who had grown together in Anne's womb and been separated at birth. The sexual and creative impulses, he had seen, were inextricably intertwined.

In the Sonnets Shakespeare investigates all kinds of mental and spiritual conditions through the person he is addressing, rather as T. S. Eliot, in the *Four Quartets*, explores different spiritual moods through landscape. Shakespeare could do this in a compact, hermetically sealed manner which would appear to be unambiguous and explicit, as in the last sonnet (126) addressed to the young man, who growing older becomes even more beautiful – "Thy lovers withering as thy sweet self grow'st" – yet whom the poet warns that nature may not continue her special dispensation: "Yet fear her, O thou minion of her pleasure! / She may detain but not still keep her treasure" – her final settlement, or "quietus", will be to surrender him. But he could also be more direct, more revealing about what the method meant to him. Imagery revives his powers, not least the self-mirroring, fantasy perfections, so that when he berates himself for his failures, choking with envy and discontent, almost despising himself, his thoughts turn to his patron,

> ... then my state,
> Like to the lark at break of day arising
> From sullen earth, sings hymns at heaven's gate.

The Sonnets were for Shakespeare as much a way of detaching himself from a subject as becoming involved in it. As W. H. Auden notes in *The Dyer's Hand*, "what makes it difficult for a poet not to tell lies is that, in poetry, all facts and all beliefs cease to be true or false and become interesting possibilities." Shakespeare's relationship with Southampton, reconstructed by later generations mainly on the slender basis of the Sonnets, was extremely one-sided, existing largely in his own feelings and imagination. Later Shakespeare would steal bits from the real-life Southampton which would help him to fashion Prince Hal and Hamlet. Yet that actual Southampton was probably pretty boring and undifferentiated. Unlike Essex, Burghley or other great figures of the time, he had no strong "voice" of his own. At his trial, a bystander, John Chamberlain, reported that the Earl talked too much, was "somewhat too low and submiss". The overriding impression was still one of youthful charm, the promise, still as yet unrealized, of a noble spirit.

As for the courtly life, who can see Shakespeare as having much time, with the intense activity he crammed into his life between 1590 and 1610, to observe such niceties? The first requirement of the dependent or courtier's life was the ability to flatter and to spend long hours in attendance. This requirement extended to the highest in the land. Burghley himself was a master of ceremony, literally a servant. The ceremonial activities he could freely undertake already generated in Shakespeare an excess of emotion, sometimes almost beyond his powers of expression, as when, like "an unperfect actor on the stage" and overburdened with his "own love's might" he would "... forget to say / The perfect ceremony of love's rite".

The Sonnets, linked and ordered in a sequence which seems to suggest a frail thread of incident, were primarily a dramatic account of emotional growth. Sometimes, far from having the poet address a young man, Shakespeare has a young woman address a man; sometimes the poems are deliberately ambiguous, with no mention of gender, like many popular songs today which have an easy unisex extensibility.

Why did Shakespeare not want them printed around 1594–5? "'Tis better to be vile than vile esteemed," he wrote in Sonnet 121. When you are not vile and people reproach you for it even so, they are giving unjustified credence to your "sportive blood" – "When not to be receives reproach of being". They are likely to have got it wrong: as the poet warns, "they that level / At my abuses reckon up their own". Barbara Everett points out that this sonnet could be the poet venting his anger at being misunderstood: imaginative sympathy is itself dangerous and misguided, especially if a mock-confession of adultery – or of homosexual infatuation – is taken to be reality.

Withholding these works at the time, Shakespeare deliberately chose a path different from that of a court poet or self-conscious literary man. Never an innovator, he saw that he was too complex, daring, his talent too revolutionary and upsetting to suit the conventional mode of the sonnet. He always adhered outwardly to conventionality and he acknowledged that his excursions into this world were experimental. He would preserve the Sonnets but draw on them as a secret source for his plays. Unpublished, collected together loosely, only in 1609 were they to emerge from storage in the family home at Stratford for unauthorized or semi-authorized publication. By this time the rawness of feelings expressed in them had healed. Meanwhile, after 1595 and for the next fifteen or more years, the Sonnets were to be an important resource for thoughts and themes all the more powerful for having been suppressed. Although some were circulated, their significance was similar to that of a private diary.

But they were not a private diary. Shakespeare interiorized images as emotions, but the intimacy he knew or experienced was not under the spell of the early nineteenth-century growth of self-consciousness. Shakespeare's – Hamlet's – self-consciousness was instinctive and unselfconscious.

Thus Shakespeare abandoned the path of sonneteer. He avoided the greatest temptation success offered him. From this time forth he was detached from any dependence on patronage, and more especially from any emotional need for it. He intensified his grip on the despised profession of actor: he submerged his poetic ego in his company's fortunes. "It is an evident token of a wicked time when players wax so rich that they can build such a [play]house," complained a contemporary chronicler.

Spenser, like Shakespeare without particular advantage of birth or fortune, had become secretary to the Bishop of Rochester and later secretary to the Lord Governor in Ireland. He dedicated *The Faerie Queene* to Elizabeth, but added seventeen sonnets trumpeting the virtues of his gentlemen sponsors. Donne had been secretary to Sir Thomas Egerton, the Lord Keeper, but when he eloped with and married Anne More, a nobleman's daughter, without her father's approval, he was hounded out of his post; left at the age of thirty without money or position, he had finally and unwillingly to enter the Church. Ability, outstanding merit, even genius, were in themselves no guarantee of success. Despising the theatre as a means of livelihood, suffering crises of faith and with a cantankerous character, Ben Jonson had assiduously sought patronage, trying to preserve an aloof independence as a man of letters, yet forced into writing masques to indulge the court's childish passion for extravagant display.

Shakespeare became through his profession an unusual form of businessman: his aims were soberly personal, the more visibly so in the light of the gradations everywhere apparent in society. Not only was he prouder than Jonson, Donne or Spenser, more autonomous and in some crucial way more deeply uncompromising, he also had astonishing resilience and recuperative powers. But one thing above all he needed: the theatre's imaginative space, its classless freemasonry, its pseudo-family bonds. When Henry V calls his soldiers his "chosen few", his "little band of brothers", Shakespeare meant actors, who shared companionship as much as did soldiers: they shared freedom with those lowest ranks in the Elizabethan age, the rogues and beggars.

The people Shakespeare employed in his companies had weird and wonderful backgrounds, claims Trevor Nunn. "The prevailing notion," Nunn says, "is that theatre people are superficial, deceitful, extravagant and precious." His impression is that relationships in the theatre are surprisingly generous, loyal and forbearing. "People's bad moods are forgiven, their temperaments are tolerated, their disasters and tragedies shared." Nunn considers that Shakespeare, influenced by the theatre, came to have a great tolerance of the disparities, weaknesses, and foibles of human beings: "You learn through a theatre company that mutual dependence and forgiveness leads to a faith in the human spirit which is very sure."

Shakespeare's life in the theatre was no longer precarious. He had a family base in Stratford, a mother still very much alive and active, a wife whom either he did not want to have join him in London – to share the burdens his confrères' wives assumed – or, more likely, who herself did not much relish the prospect of metropolitan life, with its great dangers of plague and infection for her children.

In the theatre Shakespeare had found his true patron: the audience. This, he recognized, was his most important benefactor, and it, as witnessed in its many-layered mixture of vulgarity and privilege, intelligence, perception and ordinariness, became the sounding board of his art and the backbone of his survival. Writing for its custom and patronage gave him the liberty – and the livery – he needed: that audience was never of one kind, but reflected the variety and range of the colourful and rich society to which he held up the mirror.

The £1,000 that Southampton is rumoured to have given Shakespeare, to enable him to purchase a share of the Lord Chamberlain's company, can be viewed as a severance payment, a "golden handshake" which Shakespeare, with typically professional cool, allowed Southampton to give – while really it should have been the poet who paid off Southampton, for serving him excellently. It was allegorical gold, signifying that Shakespeare no longer had need of a close connection with the nobility. He was now his own master, his own sword of light. As such, as a fully professional poet and playwright of the time, unsupported by private means or any secretarial or administrative sinecure, he had become unique.

# Investigation of marriage

The Elizabethan William Harrison, who described assiduously the features of his land, speaks enthusiastically of the yeoman class of England, which rose so powerfully during the years in which Shakespeare grew up, and who, as Harrison says, "come to great wealth in so much that many of them are able and do buy the lands of unthrifty gentlemen, and often sending their sons to the schools, to the universities, and the inns of court, or otherwise leaving them sufficient lands whereupon they may live without labour, do make them by these means to become gentlemen".

Shakespeare shared this outlook with his audiences and wrote for it. He flattered the self-satisfaction of individuals who regarded their newly acquired status as glamorous – family, ancestors, native soil, the history and antiquity of his island, all came in for glorification: every connection was cultivated and inflated.

In *The Taming of the Shrew* Shakespeare made the framing story of Christopher Sly carry a similar *Arabian Nights* trick of transformation: instead of being whipped or jailed, or having the gristle of his right ear bored through, the drunken beggar becomes the butt of a passing lord, and is abducted into a dream world of leisure. His bedchamber is hung with lascivious paintings; he is bathed, anointed, supplied with sherry and conserves, and offered a lady wife for his bed, and a play to watch. Here, neatly presented in Warwickshire colours, is the greatest wish-fulfilment of Shakespeare's times:

> Am I a lord, and have I such a lady?
> Or do I dream? Or have I dreamed till now?
> I do not sleep. I see, I hear, I speak.
> I smell sweet savours, and I feel soft things.
> Upon my life, I am a lord indeed,
> And not a tinker, nor Christopher Sly.
> Well, bring our lady hither to our sight,
> And once again a pot o' th' smallest ale.

Shakespeare had not provided such basic realistic comedy before, nor had he pitched his endeavours at so earthy and unintellectual an audience.

Shakespeare based the nub of the play Sly watches on the much more traditional ballad or comedy theme of the railing wife. Socrates was supposed in popular Greek legend to have had such a wife, Xantippe. In the Miracle Plays she was Noah's wife; in Chaucer the Wife of Bath. She was a common, everyday figure and therefore easily recognizable in Elizabethan society, in which woman's traditional weapons against man – of abrasive vituperation, of fears and heartfelt appeals, of violent passions – were not only deified in the ruling Queen (with her many traits of a disordered temperament), but had not yet been repressed by Anglo-Saxon puritan, or imperial, male morality. There were few lovey-dovey wives in Shakespeare's time, and most of these were figures of fun. Woman's nature, as man's, was not only closer to nature but closer to its own sex. Although Shakespeare has many instances of woman being the weaker vessel, or being of a more timid disposition, he hardly paid more than lip-service to the male ideal of the perfect submissive woman. Indeed, women in Shakespeare's England seemed to play roles more near to those occupied by Hindu women in Indian society: they embodied the principle of *shastri*, which makes women not inferior to men but powerfully different. "It was accepted", says Peggy Ashcroft, "that a woman could dominate in this time. In the nineteenth century it would be almost impossible."

Having married a woman eight years older than himself, Shakespeare knew the extreme moods that affect a woman during her menstrual cycle and even menopause. He may even, at times, have fed off her anger and moodiness, unaware of goading her, then rising above her in his sense of virtue, creaming off energy to be used in his writing. Anne was now approaching forty, in the puberty of the critical change. Her twins, nearly ten, were in that time of precocious adulthood, themselves not far off early maturity. At almost every level of society, up to a certain point and before the privileges of education took over, family upbringing was similar. Because of the conflicts in religion there was no secure foundation of shared faith. The atmosphere was like that in an Eastern-bloc country before *perestroika*, yet a country which already had an expanding capitalist economy and a ruling class as spoilt and as corrupt as that in Hollywood. "I think if they had a Shakespeare with *perestroika*," says the Bulgarian critic Pierre Rouve, "Gorbachev could feel much happier." Conformity to an ideology was enforced by the establishment, while traditional and individual liberty was not allowed much scope for expression. Conformity of thought was imposed from above, by spies and preachers. Life outside the home in the city streets could at any moment become violent. Every man over eighteen carried a dagger, a broadsword or rapier, and sometimes a dagger and a rapier. Women took bodkins (such as Hamlet suggests to himself for his quietus), apprentices knives, while labourers bore weapons to work, and laid them down in a corner of the fields they tilled.

Within the family there was an atmosphere of deference to parents, manipulation, and of distance. Intimate and affectionate relationships were rare, and the fleeting nature of life meant to some extent that no great emotional investment could be made in another person that might not suddenly be cut short. Marriages were arranged by parents with only minimal consultation with the children; evidence of close affection between husband and wife is seen more often in the first three decades of the seventeenth century than in the last three of the sixteenth. That Shakespeare had strong affection for, and more than this, complicated and deep feelings towards his mother, father, sister and brothers cannot be doubted;

he made dramatic and entertaining capital out of the gap between what family and marriage relationships could be, and what they actually were.

The long and intricate, and above all realistic scenes between Katherine the Shrew and the swashbuckling Petruchio have the ring of marital truth, rather than wooing: this is a back-dated marriage play, a depiction, ironically presented, of what makes marriage work. The other plot in *The Taming of the Shrew*, the wooing of Kate's sister by Lucentio, Gremio and Hortensio, is mere confectionery by comparison. Shakespeare's treatment of Kate by Petruchio has a definite personal feel to it, as if Petruchio's victory at the end is grim and necessary wish-fulfilment.

But did Shakespeare make Kate's obedience too perfect, too pat, too easily the gratification of the male's dream? Directing this play at Stratford, Jonathan Miller became overwhelmed with curiosity about these scenes: "I used to walk in the churchyard and sit in the pew opposite the grave: pure sentiment on my part, but I did want to ask him if he meant Kate to be humiliated. 'Look', I would have liked to say to him, 'Can you just settle this for me?'" Shakespeare, in showing Petruchio win, generates a curious sense of rage about women, but it is not entirely straightforward. It seemed that he was winning a victory in the play over what, in his own life, was defeat. Anne's refusal to join him in London and the cooling of their marriage was at the heart of that defeat.

The playwright may dress up his characters, but ultimately he has only his own family and his neighbours and friends to write about. The further he strays from what he has himself experienced, the less vital the impetus that drives his figures. "The unconscious mind", as a character observes in Iris Murdoch's *The Black Prince*, "has only a few characters to play with." Shakespeare's genius resided in his catching those impulses from that unconscious on the wing, when they were still only rough and affective states of mind and feeling. He fleshed them out in the colours and lineaments of other people before he reached the narrower and more rational awareness that they were parts of himself. "Nature has no outline," William Blake wrote, "but imagination has."

Kate and Petruchio have strong unconscious shapes – those of Anne and Shakespeare. *The Shrew*, for all its woodenness, has been one of Shakespeare's most often revived plays, the subject of adaptations into opera, musical, film. To say that Kate and Petruchio deserve each other is a necessary cliché; they suffer from the psychotic rage, low-grade depression and protective defences of paranoia that were the common lot in Shakespeare's day. Raising children was, from an emotional point of view, not then a developed sub-culture: some men who as boys read Ovid fluently behaved like barbarians in the treatment of their wives. Most men and women, by 1990s standards of behaviour, showed painfully clear symptoms of parental deprivation.

Petruchio is such a one: a brawler from the start, newly released from being under his father's thumb, he is all too ready to up-grade his status of gentleman by grabbing the huge fortune lying in the unfortunately scalding (and scolding) lap of Kate. Shakespeare couched the wooing in terms which are at once, in the pair's first scene together, ambiguously crude and vital. The taffeta phrasemonger of *Love's Labour's Lost* lavished upon these emotional cripples a new, more monochrome and biting, down-to-earth wit:

> PETRUCHIO: You lie, in faith, for you are called plain Kate,
> And bonny Kate, and sometimes Kate the curst,
> But Kate, the prettiest Kate in Christendom,
> Kate of Kate Hall, my super-dainty Kate –
> For dainties are all cates, and therefore 'Kate'.

He served up erotic wordplay which is graphic, and suggestive of cunnilingus – and therefore outrageous for a gentleman wooing the well-off daughter of a noble house:

> KATE: If I be waspish, best beware my sting.
> PETRUCHIO: My remedy is then to pluck it out.
> KATE: Ay, if the fool could find it where it lies.
> PETRUCHIO: Who knows now where a wasp does wear his sting?
> In his tail.
> KATE: In his tongue.
> PETRUCHIO: Whose tongue?
> KATE: Yours, if you talk of tales, and so farewell.
> PETRUCHIO: What, with my tongue in your tail? Nay, Come again,
> Good Kate, I am a gentleman.

Shakespeare's best and least expected comic reversal is supplied when Petruchio himself plays the shrew and spurns the meat brought by the servant, and "rails and swears, and rates" so that, as a servant remarks, "He kills her in her own humour". For all the violence and shock of the language, Shakespeare demonstrated great subtlety in showing the difference between the pair, and offering justification for Kate's becoming obedient. That Petruchio is a man and Kate a woman is not the important difference. That Petruchio has understood himself, understood what it has taken for him to become master of himself, is the critical factor, so the obedience Kate needs and Petruchio has to impose is the only bond within which they feel comfortable, and can become free to enjoy civilized qualities.

Shakespeare afforded ample proof that Kate is the neglected daughter. Bernard Shaw, himself a deprived son, urged men and women who respected one another to boycott this play until it was driven off the boards – in it glimmered a crude reflection of himself that he found too painful to contemplate. But Shakespeare's observation of the pair cuts clear and deep; the type each is, the painfully sharp dynamics of their relationship, the strong and gratifying comic release, the razor-edge sense of contrariness that lies under the surface, offer a huge potential for good acting. The text itself does not make explicit the understanding underlying Petruchio's harshness, the tender and absorbing humour, the warmth of feeling which emerges from Kate:

> PETRUCHIO: I say it is the moon.
> KATHERINE: I know it is the moon.
> PETRUCHIO: Nay then you lie, it is the blessèd sun.
> KATHERINE: Then God be blessed, it is the blessèd sun.
> But sun it is not when you say it is not,
> And the moon changes even as your mind.
> What you will have it named, even that it is,
> And so it shall be still for Katherine.

# La Passionata

Ever since he became part of the Southampton circle Shakespeare had been a friend of John Florio, the Earl's Italian tutor, who was some eleven years older than Shakespeare. Born in London, Florio came from a family of Italian Protestant refugees: a protégé of Burghley, he taught Italian to others in the wider circle of Shakespeare's patrons, and later translated Montaigne from the French.

He and Shakespeare had a natural sympathy with one another: he led the captive life of a servant of the nobility such as Shakespeare could easily have fallen into. Florio's *A World of Words*, his influential Italian dictionary, although not published until 1598, indicated how close its maker's mind and spirit was to Shakespeare, for Florio delighted in dazzling turns of expression, and grasped the wonderful range and rapidity of Elizabethan English: *nicchiare* is to "wallow or twiggle up and down as doth a woman on the point of being delivered of a child ... to lament in corners, grumble secretly"; *schinchimurra*, "a skummering of a dog ... a filthy great stinking turd". The man who coined these definitions could well have been the block from which Shakespeare carved some of his verbally dextrous characters.

If it was not Shakespeare, then it was someone close to both men who expressed his feelings, who in a prefatory sonnet to Florio's *Second Fruits* (1591) extolled the Italian's seminal power, comparing him to the spring, when herbs, gums and plants do "vaunt of their release". When our English wits lay dead, the sonnet ends, Florio came with his riches to overspread the English barrenness: "Such fruits, such flow'rets of morality, / Were ne'er before brought out of Italy."

Since the savage continental counter-Reformation started in 1570, with its massacres, its barbarous use of the Inquisition, and its sentence of excommunication passed on Elizabeth, England had virtually severed all connection with Italy. But the Protestant English, particularly the flower of the élite – including the Queen – continued their paradoxical passion for their cold-war enemy. And some but by no means all of the aristocracy who loved Italy, and did their best to travel there, had Catholic connections, either from recent exile or dating back to Marian times.

The aristocracy and the better-cultured *nouveaux riches* English journeyed to Italy and elsewhere in Europe to broaden or complete their educations, to observe foreign judicial systems and customs, and to learn languages, often as a springboard to a career in diplomacy. In politics, as in court behaviour, in public health, literature, painting and architecture, Italy dominated. The first Italian grammar in English, published in 1550 with a pioneering dictionary for the "better understanding of Boccaccio, Petrarch and Dante", had gone through three editions in the 1560s. Niccolo Machiavelli's *The Prince* and his *The Art of War* were widely read, while Baldassare Castiglione's *The Courtier* focused on the arts of peace, and the ideal courtier, who had to be proficient in music as well as etiquette.

But Italy was also a subject for hot dispute, a further extension of the good–evil battleground. The Earl of Oxford (supposed later by some cranks – including, in this context, a perhaps envious Sigmund Freud – to have written the works of Shakespeare), "abashed and ashamed" of a fart released in the royal presence (when bowing to the Queen), fled his native land and voyaged widely in Italy. On his return he secretly became a Catholic for a time, and also waxed so Italianate he was accused of "buggering his boy that was his cook and many other boys". Oxford, like his great rival Sidney, had mixed with dangerous papists; he had even gone as far as the dangerous, inaccessible shores of Sicily, though in Italy Englishmen voyaged in fear of local ill-feeling and of arrest by the Inquisition.

Venice particularly attracted the English, not only for being, as Emrys Jones says, "a stunning example of a successful and working republic" – Shakespeare would later set two of his plays there – but also for being, with its legendary tens of thousands of licensed courtesans, "esteemed so loose that they are said to open their quivers to every arrow", "the best flesh shambles in Italy", as John Day called it. Robert Greene, a follower of the Earl of Oxford, had distanced himself from his master's peregrinations, complaining that he was not "a devil incarnate because I am Italianate". Marlowe, as well as Shakespeare, and later Webster, brought popular force to the idea that Italy was the land where thrived the "liberty to sin": he had Machiavel introduce *The Jew of Malta*, while his most negative and diabolical character, Lightbourn, had learned his homicidal arts beyond the Alps: how to poison flowers in Naples – "To strangle with a lawn thrust down the throat; / To pierce the wind pipe with a needle's point".

Shakespeare, it seems, in the end never did see Italy, relying for his vision on secondary sources like Florio, but also on the works of Ariosto, Bandello, Boccaccio, Cinthio and Petrarch. A little reality, in Shakespeare's imagination, went a long way.

*The Most Excellent and Lamentable Tragedy of Romeo and Juliet*, Shakespeare's first great universal play and popular masterpiece, was saturated in the romantic yet dangerous image of Italy. He first picked up the idea from an Italian novella by Matteo Bandello which he bought in the open-air bookstalls behind St Paul's, but a leisurely English poem of 1562, Arthur Brooke's *The Tragical History of*

*Romeus and Juliet,* which Shakespeare had already drawn on for parts of *Two Gentlemen of Verona,* served as a direct source. Brooke originally saw the story on the stage on tour with an Italian company of mixed sexes; he died unfortunately by drowning on an expedition to help the Huguenots.

Shakespeare's unassuming yet transforming imagination embraced another writer's inferior efforts with the kind of humility that would draw out the best. Brooke's poem often reads like the Pyramus and Thisbe playlet from *A Midsummer Night's Dream.* "What if your deadly foes, my kinsmen, saw you here," Juliet asks Romeo on the balcony:

> Like lions will, your tender parts asunder would they
>     tear.
> In truth and in disdain, I, weary of my life,
> With cruel hand my mourning heart would pierce with
>     bloody knife.

Yet Shakespeare treated Brooke's work as he did when adjusting himself to those many plays he acted in, with an unselfconscious equality: he had no artistic arrogance or sense of superiority. He hardly rated his own version higher than his source's treatment of the story. He transformed, but without any self-regarding instinct or need to applaud his own effort.

He also eradicated the didacticism; he generalized Romeo's initial love for Rosaline, removing the lustful aspects from it; he cut the nine months of the Brooke treatment down to a week of hot days and nights, reducing Juliet's age from fifteen to thirteen. All this, and especially the way he fashioned the imagery as an integral part of both theme and atmosphere, by employing "running images" which underlined certain aspects of the narrative, characters or background, helped to create imaginative unity. While writing the Sonnets he made images constantly recur and tried out new poetic or linguistic constructions against a demanding metrical and rhythmic pattern. This method was gloriously vindicated by *Romeo and Juliet.* The prologue is a complete sonnet; so is the first encounter between the lovers:

> ROMEO: (*to Juliet, touching her hand*)
>     If I profane with my unworthiest hand
>         This holy shrine, the gentler sin is this:
>     My lips, two blushing pilgrims, ready stand
>         To smooth that rough touch with a tender kiss.

> JULIET:  Good pilgrim, you do wrong your hand too much,
>        Which mannerly devotion shows in this.
>        For saints have hands that pilgrims' hands do touch,
>        And palm to palm is holy palmers' kiss.
> ROMEO:  Have not saints lips, and holy palmers, too?
> JULIET:  Ay, pilgrim, lips that they must use in prayer.
> ROMEO:  O then, dear saint let lips do what hands do:
>        They pray; grant thou, lest faith turn to despair.
> JULIET:  Saints do not move, though grant for prayers' sake.
> ROMEO:  Then move not while my prayer's effect I take.
>        (*He kisses her*)

He dispensed love as a form of religious celebration, both pagan and Christian. Caroline Spurgeon tabulates the prevalence of images relating to light and darkness: perhaps not quite so methodically, Shakespeare did select images which echoed one another and built up to a complete structure, like repeated musical phrases. Again the model is Italian: both the form and the decoration of baroque architecture. He mirrored the exterior imagery of action – the meetings, the fights, the forms of social intercourse, the letters and the vows – in the interior imagery of light and dark. Love was as sudden as the lightning, as violent as an explosion of gunpowder. He added to the images of death a glowing, sapphirine interior landscape of sympathetic nature – pomegranate and sycamore trees, the nightingale singing passionately in warm darkness, the wind wooing the frozen bosom of the North – while he induced Capulet, on finding Juliet apparently dead, to lament: "Death lies on her like an untimely frost / Upon the sweetest flower of all the field".

But the crowning image he effected was that superlative beauty which, with massive irony, he allowed Romeo to find upon discovering his love supposedly dead. Shakespeare displayed in this climax a supreme unselfconscious confidence which revealed how little the playwright needed ordinary mortal forms of vanity to sustain him. His art gave back as much, if not more, than the effort it cost him. Death has no power over Juliet's beauty:

> Death, that hath sucked the honey of thy breath,
> Hath had no power yet upon thy beauty.
> Thou art not conquered.

It was fate rather than any individual flaw which enabled Shakespeare to bring about the death of the lovers in *Romeo and Juliet*. Here was the secret of Shakespeare's marvellous achievement: he was dramatizing a story which as myth incorporated a permanent truth about the human condition. Romeo and Juliet symbolize the power of Eros, "So rash, so foolish, so ill-advised", the opposite of Christian love, in which the pair would have accepted their limitations. They symbolize the abandonment to passion that lovers who love love and being in love ultimately succumb to. Psychologically Romeo and Juliet are hardly people of any individual soul or quality; their most lively encounter – in terms of crisp dialogue which reveals character and contact – is their first. Passion has not yet geared itself; so Juliet pushes her would-be lover around like a precocious fifth-former. Had they ever settled down to married life, Juliet would have been a frightful, egging-on shrew.

But from the moment their love catches fire they lose touch with reality. Romeo never comes to know who Juliet is, nor does she see in him more than an excuse for a rising inner intensity. Their love is not a love for one another as they really are: their love is based on a false reciprocity, which conceals a twin narcissism. They love in one another the reflections of themselves. Their passion is blind and undifferentiating, and therefore must lead to mistakes, to mutual blindness and ultimately to the fate of any love that is based on egocentric passion: to death. It could be argued that their love contains a great yearning for death, for, not able to know one another, each wants self-obliteration in a glorious form of sacrifice that will transcend life and raise them to a permanent, eternal plane of love. By their martyrdom to love they give love immortal power, but reality would have killed their passion and made them ordinarily happy. In European literature, at least, happy love has no history.

In the way Shakespeare realized this story of woe there was nothing abstract. Although ostensibly set in a distant time and place among noble foreigners, the domesticity of the Veronese touches is so recognizably that of provincial and Elizabethan England that no one could be fooled for a moment. The Capulets, with their bourgeois habits of running a house, do not seem particularly exalted; Shakespeare filled them out with loving care and comic observation. Mercutio's lewd and graphic humour with the Nurse; his high-spirited repartee with his best friend; the frequent street fighting – Benvolio is taunted by Mercutio, "Thou wilt quarrel with a man for cracking nuts, having no other reason but because thou hast hazel eyes ... Thou hast quarrelled with a man for coughing in the street because he hath wakened thy dog that hath lain asleep in the sun . . ." – which the authorities try in vain to suppress: these would have been happily familiar to the audiences which first came to *Romeo and Juliet.* So would the young man ambling in the grove just outside the built-up area; so would a garrulous old windbag recalling the weaning of her employer's little girl, reminiscent of the Nurse in *Dido, Queen of Carthage* who describes Cupid, "How prettily he laughs / He'll be a twigger when he comes to age"; or an old scholar gathering medicinal herbs in the early dawn. The middle-class commercial population that lived by London Wall and Bishopsgate, which sought solace and pleasure by frequenting the playhouses, knew only too well how sudden fights flared up, or how London's authorities might, on the slenderest pretext, slap people suspected of the plague into quarantine.

The public of Finsbury also was, broadly, a "sword-and-buckler" public and likely to enjoy Mercutio's cavalier disparagement of rapier play, and Tybalt's punctilio of quarrelling. The sword and buckler was on its way out, but it still commanded old-fashioned affection. Mercutio, who constantly sends up Romeo's romantic excesses, switches to down-to-earth prose when he receives his wound: "Ay, ay, a scratch, a scratch; marry, 'tis enough". After two more lines of verse Shakespeare allowed the grim reality of death full play in the mind of this sardonic, tough, and self-mocking man: "No, 'tis not so deep as a well, nor so wide as a church door, but 'tis enough. 'Twill serve. Ask for me tomorrow, and you shall find me a grave man."

Mercutio is real: he wants to live and to be his own master, while the protagonists of passion seek to be defeated, to lose self-control, to be entirely beside themselves and in ecstasy – except for that semi-divine control of the artistic artefact. In such counterpoint of dramatic action did Shakespeare demonstrate the painful quality of life, and unify opposites in the harmony of form and imagery. He mythicized a purity which invites comparison with Mozart and Beethoven.

*Romeo and Juliet* is also Shakespeare's first perfectly told story. Concentrating on the two main characters, he stretched the pro-gressive complications of their love, in an atmosphere of feud and death, to yield the fullest possible dramatic harvest. Shakespeare handled the crisis – how shall Juliet escape the marriage to Paris? – perfectly, although he conceived the passionate climax perhaps too predictably, by modern unliterary standards at least, and sustained it too lengthily through arias of great lyric poetry. He never faltered in the cycles of rising and falling action; he delineated sharply the contrasts between the vulnerability of sensitive emotions and the violence of closed implacable hatreds; meanwhile mingling comedy and sexual banter to create variety within the unity of intense feeling:

> MERCUTIO: The pox of such antic, lisping, affecting phantasims, these new tuners of accent! 'By Jesu, a very good blade, a very tall man, a very good whore.' Why is not this a lamentable thing, grandsire, that we should be thus afflicted with these strange flies, these fashion-mongers, these 'pardon-me's, who stand so much on the new form that they cannot sit at ease on the old bench? O, their bones, their bones!

If Romeo is, as Hazlitt says, Hamlet in love, Mercutio has the accent of Hamlet the jester.

Shakespeare did not know (unlike the more scholarly Marlowe, had he been alive) that in reviving the potent myth of the doomed lovers with a Renaissance setting of Catholic magnificence – and with a Franciscan friar sympathetically portrayed – he was appropriating the setting of violent struggles between the Orthodox Church and the Manichaean heresy of the Catharists, who, like English Puritans, professed superior purity. This may explain the otherwise inexplicable feud between the Capulets and the Montagues. Not that Shakespeare would himself have ventured into such spiritually dangerous territory on the stage: he played safe, gratifying well-established expectations rather than delivering devastating surprises.

Nearer at hand, audiences must have recognized in Shakespeare's love story an echo of the Wiltshire feud of the Danverses and the Longs from the autumn of 1594. First one of Danvers's servants was killed by a Long servant, for reasons unknown, but the Long retainer cunningly avoided justice or revenge; the feud escalated until the Danverses, notably the headstrong sons Sir Charles and Sir Henry, both young men who were close to the Earl of Southampton, irrupted into a private dinner party in Corsham attended by the Longs, and engaged Sir Walter Long and his brother Harry in a violent dispute during which they resorted to long swords. Charles was wounded in the hand, Harry Long stabbed to death by Harry Danvers. The Danverses fled, but they escaped justice through the protection of South-ampton, based on Titchfield in Hampshire, and were ferried over to France where Henry IV, a friend of Essex, sheltered them, and sought Elizabeth's pardon on their behalf.

John Florio was in the party that aided the Danverses, and so were thirteen of Southampton's servants – his steward, keeper of his wardrobe, gentlemen of his horse, his bailiff, falconer, barber, stablemen and grooms. As a result Charles, Henry Danvers and Southampton became bonded in danger – and bound to future mis-chief. Shakespeare, free of his ties with a Southampton whose repu-tation was becoming increasingly stained, removed this explosive Wiltshire saga to Florio's homeland, even-handedly putting a plague on both houses.

With the continual invocation of love in spiritual terms, with broad Italian feeling and its explosive emotions which must be expressed and atoned for, Shakespeare embedded in *Romeo and Juliet,* for all its English domestic trappings, a Catholicism of feeling which revealed the power of the old faith over his imagination. Some who argue that Shakespeare could never have been a Roman Catholic point to Juliet's line in Act IV, "Or shall I come to you at evening mass", as an indication of his ignorance: but mass could be cele-brated in the evening. Apart from this, *Romeo and Juliet* abounds in biblical echoes and mentions, as well as religious images: these were Shakespeare's own, not taken from his source Brooke. Shake-speare also, in spite of the Catholic setting and atmosphere, para-phrased the Anglican marriage service at certain crucial moments; he used common biblical expressions from his Geneva Bible, such as when Romeo, arguing with Paris, says, "Put not another sin upon my head / By urging me to fury".

*Romeo and Juliet* became instantly popular, especially with the young, who liked to quote in their wooing from the latest thea-trical success, and would jot down passages in their commonplace books. Robert Allot's popular anthology, *England's Parnassus* (1600), has more lines from *Romeo and Juliet* than from any other play by Shakespeare. The script of the play, 800 lines shorter than the full text, was pirated by the printer John Danter in 1597, probably from the memories of actors who played Romeo and Juliet.

But the text itself could not have been filled with such perfectly drawn and vital characters had not Shakespeare worked, and written for, such an outstanding company. The ability of what was now called the Lord Chamberlain's Men, under the patronage of Henry Carey, Lord Hunsden, and led by Burbage and Heminges, Shakespeare, and the "most comicall and cavalier" Will Kempe, was an integral part of Shakespeare's development. Their flexibility of style and the adaptability of their powers of impersonation found expression in Shakespeare's already wide range. It gave the playwright security to know that he could return, in a new play, to write for the same cast: he knew their work backwards and, in tempo and technique, borrowed from their playing to fill out a particular role with naturalistic or dramatic touches. Yet he could also blank out of his mind the reality of Juliet being played by a boy whose voice had not yet broken, and the Nurse by a man of forty or more. To unravel what traits of character come from the actor (or the actor's imagination) and what from the playwright is impossible, but Shakespeare jotted down and swiftly incorporated in the parts he wrote for this company hundreds of mannerisms, tricks of mind as well as of behaviour, and physical characteristics – even dreams and fantasies of his faithful performers. A modern instance of such practice happened when David Storey wrote *Early Days* for Ralph Richardson in 1979: in *Early Days* Storey contrived a play around a character somewhat based on Richardson, as well as for Richardson to play. The result was a complex many-sided character with a teasingly ambiguous life.

This also happened with the major members of Shakespeare's company, even the hired men and extras. But there was no typecasting. The highly intelligent actors in the Chamberlain's company switched to play roles totally opposite or different from those in which they had made their names, or those that might be assumed a natural choice. The whole protean, chameleon nature of the Elizabethan theatre testifies to tremendous versatility on the part of its practitioners, from leading actors and playwrights to apprentices who played women, the bookkeeper, the tireman who attended to costumes and properties, and the stage-keeper, the musicians, and gatherers of entrance money, who sometimes could not resist cheating, scratching their heads when they itched not, and dropping, as noted in *The Actors' Remonstrance*, shillings and half-crown pieces in at their collars. The Chamberlain's company, for instance, refurbished for Juliet's tomb the one used for *Titus Andronicus*: old costumes were always being "translated". As Marchette Chute notes: "If the Revels office" (the Clerkenwell offices and storerooms where plays were rehearsed and equipped for performances at court) "started with eight jerkins of purple cloth-of-gold for mariners, the jerkins made their next appearance translated into six costumes for Hungarians and then into four kirtles for Diana's nymphs." One of *Romeo and Juliet*'s merits from the costumier's point of view was its lack of battle scenes requiring armour: this could prove expensive, needed special underwear, and was difficult to get on and off. The principals despised painted imitations.

# Lawful magic

### i

Shakespeare went straight on from *Romeo and Juliet* to write *A Midsummer Night's Dream*. Success must have encouraged a certain autobiographical flourish, even in the self-effacing Shakespeare, who put into the mouth of Mercutio, with whom he probably had more sympathy than with Romeo, the self-indulgent words of a poet discussing his own profession:

> True, I talk of dreams,
> Which are the children of an idle brain,
> Begot of nothing but vain fantasy,
> Which is as thin of substance as the air,
> And more inconstant than the wind, who woos
> Even now the frozen bosom of the north,
> And, being angered, puffs away from thence,
> Turning his face to the dew-dropping south.

The Queen Mab extravaganza fits oddly in the mouth of Mercutio, and might, anyway, have been dashed off for the "fairy" entertainment forming in Shakespeare's mind – but then finding no place there, have suggested itself as a teasing foil to Romeo's passion. It does not altogether fulfil this function, for the personality behind the imagery is more naïve – more carried away with his fantasy – than Mercutio would ever have been, which is why, although it makes a good set piece for actors' auditions, it has provided every Mercutio with his toughest assignment in the role. Shakespeare possibly intended it for delivery by one of the schoolchildren who played the first fairies in the *Dream* itself. Theseus also expatiates in the poet's own voice on the imaginative faculty:

> The poet's eye, in a fine frenzy rolling,
> Doth glance from heaven to earth, from earth to heaven,
> And as imagination bodies forth
> The forms of things unknown, the poet's pen
> Turns them to shapes, and gives to airy nothing
> A local habitation and a name.

Shakespeare was still in a Berowne mood: "forms of things unknown" were hardly a lusty, hunting Duke's life concerns, just as Mercutio was unlikely to be spinning elaborate conceits on the nature of a fairy queen. But in these speeches the anonymous, invisible poet spoke out. George Rylands suggests that he inserted such passages from a notebook in which he jotted down random poetic thoughts. Shakespeare also changed the character of English fairies, who, before he placed them on a bank with the wild thyme, were malignant and earthbound little folk, perhaps more like Irish leprechauns or Norwegian trolls. Shakespeare found their good side.

He wrote *A Midsummer Night's Dream* for an occasion: a Tudor courtier's private wedding, that of William Stanley, the new Earl of Derby (Lord Ferdinando Strange having died in 1594), early in 1595, to Queen Elizabeth's chief minister's granddaughter, Lady Elizabeth de Vere, the twenty-year-old daughter of the wayward "lewd" Earl of Oxford, whose hand had been spurned by Southampton five years before. Shakespeare carefully differentiated this play from solid family entertainment (*Romeo and Juliet*), nor did he try to give it the slickness and intellectual appeal of *Love's Labour's Lost*. He simply hatched it as upper-class entertainment – richly dressed, elaborately scored, bold and rather silly, obvious in its jokes. He angled it to appeal to snobbery: he even included in it a mention of Elizabeth's visit to Leicester's Kenilworth entertainment in 1575 (which he himself had attended).

Shakespeare liked to mirror his clientele in his plays: the court and country gentlemen, with their riding-and-hunting society, were here uppermost in his mind. He opened the *Dream* not with a sordid fight, or lecherous wit, or verbal fireworks, but with a great prince dispensing lavish hospitality. He gave the play many features of a great tapestry hung in an Earl's manor, depicting the life of the patron: it is alive with country pictures, woodland beauties, and dreaming summer nights. Like bright, repeated threads in a tapestry he established running, or repeated, metaphors out of which he wove an imaginative unity – birdsong, the sunrise, animals, the birds themselves.

He had been back and forth to Stratford during the writing of the *Dream*, and he mentioned explicitly, in Titania's description, the bad summer of 1594. Titania sees the seasons alter, for "in the fresh lap of the crimson rose", fall the hoary-headed frosts:

> And on old Hiems' thin and icy crown
> An odorous chaplet of sweet summer buds
> Is, as in mock'ry, set –

That summer had been notably more wet and boisterous than the "aged'st man is able to recount".

Shakespeare summoned up comic figures, too, very differently conceived for the different audience. To fit the aristocratic slant he painted rustics continually grovelling and in forelock-tugging mood, gravely concerned over the general level of entertainment, and whether they could contribute usefully to it with the play they had chosen to fit the grand occasion – their interpretation of the latest London hit. Shakespeare picked for their pathetic rendering – and it was hardly a coincidence – the tragedy of Pyramus and Thisbe, which itself was a broad and concentrated joke on *Romeo and Juliet*. Shakespeare made the joke be on him.

Thus the star-crossed lovers meet at a secret place, there is a last encounter at a tomb, and a tragic misapprehension of death – Quince's play is not only presented as a skit of his previous success, but the jester Shakespeare even set himself up as the Prologue Quince, when he comes on to announce: "If we offend, it is with our good will [or Will, i.e. Will Shakespeare] / That you should think: we come not to offend / But with good will [W.S. again]." The pun was crystal-clear to Shakespeare's audience, and it is not lost even today. When Shakespeare played Quince (which was likely, for Quince is the bookkeeper of the play, in charge of its highly rudimentary production), then the laugh was even greater.

Shakespeare practised much witty recapitulation in his own organization of the action of the *Dream*: he built his own plot from *Love's Labour's Lost* (the amateur theatricals), *Two Gentlemen* (the entanglement of two pairs of lovers) and Mercutio's Queen Mab speech. He also seized other ideas from here and there – the opening looks back to Chaucer's *Knight's Tale*; the fairies' presence owes something to Spenser's "Epithalamion".

The portrayal of Bottom was a parody of Edward ("Ned") Alleyn, tragedian and leader of Shakespeare's rivals, the Admiral's Men; Alleyn was now a wealthy man, having, with his father-in-law Philip Henslowe, built the Fortune theatre in Finsbury in 1600 and having invested in property in London and Sussex. Alleyn had played (and continued to play) Tamburlaine, Doctor Faustus, Hieronimo in *The Spanish Tragedy* and Barabas in *The Jew of Malta*. Later, when an old man and single, he was to marry one of John Donne's daughters.

For the occasion of the Derby wedding, which had semi-royal status, Shakespeare had a large number of potential extra participants to hand; in *A Midsummer Night's Dream* he could therefore juggle with, uniquely, three different casts, as well as plots, constructing a many-layered entertainment with the larkishness of an elaborate architectural folly. The scenes of the fairies were played by amateurs; the speeches were mostly declaimed or sung, and their verse was packed with striking imagery which hardly needed acting. Shakespeare wrote them to be actor-proof – the fairies could also be rehearsed independently of the rest of the cast.

Shakespeare had his monarch subtly, indirectly, in mind when he conceived the warring, passionate figures of Oberon and Titania. Was he not, in the most delicately disguised way possible, writing about the high-handed Elizabeth and a composite of her lovers, including Leicester and Essex? His audience included the Queen, Burghley and his family; they would have responded to such figures as being near to their everyday experience, although harmless and comically exaggerated. There was more than a whiff of Whitehall about the sudden and arbitrary way the rule of fairyland was exercised, and what other great figure was there on whom to base Titania but the Faery Queen herself? Shakespeare, never explicit, always tactful, was adept at such games.

Twice in the *Dream* Shakespeare directly flashed Elizabeth on his memory screen. In the early 1590s Elizabeth had visited Oxford and, seated on horseback, listened to dissertations by the great clerics. She had once heard Edmund Campion so declaim. But on certain occasions her intellectuals let her down. Theseus says of his princely progress,

Where I have come, great clerks have purposèd
To greet me with premeditated welcomes;
Where I have seen them shiver and look pale,
Make periods in the midst of sentences,
Throttle their practised accent in their fears,
And in conclusion dumbly have broke off,
Not paying me a welcome.

The other reference would also not have been wasted on the Cecil and Derby families. Oberon recalls to Puck hearing a mermaid sing on a dolphin's back: the fish was part of the Kenilworth aquatic display which had also included Cupid, who fired a bolt of his love shaft at the visiting Queen (the fair vestal, throned in the west):

But I might see young Cupid's fiery shaft
Quench'd in the chaste beams of the wat'ry moon,
And the imperial vot'ress passèd on,
In maiden meditation, fancy-free.

Shakespeare dipped this gentle, flattering image in the love juice of an indirect, if ingratiating, appeal to the monarch herself: who knows but that she was delighted by this striking and yet tactfully coded form of literary homage?

## ii

"Thus play I in one person many people, / And none contented", said Shakespeare of himself in the shape of the kingly protagonist in his next play: it showed the freedom the author now felt in projecting himself in royal trappings. But while he could represent his melancholy in Richard II's final great soliloquy, begetting images on the intimate qualities of his own mind and soul, peopling his prison world with his thoughts "In humours like the people of this world, / For no thought is contented" (harping still on the poet's generative discontent from which Shakespeare continually suffered), there were serious shortcomings in *Richard II* as a play. Shakespeare, with his twelfth or thirteenth complete play, had not, in his treatment of history, quite found what he was looking for. He had mastered, as far as possible in that age, the High Renaissance comedy which stemmed from a classical or Italian tradition: he had written the perfect lyric tragedy of young love. But the chronicle play remained a genre which he could not quite integrate into a final form that satisfied him.

He moulded *Richard II* on Marlovian principles, which he could now, two or three years after the other playwright's death, shamelessly employ. Shakespeare was attempting to iron out the dead spots of a shapeless and episodic form by consciously emulating the best example he could find, namely *Edward II. Richard II* was therefore, for Shakespeare, a deeply experimental play.

Richard's last great soliloquy, as Swinburne wrote in *A Study of Shakespeare*, showed Shakespeare imitating Doctor Faustus' way of thinking in the opening scene of Marlowe's play – "in the curious trick of selection and transcription of texts for sceptic meditation and analytic dissection" –

> Si peccasse negamus, fallimur,
> Et nulla est in nobis veritas:
> If we say that we have no sin,
> We deceive ourselves, and there's no truth in us.
> Why then, belike we must sin,
> And so consequently die.
> Ay, we must die an everlasting death
> What doctrine call you this – Che sera, sera?
> What will be, shall be?

But Marlowe concentrated on the man. Edward, in his other play, is destroyed by his creature traits, his defiant love of favourites, bold clear strokes of brushwork about which there is no ambiguity.

Shakespeare was at pains to show something more complex, both about kingship and about worldly success – a reflection, if indirect, of St Luke's, "Render to Caesar what is Caesar's, and to God what is God's". Good people, he was saying, interesting people, the poetic, saintly, spiritual, witty and the noble, do not make successful kings. He was reversing, in a typical English empirical and Protestant spirit, the Platonic ideal of the philosopher king being the perfect ruler. Shakespeare's "good king" had Machiavellian qualities: bluntness, ordinariness, ruthlessness, cynicism and callousness. He was controlling reality, and was often nasty and brutish.

In *Edward II* Marlowe had concentrated entirely on simplicity and on the dramatic utility of the verse. But Shakespeare slipped away from such clear treatment by becoming absorbed entirely in Richard's own sad feelings. He removed – unusually for him – from the audience its power of objective pity, and tried to show that it was Richard's *good* qualities, his Christian humility and inability to rule, his ineffective but poetic charm, that, as much as his bad qualities, caused his downfall. The result was that much of the play seems immature – as Derek Jacobi says, "Shakespeare hadn't quite found the human being in the King" – and while Shakespeare searched in vain for a unifying theme amid the disparate historical material, its construction became uneven. Even the many references to the Bible and religion did not help, because the theme of the Divine Right of Kingship would not yield much dramatic satisfaction, whatever resources of imagery and verbal music the poet threw in. There is a superfluity of fine passages in *Richard II*; these are retained in present-day productions, while whole scenes or passages relating to the complex historical situation are cut or glossed over.

An Elizabethan audience would have understood at once that the Duke of Gloucester had been murdered on the king's instructions; Bolingbroke's accusation of Mowbray, the king's loyal servant, of the crime is meaningless unless this fact is tacitly understood. Mowbray was tried by combat in the lists at Coventry, but if he fell – in other words if divine intervention vindicated the right – would he betray Richard?

Intricate technicalities like these the audiences at the Theatre who knew their Hall and Holinshed would pick up immediately, but they were intractable materials for the playwright. Certain stories will never work on stage: and writers – even Shakespeare – have to learn the limits of their godlike gifts. Completely uninterested in chronicle history as such, Shakespeare "allowed himself", as E. K. Chambers has written, "to slip into a perfunctory and traditional treatment of all that was not directly concerned with that tragedy".

But *Richard II* had a dangerous popular theme. All history was eternally present to the Elizabethans, and they identified in a complete way with the figures of Bolingbroke and Richard: they felt none of the twentieth-century barrier of circumspection and alienation from past figures. Every noble at Elizabeth's court was a potential Bolingbroke.

Later, in 1601, after the execution of the Earl of Essex, William Lambarde, the lawyer and keeper of the Tower records, who once called the Pope "the witch of the world", made note of a talk he had with Elizabeth just before she died. She "fell" upon the reign of Richard II, "saying, 'I am Richard II, know ye not that?'" He answered, speaking of Essex, "Such a wicked imagination was determined and attempted by a most unkind Gent. the most adorned creature that ever your Majestie made". Elizabeth commented, that he that will forget God will also forget his benefactors: "this tragedy was played 40tie times in open streets and houses."

She was right. As well as other versions of the story, Shakespeare's play was popular, even before it acquired these more directly sinister overtones. At the end of 1595, on Tuesday, 7 December, Sir Edward Hoby, son of Thomas Hoby, the illustrious Italian traveller and translator of Castiglione's *The Courtier*, invited Robert Cecil to his house in Canon Row, Westminster, "where as late as it shall please you a gate for your supper shall be open: and K. Richard present himself to your view". Hoby thought nothing of keeping his actors waiting up. *Richard II* became increasingly in demand as the decade wore on, so that by 1598 it was the only play of Shakespeare's to have run through three quarto editions in two years: by this time the potentially incitatory scene of Richard's deposition had been censored both from text and performance. John Davies, in *The Scourge of Folly* (1610), suggests that Shakespeare himself played Richard:

> Had'st thou not played some Kingly parts in sport,
> Thou had'st been a companion for a King,
> And been a King among the meaner sort.

That Shakespeare had the need to become his own best critic, and take to heart the lessons he learned from the experiments he had embarked on, was demonstrated even more by his next play – and then by the ultimate sequel to both it and *Richard II*, a year or two later: the triumphant play of *Henry IV*.

# The shape of a grief

Shakespeare's rejection of Southampton was overtaken by an even greater turning-point in his life during the 1590s, the most crucial turning-point of all, which enabled him, by the conscious professional development of his craft, to transform himself into the great tragic playwright of the first decade of the seventeenth century. This propulsion was self-willed: Dr Johnson rightly stated that Shakespeare was a comic writer by instinct, a tragedian by art.

The first turning-point, the dismissal of Southampton, led naturally to the second. The first showed that, financially, Shakespeare
had become self-sufficient; the second was an even greater achievement. He managed to become secure in – or at least positively
resigned to – the values of bourgeois married life.

Of Shakespeare's liaisons with other women – whether with the
fair-haired and grey-eyed Mary Fitton, lady-in-waiting and one-
time favourite of the Queen, who bore William Herbert, Earl of
Pembroke, an illegitimate child and then was turned away; or with
the dark beauty of an Italian musical family, Emilia Bassano (or
Lanier), former mistress of Lord Hunsden, the Lord Chamberlain
and Shakespeare's patron from 1595 onwards; or with more fleeting
and temporary objects of attachment, such as the wife of John
Davenant, an Oxford wine merchant and later mayor (early-
eighteenth-century gossip had it that Shakespeare sired an illegitimate son on her); or with a black whore, Lucy Negro – it can be
authoritatively affirmed that these ended in the middle, or towards
the end, of the 1590s. Like Ben Jonson, who was finally reconciled
with the wife from whom he had more than once parted, like John
Donne, and, later, John Milton, Shakespeare came to recognize that
his gifts as a writer, as well as his destiny as a man, were inextricably
bound up with the practice of monogamy.

One lady, known as "dark" from the often-repeated description
of her eyes, her countenance, and complexion or skin, undoubtedly
gifted with a capacious desire, did exist for Shakespeare, and she
set off every kind of imaginative possibility, for she belonged to
the species of which a misogynist, the Elizabethan musician Thomas
Wythorne, complained bitterly: "Though they be weaker vessels,
yet they will overcome 2, 3 or 4 men in the satisfying of their carnal
appetites."

The Dark Lady, as anatomized in the Sonnets, and inferred
through several of Shakespeare's heroines, had a real-life counterpart. She may also have been based on certain unrealized sides
of Anne Shakespeare's character, or fleshed out with the behaviour patterns of other, demi-monde beauties Shakespeare
admired.

When Shakespeare lodged in Bishopsgate, before moving over
the river to the Liberty of the Clink, he was part of a fluid, middle-
to upper-class fringe society surrounding the court in which having
mistresses was commonplace, and in which, despite the rigid patriarchal code prevailing in Elizabethan society, sexually appetitive

women, either married or of the courtesan class, consorted easily enough with men who responded to, or could pay for, their attractions. Sexual sophistication was not generally available to all classes of society, but Shakespeare, in the course of his successful rise, partook of its delights until, as can be gauged from the powerful and increasingly authoritative moral tone of his more mature work, these wore thin and turned to disgust. The man was not a hypocrite; he was all of a piece.

Shakespeare found his sexual needs caused him stress; with him, in this area of life as in others, a little reality went a long way. He identified naturally with the pain and sensitivity of others: he suffered with the nervous, the ill, the weak, the insane, by putting himself in their shoes. But the main task, and the most demanding to which he could apply himself and still discharge his potential for sexual athleticism, was his performance in blank verse. As Laurence Olivier says in his *Confessions of an Actor*, one cannot be more than one kind of athlete at a time; "the most magnificent boxers, wrestlers, champions ... proved to be disappointing upon the removal of that revered jock strap."

The allegorical significance Shakespeare's involvement with the Dark Lady has taken on is quite out of proportion to whatever may have taken place between the two – if indeed anything more than a short-lived affair had. As with the poetic tussle with Southampton in the Sonnets, Shakespeare's relationship with the Dark Lady was essentially a vivid and dramatic form of *extrication*. He was as much pin-pointing the dangers of sexual licence, immorality and unfaithfulness which existed in superabundance – though often only potentially – in his quick sexed and profligate nature, as he was describing an actual relationship, or providing an intimate diary of amorous confidences.

The husband who, "transported by immoderate love", wrote J. Benedicti in 1584, has sexual intercourse with his wife "so ardently to satisfy his passion that, even if not his wife he would have wished to have commerce with her", is committing a sin. Shakespeare could have made his wife Anne his mistress, could have dressed her in adulterous trappings and settings, fantasized about her in a way strongly disapproved of by Puritan theology – which condemned even lusting after a wife as committing adultery in one's heart – and could thereby have explored and defined the health and validity of these emotions (as a modern sex therapist might encourage his patients to do). But it is unlikely that he did so. His fortunate circumstances in these years gave him opportunities for adventure that were so much greater, requiring on his part so little effort. The world lay at his feet.

There were indeed rumours and gossip to the effect that Shakespeare had a mistress or two. The later sonnets in fact confirm the specificity of a woman, not just in the dark (unlikely) details of her appearance but in her physical appeal, which is registered subjectively, as if it happened, whereas the outpourings to the young man, or the less specific love object of the first 126 sonnets, tend towards the notional and platonic. Hamlet, talking to Rosencrantz and Guildenstern, draws on and laconically adapts the image taken from playing the spinet or virginal, which the poet very directly applies in Sonnet 128 to his mistress's sexual attractions:

> How oft, when thou, my music, music play'st
> Upon that blessèd wood whose motion sounds
> With thy sweet fingers when thou gently sway'st
> The wiry concord that mine ear confounds,
> Do I envy those jacks that nimble leap
> To kiss the tender inward of thy hand
> Whilst my poor lips, which should that harvest reap,
> At the wood's boldness by thee blushing stand!

W. H. Auden is certain Shakespeare wrote many sonnets for himself alone, without thought of a public. Sexual love is non-existent in the first 126, he claims, and had Shakespeare thought he was expressing homosexual love, as has often been held, he would certainly have destroyed them. With sodomy still a capital offence, poets whom we know were homosexual, such as Richard Barnfield and Marlowe, never expressed their love in the first person, only through classical or historical personifications. Shakespeare was far too mindful of his own skin to write sonnets of homosexual love. The homosexual reader, writes Auden, "has been uncritically enthusiastic about the first 126 of the sonnets, and preferred to ignore those to the Dark Lady in which the relationship is unequivocally sexual, and the fact that Shakespeare was a married man and a father."

The enticing candidate conjured up by A. L. Rowse for the position of Dark Lady he names as Emilia Lanier, identified through the notes of the astrologer Simon Forman (who later viewed and commented on three of Shakespeare's plays) as a harlot who "useth sodomy". Forman supped with her and stayed all night, she was friendly and familiar with him, but while he felt all the parts of her body "willingly" and often kissed her, she would not "halek" with him. (A "halek" is a little fish used for making pickle; to be in a pickle is to be in a hole.) Whether she was or was not Shakespeare's Dark Lady, the case history Rowse draws of Lanier gives a convincing picture of the Elizabethan cocotte, and especially of how such a creature of sexual dalliance never felt the need to go the whole way in terms of intercourse. Elizabethan men were great fumblers and feelers of women.

But in spite of there being, as Barbara Jefford notes of Shakespeare, "something very Italian about his Italian women", Lanier was a bit too dark to be the real thing. Moreover, Shakespeare would surely never have rendered her so literally, but would have disguised her at the very least as "fair", especially as he was supposed to have inherited her from his patron, the Lord Chamberlain Hunsden, one of Elizabeth's most formidable warriors and protectors. The aristocracy were touchy about family scandal.

The constraints in Shakespeare's time upon full sexual licence must have alarmed even the toughest lecher, and it was common to mock sex as, in the words of Thomas Browne in *Religio Medici*, an "odd and unworthy piece of folly" – a disturbing notion to the libertarian fundamentalists of the 1990s. Deficiencies in personal hygiene and widespread gynaecological disorders made intercourse often disagreeable or uncomfortable; rotting teeth, bad breath, nauseating skin conditions and constant stomach complaints cannot have helped – and these were apart from the ever-present pox. A man rarely washed anything but his face, neck, hands, and teeth, while a woman neglected her "concealed parts" – witness the Earl of Rochester's later plea:

> Fair nasty nymph, be clean and kind
> And all my joys restore
> By using paper still behind
> And sponges for before.

Yet Shakespeare still had to cope with the demands of a strongly sexed nature. With repression and constraint on all sides – at one end of the scale the cuckolded husband and his delinquent wife publicly humiliated in a village "skimington", at the other end the nobleman banished from court for sexual misdemeanours – it is not surprising that he was tormented with unsatisfied need: "frantic-mad with ever more unrest". Shakespeare joked tartly about being a sad and distempered guest at the curative baths for his "disease" of lust, but no one knew how to "shun the heaven that leads men to this hell". The "hell" of the forfended place, which he also called "the wide world's common place", dominated his thinking in the later sonnets. Passionate kissing in public and the full view of "bared breasts seducing", not only to be seen but touched, even in highly respectable women, added to the hothouse of sex in his head.

Turned back in upon himself, Shakespeare's observation in these later sonnets became self-observation, the poet uncovering the meaner mechanics of his own lust, the nakedness of his own desire: "Th' expense of spirit in a waste of shame / Is lust in action . . ." He may well have equated, as John Bayley has suggested, the "friend" of Sonnets 133, 134 and 144, with his own penis. If so, here was the spur for the further self-limiting effort of renunciation on Shakespeare's part: he grew by facing difficulty. Writing it down, he discharged the painful side of an instinct or an emotion, dumping it on his readers or audience: "Show me a mistress that is passing fair," says Romeo cynically of the bright-eyed and scarlet-lipped Rosaline; what other use does her beauty serve than as a note, "Where I may read who passed that passing fair"?

During the time Shakespeare was dallying with real or putative pleasures of the bed, his son Hamnet died. His grief over this was extreme and shattering. Hamnet, aged eleven and a half, was an adolescent or near-adolescent who had not yet left home for college or been fostered out. The tie between father and son had become binding and profound. Shakespeare was child-centred, and he was charting that raw moment when the emotions of family life, for centuries impersonal or religiously ordained, were being born pain-fully into individuals' consciousness. Here was a grief which sent an uncontrollable echo reverberating back and re-opening that first great cause of pain and grief in Shakespeare's life: the black disgrace of his father and the fall in the family fortunes.

As on the first occasion, he blamed much of it upon himself. He could have been around at Stratford, as his father had when he was small; he had, on the whole, taken more out of his family in terms of emotion than he had put into it. Recently, too, there had been the turmoil of his London attachments, the drain on his resources of his court connections, as well as the unremitting demands of his work. In the nightmare life he led it had been hard enough to keep his head, let alone to keep writing. And then some word or rumour of his sexual release and entertainment may have reached Anne in Stratford: it affected the whole family, its shame corroded Anne's feelings, and Hamnet, seeing his mother dishonoured, had declined and drooped, fastening and fixing the shame on himself. He lost appetite and spirit, and laid himself open to the first chill or germ that he caught: "So then we do neglect / The thing we have, and all for want of wit". Hamnet and Judith Sadler, the oldest friends of Anne and William, godparents of the Shakespeare twins, attended the burial ceremony of their godson in Stratford church on 11 August 1596.

*King John*, Shakespeare's next play, bears the unmistakable marks of grief: it was a notable failure. Half-heartedly, it seemed, Shakespeare, now abandoning the example of Marlowe, still tried to get a purchase on the slippery historical process; but, heavily fatigued, he fell widely short of the mark. He had shadowed forth Richard II, the player king, bewildered, lacking in under-standing of himself; Richard's tragedy was not quite a tragedy because the King enjoyed, with aesthetic pride, his own decline – likewise Shakespeare was always watching himself, and taking note. But Shakespeare's self-conscious process overwhelmed the objective action of that play, and the correlative element was distorted and lost. When he turned once again to the dramatizing of self-consciouness, in *Hamlet*, he had through some hard think-ing and by his natural habit of absorption, brought the process much better under control. By playing Richard himself and sensing the reactions of the audience – or by watching Burbage, or whoever played the King – he could gauge where, in the writing, he had taken Richard too far into soggy self-regard.

But *King John* was overwhelmingly affected by the death of Hamnet. In his adaptation of the old piece, *The Troublesome Raigne of King John*, Shakespeare generally stuck to its errors, but consciously changed the character of Prince Arthur from a pushy youth into a powerless and innocent child. He has his mother Lady Constance refer specifically and movingly to his death *before* it happens. Shake-speare, broken-hearted and crushed by the loss of his son, was not the sort of person to declare philosophically, with Montaigne, that he had lost two or three children in infancy, "not without regret, but without great sorrow": he went straight to the heart of grief. Not an intellectual, he may have disguised himself but he never disguised his feelings, particularly those of pain or grief; he knew instinctively that such feelings needed acknowledgement and expression if they were not to become poisonous. With this terrible blow Shakespeare utterly lost his way. He was like Richard as described by Bolingbroke in the previous play: "The shadow of your sorrow hath destroyed / The shadow of your face". Grief made him unsure of himself: the only vitality he could muster was cynical, that of the bastard Faulconbridge. He avoided the anti-Catholic tone of *The Troublesome Raigne* because much of his religious feeling, in common with that of his audience, was broadly Catholic. He found refuge, instead, in patriotism, a safe alternative to dissentious feeling: "No Italian priest / Shall tithe or toll in our dominions": thus weakening the cause of John's death.

But perhaps the most striking example of Shakespeare's tiredness of invention – apart from keeping the original characters of the earlier play and adding only one of his own (who speaks just four words) – was his failure to supply any overall unity. Each scene seems to throw up different central characters.

Hamnet's death had robbed him temporarily of his centralizing artistic force. His twins, handfast wherever they went at eight years and at ten, had been the wonder of Stratford. In their very early years the goodwives had speculated endlessly on this pair of unfolding buds, together night and day like love-birds – the twinned lambs frisking in the sun, bleating one at the other, exchanging "innocence for innocence".

Not only did Shakespeare saturate the verse of *King John* with images of death, which he conceived in concrete, bodily forms; in reaction to the blow, he stuffed the play with an extraordinary number of personifications. The recurrent figure, which requires little sustained effort of imagination, suggests that the influence of personal grief over *King John* was considerable. But his redemptive knack made *King John*'s most famous visualization, the lament of the lady Constance, one of Shakespeare's most moving. Hamnet's bed in the room in Henley Street he had shared with his sister was empty.

> Grief fills the room up of my absent child,
> Lies in his bed, walks up and down with me,
> Puts on his pretty looks, repeats his words,
> Remembers me of all his gracious parts,

Stuffs out his vacant garments with his form;
Then have I reason to be fond of grief.
Fare you well. Had you such a loss as I,
I could give better comfort than you do . . .
O Lord! my boy, my Arthur, my fair son,
My life, my joy, my food, my all the world . . .

From this date, from August 1596 onwards, when Hamnet was buried in Stratford, Shakespeare, now a share-owner in his theatre company, began to put life back into his marriage and into Stratford. He meditated on, consolidated and deepened the emotional experiences of his previous years. He did not expand, repeat past patterns, or dissipate his energies further. What was left now of his sexual drive, so long expended on iambic pentameters or on dressing up as other people, was re-invested in wife, family and property development. He settled for being the successful and prosperous businessman who made shrewd investments for the future. Here now was the prototypical bourgeois artist so beloved of the nineteenth century, especially of Scott, Dickens and Jane Austen – Shakespeare, having now no particular need or desire to be anyone other than his ordinary, middle-class self, could fulfil in security his great gift for creating other people. He was content, otherwise, to carve out a stock heraldic figure, recouping for his family its lost wealth, his father John's unsatisfied aspirations to gentility, insulating himself against future debt by buying land, and enjoying the cultivation of a large and well-stocked garden.

Inwardly, though, the secret vitality went on pulsing remorselessly. Had Shakespeare not learned and put into effect the power of renunciation, this vitality would have died in him. Hamnet's death, in so far as he managed to survive it – and it brought him back to Stratford, closer to his wife, and to his mother – had a crucial formative power over his future. For, as he had prophetically written, "If children predecease progenitors, / We are their offspring, and they none of ours".

# The absence of mothers

i

The execution in 1594 of the Portuguese Doctor Lopez – a Jew by race, though not in religion – had brought the unfamiliar figure of the Jew into lurid prominence in the popular consciousness some two years before Shakespeare turned his hand to the creation of his first great antagonist: Shylock, huge predecessor to the even huger Falstaff.

Lopez, Elizabeth's physician, had been accused of planning to smear poison on the pommel of the royal saddle, and on the arms of a chair of state – an example of life imitating fiction. Barabas, the Hebrew of enormous and depraved evil in Marlowe's *Jew of Malta*, tries to poison a whole city of Christians; Marlowe had also had a character employ poisoned gloves in the *Massacre at Paris*. Outwardly Lopez had little in common with Shylock, who is powerful, Hebraistic, the opposite of pathetic – yet the sense of being outcasts links them, as does their antithetical character. Shakespeare delighted in changing qualities and attributes into their opposites.

He made a sidelong reference to the trial of Lopez, so typical of Elizabethan trials, in Portia's witty sally to Bassanio, "but I fear you speak upon the rack, / Where men enforcèd do speak anything." Topcliffe's rack was hardly an abstract torture. Lopez confessed that he had received Spanish money, but claimed he had not conspired to kill the Queen. Lytton Strachey catches the flavour of the trial:

who could disentangle among his statements the parts of veracity and fear, the desire to placate his questioners, the instinct to incriminate others, the impulse to avoid, by some random affirmation, the dislocation of an arm or a leg? Only one thing was plain about such evidence: it would always be possible to give to it whatever interpretation the prosecutors might desire.

Lopez was later believed completely innocent. That he had known and been mixed up with England's Spanish enemies was incontestable; but that he took their money without intending to commit murder was harder to prove, in that muddied and claustrophobic society.

Marlowe gave Abigail, Barabas's daughter, the chance to take a holy vow and become a Christian: Shakespeare followed this device with Shylock although, more conventional in belief, he did not arrange a polyphony of voices as Marlowe had done to present other religious points of view. Christianity was absolute: when Jessica, a Jew by race, states, "I shall be saved by my husband. He hath made me a Christian", this was fine by Shakespeare.

The part of Shylock, by comparison with other great roles that Shakespeare wrote, is very short: the character appears in five scenes, one of which is hardly more than a fragment. But so great was the force Shakespeare gave him in his complexity, his mixture of comic and tragic possibilities, that he assumed a life of his own, and became the first of Shakespeare's characters who can be imagined apart from the play. As Dustin Hoffman, a recent interpreter of the role, says, Shylock is a "hot date" – his usury gives his sense of identity, "like a black kid out of the ghetto who becomes a boxer". He was an incubus that sprang fully formed from the nightmares of the Shakespeare family's financial losses and shame. John Shakespeare had broken the Elizabethan laws of usury. Like the evil, grasping characters of Charles Dickens, Shylock came out of unquelled fears that were once the centre of reality for Shakespeare.

Shylock was quickly established as one of Shakespeare's best-known characters – just as Fagin was, later, for Dickens. In time he gathered accretions: Henry Irving invented a scene, after Jessica's desertion, of his return to his house. After the trial scene Edmund Kean went through a startling physical transformation; Edwin Booth devised an elaborate tailpiece for the play. Irving sighed – and Laurence Olivier howled. But Shakespeare, deliberately, had provided nothing for the character to do: this was his considered comment on the reversal of Shylock's fortunes. His dismissal of Shylock, for all the momentous, almost tragic status and humanity he gave the character in his poignant appeal of "Hath not a Jew hands, organs, dimensions, senses, affections, passions; fed with the same food, hurt with the same weapons, subject to the same diseases, healed by the same means, warmed and cooled by the same winter and summer as a Christian is?", shows, ultimately, an aristocratic disdain. He rejected him without greatness, almost as a figure of farce (which is why, to salvage their egos, the great actors made their interpolations). The romantic atmosphere of much of this play has subsequently been overloaded with the weight and problems of Shylock, and with his sombre humanitarian challenges.

Harley Granville-Barker asserts that *The Merchant of Venice* has no more reality than the fable of Jack and the Beanstalk. Yet each of the four stories (the bond theme; the choice of caskets; Lorenzo's elopement with Jessica; the Gratiano–Nerissa subplot) which Shakespeare so intricately wove together – once again from mainly Italian sources – has a vital issue at its centre. Shakespeare contrived *The Merchant* on one level as a savage tale of fortune-hunting, loading the text with cynical references to money; none of the glamour and moonshine conceals the viciousness of appetite and greed. Lead is measured against gold, colour against faith; outward shows against inward intentions – blood against flesh: Portia's great speech on mercy he designed to tip the scales against Shylock's hatred.

Portia was the first of Shakespeare's great romantic heroines, able to laugh with wonderful swiftness of mind, capable of generous surrender of heart, and endowed with an unassuming power of goodness. But he made her by no means wholly sympathetic; in her first scene with Nerissa she is shown as extremely bossy, while her discussion of her suitors, though popular with the audience for its destructive wit, hardly breathes sympathy and charity. Shakespeare had her pour invective on different national traits almost at the pitch of John Osborne's Jimmy Porter in *Look Back in Anger*. She says of a Frenchman: "God made him, and therefore let him pass for a man"; of an Englishman: "He is a proper man's picture, but alas, who can converse with a dumb show?"; of how she likes a German: "Very vilely in the morning when he is sober, and most vilely in the afternoon when he is drunk. When he is best he is a little worse than a man, and when he is worst he is little better than a beast." Yet Shakespeare stopped short of making her shrill, and dropped this side of her character.

This kind of unladylike talk went down well in Finsbury Fields. Shakespeare caught perfectly the new City of London mercantile puritanism. The "quality of mercy" speech was priggishly, deliberately misplaced: what could be less likely to appeal to a Jew's heart than a specifically Christian plea for mercy? Meant to be an Italian,

Portia's spirit is nearer to that of the Swiss–French John Calvin, with its Protestant insistence on godly behaviour.

Shakespeare could now develop a fully rounded view of character: he knew that in any striking woman he presented on stage there was often a mixture of primarily male characteristics with the more expected female traits, and that the first had ultimately to be subordinate to the second. "O love, be moderate!" Portia cries when Bassanio picks the right casket,

> Allay thy ecstasy.
> In measure rain thy joy; scant this excess.
> I feel too much thy blessing: make it less,
> For fear I surfeit.

Attractive did not mean sickly-sweet, for Shakespeare made Portia quite sympathetically hard, as when she refuses, although now married to Bassanio, to have sex with him until Antonio is saved – "For never shall you lie by Portia's side / With an unquiet soul."

Certain aspects of *The Merchant* remain flawed and uneasy in their combination of personal and popular elements. Shakespeare had not quite resolved the question of genre, and sometimes Shylock seems too brutal and realistic an intrusion. When he next returned to the flourishing independent Republic of Venice for a play about a racial outcast, Shakespeare concentrated on the realistic, sexual and emotional, content. There are signs, too, in *The Merchant*, that he had not integrated certain themes that obsessed him, and which he had explored or would continue to explore, more nakedly, more privately, in the Sonnets.

The central, and yet pathetic and self-chastising figure of Antonio has been described as autobiographical. Shakespeare was reputed to have played the role himself. The speculation that he "lost" Southampton through a woman can be revived through Antonio's "loss" of his friend, Bassanio. E. K. Chambers points out that it was not inconsistent with his popular appeal that Shakespeare should "reserve something behind the arras of a play for his own ear, for the secret consolation of his private trouble". Such was the secret impetus Shakespeare gave to Antonio's lines to his friend during the trial:

> Say how I loved you. Speak me fair in death,
> And when the tale is told, bid her be judge
> Whether Bassanio had not once a love.

Antonio's devotion to Bassanio has the same subservient moodiness as certain of the Sonnets.

ii

Success as a playwright, actor and theatrical manager had not led to an easing of life for Shakespeare, but rather the reverse. The mercantile Christian community of London, with its puritan work ethic and its narrow moral code, had its knives out for new prey, especially any that could be turned into a legitimate victim and persecuted as an immoral outsider. Shakespeare fought hard for status and respectability. To be rich, as he now was, meant to be alert. He had acquired extensive property. More financial facts are known about Shakespeare at the approximate date of *The Merchant* than at other periods. Antonio, therefore – a name which recurs in connection with possibly autobiographical figures – could well be a fantasy self-castigation by the playwright.

For William Shakespeare was now a gentleman: on 20 October 1596, John Shakespeare, having applied again on William's insistence, had succeeded with his re-application, after twenty years, to the College of Heralds for a coat of arms. The College acceded to the grant on the grounds that John's great-grandfather had performed "faithefull & approved service to H7 ... & rewarded with Landes and Tenements ... in ... Warwikeshere"; John Shakespeare himself had "maryed the daughter & one of the heyr of Robert Arden of Wellingcote". The coat of arms had, across a black incline, on its field of gold, a silver-tipped spear, point upwards, while for the "crest or cognizance" it displayed a falcon with outstretched wings, standing on a wreath of his colours, "Supporting a Speare Armed hedded or & steeled sylvor fixed uppon a helmet with mantelles & tasselles". The motto, never used by the Shakespeares, was "Non Sans Droict". Sogliardo, in Ben Jonson's *Every Man out of His Humour*, a play put on with Shakespeare's approval by the Chamberlain's Men two years later, explains his coat of arms as "on a chief argent, a boar's head proper" – to which Puntarvolo suggests as motto, "Not without mustard" – a typical irreverence of the younger playwright on the Globe shareholder's new status. But in his next play that shareholder was to mock the whole idea of nobility and quality, and to reduce social distinctions to absurdity.

Shakespeare, when he wrote Part One of *Henry IV*, probably in 1596, was strongly aware that Robert Devereux, Lord Essex, had recently climbed to the height of fame and fortune. The potentiality of rebellion was in the air from 1595 onwards; obliquely, and at a distance. Shakespeare, like Wilfred Owen, thought that the duty of the poet was to warn. He pointed out to his informed and influential audiences the danger of such a figure as Essex.

Anthony Bacon, director of Essex's secret service, wrote exultantly to a Venetian friend about him, "Our earl, God be thanked! hath with the bright beams of his valour and virtue scattered the clouds and cleared the mists that malicious envy had stirred up against his matchless merit; which hath made Old Fox [Lord Burghley] to crouch and whine." But Essex could not exploit his popularity judiciously. His love of fighting was the strongest self-motivating element in his exuberant spirit: arrogant, vehement, uncontrollable, he disguised his feelings badly, like Hotspur before King Henry. When thwarted, Essex "could fret and fume like a child" and he showed contempt for the Queen. When Hotspur, like Essex a melodious classicist, exclaimed that it was

> an easy leap
> To pluck bright honour from the pale-faced moon,
> Or dive into the bottom of the deep,
> Where fathom-line could never touch the ground,
> And pluck up drownèd honour by the locks,

most of the audience, trained and attuned to contemporary allusiveness, thought immediately of Robert Devereux. As Camden writes, "No man was more ambitious of glory by virtue, and no man more careless of all things else."

Shakespeare, delighting in domestic minutiae, has more specific contemporary allusion issue from Hotspur's mouth when Hotspur dismisses Owen Glendower and his poetry. He says he would rather hear "a brazen canstick turned, / Or a dry wheel grate on the axle-tree". Lothbury, near the Curtain, was a nightmare of industrial noise, for metal-turners worked in the open air – John Stow mentioned this in his *Survey of London*, printed in 1598. Dry wheels – wheels that needed oiling – were a phenomenon of the new London traffic problem, as four-wheeled vehicles clogged the narrow streets.

But Hotspur's (and Shakespeare's) local allusiveness grows even more pronounced when he says that instead of listening to Glendower, he would rather feed on "cheese and garlic, in a windmill", which is a reference to new pinnacled and towered buildings in nearby Moorfields, and rallies his wife for her genteel expletives, saying that she swears "like a comfit maker's wife ..." as if she had never walked "further than Finsbury". Shakespeare put these words into the mouth of a particular actor, knowing that he could raise a laugh with them. He may well have copied that same actor's speech rhythms, and drawn on his vocabulary.

In killing off Hotspur in Part One of *Henry IV* Shakespeare needed another part for the same actor in the sequel. The result was the creation, quite gratuitously, of an "ancient" for Falstaff: Pistol, a comic virtuoso braggart who rants like the Marlovian Alleyne. Both parts of *Henry IV* were written to be played together by the Lord Chamberlain's company, although, by the time Shakespeare finished Part Two, the company had moved theatre.

Sir John Falstaff was first called Sir John Oldcastle, a name taken from the chronicle play *The Famous Victories of Henry V*, until it was pointed out that Lord Cobham, Elizabeth's Lord Chamberlain, was actually a descendant on his mother's side of the Lollard – or low-church heretic – knight, Sir John Oldcastle, one of the companions who surrounded Prince Henry in his wild days. The name carried, as in the morality play *The Castle of Perseverance*, a sense of Shakespeare interiorizing old battle images, and adapting them to a new, less warlike identity.

Of the five greatest parts Shakespeare wrote for actors, the other four all being tragic, only Falstaff – according to Ralph Richardson, a great interpreter of the role – is permitted to retain and enjoy his basic character without terrible "translation". Unlike the other four, Hamlet, Othello, Macbeth and Lear, he is not catapulted at breathtaking speed to his doom. "Falstaff proceeds through the play at his own chosen pace," says Richardson, "like a gorgeous ceremonial Indian elephant."

James Joyce observed (or has Stephen Dedalus observe) that Falstaff had no family and that this reflected something very crucial about the playwright himself: "What do we care for his wife and father? I should say that only family poets have family lives. Falstaff was not a family man. I feel that the fat knight is his supreme creation." But is not Falstaff a family man? Accused by the Lord Justice of misleading the Prince, he answers in terms of the utmost insolence and sacrilege, "The young Prince hath misled me. I am the fellow with the great belly, and he my dog." Like Shakespeare he *is* a family man but in exile, adopting his companions and fellow rogues as his family, making Prince Hal into his son, domesticating him to the point of a father playing doggy and master with his little boy.

Shakespeare, the family man, drew much on his father John for Falstaff's irreverent humour, his glorious reversal of failure, and the nimbleness of his spirituality within his corpulence. Shakespeare mocked his father in having Falstaff wreak comic revenge on those noble qualities John Shakespeare had fought to establish for his family, and yet had not truly resolved within himself – and which therefore existed in a warring, love–hate relationship.

In Falstaff Shakespeare also incorporated the self-awareness which had led to his own rejection of the glittering court of Southampton/Hal. For Falstaff was a fantasy projection of himself, manifoldly disguised, gambolling in the reflected light of Southampton's majesty, leading the Earl astray with his drinking and wild self-indulgence – or, in other words, his creative powers (for drink, as Falstaff shows supremely, is a debased creative art: witness the expression "piss-artist"). However wild the fantasizing of a past relationship may have been, there is love and affection without any physical homosexual attraction underpinning the friendship – although, as Barbara Everett perceives, " the sheer fatness of Falstaff, most male of men, allows him some of the freedoms of the female role – and [when Falstaff puts a new wound in Hotspur's thigh] some of its betrayals, too."

In claiming that Falstaff is Shakespeare's supreme creation, Joyce also fails to take into account that Falstaff does not (perhaps sometimes like Joyce himself in *Ulysses*) really appeal to women: as Michael Holroyd observes, he is a "dumb note" on the piano as far as they are concerned. It cannot be a supreme creation that leaves half the audience cold.

Unable to use the name Oldcastle, Shakespeare created Falstaff after the cowardly knight in *Henry VI* Part One, Fastolfe; but this led to protests from Fastolfe's family. It also sounds like a corruption or paraphrase of "Shake-speare"; "Shake" and "Fall" have a certain connotation, as do "Staff" and "Spear". A lover of anarchy, Shakespeare also made the fat knight a visionary who imposes his lordly vision of himself on a disrespectful world. W. H. Auden sees him as a comic symbol of Jesus, giving, in his inertia, an impression of infinite energy. He is never tired, never bored, and, until rejected, radiates happiness – "as Hal radiates power". This unflagging devotion to making others laugh, writes Auden, "becomes a symbolic image for a love which is absolutely self–giving".

The unique power of entertainment was also given to Falstaff's creator, who knew the limit to that power – a limit he had to exercise ruthlessly. Shakespeare was much nearer to Dr Johnson than to Auden in the way he could pull back from complete surrender and drop down a portcullis. He would not have sympathized with what Auden then goes on to say, namely that when the Christian God presents himself on earth, "the highest religious and temporal authorities condemn Him as a blasphemer and a Lord of Misrule, as a Bad Companion for mankind". This would have struck Shakespeare as blasphemy. He would sooner have agreed with Johnson, who said of Falstaff that "No man is more dangerous than he that with a will to corrupt hath the power to please".

When Hal grows up and assumes the crown, his rejection of his old company remains perfectly in tune with the dislikable side he shows in being so calculating at the beginning of Part One. Order, both in the state at large and in the family, has to be maintained: Hal has lived out his Janus-faced adolescent rebellion and now has no place for Falstaff. This is what, unsentimentally, it means to grow up: he has long dreamt of such a man, "so surfeit-swelled, so old, and so profane". Becoming awake he finds he despises his dream. Thus does he "turn away" his former self.

This was a profoundly Christian moment: a conversion as fundamental and as optimistic as any man or woman in the audience could hope to see. It celebrated the triumph of self-determination. But the new king is charitable as well, and pays Falstaff, too, the highest compliment one man can pay another, the chance for change: even promising material reward as a result, saying that as he hears of Falstaff's reform: "We will, according to your strengths and qualities, / Give you advancement."

*Romeo and Juliet* and *A Midsummer Night's Dream* had, with brilliant verbal music, fortuitously combined action and theme: but they were essentially glittering arrangements, the themes did not spring from within the plays through the personal medium of character. Nor did they in the history plays, which had plots from which Shakespeare had, up to now, tried to extract themes. Only in a number of the as yet unpublished Sonnets had themes successfully permeated the whole structure.

With *Henry IV*, Shakespeare succeeded in producing a history play with theme and character inextricably planted at its centre, a play at the same time optimistic and appealing to audiences in an expanding, thrusting, and thriving commercial society. Everything found its true proportion in this hard-won reward – a reward not only for the effort of finding unifying themes in previously intractable historical material (*Richard II* and *King John*), but also for the perception and experience of character gained from writing *The Merchant of Venice*. He centred the two-layered plot of *Henry IV*, one parodying the other, round the theme of rebellion in the political world, and family duty and responsibility in the private world. Above all, and from this time forth, Shakespeare was settled in his view of the determining factors in human life: his central figures, supremely, but virtually all the others in so far as Shakespeare can show them, have the power of self-determination. The drama comes straight from the heart of the characters, from the essence of what they are. This centring of Shakespeare's power in character has gone out of fashion academically, as Barbara Everett points out: "We now tend not to believe in character in general, or in Falstaff in particular." (Everett advances as the probable cause for this the "full professionalizing of literary studies into the academic: the process by which the thing worth knowing was standardized into the thing capable of proof".)

*Henry IV* was loved by the playwright's public; it appealed to the apex of society, and Lord Hunsden had it played in his Blackfriars house before Vereiken, the Flemish ambassador, "to his great contentment". Elizabeth Southampton wrote to her husband that "all the good news I can send you that I think will make you merry, is that I read in a letter from London that Sir John Falstaff is, by his mistress Dame Pintpot, made father of a goodly miller's thumb, a boy that's all head and very little body. But this is a secret."

For the literate merchants in the audience at the Curtain there were the serious preoccupations of a king who had just quelled rebellion, and was also struggling with the problem of an irresponsible son; for the merchants' wives there was passion and romance in Hotspur's rise and fall; for humbler apprentices and groundlings Falstaff cast his more uncomplicated spell.

But everyone in the play has freedom of action and freedom of will: they are not "star-crossed" lovers, or drugged or fairy-bewitched romantics. They are not foredoomed by race or creed. Fittingly, in a play about choice and responsibility, and about a young man's arrival at maturity, self-determination was Shakespeare's keynote. Hal plans his own life as the playwright plans that of his characters, educating himself in the "unyoked humour" of idleness, yet imitating the sun that "when he please again to be himself", breaks through "the foul and ugly mists . . . that did seem to strangle him".

Shakespeare's skill in versification, miraculously, leapt forward into greater diversity and individuating difference in *Henry IV.* In Part One, in particular, the rhythm and vocabulary, far from being standardized – so that they become interchangeable between the various acting parts – begin to take on a beat and verbal colour which is specific for each person. This was by now a semi-conscious, or unconscious, practice: for in the heat of creation, and in the pace of putting down speeches on paper, Shakespeare acted out roles in the distinctive verse and prose of each. Thus Hotspur uses verse as an extension of his personality: proud, splintery, saliva-loaded,

> for he made me mad
> To see him shine so brisk, and smell so sweet,
> And talk so like a waiting gentlewoman
> Of guns, and drums, and wounds, God save the mark!
> And telling me the sovereign'st thing on earth
> Was parmacity for an inward bruise . . .

The garden scene in Part Two, at Shallow's house, when Silence and Shallow discuss the death of Old Double, and the tavern scene with Mistress Quickly and Doll Tearsheet at the end of Act II, each reveal that Shakespeare now had little more to do than to think of something in order to become it. William Hazlitt later formulated an apt image of this instantaneous process, saying that "all the persons concerned must have been present in the poet's imagination, as at a kind of rehearsal", so that whatever passed through their minds on this occasion, Hazlitt goes on, "passed through his".

# Green fields

In May 1597 Shakespeare bought the finest house in Stratford, New Place, second in size only to the old College, a Crown property leased in 1596 to his friend Thomas Combe. He paid for it an unknown sum in cash which included a loan redemption of £60. With a frontage of 60 feet, a height of 28 and a breadth, at its widest, of 70 feet, this ten-room structure of brick and timber had three storeys and five gables and had formerly been the local grandee Clopton's town house. Two barns, two gardens and two orchards were also included in the purchase. Reconstruction and planning occupied Shakespeare's mind at this time: when meaning to build, says the rebel Lord Bardolph in *Henry IV* Part Two, we first survey the plot, then draw the model.

> And when we see the figure of the house,
> Then must we rate the cost of the erection,
> Which if we find outweighs ability,
> What do we then but draw anew the model
> In fewer offices, or, at least, desist
> To build at all?

In the months before Shakespeare bought New Place James Burbage, owner of the Theatre, had applied for a ten-year extension of his lease on the land, which was refused, so on 13 April 1597 Burbage lost the building as well as the land. For the time being Richard Burbage and Shakespeare went on using the Curtain, where possibly both the first and second parts of *Henry IV* were first played, in 1598–9.

James Burbage responded to the loss by paying £800 for property and a site for a new theatre at Blackfriars, within the City's walls but outside its jurisdiction: he transformed the interior of the hall into a select private theatre – fully roofed in, properly illuminated. But the residents of Blackfriars, with the usual Puritan objections to playhouses, successfully petitioned the Privy Council to suppress the new theatre. James Burbage died heartbroken only two months later.

Richard Burbage, with his brother Cuthbert, tried further to obtain a new lease for the Theatre; failing with this, they drew up a plan by which the five leading actors of the Chamberlain's company – Shakespeare, John Heminges, Augustine Phillips, Will Kempe and Thomas Pope – would provide financial backing in return for a share (one-tenth for each of the five actors) in the new venture. A clause in the original lease had stipulated that James Burbage might "have, take down and carry away to his own proper use" the Theatre; so three days after Christmas 1597 a carpenter, Peter Street, the Burbages and others assembled a crew with wrecking tools, demolished the Theatre, carted away the valuable heavy timber and fittings, and spirited the whole assembly across the Thames.

Giles Allen, owner of the site, sued the new consortium, but lost the case. The new site on the south bank of the Thames was just east of the Rose theatre in Southwark. The area in which Henslowe had built his Rose had the greatest concentration of prisons – the Marshalsea, the White Lion, the Counter, the Clink and the King's Bench – and therefore the largest prison population in Elizabethan England. There were choicely appointed inns in this district, such as the Tabard, well known in Chaucer's day, and with moneyed prisoners ensuring their comforts, and with no particular stigma attached to being in prison – for as in post-Revolutionary Russia the prison population comprised a significant proportion of the populace – a great deal of ready money was available for entertainment. Southwark, its teeming prisons and watering-holes apart, was a thriving community, characterized by Stow in the *Survey of London* as being of "divers streets, ways and winding lanes all full of buildings inhabited". When the new theatre had been constructed, it, together with the existing Rose and the Swan, drew 3,000 or 4,000 people in boats across the Thames every day. Nearly 40,000 people contributed to the prosperity of the watermen. A list of baptisms perused by Marchette Chute reveals the names of four bakers, four glovers, one innkeeper, one actor, one schoolmaster and seventy watermen.

Garbage had preceded actors on the marshy land where the new playhouse was erected: "flanked with a ditch and forced out of a marsh", according to Ben Jonson. Its cost of £400 included the provision of heavy piles for the foundation, and a whole network of ditches in which the water rose and fell with the tidal Thames. The smell, to begin with, could not have pleased the sensitive nostrils of Shakespeare, but here was fertile ground for his observation in later plays: the crowd like the vagabond flag in *Antony and Cleopatra*, that rots itself with motion; the ooze and mud images of the Nile in the same play; most remarkable of all, perhaps, Macbeth's great river image:

> I am in blood
> Stepped in so far that, should I wade no more,
> Returning were as tedious as go o'er.

The new theatre, called the Globe, became the finest in London, giving the Chamberlain's Men the edge over their rivals. Though Shakespeare owned only a tenth, the inventory of Sir Nicholas Brend describes the Globe as belonging to "William Shakespeare and others". Here, from the summer of 1599 onwards, possibly as many as twelve out of Shakespeare's remaining new plays were produced, while many earlier ones were successfully revived.

Shakespeare moved his own lodgings, too, with his company. He had lived in Bishopsgate Street, on the route from the City to the Theatre and the Curtain, and now he moved to the Liberty of the Clink, where he became a neighbour of Thomas Pope, the comedian and acrobat, a bachelor who with a "good-wife" raised fatherless children; William Sly, soon to play Osric; and Augustine Phillips, his wife and five children. Southwark now became the new centre of Shakespeare's working life. "In this rather rough end," says Coleridge's biographer Richard Holmes, "we can imagine him looking across at all those centres of power".

The Liberty of the Clink was in the Bishop of Winchester's jurisdiction, and as well as criminals it contained the highest density of brothels in London: a special burying ground was designated by the local church as the Single Woman's graveyard. Theatres were notorious places for picking up women. In the London playhouses it was the fashion of youths, writes Stephen Gosson, to carry their eye through every gallery, "then like unto ravens where they spy the carrion thither they fly, and press as near to the fairest as they can ... He thinketh best of his painted sheath, and taketh himself for a jolly fellow, that is noted of most to be busiest with women in such places." Thomas Dekker corroborates this: "By sitting on the stage, if you be a knight, you may happily get you a mistress; if a mere Fleet-Street gentleman, a wife."

Globe audiences were significantly different from those of the Curtain; Part Two of *Henry IV* set against Part One underlines that difference, as well as providing evidence of how sensitive Shakespeare was to the specific needs and tastes of his clientele. Part One was printed in quarto in 1598 before the move, Part Two in 1600, when the two parts were being played at the Globe. Shakespeare wrote for his Shoreditch audience more gentle and rustic comedy: Hotspur jokes about the local windmills; while for Part Two the humour was made more dark, subtle and sexual, with greater emphasis on disease. Shakespeare had found the air and atmosphere of Finsbury Fields, with its (according to Stow) "many fair summer houses", more salubrious. But on the move to Southwark, with its much higher incidence of fever and venereal disease, he purged fears and apprehensions with gloom and pestilence, summed up by the Archbishop who observes that we are all diseased:

And with our surfeiting, and wanton hours
Have brought ourselves into a burning fever,
And we must bleed for it.

The inns of Part Two are no longer innocent fun parlours, but infested with criminals, whose prime occupations are drinking, whoring and fighting; a man might easily be beaten to death there. Divine retribution is ever at hand: Falstaff has little delicacy left, as a gentleman, although wit and gusto are as rich as ever. "Thou whoreson little tidy Bartholomew boar-pig," Doll Tearsheet harangues him, "when wilt thou leave fighting o'days, and foining o'nights, and begin to patch up thine old body for heaven?" To which the old reprobate answers, "Peace, good Doll, do not speak like a death's-head, do not bid me remember mine end." Prince Hal and Poins overhear this colloquy. "Look", observes the Prince, "whe'er the withered elder hath not his poll clawed like a parrot"; Poins adds, "Is it not strange that desire should so many years outlive performance?"

But Falstaff's spirit, challenged by this encroaching infrastructure of darkness, triumphs over pessimism: if not exactly a symbol of Jesus, then that spirit is a great and everlasting symbol of life, which is put to most challenge by darkness and nothingness, and conquers it in order to please. Creating Falstaff Shakespeare had to look into the heart of darkness – his father's failure and the grief of his family: instant, as well as everlasting, popularity was the reward, as a contemporary wrote,

Let but Falstaff come,
Hal, Poins, the rest – you scarce shall have a room,
All is so pestered.

Yet Shakespeare was not much bothered to reap the accolades as creator of Falstaff; he was inclined to continue as medium for a greater voice, and move on. He was now tired: he did not sleep well: he identified with his careworn monarch at the centre of the Essex rebellion; uneasy lay his head that not only wore a crown, but had to continue with such zeal and industry spawning kings, often without proper space for recuperation.

Although peace was to be found in Stratford, there was not much in the way of personal happiness. John Shakespeare had been taken seriously ill. Robust, to have lived as long as he had, he was now highly gratified, after his own reversals, to see his thirty-five-year-old son so well rewarded financially and so prominent a figure. But that son, more than anything, ached with grief at the absence of his own son.

Remorselessly Shakespeare had for twelve years gone on pushing out the boundaries of his drama – he had written at least seventeen plays, and had a hand in several more. He had peered as deeply and closely as he was capable at that point into dark and bad people – into despair and other black conditions in his own soul – to fill out the life of his plays with truth. He could now afford to free-wheel for a year or two, to repeat effects in new disguises, gather together well-used threads and turn them inside out, before once again extending himself, testing his poetic and story-telling power in new conditions.

For some time he had been thinking, given the sweep and powerful design of his mind (and he had begun with a historical trilogy), that he could hang up his spurs and retire from the chronicle play with one more resounding success – spirited and vigorous, if not exactly original and challenging. His partners in the new playhouse wanted him to write a patriotic play to make their position at the Globe impregnably secure. He had shown England so variously embroiled in civil war that a straightforward work of triumph and domination could make a fitting conclusion to the systematic pillaging of Hall and Holinshed:

> We bear our civil swords and native fire
> As far as France. I heard a bird so sing,
> Whose music, to my thinking, pleased the King,

says Prince John at the end of *Henry IV*. The Epilogue promised more scenes with Falstaff ("I shall be sent for in private," the old knight consoles himself, predicting a new scene with Hal) and will make "merry with fair Catherine of France".

Shakespeare ("My tongue is weary," adds the Epilogue) wrote the Chorus speeches of *Henry V* for himself: they contain numerous references to the Globe theatre, as if the proprietor, like Ben Jonson's Host in *The New Inn*, is showing his clientele the limits and possibilities of the new circular marvel, with its platform stage, covered in thatch, thrusting well out into the auditorium: "Piece out our imperfections with your thoughts," he tells the crowd, and then, recognizing that he must be a well-known figure as an actor – they must be wondering which part he is going to play – declines to take more than a back seat: "Admit me Chorus to this history."

Shakespeare allowed little to get in the way of the great rallying cry that *Henry V* builds towards, but he adumbrated the darkness of civil dissension and war in the Grey, Scrope and Cambridge plot to assassinate Henry at Southampton, and made his own aside:

> O England! – model to thy inward greatness,
> Like little body with a mighty heart,
> What mightst thou do, that honour would thee do,
> Were all thy children kind and natural?

He also honoured the Archbishop of Canterbury, in the longest and most tedious, rhetorical, and legal defence of a king's legitimacy in all his plays. One of Canterbury's speeches is sixty-three lines long, another supports Henry's claim to the throne with a quote from the book of Numbers. Most of this obvious padding was recycled, almost at equal length, from his sources – the audience, who knew the story backwards, expected it.

The patriotic scenes in *Henry V* do not rise to the level of John of Gaunt's death-bed lines in *Richard II*, with their majestic, rolling images of England as

> This other Eden, demi-paradise,
> This fortress built by nature for herself
> Against infection and the hand of war,
> This happy breed of men, this little world,
> This precious stone set in the silver sea.

Much of *Henry V*'s imagery is forced, as if Shakespeare was no longer prepared to try and rival Marlowe in magnificent images of conquest. Aware of growing too old to bang the drum of military glory, more often than not, from now on, he would present it obliquely and ironically.

But if – apart from those gems Shakespeare as Chorus reserved for his own motley display and goring of thoughts – much of the verse has at best a snarling, virile rhetoric and show-piece pageantry, Shakespeare made the prose of *Henry V* relaxed, realistic, and often discerningly compassionate. He boasted his "small Greek", from Xenophon's *The Retreat of the Ten Thousand*, in Fluellen's account of a river in Macedon just like one he knew in Monmouth, with "salmons in both". The King woos his bride-to-be in unforced prose that gently echoes Petruchio. In disguise and like Xenophon "a gentleman of a company", he surveys his ragged band of followers and explores the problem of kingly responsibility in sentences that could serve as a model for the future Authorized Version: "I think the king is but a man, as I am. The violet smells to him as it doth to me; the element shows to him as it doth to me." Shakespeare observed the ordinary soldiers of Henry's army beautifully, almost taking them, in their full vernacular glory, straight off the streets outside the Globe.

Enabling *Henry V* to be dated almost to the month – or at least between the end of March and September 1599 (after which a return in triumph would have been inconceivable) – Shakespeare pointed directly to Lord Essex, and the Irish expedition which ended in débâcle:

> Were now the General of our gracious Empress –
> As in good time he may – from Ireland coming,
> Bringing rebellion broachèd on his sword,
> How many would the peaceful city quit
> To welcome him!

It made that link to the Globe audience in his own person even more credible and contemporary.

With the creation of Macmorris, Shakespeare – again with topical skill, and with lavish blasphemies rare in the printed texts because of censorship – invented the first stage Irishman, that poltroon and vagabond who was to become embedded as a comic virus in the English theatre for centuries until he emerged as a hero to win victories in his topsy-turvy defeatism. "It is no time to discourse, so Chrish save me," says Macmorris, "the day is hot, and the weather and the wars and the King and the dukes . . ." Discourse is just what Macmorris does. Here Shakespeare sowed the seeds of *Waiting for Godot*: "So God sa'me, 'tis shame to stand still, it is shame by my hand. And there is throats to be cut, and works to be done, and there ish nothing done, so Chrish sa' me law."

The most remarkable prose passage of all reports Falstaff's death. The reason for his non-appearance – despite Shakespeare's promise – was patriotically as well as aesthetically sound. His ceremonial elephant's progress would have swamped the glory and smashed like matchsticks the brittle patriotic rhetoric of Harry. The comic figures had to submit to the play's overall panegyric intention: none doubts the seriousness of the war, or the overriding importance of national unity.

Exhausted when writing *Henry V*, and wavering in his belief in the value of military glory, Shakespeare nevertheless had his timing right for the mood of the country. The larger topicality and victory he celebrated in this play was that other event of commanding importance as far as the survival of England mattered. After fifty days and fifty nights of absolute piety, Philip of Spain – more than forty years before king-consort of England, one-time suitor for the hand of the imperial votaress herself and since then her scourge, her wolf, her eternal persecutor – died in indescribable torment. On hearing of the Irish rebel Tyrone's defeat of Elizabeth's army at the river Blackwater he received pyrrhic consolation, but the release and relief from his own threat meant a freedom from danger and the constant likelihood of annihilation which had always been present in the island kingdom. Powerful and implacable enemies, the two great monarchs had propped up one another with their undying hatred, to rule their respective countries longer and more absolutely than any monarchs before or since. Philip having departed, it would be only a matter of a year or two before Elizabeth herself would die. Shakespeare managed his deaths more lightheartedly, in matchless prose:

> A parted ev'n just between twelve and one, ev'n at the turning o' th' tide – for after I saw him fumble with the sheets, and play with flowers, and smile upon his finger's end, I knew there was but one way. For his nose was as sharp as a pen, and a babbled of green fields. 'How now, Sir John?' quoth I. 'What, man! Be o' good cheer.' So a cried out, 'God, God, God', three or four times.

# Life measured by the act

The first great and lasting influence on Shakespeare's life and development had been Christopher Marlowe: this influence, reaching its climax in *Richard II*, prevailed until Shakespeare became able to define what was essentially himself, what Marlowe. In the first half of his career he paced himself against Marlowe, innovated on the basis of Marlowe, heard echoes of Marlowe being played back to him. But Shakespeare *was* essentially change and development: no ivory tower poet, he was quick to catch and assimilate a new voice.

Primarily an actor in mentality, he imitated other voices, other characters, he drew on everything as raw material.

The sudden horrific death of Mercutio in *Romeo and Juliet* had been a replay of Marlowe's needless and tragic end. Mercutio was not meant as a direct presentation of Marlowe, but that shock of loss the play provides (more realistic and shaking in the grief it produces than the love of the protagonists) had an intimate rapport with the playwright's own life.

Ben Jonson's life had parallels with Marlowe's, but his appeal was to the mature Shakespeare more than to the young aspirant. Jonson himself matured slowly and outlived by far other writers of his time. He was devilishly clever in that age of verbal power and dexterity, where words had virtuoso appeal. He was superbly equipped with every gift and weapon the word-merchant could command. Above all he had a phenomenal, elephantine memory. It was said of him, later on, that he knew all his own plays by heart.

If ever one playwright envied another's happiness, Jonson, struggling in the mire of prison, religious persecution and satiric bitterness, must have envied Shakespeare his output and the success of his next three plays.

In these dark and gloomy times Elizabeth faltered and showed more signs than usual of indecision and weakness. The *fin de siècle* feeling grew, with no significant change in the air; the eternal presence of that great character who overlooked all plays written at the time – namely Death, the ever-busy Patron – daily supplied new roles for actors, new places for courtiers. But Shakespeare gave himself up to pure entertainment. He, too, needed space in which to recover after his great spurt of ambition.

i

*Much Ado About Nothing* – the title conveys the importance it held for its author – was, like *Henry IV* (and *Henry V*, in a pirated edition), printed as soon as it was played. It had for the main part a romantic central plot, written in verse, based on Shakespeare's usual Italian sources, but the best scenes, those in which Beatrice and Benedick are deceived into admitting they love each other, were written in prose and wholly invented. Will Kempe was cast as Dogberry, the constable whose humour Shakespeare "happened to take", Aubrey wrote, "at Grendon in Bucks which is the road from London to Stratford". As Kempe left Shakespeare's company in 1599, sold his interest in the Globe, "and went dancing and japing about the continent", it is possible that *Much Ado* was first performed at the Curtain, then revived at the Globe. It was the first of Shakespeare's plays, as listed in the Stationers' Register on 23 August 1600, to be ascribed directly to "Master Shakespeare", an indication of Shakespeare's popularity – plays were rarely credited to a specific author.

As in *Henry IV* and *Henry V*, the prose scenes of the play far surpass the verse scenes in quality. The more vital Beatrice and Benedick put the naïve Hero and Claudio in the shade in a way reminiscent of the weaker, less realistic subplot of *The Taming of the Shrew*. And Beatrice, although softened and humanized, has much in common with Kate; played by a boy – in the context of an Elizabethan audience's tastes – Beatrice's involvement with Benedick had at first been downgraded as light comic relief for the main plot of Don Pedro's deceptive wooing of Hero for Claudio. But Beatrice and Benedick became so popular that Shakespeare expanded and rewrote their scenes, and abridged the rest.

In the fresh advance he had made since *Henry IV*, Shakespeare gave *Much Ado* a unifying theme, that of the way gossip or overheard information can change people's lives. He fastened on to the dramatic possibilities of the eavesdropper's discovery, which is allied to the evil but widespread art of the informer. He exploited its tragi-comic potential in a masterly way, with an overriding emotional vibration, already explored in the Sonnets and elsewhere, of love's inconstancy.

*The Merry Wives of Windsor*, his second comedy of this period, fits perfectly the tradition that Queen Elizabeth commanded Shakespeare to show her Falstaff in love, and gave him a fortnight in which to do it. Like *Henry V* he wrote the play in a hurry, mostly in prose, so that it became, with Shakespeare in free-wheeling mood, his purest potboiler, the least contaminated by quality or originality. Stripped down as it is for popularity, it is hardly surprising that it became the libretto for an opera by Giuseppe Verdi. But the true Falstaff of *Henry IV* was not shown: amorous manoeuvre could never soil his hands. Falstaff and the direction and intention which come from being in love are a contradiction in terms. With the subtlety of an escapologist Shakespeare fulfilled his daunting commission by making it Ford who is in love: and there is little trace of sensuality in that character's self-willed masochism, which achieves ferocity in its torment. This was middle-class comedy at its most typical and farcical, piling on the deceptions to be unmasked, elaborating them with jealous fantasies and then duly exploding them. Ideally – or so it feels in the writing – Shakespeare would have given the whole play to Ford. "God be praised for any jealousy," Ford spits out with rhapsodic obsession: his "humour" is a perfect piece of borrowing from Ben Jonson.

But the shaky structure of *The Merry Wives* had to be made to support the corpulent knight, and, in anticipation of the Host of Jonson's *The New Inn*, Shakespeare dipped Falstaff in infectious hospitality, so he could preside over the frivolities with an even-handed, condescending sense of his own absurdity. But he could not hide that Falstaff was in Windsor on the flimsiest of excuses; too often, compared with the earlier creation, he is a gallivanting moron.

*The Merry Wives* did provide some flattery for its royal patron's susceptibilities. On her mother's side Elizabeth came from quite a humble middle-class background, which Shakespeare flattered; the comedy also pandered to her much-exercised dislike of husbands, and the state of matrimony. Shakespeare directed *The Merry Wives* not only at the Queen, but at the bourgeois ladies in the audience, housewives as well as courtly ladies. Shakespeare ranged himself on the side of the women, although, to honour the surroundings of Windsor, he allowed Pistol a gain in respectability.

The prose was highly conversational: citizens and their wives were paraded for the Queen and court; Shakespeare sprinkled the text with mentions of local landmarks, employing the Garter Inn, Herne's Oak and Datchet Mead as settings. Mistress Quickly works in an explicit reference to the Queen's highest order of chivalry, and *The Merry Wives* may well have been written for the St George's Day ceremony of 23 April 1597 when the Garter was bestowed at Westminster on the Count of Mömpelgart:

> Like to the Garter's compass, in a ring.
> ... *'Honi soit qui mal y pense'* write
> In em'rald tufts, flowers purple, blue, and white,
> Like sapphire, pearl, and rich embroidery,
> Buckled below fair knighthood's bending knee.

Mistress Quickly also compliments Elizabeth, saying of Windsor Castle, "Worthy the owner, and the owner it", although this compliment may be taken as somewhat opaque.

But Shakespeare seemed finally to be aware that *The Merry Wives* was putting to ill employment his greatest comic creation: "Have I laid my brain in the sun and dried it", he has Falstaff say, "that it wants matter to prevent so gross o'er-reaching as this?"

ii

*As You Like It*, the third and by far the best of this trio of comedies, demonstrated that Shakespeare was frankly tired and needed the countryside in order to recuperate. He may have gone to write it in Stratford, or he may have written it in the Liberty of the Clink after an extended visit to the rural peace of his infancy and youth; but, typically with Shakespeare, there was little difference between the action itself and the real need for enactment the work satisfied. Shakespeare hungered after the countryside, and hey presto, here it was in his next play. Setting it down and living in it imaginatively refreshed him, as it refreshed the play's audiences.

There was, between the courtier and the London citizen, still a real difference. During the previous ten years the City of Westminster, which had depended entirely for its life upon the presence of the Queen, had significantly expanded. The Queen, tired and ageing, made neither so many nor such wide-ranging visits to the country, so it became *de rigueur* for noblemen, up to then based in their country seats, to have establishments in town. Thus the new residential district of Whitehall brought into being an entirely fresh audience for plays.

The courtier was easily distinguishable from the citizen of London: with starched ruff, high-crowned hat, sword and cloak, he expressed confidence in the future; his eyes trained on the new century, his influence in the ascendant. The citizen was more tradition-bound, a figure with wasp-waisted doublet, round-hose, flat cap and "guarded" gown. The citizen's life-style was blunter, more open, where the courtier's world was secret, his loyalties murky, advantages gained by ambiguity: trust and constancy were perceived as rare qualities which hardly served to procure advancement where there were rich pickings and whole new areas of influence and patronage to be canvassed.

Shakespeare increasingly – but indirectly and in non-literal settings – reflected these changes. The end-of-the-century disillusionment continued to grow alongside a feeling of insecurity about the lack of succession, and the stability of national rule after Elizabeth's death. Civil disturbance was already brewing between puritanical fundamentalists and traditional ritualists. Exile, insubordination, rebellion, the threat of plots both at home and abroad, filled the air.

Shakespeare had tired of the painted pomp of Westminster and London: he appropriated a prose romance, *Rosalynde*, by Thomas

Lodge, as a basis for *As You Like It*, but whereas Lodge dispatched his characters, following the old tale, to the Ardennes, Shakespeare with his benign insularity brought them home to the forest of Arden. This, for him, had strong family associations (some editions keep the French spelling Ardenne).

Here, through the characters in exile, Shakespeare was yearning for a lost world. The enclosure of land, which destroyed its open character as common land available to all, was transforming the countryside into something prettier and less wild and rugged, but Shakespeare, unlike Chekhov, had no feelings about the future. In *As You Like It*, he harked back constantly to the golden age as he believed it was worshipped in classical antiquity. The past was a source of hope and inspiration, permitting a return to more primitive feeling and simplicity, qualities now vanished from the earth:

> Who doth ambition shun,
> And loves to live i'th' sun,
> Seeking the food he eats
> And pleased with what he gets,
> Come hither, come hither, come hither:
> Here shall he see
> No enemy
> But winter and rough weather.

Exhaustion, suspicion, insecurity sent Elizabethans back to that golden age: their philosophical mentor was Plato. They were not bored – unlike characters in Chekhov, who set the standard of decaying bourgeois feeling – or totally beyond society or inoperant, like the vagabonds of Samuel Beckett. They did *not* look forward to the future, but were pragmatists: hence Shakespeare conceived the whole of *As You Like It* as an elaborate mating ritual, important because of the immense difficulty – in face of recurrent plague and other hardships and infections – of increasing the population.

His depiction of a golden age underlines how much Shakespeare experienced a happy childhood, on which he drew all his life, before the blow of his father's disgrace fell. Marlowe, at heart a classicist, had attempted in *Doctor Faustus* to fulfil the greatest wish of his life: to return to the lost golden age, the period of innocence and purity before the world became corrupted. Hence the incarnation of Helen of Troy as a central figure in *Doctor Faustus*. Greek mythology linked up with Christian and particularly Protestant theology at the point at which the golden age became merged imaginatively with the world before Adam was driven from Paradise. If Troy was recoverable for Marlowe, for the Protestant, now secure in his political ascendancy in England, man had definitely tumbled from a state of grace. Milton, the greatest and purest English Protestant poet, was to celebrate that lost golden age in *Paradise Lost*. Yeats, another Protestant at heart, revived it fleetingly in his poems about Byzantium.

Marlowe had become topical a second time with the posthumous publication in 1598 of *Hero and Leander*, prefaced by a compliment on behalf of the editor, Edward Blunt, to Marlowe's old patron, Sir Thomas Walsingham. That Shakespeare in *As You Like It* recalled Marlowe and the lost golden age is apparent in the backward glances of Rosalind's love mockery, when she mentions how Troilus had his brains dashed out with a Grecian club, yet "did what he could to die before". He was one of the patterns of love. So was Marlowe's Leander who "would have lived many a fair year though Hero had turned nun if it had not been for a hot midsummer night ... he went but forth to wash him in the Hellespont and, being taken with the cramp, was drowned". Phoebe the shepherdess quotes directly from *Hero and Leander* – a warm tribute invoking Marlowe as the "dead shepherd" – "Dead shepherd, now I find thy saw of might: / 'Who ever loved that loved not at first sight?'" Touchstone obliquely recalls Marlowe's death by Frizer's dagger over "le recknynge" in the Deptford tavern, when he chides Audrey: "When a man's verses cannot be understood, nor a man's good wit seconded with the forward child, understanding, it strikes a man more dead than a great reckoning in a little room." The allusion is the more trenchant for being double: to Marlowe's death, and to the well-known line from his *Jew of Malta*, "Infinite riches in a little room".

But Shakespeare had his eye on the court, too, and with his usual aplomb both flattered and mocked at the same time, as he did through the character of Touchstone. The eccentricities of this jester, the first of a celebrated line, owed much to the personal foibles and fantasies of the Lord Chamberlain's company's new clown, Robert Armin, who had replaced Will Kempe after the latter left the Globe, or, as he said, "danced myself out of the world". Kempe, besides being an excellent jigger, had specialized in the broad comic butt – the last he played in this line was Dogberry – but the subtler age required a new sophistication. Armin, who later spoke of being "writ down an ass in my time" – though he had been a goldsmith's apprentice, and a pupil of Tarlton – supplied this. Many-sided and more fantastical than Kempe, Armin extended himself easily into the new witty logic – as when Jaques asks Touchstone about the quarrel upon the "seventh cause", and Touchstone replies that he disliked the cut of a certain courtier's beard, and the courtier sent back "the Retort Courteous" ... and so on through the well-known series, ending with "the Lie Direct".

Touchstone was a stage on towards the wry commentator here-after increasingly personified, as Shakespeare began shifting into his dark period. His characters had always had the capacity to evaluate, or generalize from, their own particular situation, but Shakespeare now started to take this capacity a stage further, into a probing self-consciousness, as well as self-awareness, that would in his future work colour a whole new dimension. This quality was pre-eminently personal, and reflected that watching, alienated young man now grown up, but still feeling himself insecure and dispossessed of his due, stripped of honour and birthright because of what his father had done. He would not paint a direct self-portrait, but from now on he did put his own anatomized emotions more and more into his plays: he wrote in the direction his inner instincts prompted him, he developed themes and preoccupations nearer to his heart.

In *As You Like It* Shakespeare expressed elegiac sorrow over the departed world of Christopher Marlowe (and also over his own departed world of courtship). But in the creation of Jaques, for whom there was no antecedent, he looked ahead to a new pro-fessional rivalry, that with Ben Jonson. Shakespeare would not have been foolish enough to satirize Jonson directly; yet it was impossible not to be aware of the other playwright's colossal self-conceit, and that Jonson himself was a "humour" such as he theorized about depicting in his plays. Jaques was conceived, ironically, as adhering to Jonson's precepts of comedy: Shakespeare carved his name out as a pun on the Elizabethan slang for lavatory, "jakes" – a mocking allusion to the fact that Jonson had as a child lived over an open sewer (and often talked about it). Jonson saw the world more as a stage than did Shakespeare, in whose work real life jostled along easily with artificiality and artefact; so although Jaques's famous speech was amplified with typical Shakespearian warmth and obser-vation, its essential perception of artificiality was inspired by Jonson's example. Jaques's credo for the exercise of his wit was specifically Jonsonian: he must have liberty, "as large a charter as the wind", to blow on whom he pleased, in the way fools had, so

that those who were "most gallèd" with his folly had to laugh most.
He appeals for licence to speak his mind and he will

> through and through
> Cleanse the foul body of th'infected world,
> If they will patiently receive my medicine.

Shakespeare never had such a patently moralistic intention. His
own attitude was never didactic and reformist, never protestant and
proselytizing like G. B. Shaw or Sean O'Casey. The bad Duke
Frederick never meets his exiled brother in final conflict because he
encounters a religious old man who converts him to the holy life;
when Orlando saves Oliver from the lion, he too undergoes a
conversion to goodness: while in Orlando's mouth Shakespeare
placed the mote and "beam-in-thine-own-eye" gospel sentiment –
"I will chide no breather in the world but myself, against whom I
know most faults." Shakespeare's instinct impelled him to seek out
and enlarge the good that could be found in evil, to find, next to
the darkness, the redeeming light; for he knew, paradoxically, how
each quality contains its opposite. Duke Senior describes their exile:

> Sweet are the uses of adversity
> Which, like the toad, ugly and venomous,
> Wears yet a precious jewel in his head;
> And this our life, exempt from public haunt,
> Finds tongues in trees, books in the running brooks,
> Sermons in stones, and good in everything.

Not only by avoidance of any nasty scenes, but in a prose variation on his mockery in *Love's Labour's Lost* of themes from the
Sonnets, Shakespeare played further games on the subject of love.
Thus Rosalind tutors Orlando on the necessity, to cure his amorous
suffering, of cynicism: "This way", she says, "will I take upon me
to wash your liver as clean as a sound sheep's heart, that there shall
not be one spot of love in't." In such lightness and free-wheeling
exhilaration, Shakespeare betrayed a need for happiness to overcome not only fatigue, but disillusionment in love and marriage. It
was only later, when he had the energy to portray grief and conflict
directly, that he was personally at his happiest. His invention of an
ideal, spirited and teasing mental companion in Rosalind (always
harping on that name, and on "rose"); the tradition that he himself
played old Adam, gluing on a long beard, overdoing the senility

(according to the eighteenth-century antiquary William Oldys, one of Shakespeare's younger brothers saw him act this); the possible personal reference to his own colouring, as Hugh Kingsmill suggests: "Your chestnut was ever the only colour" – all these point to a desire in him for compensatory cheerfulness.

But he was wise enough to know that he could not run away for more than a play or two, and that the countryside could be no more than a refreshing interlude: any self-deception about fleeing the court in order not to face himself quickly evaporated. As Touchstone remarks, "Ay, now am I in Arden; the more fool I. When I was at home I was in a better place." He adds that travellers must be content.

In *As You Like It* Shakespeare infused the imagery with the theme of betrayal, but kept his foot away from the clutch. A serious crisis had happened over the previous years and the artist's personality had become "worn to a husk", as John Masefield expresses it. He had faced and come to terms with a terrifying experience just before he got down to writing his next play, *Julius Caesar*. He had sat in judgement on himself and annihilated his past; former flowerings could be dismissed, as new opposites were ready to fuse and germinate new life.

*Julius Caesar*, whose subject is betrayal on a worldly and political canvas instead of on a personal one, would be the gateway or *arc de triomphe* to the great tragedies which followed.

# The cockle of rebellion

*Julius Caesar*, the first of Shakespeare's three most famous Roman plays, was more directly related to contemporary Elizabethan politics, and made more of what could be inferred as direct political comment on the world in which Shakespeare lived than any other play he wrote, except perhaps *Hamlet*, which may well already have been started. *Julius Caesar* reads like no other play he had written: this was the playwright's critical or pivotal moment.

The play was a powerful study of political types, whose models

Shakespeare had circulated among, or near, all his life. London and Westminster seethed with powerful political figures, while the times promised, or threatened, sweeping political change. Although September 1598 had seen the death of Philip of Spain, removing the great external threat to England's survival, in the month before William Cecil, Lord Burghley, for thirty years Elizabeth's chief minister, had also died, arguing to the very last the need to make peace with Spain.

After his death the parties following the rivals Robert Cecil and Essex became more sharply divided than ever. Essex was immensely popular – as Earl Marshall, the Queen's favourite, he was the supporter of King James of Scotland as successor to the English throne. Cecil, the only man who could stand up against Essex and had a chance of winning, had no popular appeal at all. He was a hunchback, known as Monsieur le Bossu, or Gobbo, after Shakespeare's clown, or, more sinisterly, as "Robert le Diable".

All during the time of Shakespeare's writing *Julius Caesar* the two factions were engaged in a life-and-death struggle. The Queen, old, irascible, presided over this perilous state of affairs, which came to a climax over the appointment of a new commander-in-chief for Ireland. In March 1599 Elizabeth resolved the situation, after much heart-searching, by sending Essex to Ireland, saying, or so it was reported, "He hath played long enough upon me, and now I mean to play awhile upon him, and stand as much upon his greatness as he hath upon [my] stomach." But Essex, like Cassius in *Caesar*, was boiling with discontent.

When the Earl of Southampton was refused permission to accompany him to Ireland – having been disgraced and imprisoned for carrying on an affair with Essex's cousin, Elizabeth Vernon, one of Elizabeth's ladies-in-waiting, then marrying her when she was found pregnant – Essex appointed him "General of the Horse", which must have seemed to Elizabeth like flagrant provocation.

This was the immediate political background to Shakespeare's play: had it been written and played after the explosion of the Essex rebellion, some seventeen months later, there is no doubt it would have been banned. Shakespeare, in the complex combination of threads and purposes he drew together in the play, no doubt intended it as a warning to Essex and his followers, as much as to Elizabeth and her court. Be sensible and moderate, he was telling the Queen through his portrayal of a Caesar who has much more in common with her moodiness than the Caesar of Plutarch. Shakespeare's *Caesar* tells us much about Elizabeth's court, but particularly about the woman herself, who now, in her old age, had more nakedly, unconcealed by feminine charm and subterfuge, the despotic traits of her father in his old age.

The conspirators of Brutus's faction are brilliantly observed characters, like the dramatis personae of a Ben Jonson play, each possessed by an overriding humour. This method was perfectly suited to *Julius Caesar*, where although the mood is dark and conspiratorial, and some of the action is duplicated, Shakespeare allowed much comedy to play about the relationships among the conspirators. Yet even while using the notion of a humour – and Cassius and Octavius Caesar conform most closely by having one complexion in charge of their character – Shakespeare, a far greater artist than Jonson, breaks out of any confine instinctively, suddenly, broadening the character of Casca, for example, from the cynical persona describing a Caesar loath to refuse the crown to, only a little while later, someone totally unnerved by the supernatural force of the storm:

> Are you not moved, when all the sway of earth
> Shakes like a thing unfirm: O Cicero . . .
> Either there is a civil strife in heaven,
> Or else the world, too saucy with the gods,
> Incenses them to send destruction.

Such an instinctive power came from Shakespeare's extraordinary optimism: he wanted to share the freedom of his many-sidedness with his audience, describing how we are a mixture of different states and feelings which are often totally contradictory. At the same time he heightened the dramatic impact by giving to the most scornful and derisive character the most vulnerable and hysterical response to the storm, switching the rhythm from prose to blank verse, so that Casca's conversion to the cause of assassinating Caesar will be easier for Cassius to achieve in the following scene. Conversion, change of opinion, a new line on an old problem, above all the *idea* of change is right at the centre of the dramatic life of *Caesar*, and reflects its creator's preoccupations concerning both society and himself. The fickle mob, able so rapidly to switch allegiance, so committed at one point to honour, the next to murdering a poet, is one aspect of that sense of change which was in the nature of the man himself at this time.

Brutus, too, is a character who points forward: the first portrayal of a wrong-headed determination which produces a result destructive both to himself and to his cause, his determination is the most precious quality of the Elizabethan Christian gentleman, namely an exercise of his free will. Brutus is no medieval incarnation of evil, like Richard III, but a man of conscience and honour. He is reflective, an intellectual who although skilfully camouflaged with a few Roman habits and attitudes of mind, has in essence an Erasmian good nature. Shakespeare was shortly to embark, if he had not already done so, on the most philosophically searching and intellectually complex play of his whole career: *Julius Caesar* can, apart from being a rousing work in itself, be viewed retrospectively as a dry run for *Hamlet*.

The character of Brutus is not dramatically exciting, and has not sufficient power to hold the centre of the play together, but in the magnificent scene of the quarrel between Brutus and Cassius in the fourth act, with the appearance of Caesar's ghost afterwards to Brutus, Shakespeare added a dramatic irony to the change in Brutus's spirit which was of a deeper dimension than anything he had given his audiences before. That Cassius should have been moved to make a reconciliation with Brutus, and then overturn, fatally, his previous realistic decision out of a desire to patch up a friendship – and that this should lead to the military defeat at Philippi – shows not only that Shakespeare had mastered a deeper complexity of character, of the interplay of action as the consequence of character, but that his audiences also found pleasure in living up to their playwright's expectations and experience of them. Their own experience of political and personal uncertainty in that climate of betrayal was on a level with the playwright's own. *"Et tu, Brute"* is the poignant, naked cry of pain at the centre of *Julius Caesar*, which Mark Antony picks up with the emotional power of a Beethoven expanding the motif into a flood of impassioned feeling:

> Through this the well-belovèd Brutus stabbed;
> And as he plucked his cursèd steel away,
> Mark how the blood of Caesar followed it . . .
> This was the most unkindest cut of all.
> For when the noble Caesar saw him stab,
> Ingratitude, more strong than traitors' arms,
> Quite vanquished him.

If Shakespeare cut back in this play his proclivity for lush verbal display to a deliberate austerity in the use of prose and extremely classical, restrained and prosaic verse, he proclaimed with Mark Antony that the force of great passion, which had grown tired in the year or two previously, was once again in the ascendant in him. But it was completely under the poet's control: *Julius Caesar* is a work of conscious and careful planning, an experiment in probing the psychology of betrayal, as well as a dramatic, even cinematic, observation of the shaping forces in any great and cataclysmic political event. Shakespeare, in a prognosticating way, imagined in *Julius Caesar* the Essex plot and wrote it up fortunately before it happened. In his treatment of the mob, he conveyed North's Plutarch into the narrow and choked byways of Bankside, displayed the cruelty of public entertainments, such as bear-baiting, and the ugliness and volatility of the crowds in the cluttered and airless streets outside the Globe.

While Shakespeare was at work on *Julius Caesar*, Ben Jonson, with the success of *Every Man in His Humour* and *Every Man Out of His Humour*, became a valuable, if short-lived, asset to the Chamberlain's Men. Shakespeare sharpened up his contemporary and realistic portrayal of character to a considerable degree by this new association. With the second play Jonson was quickly becoming the leading comic writer of the age; Shakespeare, as ever sharp, had chosen the first play for the company to perform. He noted that tastes, in the complex, interlocking worlds of city and court, had changed: in the intellectually more sophisticated climate, the demand of a highly educated public was no longer for the broad, unsophisticated romance of his own early comedies. In order not to compete with Jonson, and because his ambitions lay elsewhere, he abandoned to Jonson (though with one later exception) the comic muse – which was, in any case, a muse with a much changed face.

Shakespeare acted in *Every Man in His Humour*, his name heading the list in the 1616 folio edition: "Acted in the year 1598. By the then Lord Chamberlain his Servants": this was the first such actors' list. Droeshout in his engraving portrayed Shakespeare as Jonson's character old Knowell. He grasped the new conventions of Jonson's powerful talent from the inside – he had them in his pulse, and in his nervous system as an actor, and could draw instinctively on them.

At the end of the performance *Every Man Out of His Humour* presented the "emaciated", impoverished scholar Macilente, the displaced intellectual, greeting a boy actor dressed as Queen Elizabeth:

"Envy is fled my soul at sight of her, / And she hath chased all black thoughts from my bosom". In the Epilogue Jonson expanded the compliment in scatological terms referring to his own background – he having lived as he said in a house built over an open sewer:

> And as our city's torrent (bent t'infect
> The hallowed bowels of the silver *Thames*)
> Is checked by strength, and clearness of the river,
> Till it hath spent itself e'en at the shore;
> So, in the ample, and unmeasured flood
> Of her perfections, are my passions drowned.

His way of appealing to Elizabeth's favour was bizarre and dangerous.

Shakespeare's company refused to repeat the performance and Jonson ceased writing for the Lord Chamberlain's company, which tried to block publication of 1,500 copies of the play that had been printed. Jonson's publishing of *Every Man Out of His Humour*, in three quartos in 1600, which the poet undertook for his own private profit when he gave up writing for the conventional theatrical companies, explains why Shakespeare the actor had such a strong interest in keeping his own plays from print (and why three of the most popular, *Henry V, The Merry Wives* and *Hamlet*, were pirated). As long as the Chamberlain's Men kept possession of the play scripts they had to make the public turn up at the theatre and pay: in print, the plays quickly lost their commercial value. By publishing his play himself Jonson, perhaps the first playwright ever to do so, claimed exclusive copyright.

Shakespeare's ego was of a different, less obtrusive kind. But his earlier reputation of having an amorous, easily aroused disposition re-emerges in Thomas Dekker's *Satiromastix*, a savage "untrussing" of Jonson, in which a playwright called Sir Adam Prickshaft joins a posse of writers wooing the fair Mistress Miniver. Dekker made good-natured sport of Shakespeare, milking the satirical name Prickshaft for its ribald possibilities. His Captain Tucca says to Prickshaft: "I'll hold my life thou art stuck with Cupid's bird-bolt, my little Prickshaft, art? dost love that mother Mumble-crust, dost thou? dost long for that whim-wham? ... if I might have my will, thou shouldst not put thy spoon into that bumble-broth." Prickshaft's response, "Would I were as sure to lie with her, as to love her", reflected some well-known difficult quality in the poet of *Venus and Adonis*. So does Mistress Miniver's malaproposed reason for rejecting him – Shakespeare was thirty-five, strongly middle-aged in appearance – "Troth I shall never be enameled of a bare-headed man for this, what shift so ever I make." But the crude caricature tells little more.

In *Satiromastix*, in the clash of petulant ill-natures, the so-called "war of the theatres" – or Poetomachia, as Dekker called it – reached its height. The fight had started primarily because of a private quarrel between Jonson and John Marston, who had shown Jonson in his youth as being "given to venery". Marston, first writing for the Paul's Boys, one of the new companies of non-professionals, had mildly sent up Jonson in his *Histrio-mastix* as the high-minded scholarly Chrisoganus, whose pretence it was to "feed the hearings of judicial ears". Jonson had replied with the inordinately complicated *Poetaster*, performed by the Children of the Chapel (in Blackfriars), in which he pilloried Dekker as Demetrius, "playdresser and plagiary", flatteringly displayed himself as the English Horace, giving the hack Crispinus (meant to be Marston) an emetic that makes him vomit his turgid words, and then placing him on a "strict and wholesome diet of the classics". Jonson completed his fantasy of self-vindication with the symbolic banishment of Ovid, patron poet of Marlowe and Shakespeare in the early 1590s.

*Satiromastix* provided not only the climax but also the final round in the war of the theatres. Dekker presented Jonson, in his insulting lampoon, as an arrogant Horace whose plays displeased the court – so was the satirist whipped (the meaning of Dekker's title), insulted and crowned with nettles. But Jonson had to desist from further reply, for the forces of the law, which he also lampooned in *The Poetaster*, threatened to arraign him, and but for the favourable intervention of Richard Field, the publisher and Middle Temple wit, he might once again have seriously fallen foul of the authorities.

The Elizabethans loved a fight between gamecocks, especially the "skipping swaggerer" playwrights who plucked each other's most resplendent feathers, and this "merry murdering" had gone on and on – "humours, revells, and satires, that gird, and fart at the time", in the words of Dekker's Tucca. Shakespeare later made Hamlet question Rosencrantz and Guildenstern about these children players who enjoyed, often outside the censor's scrutiny, what Guildenstern called "throwing about of brains". He was proved right, for while the private theatres continued to attract plays for their small, captive audiences, three of the *Poetaster*'s cast, Nat Field, John Underwood and Will Ostler, joined Shakespeare's company, which had cashed in on the scandalous appeal.

# I am that I am

*Hamlet* is Shakespeare's longest and most lavish play. He took time over its composition. He revised it. It was his considered response to Marlowe's *Doctor Faustus*, an exploration of goodness to answer a portrayal of evil, but now refracted through the novel and intricately cut glass of Jonson's theory of humours, and through his own deepened mastery of psychology and emotional perception. Some have suggested that Shakespeare wanted to explore the pathology of crime (like *Crime and Punishment*):

> Between the acting of a dreadful thing
> And the first motion, all the interim is
> Like a phantasma or a hideous dream.
> The genius and the mortal instruments
> Are then in counsel, and the state of man,
> Like to a little kingdom, suffers then
> The nature of an insurrection.

These are Brutus's words, which prefigure *Hamlet* in the way Mercutio's Queen Mab speech anticipates *A Midsummer Night's Dream*. The *Dream* also replays *Romeo and Juliet* in its mock tragedy, while *Hamlet* echoes *Julius Caesar*, notably when the storm is recalled:

> In the most high and palmy state of Rome,
> A little ere the mightiest Julius fell,
> The graves stood tenantless, and the sheeted dead
> Did squeak and gibber in the Roman streets.

Hamlet jokes with Polonius, who boasts that he played Caesar at university (Caesar and Polonius were acted by the same man in the Chamberlain's company) – and then, of course, Hamlet meditates on Caesar in the graveyard: "Imperial Caesar, dead and turned to clay, / Might stop a hole to keep the wind away".

Yet Shakespeare made Hamlet's crime incidental to his perturbation of mind and soul: the accomplishment of the revenge theme, although brought forward to generate dramatic life, was secondary to the exploration of character. The gaps, the delays in action, were primarily caused by Hamlet's need to find himself, by Shakespeare's desire for an answer to the problem of the melancholy man, the new, pre-eminent type of young man of the day. For as much as being a study of a specific prince in a court, and an exploration of the primal family with the curse of Cain upon it, *Hamlet* was a tragedy of reflection – but also a study of genius in crisis.

The identity crisis of a nation which *Hamlet*, in its breadth and many-sidedness, so amply demonstrated, was also personal. Shakespeare knew the story of Oedipus through Latin accounts, perhaps even through translations of Sophocles, with the sickness of the land mirroring the sickness of the ruling family. Again, heavily disguised, for Hamlet was in no sense a replication of himself, Shakespeare projected through the central character the whole of his own mid-life crisis of identity, which was in itself a direct response to his adolescence. He was recalling, as much as living at first hand, that crisis. For Shakespeare *Hamlet* was not a passionate play in which he as a writer discharged a whole incubus of stored-up feeling; it was circumspect, controlled, beautifully organized; it was also literary and explorative of idea and motive in the way of a novel.

No doubt, as in most parent–child relationships, Shakespeare's mother and father had let him down: the curse on his own family had been his father's disgrace, when he was twelve, a kind of death of his father as an ideal hero-figure. The new father he saw, a seeker after status, a fallen idol, he may unconsciously have drawn on for Claudius. Every son's image of his father has some time in the process of growing up to be shattered. Every son feels a certain betrayal by his mother when he sees his father's limits (exaggerated in Claudius by being made into vices) still attracting her, rather than the ideal manly qualities. Every son feels a loss of self-esteem (exaggerated in Claudius) when he sees his mother's individual needs and feelings serving herself, rather than him and that ideal part of his father. Every son has to separate, which is the beginning of growing up. Hamlet's "revenge", viewed in this light, is highly symbolic.

But if Shakespeare was facing and recalling – and not recollecting in tranquillity, because *Hamlet* is above all the work of a man who could face pain – his own difficult passage through adolescence, he was also confronting that second death or sense of change which comes with middle age (and which may take place at any time from mid-thirty to sixty). Shakespeare had married young, at eighteen; his family and sexual life had now reached a crucial stage, as his two daughters were themselves reaching the end of puberty. His wife's procreative days were over, and he himself would never, at least legitimately, be a father again. *Hamlet* became a means of recreating that dead son and heir, Hamnet, whose name, even, is echoed in the great protagonist (for the pun-loving poet this was important). Guilt, as well as grief, had been stored up for five years now, and Hamnet, had he lived, would at the time Shakespeare wrote have been sixteen – roughly the age of the students who made up his audience. Hamnet would be leaving home. Although Shakespeare had been in no way directly responsible for his son's death, guilt, inevitably, is the lot of any sensitive parent whose child suffers deep reverses, or dies. Shakespeare felt responsible for Hamnet's death, and *Hamlet* was his attempt at atonement, as well as powerful wish-fulfilment: a realistic romantic vision of an ideal prince such as he would have liked his son to become.

Even that prince's so-called "mad" sides, blown up to enormous proportions by the nineteenth-century *Weltanschauung* and the twentieth-century psychiatric industry, in so far as they are grown through and discarded in his arrival at maturity, are an enhancement to Hamlet's character and his appeal. Never had Shakespeare, this writer above all intent on pleasing and reassuring his audience, been more careful to make a character likeable. This was, as he knew, his greatest opportunity to bring his dead son back to life, overcome through the exercise of his art the terrible grief he suffered. In the superb deployment of every skill of adaptability and protean resource he unravelled, in his depiction of the Danish court, the riven moods and volatile pains of a young man confronted with the horror of having to grow up, of moving on to the next stage of human life: like Jaques in *As You Like It*, Shakespeare saw that life as a series of stages, each of which required the letting-go of some illusion or power: in Hamlet's case the distorted view of his parents.

So the supreme pragmatist moved on. Hamlet the playgoer would never have applauded *Hamlet* the play.

\*　　\*　　\*

But how had Shakespeare found the key to creating objectively a character modelled on himself? He did this primarily by the device of interiorizing experience as chorus to the main action of the play, namely the working of Hamlet's own mind.

This he based on his practice with the Chorus speeches of *Henry V*, which he himself delivered, and each of which was the prelude to an act of the historical chronicle. He wrote five of these, each containing material that could not be shown on stage by any other means, and each, in reverse, he mirrored, or almost mirrored, in *Hamlet*: even the positioning of the soliloquys there echoes *Henry V*, although more informally.

In *Henry V*'s first chorus Shakespeare appealed to the imagination to expand the stage's limited resources, while in Hamlet's first outburst he revealed the rottenness of outward appearance – a deficiency in what is seen, although Shakespeare meant, in contrast to *Henry V*, that what he showed on stage should be taken for real. In Hamlet's second soliloquy Shakespeare contrasted the actual event that had just taken place – the First Player's performance – with the inner, unrepresentable action of Hamlet's soul and feelings (in *Henry V*'s second chorus he described the treachery in the bud). In the third, most famous soliloquy of all (Act III, scene i), "To be, or not to be; that is the question", Shakespeare punctuated the action in a mood uncannily similar to the pre-battle speech of the Chorus in *Henry V*, Act IV: "Now entertain conjecture of a time / When creeping murmur and the poring dark . . .". Both set the scene for intimate revelations made by the central character in the play.

He echoed *Henry V*'s more vigorous Act III prelude, "Thus with imagined wing our swift scene flies . . .", in Hamlet's self-laceration over Fortinbras' army:

> Witness this army of such mass and charge,
> Led by a delicate and tender prince
> Whose spirit with divine ambition puffed
> Makes mouths at the invisible event.

This fifth soliloquy, on the passage of Fortinbras' army "over the stage", was omitted from the folio (and possibly cut later when Shakespeare revised the play). The Act V chorus of *Henry V*, opening with "Vouchsafe to those that have not read the story / That I may prompt them", was contrived as a bridging passage, crudely and functionally, to move the action forward; similarly, Hamlet's

short explanation of why he does not kill Claudius at prayer fulfils
a purely choric function.

Shakespeare, writing *Hamlet* at night in the Liberty of the Clink,
a frequent user by now of the ever more popular and addictive new
American import, tobacco, which cost 3s. per ounce and which he
smoked through a pipe, had his own part sheets of *Henry V* – those
with only the Chorus speeches written out – on his knee or on the
floor beside his table. By such an astonishing and yet simple trick,
originated from within his own practice, did he render the mind of
Hamlet as he observed the outward world of court from which he
felt alienated, and his own profoundly unsettling thoughts about a
family crime.

*Hamlet* also became for Shakespeare a secretive version of the
story he would never write. The popular Faust legend played on
its audience's deepest fear, deeper by far than the likely occurrence
of premature death – its fear of eternal damnation. Typically Shakespeare turned Marlowe's version of the story upside-down. The
Ghost is Mephistopheles: is he a tempter, or is he a genuine and
good spirit? Hamlet, acting within the confines of what his reason
will allow, has to find more than supernatural, hearsay evidence for
his uncle's guilt. He has to translate an inner prompting which
has supernatural authority into proven fact. Shakespeare knew the
murder of Hamlet's father lay outside the play – this was the inciting
action of the drama – and he focused the main attention on Hamlet's
effort to do his duty, not as a rebellious atheist, like Faust, but as
a man of conscience. The gap between his unfulfilled ambition,
his half-baked revenge awoken by the Ghost, and its fulfilment in
Claudius's death is widened not by his pathological uncertainty, or
other qualities on which Freudian speculations have been based
(although Shakespeare would not have been one to miss a trick of
feeling or motivation), but by his sense of justice.

Hamlet himself rages through every kind of style: obscene, cynical, choric, sublime; he can pass from scorn and ironic incongruity
to soul-searching meditation with effortless ease. The pseudo-
insanity is both real and assumed: comedy always exists in potentiality, breaking out sometimes in the darkest moments; Hamlet's
cutting wit, his cunning and boldness, his almost supernatural gifts
of perception both of himself and others – all belie the Romantic myth
foisted on him by Goethe and later Romantics, who sentimentalized
his goodness to suit their own feelings and needs. Shakespeare
created Hamlet's appeal through his strength as a dramatic character,

in which even his victimized traits have their rich and differentiated colour. In this particular *Hamlet* is a joyous play, written by a happy man who in no way felt trapped by the feelings and preoccupations, or even the darkness, he uncovered. W. B. Yeats noted in verse, correctly, that "*Hamlet* and *Lear* are gay": this is not to assert that Shakespeare had not himself felt and explored the play's darkness and its suicidal moods. But the way in which he depicted them, with such generosity, amplitude, and underlying stability, made audiences secure in their contemplation, as he was himself – so that, ultimately, the effect of the tragedy is life-affirming.

Shakespeare even prodigally endowed a minor worm like Osric with character. Osric has the function of releasing a "significant reflex of Hamlet's temperament and state of mind", yet he could have been disposed of summarily and still have been dramatically effective. But Shakespeare, with his own typical reflex of mind, could not deny Osric his own gorgeous salience.

Shakespeare set man free with abundant life, but the freedom he showed him enjoying was permeated not only with sacred and ethical values from the past, but with eternal values which held that the universe was in sympathy with man – that he, aware of his power of free choice, could explore a personal life and submit himself to self-scrutiny. Medieval Christianity, like each individual in his or her own life, had run its course through a series of great crises, and had brought a "dynamic need for self-orientation, and will to trace the secret forces of life", according to Erich Auerbach. Hamlet tapped a deeper vitality from his creator's profound and happy awareness of where man his faith, and his relationship to the world around him stood. Basically he is completely delightful. As Kingsley Amis ironically comments through a female character in *Jake's Thing*, "Hamlet is far too nice and intelligent to be a man, he must be a woman." He does not return aggressively or in any way confused from England to Denmark – physical separation from Gertrude and Claudius has been the pre-condition of growth. He has achieved complete mental balance by coming to terms with his past: he has begun to know where he himself ends and God, or fate, takes over,

>          ... let us know
> Our indiscretion sometimes serves us well
> When our dear plots do pall, and that should teach us
> There's a divinity that shapes our ends,
> Rough-hew them how we will –

in such accepting terms does he tell Horatio of his discovery of Claudius's plot to have him killed in England. His acquiescence in his summons to court, to the enactment of Claudius's double revenge over him, is similar to that of the many martyrs Shakespeare knew who had died during the reign of Elizabeth: it proved Hamlet's ultimate nobility and power of growth. Although the tragic sense of waste and pity was not denied the audience, and although Shakespeare was not ultimately writing a play with a Christian message, he made acquiescence the expression of Hamlet's goodness:

> It if be now, 'tis not to come. If it be not to come, it will be now. If it be not now, yet it will come. The readiness is all.

His moving and tender reconciliation with Laertes, who, unwittingly, has killed him with the poisoned rapier, is too often glossed over in production, yet Shakespeare meant this to be crucial as an expression of Hamlet's maturity. When he dies he has, while changing inside, remained true to what he was in the beginning.

*Hamlet* was Shakespeare's most contemporary play. Leviticus, one of its sources, lists marrying one's sister-in-law as unlawful: "Thou shalt not discover the shame of thy brother's wife; for it is thy brother's shame". Gertrude commits incest by marrying Claudius: as Hamlet damns her, "You are the Queen, your husband's brother's wife." The audience that first saw the play would have been well aware of that broken law that underlies the rottenness of Denmark, the decaying body politic. Furthermore they, and specifically the court, would have known that Elizabeth's own legitimacy as Queen of England depended on Henry VIII's divorcing Katherine of Aragon on the grounds of incest, as she had been married to his brother Arthur (and no explanation was offered as to why he could not have thought of this before the marriage). Henry VIII based his argument for divorce largely on Leviticus.

There are other recognizable and deliberate parallels, although hidden – for Elizabeth and her ministers forbade public discussion on the subject of Elizabeth's succession. Open talk about who was to take over was treasonable, yet no question could have been more important.

Shakespeare had Lord Essex on his mind, and it is quite likely that, given that *Hamlet* has every aspect and feel of being written at a leisurely pace, he might have written a draft, or some, of the play before the Essex rebellion, which came to a head in November 1600 (*Hamlet* was acted in 1601, possibly; certainly before July 1602). Much of Hamlet's behaviour mirrors that of the headstrong and moody Earl. For some of late 1599 and the first six months of 1600 Essex had been confined to Sir Thomas Egerton's York House in the Strand for disobedience to the Queen's will and other charges relating to the débâcle of his campaign in Ireland. He would, by turns, talk wildly – the Queen, he said on one occasion, was "no less crooked in mind than she was in carcass" – then protest devotion, or express repentance.

One of the accusations centred on the incredible passion of his return from Ireland, when, mud-bespattered, in riding boots after a break-neck ride, he arrogantly assaulted the Queen's privacy at Nonesuch, bursting in on her in her bedchamber where she was *en déshabillé* among her ladies, "in a dressing-gown, unpainted, without her wig, her grey hair hanging in wisps about her face, and her eyes starting from her head". Her immediate response was to dissimulate – second nature with her – and to speak him fair. Here is the essence of the great Gertrude–Hamlet scene of Act III; for as well as being unconsummated lovers, Essex and Elizabeth had a mother–son involvement, and Essex a deep sense of betrayal:

HAMLET:              Peace, sit you down,
    And let me wring your heart; for so I shall
    If it be made of penetrable stuff,
    If damnèd custom have not brassed it so
    That it is proof and bulwark against sense.
GERTRUDE:    What have I done, that thou dar'st wag thy tongue
    In noise so rude against me?

Hamlet was not in any way a portrait of Essex: he was Shakespeare imagining the character and actions of Hamlet, into which he poured feelings and observations gathered from his everyday experience and that of his friends and audience, in which the actions of Essex loomed large.

"By God's son," said Elizabeth to Sir John Harington, also just back from Ireland, "I am no queen. The man is above me. Who gave him commandment to come here so soon?" She stopped his monopoly of sweet wines: "An unruly beast must be stopped of his provender."

Like Essex, Hamlet in revolt against Claudius and Gertrude has the entire populace with him. Essex, too, according to Harington, seemed "devoid of good reason as of a right mind ... The man's soul seemeth tossed to and fro like the waves of a troubled sea." There the stories diverge. Essex felt everyone was plotting against him, and turned plotter to destroy a plot. His extreme paranoia triggered off the Queen's, and they became engaged in something approaching a Strindbergian Dance of Death.

In early February 1601, a group of Essex's supporters, including the Earl of Southampton, Sir Charles Danvers and his brother Henry, former hot-headed outlaws whom Southampton had protected from justice, organized a plan of action. Essex did not want to depose Elizabeth, or take the crown for himself, he wanted to secure the succession for James VI of Scotland, who eventually did succeed, and to ensure that his party and followers, rather than Robert Cecil's, controlled the Queen. He planned therefore to seize the court in order to bring pressure to bear.

Shakespeare's Globe itself became part of the scene of rebellion, as sympathizers such as Catholics, Puritan preachers, unemployed mercenaries, adventurers and general malcontents flocked to Essex House. Burbage, Augustine Phillips and the playwright were dragooned by the fiery Sir Gilly Merrick into staging *Richard II*, so that "the people could see that a sovereign of England could be deposed".

At first they said no, as they had no wish to be implicated. But Merrick and his friends insisted, and offered the Globe players forty shillings for a Saturday afternoon performance, which duly took place on the afternoon of 7 February 1601. Although on the very fringes of the uprising which Essex, with his love of theatrics and increasingly hazy grasp of reality, attempted, with the support of Southampton, Rutland, and 200 armed swordsmen, to stir up in the City the next day, Shakespeare and the Globe company had little choice but to give way to the intimidating Merrick and his followers. The performance of *Richard II*, not very enthusiastically advertised, but with the deposition scene restored, must have evoked some wry comment in the Chamberlain's Men – after the plot was broken.

Westminster had prepared itself against the Essex plot, and although four leading members of the court were captured by Essex, he bungled his leadership of the mob he incited, and in extravagant style shouting, "For the Queen! for the Queen! A plot is laid for my life," dissipated "the shame of action" in pathetic bravado. A vindictive monarch could well have taken revenge on the players (although such a thought does not pass through Claudius's mind at the play instigated by Hamlet). Augustine Phillips, senior actor and shareholder of the Globe, as well as its master musician, pleaded their case on oath before the Council. He answered his examiners, the chief of whom was Francis Bacon, who had switched his allegiance to Essex only months before his rebellion, that they had not wanted to play *Richard II*.

If the other shareholders of the Globe were rattled, Shakespeare himself supped on nightmares – the offending brain-child was solely of his generation. He recalled how Kyd had been tortured and informed on Marlowe just before the latter's death: what if someone informed on him and alleged sexual scandal with Southampton, already charged with homosexuality (Elizabethan courts were alacritous in the supply of dirt), or about him and a mistress. Fortunately for him Shakespeare rested secure in his masters' good will: only five weeks before the rising he had played before the Queen at Blackfriars: Lord Hunsden, son of Henry Carey, Shakespeare's first Lord Chamberlain, had entertained the Queen to supper. Had Shakespeare indeed taken up with the elder Carey's discarded mistress, Emilia Bassano (or Lanier), it could not have gone well for him; he almost certainly would not have been protected from charges.

It was Francis Bacon who, judging by his sympathetic report, was instrumental in saving the actors. Becoming at the trial Essex's chief and most ruthless prosecutor, Bacon insisted that Merrick had "procured" *Richard II* to be played before the Essex faction, "so earnest he was to satisfy his eyes with the sight of that tragedy which he thought soon after his lord should bring from the stage to the state, but that God turned it upon their own heads".

All decisions ultimately were taken by the Queen and reflected her feelings, which were often as wide-ranging and universal as that of her leading playwright. And she had grown thoroughly tired of persecution. The torture of the religious poet, Robert Southwell, by Topcliffe at his Westminster home had induced revulsion at her servants' methods, and they now knew she was just as likely to turn on them as support them. Sick with despair and anger, she had rounded on her Council: if Protestants wanted to convert Catholics, let them do so by the example of their own lives, she cried out, "For I will persecute no more as I have done".

In an act of public forgiveness Shakespeare and his troupe were bidden to play at Whitehall again for the Queen on Shrove Tuesday, 24 February 1601, the night before Essex was executed (wearing a scarlet waistcoat) in a Tower courtyard, while his old enemy,

Raleigh, stood watching from a window. This was only sixteen days after the uprising. The Chamberlain's Men could not have felt too cheerful: Southampton lay under sentence of death in another corner of the Tower. Some speculate that the company revived *A Midsummer Night's Dream*. If so, the fairy magic stuck in their throats, as did the compliments to their sovereign. Outside, the people in the streets soon would sing, in a bitter and mournful minor key, a setting of "Greensleeves": "our jewell is from us gone, / The valiant knight of chivalry."

There were further parallels to the succession plot in *Hamlet*: Shakespeare casting the universal net of a story, and tugging on the right strands, could gather in contemporary attention as well as universal application. Hamlet's family background was remarkably similar to that of James VI of Scotland, the successor Essex supported, in one horrifying detail. Thirty-four years before, James's father, the weak and promiscuous Lord Darnley, husband of Mary Queen of Scots, just after the baptism of his son with full Catholic ceremonial, was strangled at Kirk-o'-Field in a house which was then blown up with gunpowder. The Scottish lords accused the Queen's lover, James Bothwell, of having instigated the crime, and the Queen of being his accomplice. Whatever the truth of the allegations – and Bothwell was subsequently "cleansed" of them and married the Queen with Protestant rites – the enigmatic murder, dark as the inside of a black cat, and subsequent (rushed) marriage lurked in the public consciousness, establishing Mary's depravity in the eyes of subsequent generations.

Gertrude could serve, then, both as Elizabeth and her "half-sister". Here was yet another family story, disguised in a Danish respectability of distance from Elizabeth's affairs, atmospherically dressed in the rotting damp and diseased political body of Ireland, that bog-ridden and misty land of ghosts, which Shakespeare appropriated for local colour, and festering with all the suspicion and self-fulfilling paranoia of the Elizabethan court which had just lived through, and purged itself of, the Essex plot. As Polonius advises the informer, only too well known to an Elizabethan audience, to spy on his son Laertes:

> See you now,
> Your bait of falsehood takes this carp of truth;
> And thus do we of wisdom and of reach
> With windlasses and with assays of bias
> By indirections find directions out.

Essex himself had been a protégé and pupil of Lord Burghley, on whom Shakespeare, now Burghley was dead, could safely base the character of Polonius: no doubt the school formed by the elder Cecil was not only a training in etiquette, but was also a college for Machiavellian self-advancement, and many of the distortions of the Essex character might well be attributed to his early mentor, on whose employer, perhaps with poetic justice, they rebounded. Yet had Essex taken Burghley's advice on Queen Elizabeth – "Conquer her by yielding" – there might have been no play by Shakespeare, or at least a very different one.

But it is significant, if one is looking for symbols rather than sources, that Hamlet should have killed, revenged himself on, Polonius for his "treachery", for the feud between the old Cecil and Essex was an important factor in the Earl's wounded pride. "Bloody and deceitful men shall not live out half their days," Burghley had warned Essex, silently pointing out this passage in the Book of Common Prayer. Although Shakespeare had selected the right story, with local as well as universal reverberations, he made no conscious allusion to its relevance to his own troubled times.

Interestingly enough, all discussion of why the succession did not automatically go to Hamlet after his father's murder was omitted from the play: Shakespeare presumably did not want to fuel any discussion which might prove to his disadvantage. As virtually the official dramatic mouthpiece of the court, he was the opposite of provocative, which is not to say he did not have his own opinions and did not show individuals – under heavy disguise – as they actually were. It was safe, several years after the old man's death, to paint an affectionate although generalized portrait of the elder Cecil. If Laertes' unexpected arrival home echoes Essex a little too closely, Shakespeare covered himself by having Claudius respond to the threat with courage, and with the unshakeable court line:

> There's such divinity doth hedge a king
> That treason can but peep to what it would,
> Acts little of his will.

Apart from reflecting the gloom and indecision of Elizabeth's later years, *Hamlet* abounds in topical remarks about the acting conditions prevailing in Elizabethan playhouses. In the form in which it has come down to us, the play was apparently written for an audience very different from that for *Julius Caesar* and *Henry V.* The populist element in the writing receded, and a witty, intellectual allusiveness was to the fore: Shakespeare was writing for the informed Inns of Court audience. It is a tribute to the Elizabethan age that such a complete, many-layered and many-sided play should, on its own merits as a piece of entertainment, have become so popular. It pleased, according to Gabriel Harvey, "the wiser sort", and as well as being much played in London, stormed the university wits' strongholds of Oxford and Cambridge, and quickly appeared in quarto editions.

Part of *Hamlet*'s popularity was that it, like *Doctor Faustus*, balanced precariously and yet brilliantly on the border between the assertion of divine will, the exercise of grace, and man's own assertion of himself. It projected a specific reflection of the glory of that age of man both as the beauty of the world and the quintessence of dust.

# A TROUBLED MIND

# Whole men sick

Shakespeare had written his greatest play to date. It is doubtful, today, whether such a complex work would pass a preliminary script-reader's eye. Certainly no play with such masterful many-sidedness would have found its way on to the stage without being drastically simplified in its wordiness and wilful obscurities, and having its meandering plot straightened out. *Hamlet* is not by any means a perfect tragedy, and certainly not a tragedy in the Aristotelian sense, for Hamlet has no flaw which causes his own downfall. It is a tragedy of wasted human growth, but the play is about growth, not destruction, about goodness, and not really about evil, although the background and circumstances of Hamlet's life are poisoned by crime. Claudius and Gertrude are much nearer the tragic characters which Shakespeare would experiment with in the great tragedies that followed – people of passion and power whose inflexibility, faults or blindness stop or impede their growth so that they become incapable, stripped of the power of free will, acquiesce in their fate: people who display hubris in the face of the divine or natural order.

Shakespeare, in writing *Hamlet*, had also written his most personal and autobiographical play, had faced, in heavy disguise, his own faults and conflicts, proved, through Hamlet's capacity for change and growth, that he was capable of these. By the end of the play Hamlet has found himself. Shakespeare, too, had come to terms with himself: with the onset of middle age, the pain inflicted on him by his parents, the grief of his less than happy marriage and with the tragic loss of the thing that had mattered supremely to this sensitive and fatherly man – his only son.

The self-confrontation and self-examination begun with *Hamlet* was, for Shakespeare, to intensify. In his early years pain had been unwittingly inflicted on him: pain which, in this most indirect of authors, had found its most direct expression in *Hamlet*. Yet until the age of eleven or twelve – or when he was roughly the age at which Hamnet had died – nothing had impeded the wholeness of his developing vision. Although he had grown up without detectable mental illness, character deformation, or – what he might have suffered in later childhood – any marked neurosis, many late-twentieth-century authorities and theatrical practitioners still attribute an extreme nature to him. Peter Hall says, "I think he would have been a lunatic if he had not been a genius." Trevor Nunn believes that regardless of how he spoke and looked, an uncomfortable electricity would have come off him, "which in your contact with him could lead you to think you had made a fool of yourself and inadequately represented yourself". Nunn senses a dissatisfied person, dissatisfied in appetite and quite scathing: "There would be signs of extremely mentally disturbed behaviour – of an obsession with these uncharted areas". "Yes," Hugh Kingsmill has his Shakespeare observe of himself, "most certainly a vein of malice".

Medical opinion, as well as a fair body of criticism, not to mention the man in the street, holds the opposite view: the psychiatrist Aubrey Lewis comments that surmises and diagnoses of an unbalanced Shakespeare are unwarranted. "The little we know for sure about Shakespeare's way of life, his steady activities, his attention to business, and how he seemed to his contemporaries – all this speaks strongly against the assumption of instability and mental illness". The mathematician and broadcaster J. Bronowski agrees: "Like Goethe he was always contented in his environment. There is a sense that whatever goes on finds him at home".

The agreeable, untormented Shakespeare is an attractive figure: he "loved to lie in bed all day for his ease, and sit up all night for his pleasure." Jonson after Shakespeare's death dramatized in *The New Inn* a self-idealization of the playwright in the person of the Host, Goodstock (the Lord Frampul in disguise): but Goodstock is affable, proprietorial, as we imagine Shakespeare, he is not a freelance man of letters, like Jonson abandoning his wife, then returning to her, embracing Roman Catholicism, then renouncing it and informing on recusants. Goodstock's Inn is the sign of the Light Heart: "A heart weighed with a feather, and outweighed too". He chooses an inn – a trade, like being one of a common cry of players. Jonson's representation of Goodstock may be the nearest we have, as a retrospective tribute, to the fulfilled, mid-life playwright.

Shakespeare's sense of balance was rare for the time, especially among those who had aspirations to gentility, or who wanted to achieve literary celebrity. Hamlet (incognito) enquires of the grave-digger why the young Hamlet was sent into England and receives the answer, "Why, because a was mad. A shall recover his wits there, or if a do not, 'tis no great matter there." "Why?" asks Hamlet. "'Twill not be seen in him there. There the men are as mad as he."

This was not only a joke. England was in the new century still a land of confused signals and contradictory principles, in many respects a mad world. "How is it that the clouds still hang on you?" asks Claudius. Conventional and hypocritical middle-class Anglican theology encrusts the surface of *Hamlet*, but the instinctive feelings of the old faith of Catholicism bubble and seethe below, like a hot spring ready to heal, but also to burn and scald.

Biblical and liturgical echoes abound. "She should in ground unsanctified have lodged / Till the last trumpet", says the Priest at Ophelia's privileged funeral (Corinthians 15:52 in the Geneva Bible reads, "At the last trumpet: for the trumpet shall blowe, and the dead shall be raised up" – in specific contrast to all other English versions of the Bible, which have "trump"). "Like the palm should flourish", as Hamlet describes the relations between Denmark and England, also echoes the Geneva Bible, "The righteous shall flourish like a palm tree". Matthew's observation, "Are not two sparrows sold for a farthing, and one of them shall not fall on the ground without your Father?" becomes Hamlet's, "There's a special providence in the fall of a sparrow"; while Hamlet's ruminations on suicide,

> But that the dread of something after death,
> The undiscovered country from whose bourn
> No traveller returns . . .

reflect again his favourite reading, Job: "Before I go and shall not return, even to the land of darkness and shadow of death: into a land . . . dark as darkness itself."

Do we read Shakespeare's submerged mind correctly in *Hamlet*, and report his cause aright, by finding in it the stored-up mourning for Hamnet, Hamlet's name a variant on his and also in Danish a variant of the word for home, similar to the German *Heimat*? The beginning scene of the play revolves round Hamlet mourning for his dead father, yet he refuses also to mourn, because it is the shadow of his dead father which is denying him life and identity; it is a huge barrier of grief which lies in his way until he can clear up its cause and its purpose, and its justification. Deep in Hamlet's inner psyche – and that of his creator – is an eldest son rebuking his mother for remaining with a husband who has let her down, who has brought disgrace upon the family, who has imposed upon a young adolescent the strain of keeping up appearances, taxing his vulnerable self with trying to remain whole and respectable, yet aware of a crime, a darkness in his family psyche. From this came much of Shakespeare's own need to hide himself away in characters, to act out again and again in many different guises the pain and the shame. From this also stemmed his hatred of vanity, of the outward false-seeming: he had stood up to the blow, suffered the sense of shame, and his life had given him a succession of further blows to prolong, recreate and echo this early pain, stretching in him the power to stand outside the painful emotions, record them while suffering them. Auden uses as epigraph to *The Double Man* Montaigne's statement, "We are, I know not how, double in ourselves, so that what we believe we disbelieve, and cannot rid ourselves of what we condemn."

Shakespeare in *Hamlet* is taunted by his sense of separation from himself, by his lack of wholeness. It is the basic predicament of the actor, denied being himself and forced, to make his living, to adopt roles with which, often, his inner feelings do not accord. Don't be ashamed to "show", Hamlet wickedly suggests to Ophelia, with a sexual innuendo – that is, to display yourself, then the player will not "shame to tell you what it means". Ben Jonson once used "show" with even more explicitness when he told Drummond of Hawthornden he "lay diverse times with a woman, who shew him all that he wishes except the last act, which she never would agree unto." I could interpret between "you and your love", Hamlet tells Ophelia, again sexually aroused, "if I could see the puppets dallying" – in other words if he could see his mother in bed with his uncle. Denied justice of the spirit, increasingly distorted into the narrow male and Calvinist ethos of puritanism and money-making, the fouled-up, murky land of England has forced its active, brilliant, intelligent young men into false identities, into becoming actors to survive, burdened with inner realities which bear no relation to the ugly and decadent outer world, and therefore trapped, explosive, mad.

Hamlet is an emergency self, a provisional persona. It is not surprising that some actors have felt nearly, if not entirely, overwhelmed by the difficulties the part presents to them: Alec Guinness

says he used to feel sick with apprehension before every performance. *Hamlet* is as much "variations on the theme of Hamlet as a
single work". It challenges above all the actor's power of inte-
gration. Guinness imagines Burbage asking Shakespeare, at a break
during rehearsal: "How can I rehearse this part? Hamlet exhibits a
different personality in each act. The part does not add up." And
Shakespeare replying, "No, I don't mean it to. Think of each act as
a different play."

Daniel Day-Lewis had a breakdown performing in Richard
Eyre's National Theatre production in London. His successor, Ian
Charleson, died of Aids. For all actors are essentially Hamlets and
to play the role, if one is to do so sensitively, is to confront and
reveal one's own vulnerability and helplessness. The last words the
famous interpreter, Ernest Milton, was reported as saying were,
"Hamlet, I knew the man – you will remember that."

Paradoxically, and with his usual flamboyance of antithesis, in
the character of greatest spirit and nobility he drew Shakespeare
exhibits his greatest sense of affinity with the actor – at the same
time his closeness to the "free" vagabond spirit. Hamlet compares
himself to a rogue and peasant slave, he talks to the Player King in
just the informal tones Shakespeare himself must have used to a
colleague at the Globe: "You could for a need study a speech of
some dozen or sixteen lines..." His advice to the Players on
realistic moderation shows the distance Shakespeare himself felt
from the showy bombastic style that held sway at the time.

Half of the double self Shakespeare reveals in *Hamlet* is the actor.
"Every day", writes Simon Callow, of the rehearsals for his one-
man feat of performing all the Sonnets, "we seemed to come closer
to the greatest dramatist in the world, who was also one of the
greatest enigmas." Callow finds in the Sonnets that incompleteness
of being which is shared with Hamlet. The difference is that in the
Sonnets it is not turned mostly upon oneself (although sometimes),
it is turned mostly upon an object of love or admiration: Callow
calls this the "idolizing, self-denigrating enslavement to one who
embodies everything one feels oneself not to be". His experience
of performing the Sonnets brought him close to the essence of
Shakespeare the man: "I felt that I knew him; and I knew what he
was, in the root of his being: he was an actor."

# Double blessing

In *Hamlet* Shakespeare had brought back to life his lost son, Hamnet. In *Twelfth Night*, in his concealed allegorical manner, he broached again in glittering terms the subject of his own twins, concentrating almost wholly on the girl and boy bond; that is the living quick of this play, although Sebastian, perhaps because of the undue concentration upon the Hamnet figure in *Hamlet*, is not as centrally important as his sister to the play's relationships. Viola stands in for them both, playing her brother as well as herself. In such a way had Shakespeare, when very young, found himself standing in for his dead sisters: in such a way, since Hamnet's death, had Judith stood in for Hamnet.

*Twelfth Night* shows the constancy of the bond of twins in the face of the fickle, transient passions of the lovers: that he substituted this pair for the brother and sister of his Sienese source, *Gl'Ingannati* (The Deceived), reveals how naturally and instinctively Shakespeare tightened the knot of any dramatic complexity, at the same time drawing on his own life. It is as if the waters of the womb are being broken in the extraordinary speech in which Sebastian describes to Antonio both his own and Viola's birth, and her supposed death by water. Sebastian speaks of his father leaving behind him . . .

> myself and a sister, both born in an hour. If the heavens had been pleased, would we had so ended. But you, sir, altered that, for some hour before you took me from the breach of the sea was my sister drowned.

Sebastian's rescue is conceived by Shakespeare as a birth, with Antonio the midwife: indeed owing to the arrangement, often, of twins in their mother's womb the first is in a position for what is known as a "breech birth", when the child's limbs and body, as opposed to its head, emerge first.

Sexuality, in Shakespeare's mind, extended to the differentiation

– 204 –

taking place in the womb as well as to the sexually charged act of birth: womb and tomb go together. In both *The Comedy of Errors* and *Twelfth Night* the quest for a lost twin of a pair dominates the action: mysteriously and potently the poet wrapped this in a suggestion of amniotic fluid: "I to the world am like a drop of water, / That in the ocean seeks another drop . . ." A lost sibling is irreplaceable. Viola's feelings often echo those of Sophocles' Antigone:

> One husband gone I might have found another
> Or a child from a new man in the first child's place
> But with my parents hid away in death,
> No brother ever could spring up for me.

But to lose a *twin* sibling is to lose a central creative bond of life. Shakespeare could see that his daughter Judith, now sixteen, was struggling with the difficulty of forming relationships to substitute for that which she had lost with her brother. Who knew what grief lay buried and unexpressed inside her? Had not her father often thought of replacing Hamnet with another son or daughter: but, by now, by the early part of the seventeenth century, that possibility was well and truly past.

Leslie Hotson, so illuminating on Marlowe's death, loses his way somewhat in the majestic and intricate reconstruction he makes of the first night of *Twelfth Night*, which he would like to believe happened at Christmas 1600 in the Great Banqueting Hall of the Palace of Whitehall. Hotson is sure this play was specially commissioned by the court on the occasion of the visit to London of Duke Virginio Orsino, special envoy of the Florentine Duke Bracciano, and that Shakespeare wrote the play in a few days after Duke Orsino's arrival, retaining his name for the main character, so that it could be played in his presence.

Hotson also has Shakespeare "block" *Twelfth Night* into the particular dimensions of the hall, so that when Fabian says to Sir Toby, "You are now sailed into the north of my lady's opinion", he means specifically the north–south lines of this well-documented Whitehall "meridian", or Noon Hall as it was called (the word "meridian" too occurs only in the play). When Feste tells Malvolio that the "dark house" has "bay windows transparent as barricadoes, and the clerestories toward the south–north are as lustrous as ebony", this means the clerestories and bay windows were jammed with hangings to keep out the light – a joke which Shakespeare might well have based on performance in such a hall, or recalling a visit he had made to the Banqueting Hall itself (Shakespeare could fill out details in plays with what he had last seen and had at the forefront of his mind: and he might, the night before he wrote this, have been at the Banqueting Hall). Or, it might have found its way into the text later from being played at Westminster.

But it is unlikely – and more insulting than flattering – that Shakespeare should have used the name Orsino for a performance given before this distinguished visitor, whom the Queen, although now a declining shadow of her former zestful self, was wooing not only diplomatically but also in person. It would have been a betrayal of the characteristically tactful and many-layered way in which Shakespeare's mind worked. What is more possible is that Shakespeare's invention picked up the name subsequent to the visit, recalled it some months later, and embroidered on the by then romantic figure of Elizabeth's last continental conquest (though never by now a possible match). During Virginio Orsino's visits she had given a last performance of her dazzling seductive powers, even dancing spiritedly, providing the Duke with much intimate attention, so that he could write to his wife of his personal reception by the Queen in her own room.

Anyway, as the Duke says, he knew no English (he was relieved to find that most of Elizabeth's courtiers could speak "Italian, many French, and some, Spanish"), and they would hardly have made him suffer a play in a language he did not know, and at that time of little importance in the civilized world. Keen though the English were on the English language, no one else in the world spoke it. In order to forestall the oblivion he dreaded, the passionless, pusillanimous Francis Bacon translated his works into Latin (or composed them directly in Latin): "these modern languages will at one time play the bankrupt with books," he complained. (Posterity had its revenge, and so did the English language, on Bacon's Latin works.)

Shakespeare knew that the Globe's hunger for new plays was greater than that of the court. In the same year in which he wrote *Hamlet*, he marked time with this bitter-sweet comedy which re-evoked the lost world of his happy comedies. Yet he injected into that lost world some of the darkness of his new and happier realization that pain – that suffering grief – could be continually embraced. No longer did this need to be escaped, indulged or wallowed in.

Having faced so much stress or psychological reality in writing *Hamlet*, Shakespeare slackened in *Twelfth Night* into a more relaxed mood of toying with unreality. Orsino is in an unreal mood of love-sick emotion; Olivia's unreal mood is one of mourning for her brother; Malvolio's of self-importance.

*Twelfth Night, or What You Will*, the only one of Shakespeare's plays besides *Henry VIII* to have an alternative title, has many "in" jokes and literary allusions to the continuing rivalry among the playwrights. The alternative title is that of John Marston's play which had been part of the public slanging match between Jonson and Marston: Shakespeare was deliberately linking his comedy to the earlier lampoon of Jonson in *What You Will* as Lampatho Doria, an uncouth *arriviste* who competes with a nobleman for a highborn lady's love. Both based on the popular *Gl'Ingannati*, the two plays have similar main plots – Olivia pursued by the Duke Orsino, in the case of *Twelfth Night*; and subplots – Toby Belch and his crew "setting up" Malvolio in his wooing of Olivia.

Ben Jonson was twenty-nine when *Twelfth Night* was given a convincingly documented, although not necessarily first, performance at the Middle Temple on 2 February 1602, in a new hall with an impressively carved ceiling. The Cambridge undergraduate authors of *The Return from Parnassus* Part 2 – a skit, in *Footlights* style, for the tradition of Cambridge satire was even then prevalent – had "Will Kempe" observe that "our fellow Shakespeare" had given Jonson "a purge that made him beray his credit" – taken to be a reference to Shakespeare's depiction of Jonson as Malvolio in *Twelfth Night*.

Jonson was thin-skinned like Malvolio, easy to rise to offence ("To be generous, guiltless, and of free disposition is to take those things for birdbolts that you deem cannon bullets"); Shakespeare aimed other jokes at Jonson for his coterie audience – mainly through Feste the clown, who is endowed with the wordy mock-solemnity of Marston, and some of his dark and malevolent humour (Armin, who had a good singing voice, having taken on Kempe's uncouth clown habit, transformed this recurrent Shakespeare role-model into a fascinating, ambiguous sophisticate who released the dark and watchful vein in Shakespeare's make-up). Feste and Malvolio battle away, and the "madly used" Malvolio is incarcerated, subjected to merciless philosophical and satirical cross-examination by Feste disguised as a cleric. To us it is cruel, but to the Middle Temple it was Jonson being subjected to the gull treatment he doled out to characters in his own plays: also – with cruelty both in pleasure and the ordering of society so taken for granted – the abuse of Malvolio had more the weight of farce than of gratuitous punishment.

The diary of a young lawyer, John Manningham, records a scrap of gossip of the time about Richard Burbage and Shakespeare: when Burbage played Richard III so successfully he arranged a secret meeting somewhere in Bishopsgate with a citizen's wife; hearing of this, Shakespeare arrived first at the lady's house, and when Burbage turned up, saying "Richard III was at the door", sent down word that "William the Conqueror came before Richard the Third." (Manningham, to make sure no one misunderstood his story, adds that Shakespeare's Christian name was William.)

William the Conqueror's reputation in that department had been publicly enhanced by his depiction as Prickshaft in *Satiromastix*. But Shakespeare the playwright, as opposed to the man, had a multiple nature, conscious of contrary moods that had to be allowed, of doubt and of contradictions of feeling, which he could now handle with such ease, in following through a story line, that narrative and character were fused with elemental naturalness. In *Twelfth Night*, when Malvolio delivers Olivia's ring to Viola, on the pretext that he is returning it to her, she responds, while picking up the ring, that she left no ring with her. Recognizing with alarm that Olivia has fallen in love with her, she comments:

> ... The cunning of her passion
> Invites me in this churlish messenger ...
> Poor lady, she were better love a dream!
> Disguise, I see thou art a wickedness
> Wherein the pregnant enemy does much.
> How easy is it for the proper false
> In women's waxen hearts to set their forms!
> Alas, our frailty is the cause, not we,
> For such as we are made of, such we be.

Viola sketches out the plot, acts it, and expresses her feelings all in one:

> ... My master loves her dearly,
> And I, poor monster, fond as much on him,

> And she, mistaken, seems to dote on me.
> What will become of this? As I am man,
> My state is desperate for my master's love.
> As I am woman, now, alas the day,
> What thriftless sighs shall poor Olivia breathe!

She passes judgement as dramatic critic: "O time, thou must untangle this, not I. / It is too hard a knot for me t'untie." Disguise, ambiguity, is at the centre of this moving sense of confusion.

In *Twelfth Night* the quality of the lyrics, endlessly set to music in later years, showed Shakespeare's response to the exceptional interpreter and musician as well as clown, Robert Armin. Feste's three great songs, "Come away, come away death", "O mistress mine", and "When that I was and a little tiny boy", surpassed in quality most that he had written before. Far from the thin, hermaphrodite pathos of Ophelia's last lament, in these songs Shakespeare yet again practised his uncanny knack of capitalizing on the talent available to him.

Music had from the start been an integral part of his sensibility; it functioned in multiple ways, as stage music for banquets and duels, battles and serenades; it established the atmosphere for miraculous or supernatural events, it provided the source for hundreds of brain coinages, from basic synonyms and metaphors for character or mood to the most cosmic and speculative of images. Underlying much of the textual use of musical sounds and instruments – in which Shakespeare delighted, being blessed with the most phenomenal knowledge, instinct and taste for such details – were displays of classical antithesis derived from the ancient world: from musical contests between Apollo's silver strings and Pan's rustic pipes, the sublime and the earthy, the music of the spheres and the discordant ill-tuned harshness of man's tragic or discordant nature. Music always had power for good: says Benedick in *Much Ado About Nothing*, of the song "Sigh no more ladies", "Is it not strange that sheep's guts should hale souls out of men's bodies?" "He hears no music," says Caesar of the spare and unsmiling Cassius. Villains and non-musicians were often one and the same; Guildenstern denies knowledge of music, saying to Hamlet: "I know no touch of it". "The man that hath no music in himself", says Lorenzo,

> Nor is not moved with concord of sweet sounds
> Is fit for treasons, stratagems, and spoils.

The motions of his spirit are dull as night,
And his affections dark as Erebus.

Shakespeare conceived music as the food of love, as well as a simile for its operation: "That strain again," says the Duke Orsino,

it had a dying fall.
O, it came o'er my ear like the sweet sound
That breathes upon a bank of violets,
Stealing and giving odour.

Like Mozart, Shakespeare cut his musical cloth according to the talents available to him: he wrote lyrics for a hundred songs, not always for the best of interpreters, so sometimes he issued a disclaimer. In *As You Like It* Touchstone says of the Pages' song, "It was a lover and his lass" – "the note was very untunable", and when they remonstrate with him, adds, "God mend your voices". The farcical pinching-song in *The Merry Wives of Windsor* has lyrics that were designed for clod-hopping amateur fairies. Shakespeare's grasp of the practicalities of stage music had its own highly professional evolution: as Guy Woolfenden, Stratford's musical director, attests, "The placing of music, time after time, is absolutely perfect: songs just have to happen where they do."

# A sense of limit

i

The year 1601 was also that of publication of the enigmatic but perfect lyrical poem, "The Phoenix and the Turtle", which Shakespeare either wrote some fifteen years before, or for which he drew on earlier circumstances as inspiration. It appeared in a collection called *Love's Martyr*, commemorating the marriage of Sir John Salusbury to Ursula Stanley, illegitimate daughter of the fourth Earl of Derby. The collection was made by Salusbury's friend Robert Chester, known to Shakespeare from his early years perhaps spent in the Lancashire Hoghton household. Salusbury's brother Thomas had been executed for his part in the Walsingham-fabricated

Babington plot and his severed head put on display in London. It was in the aftermath of this grisly event that Salusbury and Ursula married, and he was therefore in the state of dejection in which the Phoenix finds the turtle dove.

Salusbury, grieving apart, was a pugnacious and colourful character who may well have reminded Shakespeare of his own father, for he soon went into considerable debt and disgrace. The poem, the only occasional piece known to have been written by Shakespeare, was a good-natured gesture of friendship. There is a mystery in the phrase "married chastity" of line 61, as the couple did have children; but Shakespeare in "The Phoenix and the Turtle" was not going to be circumscribed by a specific context. The poem no doubt had its genesis in death, treachery, conspiracy and grief, but ultimately it is condensed and allusive, as if Shakespeare had been listening to the new poetical tunes of the Metaphysical poets, and wanted to make his own token experiment in this direction.

"The Phoenix and the Turtle" is a glancing, almost abstract distillation of the nature of self-hood in love:

> So they loved as love in twain
> Had the essence but in one,
> Two distincts, division none.
> Number there in love was slain.
>
> Hearts remote yet not asunder,
> Distance and no space was seen
> 'Twixt this turtle and his queen . . .
>
> Reason, in itself confounded,
> Saw division grow together
> To themselves, yet either neither,
> Simple were so well compounded . . .

Shakespeare was probably surreptitiously preening himself, beholding himself in a glass, wearing a headband of Metaphysical feathers. Donne's "Extasy" was at this time circulating in the Inns of Court, although not printed until 1635:

> But as all several souls containe
> Mixture of things, they know not what,
> Love, these mixed souls, doth mix again,
> And makes both one, each this and that.

Shakespeare was still attached to the old Essex circle in the early years of the seventeenth century. Elizabeth was lonely in old age, with a failing memory and a troubled conscience. The character disorders she had been keeping at bay with royal privilege and instantaneity of command over the destiny of others came creeping out of their dark corners. She now no longer had ministers of grace to defend her, or other legitimate channels for her "thralled discontent". Leicester had gone in the years of the Armada, Warwick and Walsingham in 1590, Shrewsbury and Hatton a year later, Hunsden the Lord Chamberlain in 1596, and – most missed of all, the Polonius of the court – Burghley, who used to advise young courtiers to "overcome [the queen] with yielding", in 1598. "She walks much in her Chamber," wrote Harington of her deteriorating behaviour in late 1600: "and stamps with her feet at ill news, and thrusts her rusty sword at times into the arras in great rage . . . so disordered is all order that her Highness hath worn but one change of raiment for many days."

She refused consolations of religion, sending away in fury her professional divines, headed by Canterbury, who had carved out for themselves great careers in the Church. She saw a hideous vision of her "own body, exceeding lean and fearful in a light of fire". Essex still troubled her and when at Christmas 1601 Harington again visited the Queen and she asked him if he had seen Tyrone, to which Harington replied that he had last seen him in Ireland with the Lord Deputy (i.e. Essex), she looked up "with grief and choler in her countenance".

"Oh yes," she told Harington, "now it mindeth me that you was one who saw this man elsewhere." The head of the Church complained of Lord Knollys who had tried, intimating it smacked of popery, to have the crucifix smashed that she kept in her own private chapel. Would they deny her the consolation of Jesus, substituting a bare Protestant cross? What more was she now than "an old perjured woman, dying without comfort? It had been a life of tumultuous drama, and it was ending, now, in silence."

The Queen moved from Whitehall to Richmond early in 1603 to escape the foul contagious vapours of the Thames. In Richmond she commanded that the ring, which symbolized her marriage to England, should be filed and taken off her finger. It had become too deeply embedded in her flesh for her comfort.

She died on 24 March 1603 without speaking. Three days and three nights she had sat upright in a chair, too frightened to be put to bed, sucking her thumb like an infant. Canterbury returned to her in the end; a movement of her hand was acknowledged by her ladies-in-waiting as consent to his presence:

Consider the tears of Richmond this night, and the joys of London, at this place, at this time, in the morning; and we shall find prophecy even in that saying of the poet, *Nocte pluit tota*, showers of rain all night, of weeping for our sovereign. And we would not be comforted, because she was not.

So did St Paul's Dean, John Donne, sermonize fourteen years after the event, trumpeting the High Anglican sentiment with his Establishment voice:

In the death of that Queen, unmatchable, inimitable in her sex; that Queen, worthy, I will not say of Nestor's years, I will not say of Methusalem's, but worthy of Adam's years, if Adam had never fallen; in her death we were all under one common flood, and depth of tears.

It was hardly very convincing. She died £400,000 in debt.

One person who was assuredly not swayed by such feeling was Southampton. Shakespeare had trod the circular stairs to the room in Bell Tower where, ironically enough, the Queen herself had been imprisoned in 1554, aged twenty-one, when she was suspected of plotting against Mary. In prison Southampton had suffered periodic attacks of the "quartern ague", but he at least had two rooms, a withdrawing chamber with a gallery window of cracked, diamond-shaped panes, and a bedchamber, and could receive visitors.

How Shakespeare would have encountered him is conveyed by the well-known portrait of the Earl in his Tower lodging, where he kept a pert, bright-eyed black and white cat to keep the rats at bay. "There is the familiar long countenance," his biographer wrote, "with the grey-blue eyes and arched eyebrows, looking paler and sadder now. The fair moustache has grown, though the beard is still only beginning; the long locks fall down on both shoulders." Southampton wears a dark cloak, in whose fold his left arm is shown resting: "The right hand, gloved, carries the other glove, both embroidered with love-knots."

They discussed plots and treason. Shakespeare had set so many scenes of his plays in or around the Tower, that a visit there sent many *frissons* along his spine and awoke voices proclaiming the hardship of prisons, or the imminent presence of death (or its unexpected enactment). Even so one imagines he smiled to himself on his own remarkable survival – and he and Southampton even shared a joke together in the prospect of better times ahead. The Queen had departed:

Not mine own fears nor the prophetic soul
Of the wide world dreaming on things to come
Can yet the lease of my true love control,
Supposed as forfeit to a confined doom.
The mortal moon hath her eclipse endured,
And the sad augurs mock their own presage . . .

Southampton had already, before Elizabeth's death, negotiated his own release with King James of Scotland: James's last action before leaving Holyrood was to authorize this release. Only three weeks after that extraordinary eclipse Shakespeare's old patron was set at large:

Incertainties now crown themselves assured,
And peace proclaims olives of endless age.
Now with the drops of this most balmy time

– and here Shakespeare is indicating the time with precision, as this means the anointing of the new King of England –

My love looks fresh, and death to me subscribes,
Since spite of him, I'll live in this poor rhyme,
While he insults o'er dull and speechless tribes.

By this time, as Sonnet 107 only too confidently proclaims, Southampton's golden husk of promise had fallen away. Indeed his muddled and ambiguous role in the Essex plot, his immaturity during the Irish campaign, model for the homosexual dalliance between Hector and Patroclus in *Troilus and Cressida*, had shown how acutely Shakespeare spotted the early flaws in his personality: indecisiveness, self-cocooning, narcissism, and a spoilt and childish obstinacy. Yet some affection remained.

Southampton revived *Love's Labour's Lost*, his favourite play and written for his patronage, for the new King in 1604, so that James and Anne could be entertained. "This is appointed to be played tomorrow night," wrote Sir Walter Cope to Robert Cecil, now Lord Cranbourne: "unless you send a writ to remove the *corpus cum causa* to your house in the Strand. Burbage is my messenger, ready attending your pleasure."

## ii

*Troilus and Cressida*, entered in the Stationers' Register of 7 February 1603, was most likely the last play Shakespeare wrote in Elizabeth's reign and saw performed before her death six weeks later. The editor who printed it in 1609 claimed that it had "never been staled with the stage, never clapper-clawed with the palms of the vulgar", so like Jonson's *The New Inn* (1629) it was unpopular and little played.

*Troilus and Cressida* is a play of dire mental confusion, involved, bitter and irritated in mood, often appearing to be the "arts and scraps" and "greasy relics" left over from *Hamlet*. Fragmented in feeling, it appeals to present-day literary sensibility, which sees in its cynicism and sense of dislocation, powerfully and bitterly expressed, a truer image of the human condition than more optimistic aspiration (as Michael Holroyd points out, "All Shakespearian criticism is a form of autobiography"). At the time and in spite of its huge set-piece fight between Hector and Ajax, it failed on the Blackfriars stage, where its often Shavian tone, its *louche* appeal through the diseased and sexually distorted underside of Elizabethan life, did not attract much following.

It is hard to know exactly on whom Shakespeare wished to focus. The Globe actors had been cleared of complicity in the Essex plot, but Shakespeare and his company had remained uneasy, so he wrote the great artificial debate between Ulysses and his fellow Greeks at Troy, on the necessity of order, to make the company's position unimpeachable. That Shakespeare felt the truth of Ulysses' philosophy was incidental to his function as a mouthpiece of Elizabethan propaganda: his appeal is to everyone to remain calm when Elizabeth dies: "So many hollow factions", exclaims the wily Greek of his own armies. This long and undramatic scene, written to please the authorities, is reminiscent of an equally long scene in *Henry V* when the Archbishop of Canterbury justifies Henry's right to the English throne, but it has even less dramatic weight. The writing is fine but irrelevant, and could easily be cut:

> The heavens themselves, the planets, and this centre
> Observe degree, priority, and place ...
> Take but degree away, untune that string,
> And hark what discord follows ...
>                               The bounded waters
> Should lift their bosoms higher than the shores ...
> Strength should be lord of imbecility,
> And the rude son should strike his father dead ...
> Then everything includes itself in power,
> Power into will, will into appetite;

> And appetite, an universal wolf
> So doubly seconded with will and power,
> Must make perforce an universal prey,
> And last eat up himself.

Much of this, on which he expanded, Shakespeare had paraphrased from Anglican homilies in the *Book of Homilies*, which originated under Cranmer and had been one of the most influential and widely circulated books during Elizabeth's lifetime. The quarrel between Ajax and Achilles, with Thersites' rasping sidelights on the nature of war, was driven by a more personal animus, still related to and harping on, the rivalry between poets. By now such parochialism had little appeal for audiences.

Shakespeare's father John had become in his older years a legendary figure – with his son by then a famous playwright: "merry cheeked ... good and honest", John could be seen in the shop in Henley Street where he practised his trade, still dressing and cutting his skins of soft white or light-coloured leather. In the autumn of 1601 he died in Stratford. Much imagery of disease, not only in *Troilus* but in *Hamlet* too, where the father–son preoccupation is central, is noticeable in Shakespeare's writing at this time. The disease imagery of *Troilus* largely revolves around syphilis, but "the pox" covered a host of degenerative symptoms of age and disease: rheumatic pains, fevers, dysentery, ague, painful susceptibility to coughs and colds – even Lord Essex, it has been suggested, suffered from Venus's curse.

Shakespeare did not, although his imagination was burdened with the possibility. Laurence Olivier seemingly prolonged his life by playing, in old age, innumerable death scenes; Shakespeare similarly, with the experience of *Hamlet* behind him, knew that to enact in words an evil or fear often purged it.

But with Thersites he went very far in his nausea with sex, not only issuing from Thersites' mouth but spreading throughout the play, especially into Pandarus. Shakespeare was returning in black, retrospective bitterness, not this time to his own adolescence, but to more recent incidents of betrayal. Still loyal to the idea of passionate love, he recognized in his deepest self that Troilus' love was not real love but self-deceptive passion, although none the less disturbing for that. He viewed it as a self-limiting fault, the very essence of the tragic figures that were now brewing up in his mind. The depiction of this passion was crucially necessary to the process of becoming objective about subjective states, never perhaps more exquisitely stated than by Troilus when he confronts Cressida's unfaithfulness to him:

This, she? No, this is Diomed's Cressida.
If beauty have a soul, this is not she.
If souls guide vows, if vows be sanctimonies,
If sanctimony be the gods' delight,
If there be rule in unity itself,
This is not she . . .
                    This is and is not Cressid.
Within my soul there doth conduce a fight
Of this strange nature, that a thing inseparate
Divides more wider than the sky and earth,
And yet the spacious breadth of this division
Admits no orifex for a point as subtle
As Ariachne's broken woof to enter.

By the end of the play Shakespeare had made it clear that Troilus never really loved – in the stronger and more lasting sense that he now knew love to consist of – false and beautiful Cressida. Troilus' passion was self-projection, a figment of his own being, a creation of his own need, and as such he was using her in an egotistical, utilitarian way – as much as she was using him. But the play remains an ungainly vehicle of self-expression, stuffed with difficult ideas and extreme poetic effects caused by muddy and swirling personal problems – sometimes self-indulgent in its psychotherapeutic outbursts, but essentially a work of transition. His thoughts pounded with preoccupations straight from the Sonnets:

ULYSSES:   A strange fellow here
          Writes me that man, how dearly ever parted,
          How much in having, or without or in,
          Cannot make boast to have that which he hath,
          Nor feels not what he owes, but by reflection –
          As when his virtues, shining upon others,
          Heat them, and they retort that heat again
          To the first givers.
ACHILLES:                      This is not strange, Ulysses.
          The beauty that is borne here in the face
          The bearer knows not, but commends itself
          To others' eyes. Nor doth the eye itself,
          That most pure spirit of sense, behold itself,
          Not going from itself; but eye to eye opposed

– 217 –

Salutes each other with each other's form.
For speculation turns not to itself
Till it hath travelled and is mirrored there
Where it may see itself. This is not strange at all.

ULYSSES:       I do not strain at the position –
It is familiar – but at the author's drift;
Who in his circumstance expressly proves
That no man is the lord of anything,
Though in and of him there be much consisting,
Till he communicate his parts to others.
Nor doth he of himself know them for aught
Till he behold them formèd in th'applause
Where they're extended – who, like an arch, reverb'rate
The voice again; or, like a gate of steel
Fronting the sun, receives and renders back
His figure and his heat.

Shakespeare had fought to discover – and successfully found – the limits of himself, testing these in love and life, and in practising his art. He meant here that he could dump on characters difficult feelings and dangerous areas of darkness which impede health and growth.

### iii

Reflecting the Elizabethan enforcement of morality from above, Shakespeare, in *All's Well That Ends Well*, imposed a dubious and rigid supposition on his married couple, Bertram and Helen, which suggested a very different love from that shown in *Troilus and Cressida*. The playwright, still experimenting his way through to the ultimate form he believed he could achieve, was further separating, in order to unravel and depict it, man's "will" or power of choice, from his powerful and yet more passive emotive and affective states (which from now on become increasingly forceful).

As shown early on, Helen is in charge of the plot, and as the play is meant as a comedy, with a happy ending lifting it ultimately above its dark undertones, reason had to rule. Although Helen would seem to be one in the line of steady and loving heroines, she overlooks some pretty unsalubrious elements in Bertram. What finally impresses her is his "conversion" to perceiving how good a person she is, transcending her poverty of blood and rank:

                                                    Good alone
    Is good, without a name; vileness is so:
    The property by what it is should go,
    Not by the title.

In theory *All's Well* is better than Shakespeare actually managed
to make it on the stage. He wrote it as an antidote to the cynicism
of *Troilus*, and also because, while abandoning the by now unsatis-
factory optimism of the early comedies, he wanted to uplift the
heart through a moral tale making the point that love – namely the
recognition and valuation of another person for his or her virtue
and goodness – was essentially different from lust. For a variety of
reasons, not least the chaste morals which Elizabeth personified in
her court, the Elizabethan public theatre never encouraged sexual
immorality. "My chastity's the jewel of our house", says Diana,
whom Bertram tries to take to bed, and whom Helen persuades to
allow her to substitute herself in Diana's place in bed with Bertram,
and so consummate her own marriage, which Bertram had entered
into unwillingly.

But *All's Well* was unconsciously self-disapproving. Shakespeare
avoided the big obligatory scenes, especially the one between
Helen and Bertram in the bedroom. He wrote it without his
customary skill in pre-planning the climaxes, while the *Decameron*
story, from which he concocted the plot, sits awkwardly with its
chivalric trappings inside the early Jacobean court atmosphere.
His gift for characterization seemed blocked. Even Paroles, in
whose relationship as servant and mentor to Bertram Shakespeare
revived the Hal–Falstaff friendship – and which he ended by the
complicated unmasking of Paroles' capacity for betrayal (the most
comic, and best, scene in the play) – dangles as a loose end by
the conclusion. Paroles is rather hurriedly tied up by Lafeu's
generosity to him, and by making him a witness to the denouement. But he is a well-drawn, realistic character, and may well
have become *de facto* a sketch for Iago. He could never have
uttered his *locus classicus* damnation of virginity within the Queen's
hearing:

    virginity is peevish, proud, idle, made of self-love – which is the most
    inhibited sin in the canon ... Virginity like an old courtier wears her
    cap out of fashion, richly suited but unsuitable, just like the brooch and
    the toothpick, which wear not now. Your date is better in your pie and
    your porridge than in your cheek, and your virginity, your old virginity,
    is like one of our French withered pears: it looks ill, it eats drily, marry,

'tis a withered pear – it was formerly better, marry, yet 'tis a withered pear.

Here, surely, are echoes of Essex's "crooked carcass" outburst against Elizabeth.

In *All's Well* Shakespeare looked forward to the emotional equation he was to set and solve so beautifully in a mood of conciliation in his last plays; but its material and form seemed intractable for the present when the playwright was clearly preoccupied with the potential tragic hero. Health and sickness, both in the kingdom and in the individual, remained a preoccupation in *All's Well*, as Shakespeare took up the ailing King and had his heroine restore him: "He that of greatest works is finisher / Oft does them by the weakest minister . . ."

Shakespeare supplied the first taste, again a purely instinctive device, of that explosive scene change roughly half-way through the action that suddenly amplifies the last comedies. It happens when the setting changes to Florence: a tucket sounds, and Diana and other Florentine girls await the arrival of the soldiers. Colour and a change of rhythm unexpectedly lift this limping play. If the King's fistula, upon whose cure the play hinges, was symptomatic of Shakespeare's mental state after writing *Hamlet*, then the King's cure betokened his own eventual recovery.

But for the most part *All's Well* plays on stage like a work of emotional convalescence, particularly in Shakespeare's pallid portrayal of Bertram, described by Dr Johnson as "a man noble without generosity, and young without truth; who marries Helena as a coward, and leaves her as a profligate: when she is dead by his unkindness, sneaks home to a second marriage, is accused by a woman whom he has wronged, defends himself by falsehood, and is dismissed to happiness". Shakespeare, feeling weak, wanted to forgive everyone, perhaps because he himself wanted to be forgiven.

He allowed the impact of John Shakespeare's recent death to affect his mood while writing *All's Well*. The text makes much mention of fathers. Both Helen's and Bertram's fathers have died: Lafeu cautions, "Moderate lamentation is the right of the dead, excessive grief the enemy to the living"; Helen weeps while the King praises Bertram's father in terms true to Shakespeare's better feelings about his own father:

> In his youth
> He had the wit which I can well observe
> Today in our young lords, but they may jest
> Till their own scorn return to them unnoted
> Ere they can hide their levity in honour . . .
>                             Such a man
> Might be a copy to these younger times.

He was trying, somewhat feebly, to convince himself in *All's Well* that all *was* well: "The web of our life is of a mingled yarn, good and ill together. Our virtues would be proud if our faults whipped them not, and our crimes would despair if they were not cherished by our virtues", is a bit of a wishy-washy generalization. The play, with its insistence on goodness and mildness, was written in a mood of exhaustion.

# The gathered self

"Peace proclaims olives of endless age." The olives soon became gifts and then corrupting bribes, or the price of favours. Shakespeare was unctuously flattering about the Calvinist-reared son of Catholic Mary Queen of Scots: in the last act of *Henry VIII* he fudged the genealogy to make James, a Stuart, appear a descendant of Elizabeth, resorting to the phoenix image once again to bridge that hiatus in the succession which had caused so much insecurity in England.

Cranmer who, in terms of great eulogy, sums up Queen Elizabeth, the newly born daughter of Henry, grows positively tortuous in identifying the Virgin Queen (bereft of turtle) with the mythical Arabian bird:

> but, as when
> The bird of wonder dies – the maiden phoenix –
> Her ashes new create another heir
> As great in admiration as herself,
> So shall she leave her blessèdness to one,
> When heaven shall call her from this cloud of darkness,
> Who from the sacred ashes of her honour
> Shall star-like rise as great in fame as she was.

James no doubt responded generously to this fulsome panegyric, which because of its air of second-rate paraphrase is denied Shakespeare's authorship by the purists who believe that their holy poet could not pen anything bad. Whoever wrote it, be it Shakespeare or Fletcher or a third unidentified hack, must have had *Love's Pilgrim* open in his lap to produce such laboured and insincere imitation.

How would Shakespeare and Fletcher have coped with a scene in which the wizened monarch with sad eyes, James, actually married Elizabeth, who was thirty years his senior? James had sounded out such a grotesque possibility through an intermediary, Archibald Douglas, some twenty years earlier.

James, indeed, was a prototypical character of Shakespeare's darkest and most paranoid period. Brainwashed by an enemy of his mother, George Buchanan, to regard Mary as wicked and heretical, an adulteress as well as his father's murderer, England's new "mountain cedar" had had much difficulty in growing straight. He had quickly become an intricate and sophisticated deceiver, and although he matured enough both to exonerate his mother and to become tolerant of Catholics, he showed little natural feeling except a need for peace and for distraction – which was hardly surprising. Elizabeth had called him a "false Scotch urchin!", declaring, "What can be expected from the double dealing of such an urchin as this?"

James erected a magnificent tomb to his Catholic mother among the kings and queens in Westminster. While Mary Tudor and Elizabeth Tudor, childless daughters of Henry VIII, were buried "lying alone together in death", under the great marble monument James also built for Elizabeth, the headless corpse of Mary Queen of Scots in its huge leaden coffin was placed in a catacomb, whose occupants proliferated in time with her descendants. As a biographer wrote, "From her every sovereign of Britain since her death has been directly descended, down to the present queen who is in the thirteenth generation."

The new age James ushered in was a prosperous one, though still with enormous contradictions. By 1603 the import of coal into London, chiefly by sea from Newcastle-on-Tyne, had increased nearly sevenfold since 1580; production from all trades including the mining of iron and salt, textile manufacture, shipbuilding, glassmaking, and of course from farming, which still engaged four-fifths of the population, had at least doubled in the same period.

London, with more than 200,000 inhabitants, was one of the richest, as well as fastest-growing, cities in the world. Demand for expensive timber for building was deforesting the land at an alarming rate. Wealth created new professions: for example, with coal being burnt on a massive scale domestically, there were, by the second decade of the century, more than 200 chimney sweeps in London, or 1 for every 1,000 persons.

Yet this powerful and absolute new king was advised, when he first came to London, to avoid the city – the nights were disturbed by the groans of dying men, women and children, bodies were being smuggled out of houses to be buried in unmarked graves. Was James "God's silly vassal", as he was called by a Scots Presbyterian, or "the wisest fool in Christendom", as a continental statesman commented? He seems to have been remarkably like Shakespeare's Richard II – although older and more seasoned, his defects were vanity and softness; but he was clever and learned, and he had a far tougher and better established government machinery behind him to secure his rule, while the traditional nobility had lost its power to the newly enriched servants of the Tudors. James created large numbers of new peers – and filled his coffers in the process.

One-quarter of James's subjects, a million people or more, were, one authority claims, practising lay Catholics when he came to the throne. Either openly or in secret, more than 200 proscribed priests celebrated mass up and down the country. At first, as James abolished the levy of £20 a month on Catholic gentlemen who failed to attend church, and as he also began negotiating directly with leading Catholic laymen, the level of tolerance increased dramatically. Had it not, Shakespeare would never have been able to write *Measure for Measure*, which takes place in Catholic Vienna, with a Duke disguising himself as a friar and hearing confession. The Protestant establishment sheltered, despite its strong Calvinist leanings, many concealed Roman Catholics. James's queen, Anne of Denmark, raised a Lutheran, had become a secret Catholic.

Anne was more interested in pleasure than in religion: from Elizabeth she inherited 6,000 dresses, and she soon gave herself up to spectacular, excessively costly entertainments in which she herself openly took part. One of the most memorable of these was Jonson's *Masque of Blackness*, performed in 1604, for which Inigo Jones supplied the scenery and stage machinery. Anne attended plays far more often than Elizabeth had, both at court and in private residences – she was even, at least on one occasion, known to visit a public playhouse. Between December 1603 and February 1604

Shakespeare's company acted eight plays at court, more than twice the average performed in any comparable period during Elizabeth's reign. From James's accession to Shakespeare's death in 1616 the King's Men would stage for the court at least twelve plays every year, many of them revivals.

"Right and wrong, / Between whose endless jar justice resides", as Ulysses observes in *Troilus and Cressida*, is a far tougher sentiment than the "mingled yarn" observation of *All's Well*. Shakespeare wanted to create a stern and yet sexually potent fable for England's – Great Britain as it soon became – new law-makers. *Measure for Measure* confronts the theme of justice head-on, not just incidentally, as in *The Merchant of Venice*. The tale of a woman who, in seeking to rescue a male relative from the death sentence (in this case, Isabella is pleading for her brother Claudio), arouses the lust of the man in authority, goes back to the classical world. It reached Shakespeare through a two-part, unperformed tragi-comedy, Whetstone's *Promos and Cassandra*, published in 1578. Adapting it to his own ends, Shakespeare committed distorting designs upon it, suggesting that he wanted to put over a specific message. The brother's crime in the original was rape; Shakespeare changed this to the less heinous one of fornication (and set the play in Vienna, where fornication was a capital offence). Angelo, the Duke's substitute who passes sentence on Claudio, is particularly harsh, although his attitude to Isabella is credible. Shakespeare changed the Whetstone ending, in which the lustful authoritarian marries the sister "to repair her erased honour", for which offence he is to lose his head; but his wife in great affection becomes "an earnest suitor for his life". Shakespeare substituted another version of the bed trick used in *All's Well*; this had gone down well in Southwark, for it contained the bawdy observation that the love-making novice cannot identify his bedmate in the dark, a variant on the old army adage, "You don't look at the mantelpiece when you are stoking the fire". Most of the characters in *Measure for Measure* reek more of the Thames than of the Danube.

Shakespeare displayed daring freedom in his study of Angelo. He felt that he was able, on account of the death of Elizabeth and the dismissal of some of the Puritan elements at court, to deal with subjects that had been up to then taboo. Angelo was not only a well-known type of Puritan, but his character contained that repressed lust and capacity for betrayal that Shakespeare must have

noted well in figures of Elizabeth's court such as Sir Thomas Walsingham and Lord Knollys. Now that Essex, who had numbered
many Puritans among his supporters, was dead, Shakespeare was
further freed from constraint. As sharply observant as ever of the
changing political climate, he continued to deepen his vision of the
polarization, no longer so much in its early stages, between the
narrow, de-sensitized Puritan line (which in its most extreme form
equated plagues with sin, and sin with the theatre, therefore claiming theatres caused the plague) and a variation on the Venus principle shown in the new libertarian, even promiscuous attitudes at
court. The ironical theme Angelo embodies – "quis custodiet ipsos
custodes" – is that of Oedipus, the ruler who, in an honest attempt
to uncover guilt, reveals that he himself is the guilty one. There is
a "gulling", Jonsonian element in Angelo's unmasking, but he is
stranger and darker, more potentially a man of chaos in his sadistic
sensuality than any Jonsonian humour; as Isabella says of him,

> man, proud man,
> Dressed in a little brief authority,
> Most ignorant of what he's most assured,
> His glassy essence, like an angry ape
> Plays such fantastic tricks before high heaven
> As makes the angels weep...

As its title implies, *Measure for Measure* began as a revenge play,
but as it had no overriding hero or villain, Shakespeare turned it
into a thesis or problem play, in which the proposition from Luke,
"Judge not, and ye shall be not judged", and "With what measure
ye mete, it shall be measured to you again", could be examined
dramatically. He also made much of an issue upon which St Paul
often preached, and which Shakespeare had seen so often abused
in the latter part of Elizabeth's reign – an issue which he hoped the
new court might heed, namely, how justice conceals the truth, and
specifically how the law can lie. The whole of Angelo's deceptive
and libidinous manoeuvring with regard to Claudio and Isabella is
a warning to the law-makers.

The Duke, who withdraws like a chorus figure and overviews
the action, passing comments on his subjects' conduct, is the author-
ial voice with which we identify, although Lucio is the cynical
filter by which the audience evaluates the everyday reality of the
characters. Shakespeare planted in the Duke some of his own strong
characteristics, especially his enjoyment of his own power in a

withdrawn, even secretive – even godlike – way. The Duke loves the people, but does not like to project himself in their eyes, nor does he relish "their loud applause and *aves* vehement". Perhaps more crucially, the Duke adds, "Nor do I think the man of safe discretion / That does affect it". Shakespeare disliked celebrity rulers and vain people in all walks of life.

Central to the difficulty of writing *Measure* was Shakespeare's refusal, after presenting a strong, potentially tragic conflict in the early part which could well have resulted in Isabella's death, to develop it in such a way that the characters were pushed further and further to extremes. Responsibility, instead of being piled more heavily on, is taken away from them. Resolutions are imposed in accordance with the philosophy of the Duke, so that Shakespeare can in the last act construct a symbolic parallel with the Last Judgement. Shakespeare made explicit reference to Jesus as an example, when Isabella pleads for Claudio's life:

> Why, all the souls that were were forfeit once,
> And He that might the vantage best have took
> Found out the remedy. How would you be
> If He which is the top of judgement should
> But judge you as you are?

But the equation with justice was not precisely formulated: the two sides are unequal, and *Measure*'s faulty construction, ramshackle legal tricks and theatrically effective stunts (the Duke dressed as a friar, the disposal of Lucio) detract from an effective Shavian solution (only Shaw, among English dramatists, ultimately mastered this kind of play). When the Duke, echoing the Epiphany, says to the Provost, "Look, th'unfolding star calls up the shepherd. Put not yourself into amazement how these things should be. All difficulties are but easy when they are known", this may be sound psychological observation, much emphasized by Shakespeare – Lear, for example, does but "slenderly know himself", while the Duke, as Escalus describes him, "above all other strifes / Contended especially to know himself" – but it does not strike to the heart of what the play shows.

What is conveyed by *Measure for Measure* are the means by which opposites of good and evil work, such as sainted purity against hypocritical self-righteousness. The Duke's disappearance creates something of a vacuum at the centre of the play, and as an "enlightened ethic" he does not order the outcome. He does not grow, as a good man in disguise, integrated into the action, as does Kent in *King Lear*, or as Henry V when he overhears and intervenes in the quarrels of his subordinates before Agincourt.

Instead of that of justice, *Measure for Measure*'s main theme too often sinks to that of chastity – as if this, underlyingly, were Shakespeare's own personal preoccupation, and that he needed to reassure himself, alone in London without an enticing love object or fascinating human being in view, that it was right to remain chaste. His powerful sexual needs remaining undiminished, Shakespeare wrestled with acute torment, in this case subjecting it to the authority and teaching of the gospels. He put lust, self-gratifying egotistical desire in plenty on display, but there was no serenity in evidence. There were self-injunctions galore (reminiscent of the philosopher Bertrand Russell holding forth on the perfect life in *The Conquest of Happiness*, and confessing afterwards that he was near suicide when he wrote it): says the Duke, "Heaven doth with us as we with torches do, / Not light them for themselves"; "Best men are moulded out of faults," says Mariana; and Claudio, on the evils of lust, declares,

> Our natures do pursue,
> Like rats that raven down their proper bane,
> A thirsty evil; and when we drink, we die.

As *Measure for Measure* goes on, Shakespeare seems to deliberate less about sin, and more about death and sex (two other opposites), which gives the play's world a very special mental atmosphere. It accelerates with reflections, disguised by some of Shakespeare's most cunning verbal artifices, on life's contradictions, even on death's contradictions – Claudio's poignantly expressed fear, "Ay, but to die, and go we know not where . . .", set against the Duke's majestic observation, "Be absolute for death . . .", both echoing the sublime personal ending of Sonnet 146 ("Poor soul, the centre of my sinful earth . . ."):

> Then, soul, live thou upon thy servant's loss,
> And let that pine to aggravate thy store.
> Buy terms divine in selling hours of dross;
> Within be fed, without be rich no more.
> So shalt thou feed on death, that feeds on men,
> And death once dead, there's no more dying then.

The ganglia spreading to all the elements and characters in *Measure for Measure*, imbuing it with a peculiar personal glow and sensitivity, was Shakespeare's guilt, his unhappy sexual instincts, especially as they had manifested themselves at such an early age with his wife Anne. He sought to replay that whole formative event in Juliet's pregnancy, to range the arguments for and against hers and Claudio's carnal act, and to duplicate it in the Pompey Bum subplot of sexual licence – and even in Isabella's temptation for Angelo. In showing Isabella not compromising with her chastity, even to save the life of her brother – the person in all the world closest to her – Shakespeare made perhaps the most extreme moral statement possible about the sexual impulse.

For all its shocking effects – beheading a man who has died of a disease and using his head to contrive a deception; substituting a live naked woman for the consummation of an intended rape – Shakespeare celebrated even more ruthlessly in *Measure for Measure* a virtue other than Isabella's chastity: her forgiveness of Angelo, who, when she is called on to do this, is revealed as her seducer, deceiver, and the murderer of her brother. Shakespeare wanted forgiveness to be viewed as the supreme act of virtue. Was he not also begging for it himself, from Anne?

Plague closed London's theatres between May 1603 and April 1604. Although scaffolding was thrown up for the triumphal processions, and the "streets plumed with gallants, tobacconists filled up whole taverns", the plague tightened its grip during the long hot summer of 1603; 1,100 people died in a week during July, when James was first due to be crowned, and London became a ghost city. Those forced to remain in the city chewed orange peel or smoked tobacco; rosemary, considered a preventative, soared to an inflationary six shillings a small bunch. Between July and December 1603 more than 2,400 of the 3,000 residents of St Giles Cripplegate died. Brave doctors like the former playwright Thomas Lodge worked heroically in the doomed quarantine areas, none realizing that bubonic plague was transmitted by infected fleas and that compulsory quarantine intensified the slaughter. Ben Jonson lost his first son Ben, and possibly another child, incarcerated in a house with a red cross nailed to the door:

> Farewell, thou child of my right hand, and joy;
> My sinne was too much hope of thee, lov'd boy ...
> Rest in soft peace, and ask'd, say here doth lie

BEN. JONSON his best piece of *poetrie*.
For whose sake, hence-forth, all his vowes be such,
As what he loves may never like too much.

The King's Men went on tour all summer: Bath, Coventry, Mortlake were on their route. In November, at Wilton House, Wiltshire, they played for the new King the first play he is recorded to have seen in England. Wilton House was owned by William Herbert, third Earl of Pembroke, who had befriended Burbage, and who fathered an illegitimate son on Mary Fitton for which he had been imprisoned in the Fleet. Pembroke, whose father was probably, and briefly, Shakespeare's theatrical patron ten years before, became a warm supporter of Shakespeare's company (later he was one of the "incomparable pair of brethren", the other being his brother, the Earl of Montgomery, to whom the 1623 First Folio was dedicated). James paid the company £30, a huge sum, even allowing for their travelling expenses.

*Measure for Measure* was written and performed in 1604. On 15 March 1604 the new King rode in state through London for his coronation, postponed from the previous year. Shakespeare and his eight other "sharers" were part of the procession: now their status had been upgraded and given royal blessing; issued livery of cloth for red doublets, and cloaks, they marched as "Grooms of the Chamber". Shakespeare headed the list of nine actors; none was salaried, but the King's Men received generous *ad hoc* payment from the royal exchequer.

# Deeds of darkness

i

The wandering nature of life for Shakespeare in 1603–4 and the omnipresence of that major off-stage character, death, was reflected in the uncertainty of the three transitional plays, *Troilus, All's Well* and *Measure for Measure*. But *Othello*, the first of Shakespeare's four mature tragedies, proclaimed a new certainty. Shakespeare reached a new plateau of achievement with *Othello*, which in its expressive power, the sweep of its poetry and the depth of its psychology seemed effortless. But the ancestry of former characters was clearly there in the rich, many-sided natures of Othello, Iago, Emilia and Cassio, while even Brabanzio and Desdemona had solid precedents.

The story of *Othello* was lifted lock, stock and barrel from a cheap melodrama published in Italian in 1565, in Giraldi Cinthio's *Ecatommiti*, which Shakespeare read in a French translation. The basic plot was romantic and unreal, but Shakespeare grafted on to it, for his ending with Desdemona's murder, the Geoffrey Fenton account of an Albanian captain who killed his exquisite wife to stop anyone else enjoying her after his death. This stemmed originally from another Italian romance by Matteo Bandello, translated into French. Thus Shakespeare's sources for *Othello*, to which can be added numerous historical and geographical reference books, were many-layered and complicated.

But *Othello* creates its own completely unified, claustrophobic world which was to be the hallmark of Shakespeare's greatness, a world which can be experienced as unique to this play. There were many reasons for this, most of them by now unconscious on the writer's part, but one huge unifying element by means of which he gave the play its dynamic, single-minded thrust (and which, as he must have been singularly well aware, was missing from the problem comedies and the failed *Troilus*) was that in it he buried a whole revenge play.

The revenge play had a fundamental dynamic drive; but now *Hamlet* was being copied almost as a format by younger dramatists, so Shakespeare was, as Trevor Nunn says, "terribly distressed and partly amazed to have fathered such a bizarre vogue". So with *Othello*, "very much a court play, with its last act in a bedroom", he thought he would go one better, and turn the tables on his competitors. He made the inciting incident, which was certainly not true but which nevertheless propels Iago into weaving his sinister plot round Othello, the seduction of Iago's wife by the Moor. He had this happen before the play begins, and so while Iago's revenge motivation embraces much wider psychological possibilities (i.e. evil hating natural goodness, underprivileged white hating black, servant hating master), this sexual cause holds the play's rationality together. Iago's evil was not, for Shakespeare, motiveless – this would have resulted in destruction of the play's meaning. It invented its own motive to be able to realize itself. Shakespeare believed in reason and will. Iago's emotion, although expressed coldly and controlledly, may be out of proportion to the cause (as is Othello's response – so, it can be claimed, Othello and Iago were fated to destroy each other), but it is not pathological.

With a certain glee Shakespeare seemed to be turning on their head the concentrated precepts of Montaigne, which he read at this time in his friend Florio's translation. Two essays, "On some Verses of Virgil" and "Of the Power of Imagination", together cover just about every topic raised in *Othello*.

Another reason for the satisfying unity of *Othello* was that Shakespeare had himself come to terms with the emotional complexities of love and betrayal which he had explored in the Sonnets, particularly those of sexual obsession and infatuation. As in the Sonnets, where the lover (Shakespeare) is trapped by his own feelings towards the beloved and overwhelmed, to the extent of losing awareness of his love for the person of that beloved, Shakespeare laid out on view, with tortured poetic compassion but clearly as a moral example, a hero with a great and good soul carried away by what he believes and calls love. It is really no such thing, for Othello fails to take into account what Desdemona's nature is (and indeed to see that not only is she not capable of meeting and dealing with such passion, but that it is quite irrelevant to her condition, and entirely useless to her). He puts, as Stanley Cavell writes, "a finite woman in the place of God". The possibility that obsesses Othello is that Desdemona exists, "is separate from him; other". The marriage is as blind and ill-advised as that of Romeo and Juliet.

Shakespeare found the story mirrored as much in contemporary reality as in fiction. In particular he knew of Sir George More's disapproval of his daughter Anne More's secret marriage in late 1601 to John Donne, secretary to Egerton, the Lord Keeper. Sir George took up arms and sued Donne (who conducted a debate with More quite like that of Brabanzio and the Duke in *Othello*): yet again Shakespeare pointed his sources towards recent contemporary scandal. The marriage, which led to Donne's dismissal and years of subsequent poverty, happened just before Elizabeth's death. The ageing Queen had disapproved fiercely of such rash marriages.

Filial disobedience as a cause of disaster is stressed recurrently in *Othello*. Shakespeare was also expressing anxiety about his two unmarried daughters, particularly the younger. The nature of Desdemona's elopement with Othello, which involves her in deceiving and defying her father, builds to shattering effect in

Othello's mind when he has been gulled (and here the Jonsonian influence on Shakespeare remained firm) into believing himself cuckolded. Although John Donne impregnated his wife Anne twelve times (and six children survived), there was more than a hint of feelings like Othello's in his constant sexual scepticism: women were fickle, Donne held (at least as the fictional "I" of his earlier love poetry), and likely to betray him.

It was an extremely masculine and reactionary ethos which saw women exclusively as love-objects: however rapturous – and he is endowed with the most perfect silvery flood of rhetorical feeling – Othello is about his love, it is, as Shakespeare signalled abundantly, to himself that Othello offers this gift of self.

Shakespeare, demonstrating the dual nature of life, was writing to further his vision of, and his need for, an ethical and emotional health. In his day this depended on a successful interpretation and implementation of the teachings of Christ, together with a judicious use of wisdom and pleasure as derived from the classical period, or filtered through humanism. The sick were not at the centre of the world picture. *Othello* positively pullulates with advice on how to achieve health in mind and body:

> When remedies are past, the griefs are ended
> By seeing the worst which late on hopes depended.
> To mourn a mischief that is past and gone
> Is the next way to draw new mischief on.

Shakespeare registered everyone in the play as continually drawing new mischief on: the claustrophobia generated comes from being caught by the past, trapped by emotion, and, in the case of the great characters that dominate the play, Othello and Iago, of being incapable of change.

Before writing *Othello* Shakespeare had to change himself from the trapped fugitive of his emotions as recorded in the Sonnets. His last three or four plays, from *Hamlet* onwards, had personated him as grappling masterfully with himself, yet with this gift for detached self-observation. Conforming to the practice of his time, he was not consciously writing an autobiography or "unlocking" his heart, but objectifying his problem, finding a detached objective correlative for his feelings. "The more perfect the artist," T. S. Eliot writes, with Shakespeare in mind, "the more completely separate in him will be the man who suffers and the mind which creates."

Shakespeare's solution was typical of him: he would use his great gift not to paint goodness directly: that had proved impossible – or more or less impossible, except in a subsidiary supportive role; rather he would show evil or blindness destroying itself. He had done this instinctively in early tragic chronicle plays such as *Richard III*, where he was fuelled by unresolved feelings of alienation towards his family. Now, in fuller control of his powers, and distanced from the immediacy of the emotions he was showing – although still affected by them, and so capable of rendering their power – he had found a tragic voice specifically through what he had always been indicating, namely the depth, many-sidedness, contradictions, and the exact identity of man's individual character.

The working out of this tragic thesis, and its relation to his audiences' lives, would go like this: when something disastrous happens – such as personal loss, or infidelity or bankruptcy – a man or a woman has to face disaster. In facing the disaster he or she has to look for possibilities of growth, or change, which are hidden within it – such as new insight, grace, or redemption through suffering. A man or woman has to discern, in that light next to disaster, some capacity for change. This was what, for Shakespeare, the Crucifixion ultimately meant: pain or suffering inflicted on an ordinary man, who found through these eternal life. "To the religious sixteenth-century mind," writes Graham Greene, "there was no such thing as a commonplace young man or an unimportant sin; the creative writers of that time drew characters with a clarity we have never regained ... Rob human beings of their heavenly and their infernal importance, and you rob your characters of their individuality." Ted Hughes echoes this in the introduction to his anthology from Shakespeare: "The poetic imagination is determined finally by the state of negotiation ... between man and his idea of the Creator."

In his tragic heroes Shakespeare deliberately painted the emotions stirred up by failing to meet this challenge, the terror and pity of likeable people – at whose centre he placed himself, the poet Shakespeare – with whom we identify, or in whom we see ourselves. The tragic figure is incapable of receiving this gift of change. He sets everything on his temporal, impermanent passion and commits his whole will and choice to fulfilling his egotistical promptings, which trap him, push him more and more into being a narrow, self-bound creature: the opposite of Hamlet's "O God, I could be bounded in a nutshell and count myself a king of infinite space". He is pushed through to the ultimate crisis, the climax of paying for his blindness or narrowness. Each tragic figure becomes a symbol, as well as a person.

In the comedies the "bad", even those with serious tragic potential, are converted to good: Falstaff will reform; so will Shylock; the Duke in *As You Like It*, Malvolio in *Twelfth Night*, Bertram in *All's Well* – all undergo change on the assumption that they can be redeemed from their folly. But not so in the tragedies: *Othello* is formed entirely of darkness, with characters moving hurriedly about half-recognized in dim torchlight; of intimacy and subtle innuendo, of whisperings behind the hand. The choice of a black hero followed the pattern set by Marlowe of the superlative and contrary hero. This brought to *Othello* an immediate, exotic flavour, and it also handed Shakespeare the freedom to exaggerate his hero's contradictory qualities, contrast his virtues with his black exterior.

Iago is prosaic, a master of underplaying and understatement, a supreme expression of the cold, analytical intellect, watching and observing, yet stripped of aspiration to do good. He is wrapped up in plausible *bonhomie* – a gift to any player wanting to show how well Shakespeare understood actors. But he is a character without feeling (which is Shakespeare's main judgement on Iago). He is the supreme last word on that most evil character in the age of Elizabeth and James, the informer: a composite personification of envy, rumour and avarice. Through him Shakespeare warned against innocent trust of a friend. Iago is the arch villain of the spy state, and Shakespeare could not have made it more obvious that he should never have been believed, and that the evil consequences wrought were caused by naïvety in those he gulled. In treason trials the prosecutors sought an Iago, whose responsibility for his evil was considered absolute, cast in the image of Satan. Shakespeare imbued his villain with the splotches and stains of his own personal acquaintance, beginning with Robert Poley and Thomas Kyd, culminating in Henry Cuffe, the "subtle sophister" who had seduced Essex into treason. Through Cuffe, writes Lacey Baldwin Smith, "Essex helped give birth to an Iago, only three years before he was to appear on stage".

But the creator of these characters stood in a position entirely of light and uncomplicated clarity. *Othello*'s effortless ease, its musical flow and intricate fullness of cadence were not those of a man struggling with himself and dark passions, but of someone who had worked them out and, with enviable freedom, could concentrate his energy on setting them down.

Shakespeare's way of serving as conscience to the new, egotistical self-assertive man of the English renaissance was individual in flavour, personal in morality, yet universal in means. *Othello* cost its author great creative effort but little torture of soul: the prodigality of towering parts – two main actors' roles – at once earned it huge popularity.

And there was a private though lighter jealousy displayed in *Othello*. In the Moor Shakespeare created the hardest part he would write for Richard Burbage to play. "Because of the big speeches, the big scenes come so fast after one another that there is no time to draw breath, no time to work up to a new climax, no room to prepare yourself," says Laurence Olivier, most famous late-twentieth-century interpreter of the role. Olivier considers that Shakespeare was jealous of Burbage for his fame and allure: "So dear old William thought – I'll get that sod, I'll write *Othello*. And he did, and he handed it to Burbage and he said, 'Right, Burbage, here is a play with unactable scenes about a man who makes no sense and the lines now and then are sublime but almost unspeakable and he's black. Get out of that!'"

*Othello* was acted before King James on 1 November 1604 in the great Banqueting Hall in Whitehall; built in 1581, the hall now posed serious fire risks because of its wooden structure, painted canvas roof, and the increased use of heat and light – and even of tobacco. According to Marchette Chute, "six men were required to haul up the great branches that held a huge array of candles and to wire them into place."

A first quarto of *Othello*, based apparently on Shakespeare's "foul papers", was published in 1622, after his death, and only a short time before the folio. That Shakespeare revised the play extensively (assuming the quarto was based on early performances) is evidenced in the 160 lines added to the folio (which may, simply, have been cut from early performances) and the 1,000 or more differences of wording between quarto and folio. Significant among these were those occasioned by the profanity laws of 1606, which provided that if an actor should "jestingly or profanely speak, or use the Name of God, or of Jesus Christ, or the Holy Ghost, or of the Trinity", he was to be fined £10 for each offence. Shakespeare had had no inhibitions about using such expressions, nor had King James's court about listening to them. But in the folio text, based on later prompt books, Emilia's cry "O God! O Heavenly God" in the quarto becomes "Oh heaven! Oh heavenly powers!"

"Heaven" was a euphemistic, more ambiguous term, and as such better suited Shakespeare's survival in an amoral or godless world. The man's instinct was for survival: to this end he wrapped up his convictions in so many different voices, engaged sensations and feelings through so many different images. The Duke's exhortation to Angelo in *Measure for Measure* was the commanding voice: he *did* see himself as a medium, and as such he could be, without scruple or qualm, himself: We *are* heaven's torches,

> for if our virtues
> Did not go forth of us, 'twere all alike
> As if we had them not. Spirits are not finely touched
> But to fine issues.

The torch of Othello's passion is lit just for himself to enjoy, and it consumes him.

## ii

*Macbeth*, like *Othello*, was not a personal play, but a completely professional tragedy, fulfilling this playwright's own destiny of writing three or four masterpieces in a particular genre before slackening off to abandon, once and for all, a form now spent. In this play Shakespeare adhered, fairly strictly, to the same formula as *Othello*, except that he painted the fault, ambition, with less ambiguity than Othello's innocence. Far from being blind to his own defect of character, Macbeth is tortured with conscience, while its interplay with his evil deeds, and his wife's extreme determination, allies him closely in doubt and self-questioning to Brutus and to Hamlet. But his crimes evoke no sympathy, and were it not for the delicacy of his soul and his self-awareness (the trait Shakespeare most shares with him), the play would be even more of an unrelieved and remorselessly dark piece than it is. Except for the Porter's scene it is virtually unrelieved by humour. (Shakespeare had to find employment for clowns, even in tragedy. Coleridge said he did not write this scene, showing his own limitation, or at least unevenness, as a critic.)

Shakespeare took Holinshed's *Chronicles* as the principal source. He conveyed the black mood of the play in starkly realistic terms, linking it to those early plot-ridden years of the seventeenth century, and the vice- and blood-filled Jacobean plays that now ruled the stage. Holinshed's hero reigned seventeen years, most of which were filled with "worthy doings and princely acts". Just as Shakespeare appropriated Sir Thomas More's view when writing *Richard III*, so now did he pack in interpretations of crime through witchcraft. He chose the subject to please King James, whose Scottish past and connections made the story particularly close. Banquo, Macbeth's confidant at the beginning of the play, was a direct ancestor of James. The "show of eight kings, the last with a glass in his hand" – Banquo's descendants – were the eight Stuarts before James:

> What, will the line stretch out to th' crack of doom?
> Another yet? A seventh? I'll see no more –
> And yet the eighth appears, who bears a glass
> Which shows me many more . . .

This flattered James's own heirs: James too had "power" to cure the "king's evil", scrofula, which Shakespeare wrote into a long irrelevant speech about healing benediction (James, sceptically, stopped dispensing the cure).

The most servile compliment Shakespeare paid to his patron – implying a meeting of minds – was a thorough reading he gave to James's own published works on demonology. James had exposed as hysterics some who had accused others of witchcraft, and later he pardoned a group of suspected witches at Leicester, establishing them as victims of a frame-up. Shakespeare duplicated some of the King's biblical references in *Macbeth*: when Banquo states, early in the play,

> to win us to our harm
> The instruments of darkness tell us truths,
> Win us with honest trifles to betray's
> In deepest consequence,

this not only echoes 2 Corinthians 11:14, "For Satan himself is transformed into an angel of light", but also a passage from *Demonology*, where James writes that the devil will cause his scholars "to creep in credit with Princes, by foretelling them many great things, part true, part false".

When Macbeth says

> every one
> According to the gift which bounteous nature
> Hath in him closed; whereby he does receive
> Particular addition . . .

he is repeating a popular sentiment already expressed in James's *Basilican Dorum*, "employing everyone according to his gifts" (Ephesians 4:7, "Unto everyone of us is given grace, according to the measure of the gift"). The whole of Macbeth's tragedy implements Jesus' observation, as reported in Mark's Gospel (and in the Geneva translation), "What shall it profit a man, though he should win the whole world, if he lose his soul". Macbeth himself describes "conscience" as an "eternal jewel" being given "to the common enemy of man". Poignantly, his understanding in full control, he commits spiritual suicide in fulfilling his wife's puritanical drive to power. At the end of the play, and of his life, he yearns for all those things – "honour, love, obedience, troops of friends" – which but for his guilt (and with which Shakespeare identifies himself personally) would have accompanied his old age. On the words "troops of friends" one can imagine Richard Burbage's voice rising to a wail of heart-rending sorrow.

Like *Hamlet*, *Macbeth* has strong links with *Doctor Faustus*, although markedly different ones. Macbeth willingly plots his own damnation, yet his will to do evil is complicated by the energizing presence of Lady Macbeth, whose ambition is greater and more ruthless than his own. Shakespeare suggests that her barren womb, and her own anger and suppressed grief over that unfulfilled power, lie behind the darkness. Macbeth asks the doctor,

> Canst thou not minister to a mind diseased,
> Pluck from the memory a rooted sorrow,
> Raze out the written troubles of the brain,
> And with some sweet oblivious antidote
> Cleanse the fraught bosom of that perilous stuff
> Which weighs upon the heart?

*Macbeth* is a short text, only slightly more than half the length of *Hamlet*, and shorter than any other of Shakespeare's plays except for *The Comedy of Errors* and *The Tempest*. It shows much evidence of cuts, suggesting that the text – which was printed in folio for the first and only time – was assembled for a special audience. Some of the scenes, such as that between Macduff and Malcolm in exile, seem inordinately long for their importance; Lennox's part is often incoherent or inexplicable, suggesting sometimes an old man, sometimes a young one. The desertion of Macbeth by his allies at the end seems hurriedly foreshortened.

Two or three scenes and some speeches of *Macbeth* may have been written by someone else – Thomas Middleton is usually cited – who wrote the Hecate scenes in octosyllabic verse in marked contrast to the abundant imagery and fluid blank verse of the rest. The play is Shakespeare's most unified and "frontal" tragedy, virtually without a sub-plot; as such it is uncharacteristic, so a much longer, more copious and varied *Macbeth*, with unstinted comic scenes – as well as greater diversity of scene and action – may once have existed. The generally well-edited text we know preserves a simple and violent thrust of action, and the important confrontations and climaxes. We can be sure the most haunting clusters of irony and imagery have been preserved, as in Banquo's speech to King Duncan:

> This guest of summer,
> The temple-haunting martlet, does approve
> By his loved mansionry that the heavens' breath
> Smells wooingly here. No jutty, frieze,
> Buttress, nor coign of vantage but this bird
> Hath made his pendant bed and procreant cradle;
> Where they most breed and haunt I have observed
> The air is delicate . . .

which immediately precedes Lady Macbeth's chilling entrance.

Other passages might have been omitted out of political expediency. *Macbeth* may have been performed before the bill prohibiting blasphemies was passed in March 1606; some of it was certainly written after the Gunpowder Plot of 5 November 1605, for Ross mentions the eclipses of the sun and moon in October 1605, and also the plot itself:

> Thou seest the heavens, as troubled with man's act,
> Threaten his bloody stage. By th' clock 'tis day,
> And yet dark night strangles the travelling lamp.

One plotter is picked out in the Porter's comment: "Faith, here's an equivocator that could swear in both the scales against either scale, who committed treason enough for God's sake, yet could not equivocate to heaven." The Jesuit provincial, Fr. Henry Garnett, was part author of *The Defence of Equivocation*, which argued that persecuted Catholics were justified in lying. Garnett himself had knowledge about the plot, but this had come from confession, and he had taken a sacred vow not to reveal what he knew. The public and the anti-Catholic laws respected no such fine distinction; Garnett was tortured and hanged. Shakespeare adhered to the popular view. Young Macduff is told that a traitor is "one that swears and lies ... and must be hanged". At the time of the production of *Macbeth* a little boy dreamed that one day he would be King of England, but, telling his schoolmaster of it, received a flogging. That little boy would one day implement the dismantling of royalty and the destruction of Shakespeare's guiding Venus to an extent undreamed of during Shakespeare's own lifetime. His name was Oliver Cromwell.

The Gunpowder Plot had strong consequences for Shakespeare. The conspiracy was the work of a small group of zealots, headed by the Yorkshireman Guy Fawkes and Robert Catesby, whose family held the manor of Bishopton in Stratford, and who had another estate at Lapworth, ten miles north of the town. On 5 November most of the chief conspirators were in Warwickshire, assembling in the rented seat of the Clopton family, Clopton House, just outside Stratford; the house had been leased by Ambrose Rookwood as a base from which to seize Henry, Prince of Wales, his sister Elizabeth, and his brother Charles, who were staying at Warwick Castle.

In London the conspirators drank regularly at the Mermaid Tavern, favourite watering-place of the playwrights. Ben Jonson, imprisoned the previous year with George Chapman ( John Marston, the third co-writer, escaped) for maligning James in *Eastward Ho*, which made comic reference to the King's corrupt practice of selling knighthoods for £30 – "Hee's one of my thirty pound knights", brags a comic Scotsman – sought release from the King's anger and the vengeful wrath of his Scottish supporters. Though he had dined with Catesby and Thomas Winter, another leading plotter, a month before the intended coup, Jonson now protested fealty to James and to Robert Cecil (who, some claimed, had acted as *agent provocateur* in the whole affair). Armed with a commission, he tried, as a Catholic with inside knowledge, to hunt down priests, maintaining that English Catholics should always be loyal subjects of the Crown.

Shakespeare with his Catholic sympathies, as expressed flatteringly to Queen Anne in *Measure for Measure*, was shocked by the Plot, and never again represented Catholic feeling, even in the most broad and generalized way, as he had done in *Measure* and, earlier, in *Hamlet* and *Romeo and Juliet*. His many quietist and recusant friends knew the Plot was a disaster for their cause. Although James promised not to turn faithful Catholics into scapegoats, the penal laws against them were strengthened and enforced. The Puritans, who had been under threat of silence and increasing pressure to conform to Protestantism, could now unleash a new wave of anti-Catholic paranoia, which they extended to include High Church ritual and conformism.

Shakespeare's family was caught in the backlash, for the church-warden and sidesmen of Holy Trinity Church, Stratford, reported his daughter Susanna for not receiving the sacrament at Easter 1606, a month before her twenty-third birthday. Hamnet and Judith Sadler were also on the list, which included a fair proportion of known recusants. Susanna finally conformed, so did the Sadlers, and just over a year later Shakespeare's daughter married the Stratford physician John Hall, who had solid Protestant low-church credentials.

iii

W. B. Yeats once wrote to Sean O'Casey, telling him that he must never impose his own opinions on his characters: "In tragedy the whole history of the world must be reduced to wallpaper in front of which the characters must pose and speak." Did Shakespeare educate Hamlet and Lear, asked Yeats, by telling them what he thought and believed? No. "Hamlet and Lear educated Shakespeare."

*King Lear*, the third of Shakespeare's great tragedies probably written three in a row, was the perfection of his tragic period, the climax of his achievement. A tragedy of blindness and misdirected will-power, *Lear* interweaves naturally and fluently two huge, many-sided plots of family relationships, those of Lear and Glou-cester, each of whom has lost his spouse, and therefore the moderat-ing and sensible hand of a woman. They are isolated figures when the play begins, and they grow increasingly isolated. But, as in *Hamlet*, Shakespeare is again exploring the primal family, and he is equally, in what could be construed as a back-handed compliment to King James, who brought a new unity to England, showing the folly – for a king – of dividing up his kingdom.

Shakespeare was warning once again. Each of the Fool's early scenes with his master emphasizes the importance of Lear's folly in giving away his kingdom – and abdicating the power of being a father. This was what Shakespeare's father did not do (and nor did Shakespeare, who imagined how horrible it would be to have fiend-ish daughters), yet it must have been inherent in the family situation, because of the blow Shakespeare's father suffered. Lear's sense of loss is so shatteringly registered that Shakespeare must have felt something akin to it and had this psychic pain re-awoken in him, perhaps by the "loss" of, or betrayal by, a mistress, or his grief over Hamnet's death.

But Lear, unlike Shakespeare, cannot face the pain of losing something, which provokes him into ungovernable rage, and then self-destruction. Shakespeare survived loss, but the hurt ran so deep that he had continually to exorcise those feelings, or at any rate acknowledge them, as a basis for transforming them into something lastingly expressive.

Although Shakespeare altered the Christian sentiment of his source play, the anonymous *True Chronicle History of King Lear, and his three daughters, Gonerill, Ragan and Cordelia*, acted in 1594, setting it in a more primitive and barbaric universe bereft of compassion and salvation, *King Lear* can still be interpreted as Christian allegory. Within the primitive shell, in the manner of a hermit crab requisitioning the carcass of another creature, Shakespeare invested the work with Christian modes of being, and with considerable vulnerability of feeling; so that one almost has a sense of Renaissance destiny being worked out through the characters' choices – and in spite of lip-service being paid to ancient deities: "As flies to wanton boys are we to th' gods, / They kill us for their sport."

It may *feel* like this, but this is exactly what does not happen in *Lear*. The King, a mature and seasoned ruler, specifically chooses his future in scene i, in the way that Titus Andronicus did, and his decision propels him and his daughter to their doom. He has several chances to rescind his choice, but refuses them, blinded by self-willed stupidity which has resulted in intemperate choler – a passion every bit as destructive as that of lust or jealousy. Lear blames everything on Regan and Goneril, but it was his mistaken decision to extend to them a chance to fulfil themselves at his expense – by giving them power, which so easily festers into appetite. How he could have believed he could go on dominating them by his authority, while rendering himself their vulnerable dependent, can only be explained by the distortion of personality caused by a lifelong exercise of power (itself a cause of character disorder). His blemishes have exaggerated and promoted the faults in his two bad daughters, whose personalities are partly the result of the upbringing he gave them. It is his inability to have learnt the right lesson that Regan truthfully points out:

O sir, to wilful men
The injuries that they themselves procure
Must be their schoolmasters.

In spite of the punishments meted out, becoming progressively more and more extreme, everyone in *Lear* continues to change throughout; Cornwall hardens cumulatively from the beginning into greater evil, like a diminutive Macbeth, overshadowed by Regan. Edmund begins likeably, generating audience sympathy. Albany, as he sees what is happening, converts after much dithering into a good person, and achieves greater stature when he throws off the influence of Goneril. He powerfully resolves the play:

You lords and noble friends, know our intent.
What comfort to this great decay may come
Shall be applied; for us, we will resign
During the life of this old majesty
To him our absolute power; (*to Edgar and Kent*) you to your rights,
With boot and such addition as your honours
Have more than merited. All friends shall taste
The wages of their virtue, and all foes
The cup of their deservings.

Kent reinforces the idea of the good person who still sticks around when the going gets bad, and is germane to the play's central idea of maintaining moral standards. Although disguised as a typical malcontent of the day, wearing a black hat like the Yorkshireman Guy Fawkes, Kent exemplifies the redemptive power of love and faithfulness.

So does Cordelia, who is prepared to forgive her father, in spite of the arrogance which has caused his mental and physical sufferings, although only when he is purged of his blind passion by the suffering he has undergone. This is not out of proportion to his fault, considering his responsibility as King: Cordelia's constancy redeems him, while his "birds i' th' cage" speech to her reads like an anticipation of heaven. There is no sense of waste, ultimately, in their relationship: statements such as "The gods are just, and of our pleasant vices / Make instruments to plague us" mean exactly what they say. They are not melodramatic, overstated, or would not have seemed so to the audience of Shakespeare's day, or to Shakespeare himself.

*King Lear* is not a nihilist *Endgame* vision of humanity, far from it. Cordelia advises the Gentleman, when Lear's temporary madness has burst and there is hope of cure, to exercise his own judgement: "Be governed by your knowledge, and proceed / I'th' sway of your own will" (these lines were added when Shakespeare revised the play two or three years after first writing it). It is in that wonderful interplay of unexpected choices and their outcome in its complex catastrophe that *Lear* is such a great play, closest of all Shakespeare's plays to *Hamlet*, and intimately reflective of the man.

Dressing up fundamentally Christian feeling as something else, Shakespeare never displayed his protean qualities better than when he sent the audience off on false scents. "There is something in the nature of this writer that resists definition . . . " avers John Barton. "What you get is massive contradiction, massive ambiguity, massive volatility." *King Lear*, supremely a play about human responsibility, has so often the appearance of being its opposite, a work about helplessness and suffering, because, paradoxically, it acknowledges human powerlessness in a Christian way. Shakespeare liked to do complicated things in a simple manner, and was never a provider of simple solutions.

*Lear* as no other play shows Shakespeare holding the spectator's hand: it is, for all its cruelties of expression, like the blinding of Gloucester, packed with detail and explanation that seek to reassure, and indicate, through a variety of chorus-like directives, who is to be believed, what is to be made of this. The putting out of Gloucester's eyes was hardly a worse punishment than that doled out every day to ordinary felons, in the public execution places of England's towns. As Jonathan Miller observes, Shakespeare was writing up the people he knew around him, "the upper bourgeoisie of Stratford and their domestic jealousies". Derek Jacobi agrees: "He related great events to the man in the street. He brought great kings and princes down to that level." Barbara Jefford sees a lot of the mysteries in his plays as just "oversights".

*Lear*'s emotional and actual storms, its bloodshed and cruelties, are also viewed always through the eyes of the most sensible characters, in particular Kent and Edgar. "The author has no desire to appal you – or to tell you the truth," says John Bayley.

Even Lear's temporary insanity is poignantly, tenderly, handled, as an affliction constantly in motion, passing through mania and delusions which have their own theatrical terror and bravura, to an inexpressibly affecting return to sanity (helped by Shakespeare's healing property of music). In the most terrifying bits of waywardness Shakespeare always wants us to know who is to be believed: when Lear meets Edgar disguised as Poor Tom, Shakespeare communicates this as alleviating Lear's inner tension. Lear's illness must be accepted, so the only way Edgar can help him is by engaging him on his own level. Yet Lear is never clinically mad; rather, he is little able to express and to come to terms with his emotions, so that the pent-up energy can only escape through hysterical thoughts. Shakespeare's feelings about madness were as compassionate as those about other aspects of pain. In depicting this pain he always kept something in reserve, or has someone watching and commenting, so that we, the audience, know exactly where we are. Most important of all, Lear's great disturbance is over: "the great rage you see is cured in him," says the doctor, while Lear asks, with full sense, indeed a new sense, instated: "You must bear with me. Pray now, forget / And forgive. I am old and foolish."

Nature, in the form of the storm, reflects the chaos and disorder caused by Lear's self-willed stupidity. All obsessives lack logic and the many expressions of "Ingratitude, thou marble-hearted fiend" are not of Shakespeare's own feeling. When he gave the words to Lear of "I am a man / More sinned against than sinning", he was palpably demonstrating that this attitude leads to self-destruction, because it is self-pitying. Lear refuses to cry; he nurtures and contains his pride – "Grief drives me mad". By his invocation of the gods Lear reveals that it is he who refuses to take responsibility: "O you gods, let me not be mad / Keep me in temper . . ." It is not up to them, but up to him.

However tempting it is to identify Lear's feelings about his family with Shakespeare's own experience, it was not Shakespeare's intention to do this; rather, he wanted to show up Lear as giving in to destructive feeling. Yet often, in blurred form, we can see the dark outlines of John Shakespeare and even the family affinity to Falstaff, the one who escapes gloriously from all responsibility, behind Lear. Lear cannot face failure: he closes himself to self-knowledge and makes his daughters and all mankind his scapegoats. Madness becomes his way not to know what he knows: he rails against women, he doles out reductive justice, he expresses sexual disgust because he cannot operate the female, flexible, forgiving side of his nature. He becomes the caricature of the puritan. Lack of self-love and self-esteem, destroyed through guilt, has stopped him being able to recognize others – stops him, literally, from recognizing those closest to him who support him most, namely Gloucester and Kent.

Shakespeare's own first direct experience of blindness, of madness, similar to Lear's, had been through his own father. John Shakespeare, isolated in his sense of failure, no longer a leading member of Stratford society, no longer the upholder of law in the town, or the bearer of civic dignities, drank heavily till he obliterated all personal individual sense of himself, trying to absorb his shame in the well-being induced by alcohol. He lost recognition of who he was. He looked upon his children as strangers. Like the chieftain's son in a primitive tribe who feels his father's old battle wounds in exactly the same places in his own body, Shakespeare carried the same hurts in his psyche: he had direct experience of the pain through his father's withdrawal of love and friendship from him. Yet through his own sympathetic, feminized nature, he identified strongly with his father: he justified him, took his side. In one less talented the consequences might have been disastrous: we know nothing to suggest that Shakespeare's brothers Gilbert and Richard led lives that were other than short and undistinguished (and possibly, in some way or other, blighted). Neither of them married.

Lear in the play falls because he is capable of making harsh statements about his children, and has presumably always made them; he gives away his kingdom not because he loves his children, but because he wants to possess them: his giving is purely selfish. As such, *King Lear* is a tragedy of character. The ancient kingdom of Britain falls apart because its king has renounced warmth and a unifying principle in human life. Lear is the opposite of Shakespeare himself, who saw grace and redemption as flexible; Lear would never have seen what lay behind Cordelia's reply, "Nothing, my lord".

Three incriminating letters in *King Lear* supply springs of action: Edmund's forged letter about Edgar's plot against Gloucester's life; Gloucester's genuine letter which Edmund steals and shows to Cornwall; Goneril's intercepted letter to Edmund, which Regan tries to read. Reality at the time of writing supplied the authority for these theatrical contrivances, for the Gunpowder Plot was uncovered by an anonymous correspondent warning a friend of the intended annihilation of sovereign and court. Otherwise Shakespeare would have used other means: as it is, the letters continually and deliberately enforced the parallel.

Lear's Fool was probably played by a boy – Armin had temporarily left the company, although he returned later – who doubled this role with Cordelia. This would explain why the Fool is not in attendance in the first scene when Lear disposes of his kingdom. It also clarifies Lear's mysterious remark, "And my poor fool is hanged". Both Cordelia and the Fool were dead – in the mind of the audience the same actor. They were twin souls and their identities had – in an unconscious slip – merged in the playwright's mind.

# Violent vanities

In May 1605 Shakespeare's closest colleague, Augustine Phillips, died at Mortlake, Surrey, where he owned a house. He left the hired men of the company £5, to be divided among them, and generous bequests of thirty shillings to his "Fellow" Shakespeare, to Condell, and to his servant Christopher Beeston. All the other sharers received bequests, but to his "late apprentice" Samuel Gilbourne he left forty shillings and his mouse-coloured hose, his white taffeta doublet, a black taffeta suit, his purple cloak, sword and dagger, and his bass viol.

Between October and December 1605, and again in 1606, there were further serious outbreaks of bubonic plague: there were in Shakespeare's mind, as indeed in that of everyone who stayed behind in London, serious doubts about how long one would or could hope to live. Jonson's courtier friend, Sir John Roe, "died in his armes of the pest", Jonson advancing money for his funeral, and prepared for the same to happen to him: "Which if most gracious heaven grant like thine / Who wets my grave, can be no friend of mine". Like Shakespeare, like the rising John Donne, Jonson had overcome the temptation to exchange adultery for matrimony, and court flattery for family. Writers conform to one another: in Shakespeare's day the pattern was married life, the aim social advancement and status.

i

Much of *Timon of Athens* seems like *Lear*'s afterbirth, for there are numerous connections between the two plays: perhaps it is not too great an exaggeration to claim that *Timon*, as part of the birth process of the greater work, was a play Shakespeare felt should be discounted. A tragedy of "humour", in the Ben Jonson mould – the humour being that of misanthropy – it does not reflect near-insanity on Shakespeare's part so much as extreme fatigue and loss of control, as he gave up active imaginative participation in its composition, and decided that it was not worth bothering about further. It failed, at a deep level, to engage his attention, probably because he was trying, unsuccessfully, to write about an existential hero who has no family ties. After *Lear*, with its remorseless concentration on family problems, it is clear why *Timon* should have appeared an attractive proposition. The idea came from a brief passage in Plutarch's *Life of Mark Antony*, with which Shakespeare was already engaged, and he filled out the idea from Lucian's dialogue, *Timon or the Misanthrope*.

Most fascinating of *Timon*'s sources is the New Testament, which underpins the idea of Timon's betrayal by his former friends by providing the comparison with Judas's betrayal of Christ:

> It grieves me to see so many dip their meat in one man's blood . . .

> The fellow that sits next him, now parts bread with him . . . is the readiest man to kill him.

> Who can call him his friend
> That dips in the same dish?

These mentions of the great betrayal serve dramatic ends: Shakespeare saw human betrayal in scriptural terms, and he may even have deepened his own experience of it in relation to the Passion of Christ, in order to identify himself, as Christians are exhorted to do, with the biblical figure. We may infer, then, from *Timon* itself the opposite of what is usually said of it, namely that Shakespeare was carried away by a subjective state of resentment, and self-hatred over success.

*Timon* bears out the view that Shakespeare's worked-up states of ingratitude and betrayal had an artistic purpose – they provided the stuff of his drama. In all likelihood he exaggerated his own experiences in order to draw on them, especially his earlier entanglement with patronage. The fact that *Timon* was a failed play, and that

Shakespeare abandoned it, indicates that while trying to deliver a homily on greed, he grew tired of what was primarily a Jonsonian exercise. The vice of greed emerges as impersonal. Timon's murderous didacticism displays Shakespeare's exhaustion of spirit after the writing of a supreme masterpiece.

There may have been therapeutic value in *Timon* as Shakespeare rid himself of, discharged or dumped on the awful characters the destructive feelings and passions which he had kept too perfectly in check while writing *King Lear*. To these feelings he now gave full rein: "To general filths / Convert o' th' instant, green virginity". I suspect Shakespeare was little impressed by Timon's ravings, which had something artificial and forced about them. But he felt better after writing them down, especially when following the vein of *Love's Labour's Lost*, and including more random jottings from his notebook:

> PAINTER: You are rapt, sir, in some work, some dedication
> To the great lord.
> POET: A thing slipped idly from me.
> Our poesy is as a gum which oozes
> From whence 'tis nourished. The fire i' th' flint
> Shows not till it be struck; our gentle flame
> Provokes itself, and like the current flies
> Each bound it chafes.

Was Shakespeare guying his own output when Timon at a later point remarks to the Poet: "Why, thy verse swells with stuff so fine and smooth / That thou art even natural in thine art"?

Much of *Timon* can be seen as a fatigued re-run of Shakespeare's thoughts about patronage, about flattering Southampton and then being betrayed. Or did he just wheel on these echoes to fill out a bad piece of work, written to pander to an audience's taste for the malcontent's invective? Since *Look Back in Anger*, written and performed in 1956, the 1960s and '70s have provided numerous examples of plays of sexual disgust, anger and near-insane bitterness which reflect the self-castigating guilt of their authors, and the need of audiences to be chastised for their wealth and ease. *Timon* has much of the same self-indulgence and narcissism of hatred, which has made it popular in modern interpretations, such as those of Peter Brook, and recently, Trevor Nunn. The Jacobean age was expanding into greater wealth, the pickings, particularly at court, were there for the asking. But there was also disillusionment after raised hopes – and London was full of Scotsmen on the make.

It has been said that Shakespeare felt he had wasted his great gifts on a harsh, indifferent world and that by writing *Timon* he was attempting to get his own back: "the hypersensitive soul rose in revolt". If so, he failed lamentably. But he knew himself, and how not to bring his heart into danger by self-injury. The notion that an uneven work like *Timon* revealed that Shakespeare was seriously sick in judgement, or mentally unbalanced, lacks substance. Was he unbalanced while writing *Timon*, and balanced while writing *Antony and Cleopatra* in the same year?

*Timon* reflects more that Shakespeare had nothing further to say about hate as a generator of dramatic power, and took refuge in attitudinizing; its motivation is as thin as, if not thinner than, that of *Richard III*, but it lacks the firm and glorious flesh of the earlier play. As Shakespeare's most unhappy and unsuccessful play, it needed family relationships at its hub. The "permanent politics of human nature", so identified by Coleridge, were missing.

ii

*Antony and Cleopatra*, on the other hand, was Shakespeare's supreme expression of love's power: the message of *amor vincit omnia*, even death, which although wrapped in and disguised by a classical and adulterous hide, was still saturated in biblical symbolism. Even the description of Antony:

> His face was as the heav'ns, and therein stuck
> A sun and moon, which kept their course and lighted
> The little O o' th' earth . . .
> His legs bestrid the ocean; his reared arm
> Crested the world. His voice was propertied
> As all the tunèd spheres, and that to friends;
> But when he meant to quail and shake the orb,
> He was as rattling thunder . . .

was rooted in Revelation:

> And I saw another mightie Angel come downe from heauen, clothed with a cloude, and the rainebowe upon his head, and his face was as the sunne, and his feete as pillars of fire. And he had in his hand a little book open, and he put his right foote upon the sea, and his left on the earth, and cryed with a loud voyce, as when a lyon roareth: and when he had cryed, seuen thunders uttered their voyces.

So, unmistakably, are other passages, which suggest that Shakespeare had engaged in much reading of the Bible at this time. This may have helped to produce the synthesis of feeling he furnished in *Antony and Cleopatra.*

Its basis was a hugely popular legend. Shakespeare made no bones about plagiarizing, sometimes word for word, large portions of North's translation of Plutarch's account: Enobarbus' description of Cleopatra, "The barge she sat in like a burnished throne / Burned on the water..." was a notable example.

From the beginning of the play the love of the dual protagonists was, as Shakespeare fashioned it, a magnificent public-relations exercise: Antony and Cleopatra are mostly seen apart, and their stature is built up cunningly, with an enormous number of scene changes, to suggest cosmic movement by depicting the effect each has on totally different minds. Each of the pair has the complexity of the battle of Agincourt, as described in *Henry V.* We are back with a vengeance inside Shakespeare's complete and uninhibited delight in character.

Cleopatra is, in her unexpectedness, on the scale of Falstaff: she is so many-sided she exists outside the play. Witty and adept at self-denigration, her sexual allure is that of a great film star, based on egocentricity of command. She is the model for the Queen in Lytton Strachey's gripping account of Elizabeth and Essex, and she radiates such spirit that Shakespeare, in writing her up, must have revived in himself his earlier fascination with Elizabeth. The great barge speech recalls the progress of the royal barge on the Thames between Greenwich and Westminster, its "cabin-tilt decorated with the Royal Arms in the blue and gold circle of the Garter", the watermen and pensioners in scarlet and gold, the myriad bright hues of the ladies-in-waiting and, in the midst of everything, the sudden visionary gleam of the pale face and red-gold hair as the indomitable, unpredictable old Queen came into view:

> Age cannot wither her, nor custom stale
> Her infinite variety. Other women cloy
> The appetites they feed, but she makes hungry
> Where most she satisfies. For vilest things
> Become themselves in her, that the holy priests
> Bless her when she is riggish.

The way Cleopatra questions the Messenger about Octavia has no basis in Plutarch, but depended on the heavily publicized new memoirs of Sir James Melvill of Hall-hill, who set down a fascinating account of being catechized by Elizabeth on the subject of her half-sister Mary Queen of Scots, and of having to make tactfully appropriate replies.

Shakespeare glorified the passion of the two great lovers with prophetic, hydra-headed amplification. No play ever wallowed with more delight in gossip about royals who are hardly ever together, and – when they are – are usually having a flaming row. From Petruchio and Katherine, who have few scenes together, through to Antony and Cleopatra, Shakespeare wrote sparingly in showing lovers together. There was cunning stagecraft in this, as well as keen observation: love scenes pall more quickly and are harder to get across than other scenes; distance and abstinence make love more arresting.

With women being played by boy apprentices (and with the ageing Cleopatra acted by an adolescent), the more lovers' passion could be shown by means other than direct confrontation, the better. Shakespeare had to conceive his female characters more fully than his male ones – he had to write in feminine traits and delineate them, or illustrate them objectively, in a foolproof way. In the short scenes given him as Lady Macbeth, the boy now playing Cleopatra had portrayed power, much more than pretty seductiveness. Shakespeare showed Cleopatra's seductiveness more in words and images than in her actions. She thinks in serene, detached and opulent metaphors, even when her lover is dead: in *Antony and Cleopatra* the power of words is everything, and the interplay of celebratory verse enables the great passion of the pair to achieve its eternal power:

> For his bounty,
> There was no winter in't; an autumn 'twas,
> That grew the more by reaping. His delights
> Were dolphin-like; they showed his back above
> The element they lived in. In his livery
> Walked crowns and crownets. Realms and islands were
> As plates dropped from his pocket.

Desire has been transformed into limitless aspiration, a pure romanticism of feeling whose true end is death, because only that will make the passion immortal.

The Greeks and Romans believed that love, whenever it went beyond the act that was its expression, was a sickness. Plutarch called love "a frenzy" – some conceived it as a madness; thus those who were in love had to be forgiven as though ill. This kind of love had nothing to do with fulfilled human love on earth, but was ultimately an egotism *à deux*, a great emotion lovers gave to each other, the climax of selfish, utilitarian love. This was mythological love: passion dreamt of as an ideal rather than feared as a malignant fever. It consumes the lovers in pure flame, it is a fate, stronger and more real than happiness, society or morality; it is above all a religion – which is how, much more explicitly, Shakespeare had depicted it in *Romeo and Juliet*.

The shared narcissism of Antony's and Cleopatra's passion is a sickness of being, a decay of the individual person: selfishness always ends in death. Shakespeare, with delightfully relaxed enjoyment, was now expatiating on that dark adulterous side of his nature which he had explored more rigorously in the Sonnets. His professionalism may have gloried in it, but it was a paradise of poetry only. He, as a mortal being, had solved his own sexual problems by returning to, and remaining with, his fifty-year-old wife, with whom he was now for ever reconciled. If the notion that Anne Hathaway was the Dark Lady had substance, then *Antony and Cleopatra* was its proof: Shakespeare had committed the ultimate betrayal and discrediting of the traditional myth of adulterous love by portraying his wife as his mistress.

For all the rowing and the tension of separation, their love, like that of the couple in his play, had strengthened, because their characters were equal and well-matched. Uniquely, for a female character in a Shakespeare play, Cleopatra develops and gains strength: she discards coquetry and advances to maturity. *Antony and Cleopatra* reposed centrally on Shakespeare's relationship with his wife, on to whose inner persona he had projected experiences undergone with someone else:

> Give me my robe. Put on my crown. I have
> Immortal longings in me. Now no more
> The juice of Egypt's grape shall moist this lip.
> Yare, yare, good Iras; quick – methinks I hear
> Antony call. I see him rouse himself
> To praise my noble act. I hear him mock
> The luck of Caesar, which the gods give men
> To excuse their after wrath. Husband, I come.
> Now to that name my courage prove my title.
> I am fire and air; my other elements
> I give to baser life.

Shakespeare had now been married to Anne for over twenty-five years; she was the mentally opulent and mysterious female proto-type for Cleopatra, as she had been for Katherine the Shrew. But there is no reason to believe that she served as a direct model for Cleopatra: he liked imagining himself as a king, so why should he not have extended the same facilities to his wife? She too may well not always have been faithful. And what had she been doing in those eight years of maturity before she met him?

Both of them were now reaching back into memory, which in Shakespeare's case he could transmute into a reality directly felt: as Proust expresses it, and as Shakespeare demonstrates it through his lovers, "we are torn loose from the slavery of the present and flooded with the intuition of immortal life". Each was becoming reconciled with the other: on the wider social scale marriage throughout Shakespeare's life had been in a continual state of crisis. From Henry VIII's reign until after Shakespeare's death, until Charles I reigned with Henrietta, no English sovereign enjoyed a fulfilling marriage. The death of marriage was an integral, if not the crucial part of the account of how England came to lose its soul: Shakespeare ceaselessly investigated marriage. The realism of his greatest love play proclaims a sense of personal fulfilment, rather than personal scepticism.

In *Antony and Cleopatra* Shakespeare resumed the practice of depicting contemporary political types which he had begun in *Julius Caesar*. Octavius Caesar was a detailed portrait of Burghley's son "Robert le diable", the icy and calculating Robert Cecil, now James I's chief minister; it showed particularly his cool, circumspect manner of dealing, using spies to keep him informed of Antony's activities (this recalls the Essex plot, with Antony the adventurous and reckless Essex figure): "I have eyes upon him, / And his affairs come to me on the wind." Pompey, the sea captain, was a sketch of Sir Walter Raleigh.

Like *Lear*, although markedly different in atmosphere, *Antony and Cleopatra* is a perfect work of art, a play contained within an epic love poem, with some of the most supple-versed, moving and reverberative love poetry ever penned: it is staggering, as poignant as Beethoven's great and final symphony, the Ninth, tracing the passions of Eros and the senses into inexpressible realms of glory – not so much a raid on, as a complete conquest of the inarticulate with vulgarly frontal, as well as cunningly elliptical, weapons. However painful it had been for him, Shakespeare had made the right choices in his spiritual and emotional development. As far as he was concerned man was still master of his fate: *Antony and Cleopatra* is a love tragedy of conscious will. The two protagonists may seem helpless in their love for one another, but their love is self-willed and as such they are not the victims of love nor of hate, or of politics, like earlier characters. There is a design behind everything.

After writing *Antony and Cleopatra* Shakespeare must have sighed with satisfaction, and reflected, with more than a shiver of anticipation and regret, that really there was not much more to do. Each of the complex propositions he had set himself to solve he had brought off with incredible naturalness and popularity. Yet there was one kind of play he had not yet coaxed into fulfilment – the proposition and problem play itself. He had come tantalizingly near to doing this in *Measure for Measure* – and erred equally far away from it again in *Timon of Athens*. He had suffered therefore the necessary element of failure to make him want to continue experimenting.

He set himself this lower target.

# The restoration of mothers

Shakespeare recognized that the power he had to imitate elemental qualities with the same force of nature as nature itself, would soon be spent. (*Lear*'s storm, and its conclusion, was an unconscious symbol of the turmoil of mind and soul caused in creating such elemental works.) What was left for him to do was to tie up ends.

Ibsen and Chekhov depicted life in terms of past guilt or future aspiration in a way similar to Shakespeare in his later plays, although with markedly different emphasis. Shaw, to some extent a parasite on both, wittily socialized and marginalized such conflicts. Shakespeare in the comedies *Pericles, Cymbeline, The Winter's Tale*, and finally in *The Tempest*, provided models for the three later dramatists. The late comedies of Shakespeare are plays of indirect conflict, post-crisis works, satisfying in their own unique and highly optimistic way, with their own special and individual laws and their own peculiar rhythm and flavour. Evil is down-graded as a dramatically generative force, and good tapped for its varied theatrical potential, although its appeal is inevitably more rarefied. The motto for Shakespeare's last plays was signalled by Antony's forgiveness of Enobarbus for deserting him: "The rarer action is / In virtue than in vengeance."

i

*Pericles* is often described as a convalescent play: it is believed, more upon intuition than evidence, that Shakespeare fell ill, and was nursed back to health by his son-in-law, Dr John Hall, and his daughters in Stratford. Also it is thought that he did not write all of *Pericles*: most of the first two acts is attributed to his collaborator, George Wilkins. But then Shakespeare, either adapting Wilkins's work or revived with new life, assumed control, and the last parts of *Pericles*, after its notably confused and depressingly bad beginning, became infused with numerous, often beautiful echoes of earlier plays. Some of these are cameos of the tragic Macbeths and failed Timon; Lear's recognition scene with Cordelia is echoed in the moving scene between Pericles and Marina, capped in the father's description of his daughter with its echoes of Viola's love –

> Yet thou dost look
> Like patience gazing on kings' graves, and smiling
> Extremity out of act.

There are echoes also of Portia:

> O Helicanus, strike me, honoured sir,
> Give me a gash, put me to present pain,
> Lest this great sea of joys rushing upon me
> O'erbear the shores of my mortality
> And drown me with their sweetness!

and of Othello, when Thaisa is restored to Pericles:

> No more, you gods. Your present kindness
> Makes my past miseries sports; you shall do well
> That on the touching of her lips I may
> Melt, and no more be seen.

No play more perfectly demonstrates how easily Shakespeare moved among emotions, transforming them to their opposites. "Inconsistency in matters of feeling", writes Tolstoy, "is the surest sign of their genuineness".

Pericles is drawn out of his depressive coma of suffering by Marina, but also by the skilled doctor Cerimon, a portrait of Dr Hall executed with baroque elaborateness; he is a sympathetic personage on whom the play's happy outcome depends:

> 'Tis known I ever
> Have studied physic, through which secret art,
> By turning o'er authorities, I have,
> Together with my practice, made familiar
> To me and to my aid the blest infusions
> That dwells in vegetives, in metals, stones,
> And so can speak of the disturbances
> That nature works, and of her cures...

Shakespeare, like Pericles, did feel the fire of life kindle again in his oppressed spirit and body, and so the compliments to a man "through whom the gods have shown their pow'r" were sincere – although fictional and figurative.

Yet something had departed from Shakespeare, as hauntingly from him as when the god of war deserted Antony. When he refused to fight on land and trusted himself to Cleopatra's ships, the Roman soldier went against Enobarbus' strong practical advice, making his "will / Lord of his reason", while the "itch of his affection ... nicked his captainship". Enobarbus feels nothing but disgust, for he fears his leader's judgement is warped and his courage empty:

ANTONY:    Hark, the land bids me tread no more upon't,
           It is ashamed to bear me...
ATTENDANTS:                              .Fly? Not we.
ANTONY:    I have fled myself, and have instructed cowards
           To run and show their shoulders. Friends, be gone.
           I have myself resolved upon a course
           Which has no need of you. Be gone.
           My treasure's in the harbour. Take it. O,
           I followed that I blush to look upon.
           My very hairs do mutiny, for the white
           Reprove the brown for rashness, and they them
           For fear and doting...
                              Take the hint

Which my despair proclaims. Let that be left
Which leaves itself...
                                        Pray you now,
Nay, do so; for indeed I have lost command.


ii


Shakespeare still loved war and all aspects of it, from weaponry, tactics, down to the minutiae of military music; just as *Antony and Cleopatra* was his valediction to passion, so *Coriolanus* (which could have been written before *Pericles*) was his brisk adieu to battle. In *Coriolanus* he echoed in a distant yet curiously potent way his own early departure for military service in the Netherlands. Then he had "lost" the father of his childhood in failure and debt, and yet felt compromised in his own recently assumed fatherhood. Coriolanus' sensual attachment to war suggests flight from his mother, and hunger for his father, with a desire to find, ultimately, the father in himself. Maternal feeding and consumption in death are the two poles of the play: its centre the body politic, pervasively imaged, as well as specifically parabled by Menenius, as the belly. Shakespeare, in *Coriolanus*, plucked new and strange vibrations from the primal feeding processes in the family.

Like Antony, Coriolanus too, although less surprisingly, is deserted by everyone: he is possibly not quite as loathsome as he is made out to be, although Plutarch called him "altogether unfit for any man's conversation". Many of his soldierly utterances are not revealing of the inner man, but conform theoretically to what Shakespeare saw as the professional soldier, as opposed to the soldier–scholar, of Elizabethan days. James had brought in a new era of peace: Sir Walter Raleigh, the impetuous sailor–warrior of a more individualistic age, lay in fetters in the Tower under sentence of death, Admiral Howard, Earl of Nottingham, was out of favour. The new kind of general existed only on the Continent, an alien figure who becomes absurd when he courts popularity and descends to canvassing (although, as Enoch Powell points out, the inexpressive Latin word for ambition means literally "canvassing", suggestive of "the external action of soliciting and acquiring office"). *Coriolanus* is a play full of Jacobean soldier–gentlemen jostling for advancement.

But the pride Coriolanus displays so icily, "disdains the shadow / Which he treads on at noon", is not a disintegrating passion, like lust of the body, greed, and the desire for power, and finally the impression he leaves behind is one of silliness: "his tragedy is," Stanley Cavell writes, "that he cannot achieve tragedy". Like a bleak and ageing Richard II, wholly immature in feeling, Coriolanus grows in isolation through the play, and as in the earlier work Shakespeare withheld – although this time more deliberately – any distinctive atmosphere. As Cavell notes, the play's language, "like its hero, keeps aloof from our attention, as withdrawn, austere, as its rage and its contempt permit". Albeit in muted form, there is still the intense patriotism of John of Gaunt in Volumnia's final appeal:

> thou shalt no sooner
> March to assault thy country than to tread
> ... on thy mother's womb
> That brought thee to this world.

Shakespeare was delineating once more, from direct observation, and now for the last time, the guiding political currents, so that, as Hazlitt observes, anyone who carefully studies *Coriolanus* "may save himself the trouble of reading Burke's *Reflections*, or Paine's *Rights of Man*, or the Debates in both Houses of Parliament since the French Revolution or our own". Above all Shakespeare, from a lifetime of observation, diagnosed in Aufidius' assessment of Coriolanus the relativity of political virtue:

> So our virtues
> Lie in th'interpretation of the time...
> One fire drives out one fire, one nail one nail;
> Rights by rights falter, strengths by strengths do fail.

Coriolanus, not Shakespeare, hates the common man: Cornwall's servants in *Lear* sacrifice themselves for justice, while Timon's establish a norm of goodness and decency otherwise absent: even in *Coriolanus* each separate member of "the common cry of curs" speaks rationally.

Before, or during, the writing of *Coriolanus*, in September 1608, Shakespeare's mother died. Coriolanus' final undoing, in his integrity of pride, is to yield to tenderness, and give in to his mother: "O my mother, mother, O! / You have won a happy victory to Rome." Volumnia's relationship with her son owes much to that of Shakespeare with Mary Arden; he caught in Volumnia universal qualities of a mother–son relationship, particularly in pride and ambition, both of which ran strong in the Shakespeare family. Also he heightened to extremity his mother's manly side, for she had, with her noble blood, become the patrician matron of the Shake-speare household, maintaining that position through all the phases of her illustrious son's self-projections in the guise of national leaders. Do as thou list, Volumnia intercedes with her son, "Thy valiantness was mine, thou suck'st it from me, / But owe thy pride thyself."

But the character of Volumnia was quite specific in design: she is the head of a one-parent family in the way that Lear is, with a resultant disorder in family feeling. No mention was made by Shakespeare of Coriolanus' father. One assumes that the mother had to be the man in that marriage, because the father was not up to it. Also Shakespeare depicted Volumnia objectively, as a definite Italian type – in her case an Italian mother, volatile, protective, ambitious.

The design of Volumnia's character owes much, too, as did Cleo-patra, to the King's Men's leading boy actor: this was his last, most manly, or most nearly male, role. It is uncanny that Shakespeare, along with everything else, could shape his casts to match and express not only his own development but that of his performers. "Anger's my meat, I sup upon myself", says Volumnia, and one feels a whole generation has passed since the previous young actor, nearly twenty years before as Queen Margaret, had expressed such manliness. The boy who played Margaret might now have been acting the ageing Menenius, who speaks often like a substitute father to Coriolanus. When women were played by boys the result, according to Barbara Jefford, was that "You get a bonus, of a more precisely, more profoundly stated womanhood". The same boy actor had played Mistress Quickly, Mistress Overdone, Cleopatra and was now Volumnia.

Shakespeare had created his last leading woman's part: the actor who had touched sublimity would have to bury his seductive iden-tity, hang up clinging gowns and titillating petticoats, buy himself a rapier and dagger, dwindling next season – plague permitting – into an insignificant young blade.

# Flying the courts of princes

i

Shakespeare, in a problem-solving mood during this final period, sought in *Cymbeline* to draw various threads together. But the play reveals an odd mixture of nationalistic concerns militating against his historical respect for classical Rome's achievements. *Cymbeline* is set, uniquely for Shakespeare, in Roman Britain, underlining how important the Roman heritage was to Elizabethans and Jacobean men of culture; and how that heritage figured in Shakespeare's literary aspiration, as he explored the unbroken continuity back to the invasion of Britain.

The action of *Cymbeline* happens within the span of a lifetime from that of *Julius Caesar*. With Shakespeare's scant respect for factual sources or chronology, it veers between being a nationalistic tract and a Renaissance melodrama, with sinister scheming and gratuitous horror thrown in for good measure. Was the playwright, old in craft and tired in expense of emotional energy, trying perhaps a bit too hard to convince younger rivals such as John Webster and Cyril Tourneur that at this late stage he could manipulate the new, cynical stock-in-trade as well as they?

In spite of writing many excellent scenes Shakespeare failed to bring to *Cymbeline* a complete unity. It was an experiment, a work of transition, and, as often happened when an idea of his fell short of imaginative realization, in it Shakespeare patently resorted to other playwrights' styles. *Cymbeline* is propped up by ancillary effects: the stage spectacle of gratuitous horrors – as Shaw notes, "the sensation scene exhibits a woman waking up to find her husband reposing gorily in her arms with his head cut off"; an interpolated masque; and a considerable quantity of music. *As You Like It*, *Lear* and *Othello*, as well as *King John* (the opening of Act III echoes the first lines of that history play: "Now say, Chatillon, what would France with us?" becomes "Now say, what would Augustus

Caesar with us?") supply fall-back situations and ideas. Now an old crow trying to pluck bright feathers from his earlier self, Shakespeare had been dredging through his own master works. His inspiration hung fire, and not even the ever-prodigal Holinshed, Boccaccio's erotic Italian fantasy, or the famous fairy-tale of Snowwhite, could lift this odd parti-coloured concoction into consistent life. As Dr Johnson wrote, "To remark the folly of the fiction, the absurdity of the conduct, the confusion of the names and manners of different times ... the impossibility of the events ... were to waste criticism upon unresisting imbecility..."

But – and yet again – Shakespeare was adjusting himself to new theatrical conditions: to the intimacy of the Blackfriars theatre, just inside the City wall Inns of Court territory. He was wooing a new audience, trying out on it a new mixture of ingenuity coupled with effectiveness. *Cymbeline* was not playwriting of broad and popular appeal, but a work for an intimate West End audience, basically cynical and blasé, that liked to watch rather than to participate, and then to applaud each "turn" or aria of feeling and thought. *Cymbeline* is often like a forerunner of the nineteenth-century music hall entertainment – itself an unstructured play, with comics, animal and magic acts, music, snippets of drama, designed to appeal to bored middleclass sophisticates and philistine royal families with a short attention span.

But even though attempting to beguile the quickly bored, Shakespeare could not help but lapse into his personal emotional flow. Iachimo bending over the sleeping Imogen when stealing her bracelet, and his confrontation back in Rome with Posthumus and Philario, brought Shakespeare right back to the peak of dramatic power. And his instinctive, even mystical, belief in the importance of the family, of the need to heal wounds and rifts, asserted its influence cumulatively, shifting the action with the introduction of Imogen's lost brothers Guiderius and Arviragus, into a completely different gear.

ARVIRAGUS:                          Brother, stay here.
    Are we not brothers?
IMOGEN:                          So man and man should be,
    But clay and clay differs in dignity,
    Whose dust is both alike.

Like the wine that peeps through the scars of Antony's drunken friends (or so Antony would have it), hidden family relationships crack the concrete of contemporary theatrical artifice as spread by the prevailing nihilism, and thrust up shoots of hope and rebirth. "But, gracious sir," says Belarius to Cymbeline,

> Here are your sons again, and I must lose
> Two of the sweet'st companions in the world.
> The benediction of these covering heavens
> Fall on their heads like dew, for they are worthy
> To inlay heaven with stars.

## ii

*The Winter's Tale*, Shakespeare's next play, was also, like *Cymbeline* and *Pericles*, full of echoes of past work, but this time he transmuted them into "fairy" gold. Perhaps his extended visit to Stratford revived his love of the countryside: the depiction of it in Act IV, scene iv, the longest scene he ever wrote, of nearly 900 lines, and twice the usual length of an act, glows with fresh observation and an intricate weave of comedy and lyricism which recalls *As You Like It*. Upon meeting Polixenes, her "father" in the once-deluded fantasy of her own father, Leontes, Perdita tells him,

> Sir, the year growing ancient,
> Not yet on summer's death, nor on the birth
> Of trembling winter, the fairest flowers o'th' season
> Are our carnations and streaked gillyvors,
> Which some call nature's bastards. Of that kind
> Our rustic garden's barren, and I care not
> To get slips of them.

She, like Leontes, wants to shun bastards, and when Polixenes asks why she neglects these flowers she answers:

> For I have heard it said
> There is an art which in their piedness shares
> With great creating nature.

But it is perfectly legitimate to graft, Polixenes points out, "a gentler scion to the wildest stock".

Stratford revived memories of Hamnet and Shakespeare's guilt over the death of his eleven-and-a-half-year-old son. He responded with the haunting portrayal of Hermione's first-born son, Mamillius:

HERMIONE:  What wisdom stirs amongst you? Come sir, now
  I am for you again. Pray you sit by us,
  And tell's a tale.

- 263 -

MAMILLIUS:        Merry or sad shall't be?
HERMIONE:                As merry as you will.
MAMILLIUS:    A sad tale's best for winter. I have one
    Of sprites and goblins.
HERMIONE:                        Let's have that, good sir.

Acutely, masochistically, Shakespeare observed that son's powerful reaction to his mother's demoralized state  –

LEONTES:    How does the boy?
SERVANT:                            He took good rest tonight.
    'Tis hoped his sickness is discharged.
LEONTES:    To see his nobleness!
    Conceiving the dishonour of his mother
    He straight declined, drooped, took it deeply,
    Fastened and fixed the shame on't in himself;
    Threw off his spirit, his appetite, his sleep,
    And downright languished.

Shakespeare perceived that something had gone seriously wrong with both *Pericles* and *Cymbeline* in the early parts of those plays, and was determined that this should not happen again. He wanted the sudden onrush and acceleration of Leontes' feeling in the early scenes carried through to its extreme, tragic impasse, and then the play's break – for time to begin its healing work with separation of Hermione from Leontes, Perdita from both – to possess unity in its disparateness. By now he had recovered his plotting ability, especially in his handling of the denouement and the final family reconciliation. He was using the plot of a popular novel, *Pandosto: The Triumph of Time*, first published in the 1580s and reprinted in 1608, when it caught his eye, turning from *Cymbeline* to dramatize this work with evident relief. He re-addressed himself to the old-fashioned world of romantic improbability, and he proclaimed its virtue in several places: "Like an old tale still, which will have matter to rehearse though credit be asleep and not an ear open".

He was also writing again for the Globe audience, as witness his return to South Bank jokes, and the pickpocket advice disseminated by Autolycus, and his peddling of "fine knacks for ladies". There was a return of clown and pantaloon figures of earlier days. He furnished the boy actor playing Mamillius with a continuity of roles by bringing him on again later as Perdita, so that Leontes and Hermione can embrace and cherish a child who has blossomed into striking physical similarity to the one they lost; again psychic compensation for a lost twin (Leontes and Polixenes had been as "twinned lambs that did frisk i' th' sun"). Perdita becomes "alone, th' Arabian bird", the incarnation of a spiritual ideal as expressed in "The Phoenix and the Turtle": "Beauty, truth, and rarity, / Grace in all simplicity".

The final reconciliation of Leontes with Hermione becomes a marriage ceremony – or a remarriage ceremony. If we are to see embedded in this, as I believe we should, the ending of the secret story of Shakespeare and Anne Hathaway, then Shakespeare was exploring yet again his sense of responsibility over Hamnet's death, this time in terms of recovery from it.

Dr Simon Forman, the bad practitioner who had tried to "halek" with Emilia Bassano, and who had already made a garbled and inaccurate stab at describing *Macbeth*, found the moral of *The Winter's Tale* to be simply, "Beware of trusting feigned beggars". He kept a tighter hold on his purse that way: and, to be fair, *The Winter's Tale* pulsates with the breeding propensity of money. "My traffic is sheets," says Autolycus, linking the play's heavy burden of sexuality with a lighter notion of bawdy ballads. As a frequenter of whores Forman knew all about it.

The date of his visit to the Globe was May 1611. The King's Men were still playing there in the spring and summer. "The Englishman . . . is most vain, and indiscreet and out of order," George Whetstone had pronounced on English drama thirty years before: "he first grounds his work on impossibilities; then in three hours runs he through the world, marries, gets children, makes children men." This succinctly describes *The Winter's Tale*.

# Sick men whole

"Magic," says Iris Murdoch, "prevents people from being good". Leontes calls the "warm" magic of Hermione becoming flesh "lawful". But Jacobean audiences viewed the hero of Shakespeare's next play, *The Tempest*, as a scientist more than a magician: Prospero has learnt to control nature and use it to his advantage, not material advantage, but for the transforming of baser affections into redeeming love and immortality. Again Shakespeare had taken an idea from Jonson, whose *The Alchemist* was performed roughly a year earlier than *The Tempest*, and turned it on its head. Jonson's Subtle is a fraudulent chemist who plays on his victims' fantasies of power and delight. He used in *The Alchemist* the idea that magic and the theatre parallel and reinforce one another: "Our whole life is like a play", he noted in his commonplace book, "wherein every man, forgetful of himself, is in travaile with the expression of another".

Even to the very end Shakespeare defined himself against those around him. Shakespeare calls his wizard Prospero, meaning "I make happy", like Goodstock, the Host of *The New Inn* (the name is evocative both of Shakespeare and of Prospero), which Jonson wrote six years after the publication of Shakespeare's First Folio, making his own subtle critique and appreciation of what a Shakespearian comedy adds up to:

> My end is lost in loving of a face,
> An eye, lip, nose, hand, foot or other part,
> Whose all is but a statue, if the mind
> Move not, which only can make the return.
> The end of love is to have two made one
> In will and in affection, that the minds
> Be first inoculated, not the bodies.

*The Tempest* contains the "playwright's last word". The invisible man is prepared at last to commit as much of a self-portrait as he can without descending to particulars: a universalized self-portrait to establish, ultimately, his insignificance.

*The Tempest* is ultimately, as Iris Murdoch points out, "a religious play", about "surrender of power and giving up magic". From *Lear* onwards the atmosphere and settings of Shakespeare's plays had been determinedly pagan; yet he had, in contradiction, elicited a moral thrust and design manifestly Christian, built not on abstract moral argument like Hooker's *Laws of Ecclesiastical Polity*, but on the interplay of character and emotion, and on language and metaphor. Shakespeare allowed his Christianity to develop *sui generis*, out of the free choices he made in the development of his skills as a poet and dramatist. There was absolutely not a scrap of dogmatism, no prose-lytizing certainty. Anonymous, he was present in his plays making decisions, meeting problems, as a highly individualized person. He faced and solved difficulties by means of his instinctive psychological insight and flexible responses. As no other writer has ever done, he demonstrated Christianity's contribution to civilization – and defined and warned against the dangers that destroy civilization.

The fruits of this approach, the climax and the final renunciation of that power, were in *The Tempest* in which, firmly astride the centre, Shakespeare enacted Christ's teaching of the renunciation of self. Suffering, sacrifice, sin – the Crucifixion – all were evident to greater or lesser degree in the tragedies; but in *The Tempest* he concentrated specifically on powerlessness and surrender to a higher kind of spirit. He stripped everything down to this purity of intention. We no longer have the cumbersome retrospective story fully played out, as in *The Winter's Tale*. The inciting incident in *The Tempest*, Antonio's usurpation of his brother's dukedom and Prospero's banishment, happens in the play's past, but Shakespeare made sure it was still omnipresent, so that the characters' unfolding, unified action could rake up as ammunition the unsolved past.

*The Tempest* had, for Shakespeare, a rare classical unity, a vision owing much to many influences, both factual and contemporary – and to his later habit of borrowing from himself. He gave it no beginning and middle, it is all ending. The storm, written with terminal economy, is bitingly realistic, evocative of Shakespeare's disillusionment with James's politicians: the advice is futuristic, with its Christian overtones of Thomas More's *Utopia* as well as echoes of Montaigne's "Essay of the Cannibals": "I'th' commonwealth I would by contraries / Execute all things . . ." Prospero, with almost comic humility, points to the playwright's fatigue: his old brain is troubled, he will have to walk a turn or two, in order to still his "beating" mind. "Be not disturb'd with my infirmity," he beseeches them.

Yet for all its teleological qualities, its apparently retrogressive insistence by Prospero on pre-marital chastity – placing the knowledge and union of two persons before their sexual use by one another – *The Tempest* proclaims the virtues of freedom. Ariel is set free and likewise the young people are liberated. Antonio resists the freedom; forced into isolation by his wickedness, he refuses choice: he never speaks to Prospero, and as W. H. Auden explains him in his poem, "The Sea and the Mirror",

> Your all is partial, Prospero:
> My will is all my own;
> Your need to love shall never know
> Me: I am I, Antonio,
> By choice myself alone

Shakespeare was saying, as he had said long before with Richard of Gloucester, that man has the power to change, to transform himself. The man who rejects this, who stubbornly asserts "I am that I am", is against nature, against the natural law, and destructive of life. Locked in egoism, in material, emotional or spiritual selfishness, it is he who upsets the order of the world.

Man must forgive, but however harsh it may be to accept, one must not forget the evil, and the lessons that showing evil can instil. Nature, the sea, has belched up Alonso, Sebastian, and Antonio, and Ariel has, as he tells them in his "You are three men of sin" final sermon, denatured them, driven them mad as "even with such-like valour men hang and drown / Their proper selves". The powers have incensed the seas and shores against their peace. When they draw their swords, Ariel proclaims the invulnerability of the higher power, amazing them with their powerlessness. They can no longer "hurt". So transfixed, reduced to potential annihilation, they have only the acknowledgement ("heart's sorrow") of having supplanted Prospero to free them from "ling'ring perdition".

Ultimately Prospero's gift to Ariel of freedom is far more important than his forgiveness of Caliban (whom Michael Holroyd equates with the Globe audience). Ariel is Shakespeare's genius, according to Holroyd: Ariel has no character, "that is part of the genius element". Prospero is the Stratford squire. His abdication of the power of his magic is Shakespeare's ultimate imaginative act, for magic, or writing plays, or being an actor has given Prospero a special power, a godlike differentiation from other people which is a gift, but not an egotistical possession. No one owns himself, Shakespeare is saying over and over again, except the mad and the bad; no one, in like manner, can give in order to possess. This is what Lear tries, giving his kingdom away so as to possess his children.

Shakespeare was significantly different from Marlowe, from Jonson, and from writers and artists who since his time have considered their gift their own possession, to use for purposes of ambition, self-advancement or trying to change the world – or who have vainly covered themselves in their own talent, like the self-regarding Angelo, "Most ignorant of what he's most assured, / His glassy essence". Shakespeare considered his creative power a loan, a temporary leasehold. He himself could not egotistically become identified with it. (Had he done so, it would have consumed itself, and vanished.) He was the medium for the wind that blew through him: "Heaven doth with us as we with torches do, / Not

light them for themselves." During the time that he "owned" his
gift Shakespeare knew that one day, like Prospero, that which differentiated him from other beings would pass, and that he would
become just like everyone else. He knew, with a combative humility
that had all the more to fight with and assert its sway over those
incredible emotional states and powers that he could express, that
only constant self-abnegation would allow him to go on wooing
and developing this gift to the end. "Sado-masochism", a modern
writer might call it – an inability to indulge himself, and to profit
from his power. But, spiritually, Shakespeare never did. Talent is
more often than not a wild thrashing about of egotistical despair
and fear that ultimately *he* or *she* the author may not be heard.

Shakespeare was not an egotist. Neither did he hide himself out
of perverse vanity or shame. He was far from being that grotesque
creature, the literary celebrity, who, as Elias Canetti writes, "collects
a chorus of voices. All he wants is to hear them repeat his name".
Shakespeare hid himself, as he did everything else, fulfilling a law
of nature – and nature for him was often an acceptable, morally
neutral synonym for God's world, or even God – knowing that
"summer's lease" had all too short a date. Prospero's Epilogue was
Shakespeare's final artistic credo – that of the old man signing off:

> Now my charms are all o'erthrown,
> And what strength I have's mine own
> Which is most faint. Now 'tis true
> I must be here confined by you
> Or sent to Naples . . .
> Gentle breath of yours my sails
> Must fill, or else my project fails,
> Which was to please. Now I want
> Spirits to enforce, art to enchant,
> And my ending is despair
> Unless I be relieved by prayer,
> Which pierces so, that it assaults
> Mercy itself, and frees all faults.
> As you from crimes would pardoned be,
> Let your indulgence set me free.

He, too, with the "defeat" – Iris Murdoch's word – of magic, wanted
to be freed from the burden of creation. He, too, at last wanted to
become the lord and owner of his face.

FIFTH PART

# PLOTS DO PALL

Portrait attributed to Frans Hals, and thought
to be William Shakespeare.

*(In private hands)*

# What's in a face?

The portrait that Alec Guinness had seen over forty years ago and found convincing was that of a man in late middle age.

No one had painted Shakespeare as a child: the two earliest fanciful representations of him as such, by George Romney and Henry Fuseli, executed at the beginning of the nineteenth century, underlined the quality of the infant prodigy. In Romney's cartoon, "Nature" unveils the infant Shakespeare, with "Comedy" and "Tragedy", the half-naked female Muses, bent in adulation over the Guardsman's child chosen by the artist as model. Fuseli's scion has Herculean overtones: his manly penis is caught on "Tragedy's" knee as he sits astride her, and she suckles him at her naked breast while the sinister, grimacing "Comedy" tempts him with a highly coloured gewgaw.

And no one, as far as we know, recorded Shakespeare directly from life at any other time. This was in contrast to other writers of the period, such as Ben Jonson or John Donne, whose own vanity or whose patrons, or both, led them to suggest themselves as subjects to painters or sculptors. Even the artists who made the two authentic representations of Shakespeare after his death, and by which he is generally "recognized", did not depict him from life. Martin Droeshout's engraving for the 1623 Folio is believed to have been worked up from an earlier portrait. Droeshout was fifteen when Shakespeare died. Ben Jonson wrote that it "hit / His face", but commended the reader not to look on his picture but his book: Droeshout's engraving is the most successful and most universally used image.

The half-length limestone bust in Stratford church by Gheerart Janssen, who like Droeshout was Flemish, is the generalized image of a prosperous burgher. Janssen, a leading London mortuary sculptor, may at least have known Shakespeare by sight, and may have worked from a death mask. The head is dome-like, with a full and fleshy face. Above is the coat of arms; below, an inscription.

Conventional features are painted in, with hazel eyes and auburn hair. The doublet is scarlet, the loose gown black; the hands rest on a green and crimson cushion with gilt tassels. The image bears no trace of youthfulness. It is respectable and concealing, the final confirmation of Shakespeare's Everyman and anonymous quality.

Shakespeare was, Rowe says, a "good-natur'd Man, of great sweetness in his Manners, and a most agreeable Companion"; Aubrey calls him "handsome and well-shaped". Twentieth-century Shakespearians corroborate these early descriptions. Derek Jacobi, although he sees him as a big ungainly man, not a graceful person, says he had a mellow voice and that he spoke "plumly, effortlessly". John Tydeman describes him as never being a young man, "never being Marlowe's age". A. L. Rowse in his biography calls attention to the "mobile, flexible features" that we know so well from the Droeshout engraving, "the sexy nose and sensuous lips, the large luminous eyes and dome of a cranium". Others have imaged a longish nose, with flared nostrils, denoting strong sexuality; weak eyes overstrained with the effort of concentration; a mobile, expressive mouth; chestnut hair (Orlando's "Your chestnut was ever the only colour" as approved by Celia in *As You Like It*).

Yet who could remain happy with the usual images when here – in Guinness's remark – was the prospect of an entirely new one? Throughout the writing of this biography the idea of an undiscovered portrait of an elderly Shakespeare has haunted me. I have come to see his face as combining elements of a J. B. Priestley, perhaps with a touch of Philip Larkin – a well-fleshed, full, provincial face – with something of the wildness, and high-arched strangeness, of Ralph Richardson made up as Face in *The Alchemist*. I am convinced that there was an element in Shakespeare similar to Richardson who said, "I never much liked my face", and once described it as a "hot-cross bun".

The portrait that had struck Alec Guinness as convincing had once belonged to Clifford Bax, the author and theatre critic; Guinness had no idea where to look for it now. I had pressed him with more questions about Shakespeare. What did he think he was like as an actor?

"Probably rather good", was the reply. "He knew what he was talking about – not at all like the young actors of today. Time-serving, I should think he was, he kept a very clever balance, for professional reasons – or for political. The idea that he had no personality is surely wrong. I see him as having a gentle, sweet personality. I do not think he wrote anything deliberately: it all came out in a white-hot madness, and then he would collapse."

When I ask J. C. Trewin if he knows of the Bax portrait, "Wait a minute," he answers. "I think I have heard of that. Do you remember . . . ?" he says to his wife Wendy. He rushes out of the room, to run several times up and down the stairs to his book-lined study.

"There we are." He re-emerges triumphantly, but panting. "I thought I had an idea where I could find it." He holds out a thinnish volume in a faded maroon binding.

*Rosemary for Remembrance* is the title of the book by Clifford Bax; sure enough, the frontispiece facing the title-page is a reproduction of the W. S. portrait; below it is the Italian inscription found on the reverse of the canvas, translated in the text. It begins:

> *Questo ritratto rappresenta il grande poeta inglese* . . . This portrait is of the great English poet William Shakespeare and was painted by the great Flemish painter Frans Hals. It was brought to Rome by the Count of Nithsdale, William Maxwell, and given to the Monastery of Saint Gregory on Mount Celio in Rome . . .

Bax writes of his first impression of the painting: "I saw the face of an elderly man, scant-haired, high-skulled, heavy-jawed, tuft-bearded and with almost black eyes, a face with a hundred meanings and deeply marked by emotional torment. Here was no Droeshout idler, no prosperous burgher of Stratford; here was a man, whomsoever he might have been, who was undeniably a genius."

But the picture I see reproduced is not, at first sight, very encouraging: it is the opposite of anything romantic or idealized. The realism with which the face is rendered throws out a strongly reductive image, perhaps made more so by the poor-quality black-and-white reproduction. The head is bald, but with long, whitish and wispy streaks either side of the crown. The neck scraggy, the goatee beard perfunctory, the expression – in eyes which are very unequal and different – somewhat more hurt than soulful. The right hand, raised above a book and holding a quill pen, is withered, almost arthritic – delivering an ecclesiastical blessing. The left hand is ham-fisted and badly painted. About the work there is, to be sure, an uncanny sense of movement, of thought caught in flight across the face, that does suggest someone out of the ordinary. Of course I have no idea of the colouring.

The overall effect is disappointing.

\*     \*     \*

My search takes me next to the house of Michael Holroyd, the wary, puckishly heavyweight biographer of G. B. Shaw. Here is already a connection with the portrait.

"Shakespeare not himself having any biography," says Holroyd as we settle down to a comfortable afternoon tea, "the biographer can put his own into him. You can complete him to your own formula.

"Shakespeare entered my life in a strange way," he goes on. He had written a book on Hugh Kingsmill; the central part of a crucial friendship in Kingsmill's life, that with Hesketh Pearson, "– who also, I knew, wrote a key biography of Shaw, as well as one of Shakespeare – ", revolved around Shakespeare. "Love of Shakespeare being a secular religion, the poet can become a kind of biographer's tool to dig out the intimate details of a life. Through this, Shakespeare became real to me."

For Holroyd, after he had written his *Kingsmill* and other books, Shakespeare became a tool, carried forward, to be used in the discovery of Shaw's life: "What it has given me is a device for locating truth." Part of Shaw's fight, in his brilliant embattled literary criticism, was to clear away, Holroyd says, "the end-of-the-century bric-à-brac that stopped Shakespeare being properly perceived". What he saw as he went on was that Shakespeare took him back to Shaw's childhood – "an imaginative rather than real world. Frightened and loveless in reality, Shaw found richness in dreams – that was Shakespeare. The child in the grown man who dreamed. Facts are not vital, and the dreams not unreal."

I am in the presence of the portrait. It hangs in an ill-lit corner of a reception room in the house of a person whose name Holroyd supplied, and whom I will call "Mr W. H." The owner has now carried it into the sunlight near the French window. I have sat down in a gilt-framed chair opposite. Mr W. H. and I have been chatting as I gradually take on board the image before me. It is at once all Bax said about it; the reproduction had completely belied it. I am excited. It is unmistakably the portrait of a real person, but, to my perception of it, also the work of more than a single painter – or, that of one painter who possibly at an early and immature stage was carried away by what he saw in the face, but had not enough technique to finish the rest of the painting well.

A number of remarkable features suggest that the face could be that of Shakespeare. The first is the shortened quill, which Bax noted, the mark of the professional writer. There is the flared left nostril of a longish, dominant nose, often thought to denote strong sexuality; this same flaring is pronounced in the Droeshout engraving. There are the features pointed out by Guinness: the strained, watery eyes, a sense moreover that the left eye is weaker than the right, with a drooping of the eyelid over the pupil, suggesting not only the wearing of glasses, but that astigmatism and constant use of the eyes were at fault. I do not see a face weak from the loss of upper teeth, simply the effect of age making the upper lip recede. The mouth is glistening and well-formed: a mobile, excited mouth in a face whose forehead is old. Thankfully the subject wears no ruff: just a loose, open-necked white shirt.

The most spectacular detail is the hair. There is in the dark and greying, straggly curls a gingery or reddish tint: where could a counterfeiter have discovered this speculative detail of Shakespeare's appearance, which has never been more than an inspired hunch on the part of sensitive biographers? And if it was a counterfeiter, trying to convince his purchaser that this was the authentic Shakespeare, would he not have made the gingery effect more pronounced? The detail is almost imperceptible: it appears, in effect, that of a young painter straining after realism.

There is so little about this face that is generalized, so little stylistically fixed. The forehead is full of stress, the two sides of the face almost unattractively equal. This is not a portrait which was painted to flatter its subject, who had written, "Light vanity, insatiate cormorant, / Consuming means, soon preys upon itself". The sitter is shy, vulnerable, full of shame, yet at the same time possessed of vanity; his is above all the face of someone who cannot disguise his need for anonymity. It is significant that both Alec Guinness and Graham Greene, who share with Shakespeare a concern for guarding their faces and their privacy, should have felt that this is the face of Shakespeare. This is the face of "Alas, 'tis true, I have gone here and there ... / Gored mine own thoughts, sold cheap what is most dear", also of Aubrey's convincing gossip on his nature: "the more to be admired of (quia) he was not a company keeper, lived in Shoreditch, wouldn't be debauched, and if invited to, writ 'he was in pain'." An unceremonious record of such a man. But of course it may not have been Shakespeare, just someone's inspired guess as to how Shakespeare must have looked.

# In one person many people

From late 1609 until his death in 1616 the density of recorded facts about Shakespeare's life thickens, like the light towards the end of *Macbeth*. Their nature remains as opaque as most of the previous information, as hard to see through or into as the badly fired, muddy glass of Elizabethan houses: the bleary "windows of thine age", Shakespeare calls them in Sonnet 3.

Shakespeare's company, the King's Men, had the lease of a second theatre, Blackfriars, which seated 700, while the Globe held 2,500 to 3,000. These 700 paid at least six times the price for entry, so it was a highly profitable concern. Shakespeare had a sixth share in Blackfriars. The annual return on this and on the Globe was roughly equivalent to the price of a substantial London house – Shakespeare paid £140 for a house in Blackfriars in 1613 – so even at the modest evaluation of £300,000 to buy a comparable house in London today, Shakespeare was, by the standards of his age and ours, a rich man with a considerable annual income which continued until his death.

Shakespeare took the ownership of property extremely seriously: it was not a burden, it represented the release from a burden, that of his father's failure in his endeavours to shake off his creditors. Judging by his underlying powerful optimism about money, Shakespeare enjoyed having it – like Georges Simenon and Jean Anouilh, both popular "classic" writers. He may proclaim the everlasting quality of his lines (in repeating the claims of Ovid, at the end of the *Metamorphoses*), but he had no sense of his own fate as an artist, as had Oscar Wilde and Proust, which could threaten his own material survival.

As most landlords do, he grew involved in the minutiae of furnishing and letting, finding tenants, collecting rents. This became a substantial and important part of his personality – few academics or subsidized theatre practitioners like to countenance this side of him. His hands were steeped in ordinary commerce. He collected rents, he hoarded security, he charged for broken possessions. Money transactions had run through every seam and layer of his work and imagination, not only in the more obvious manifestations in early works such as *The Merchant of Venice*, but especially in the later plays; in *The Winter's Tale* the ideas of commerce and sexual generation are inextricably intertwined. Shakespeare's later imagination hummed with economic reckonings.

The facts which can now be dug from the margins of this proprietor and playwright's life towards its end almost wholly concern the disposal of his wealth; they are dull. Namely that he subscribed to the cost of repairing a highway (in 1611); that he testified in a lawsuit brought by a fellow-lodger, Stephen Beloff, against Christopher Mountjoy, Beloff's father-in-law, for an unpaid dowry (Shakespeare is reported to have forgotten the precise details); that he was paid 44 shillings for an *impresa* won by the Earl of Rutland in a tournament – he wrote the motto while Richard Burbage cut out and painted the pasteboard shield; that from 1614 onwards he became caught up in various disputes over enclosures in Stratford.

Shakespeare's three brothers pre-deceased him in the last decade of his life. The youngest brother, Edmund, the actor, had lost an illegitimate son, also named Edmund, who was buried in St Giles Cripplegate in 1607. Edmund died in the same year, given, presumably by his brother, an impressive funeral which cost 20 shillings. Gilbert, nearest the playwright in age, a bachelor, profession unknown, died in 1612 aged forty-five, while Richard died in 1613 not quite twenty-eight years old.

Their sister, Joan, now called Hart, outlived her remaining brother by twenty-five years, while her issue stayed on as proprietors of the Henley Street house until 1806, after Shakespeare's last lineal descendant and granddaughter, Lady Bernard, died in 1670.

From 1610 onwards, his mother now dead but his first granddaughter, Elizabeth, then two years old, Shakespeare lived more of his life in Stratford. The first and most public signing-off gesture (like a prima donna's first "Farewell Concert" of many) had been *The Tempest*. He did not stop writing. He had, as Henry James pointed out, too much abundance left in him: "By what inscrutable process was the extinguisher applied and, when once applied, kept in its place to the end?"

\*     \*     \*

The Jacobean age became even more of a scribbling age than its predecessor. As "T. T.", the printer Thomas Thorpe, addressing the Earl of Pembroke, made clear when in a bid for patronage he listed all the great lord's attributes, noblemen were pestered daily with dedications. Certainly Shakespeare's Sonnets, dedicated by the same printer to the "onlie begetter of these insuing sonnets", which in the most simple reading of such a message would mean Shakespeare himself, were not dedicated to Southampton. In 1609, the year of their publication, Southampton was himself the father of two sons, now a successful courtier who ran Hampshire and the Isle of Wight, and occupied himself with the expansion of overseas trade, especially as patron of the new colony, Virginia.

The ambiguous dedication, matched by the book's mixed and diverse contents, and sold at the shops of William Ashley and John Wright for the price of 5d, has created more widespread controversy and more elaborate, often misguided research, than any other single factor, or single non-factor, in the life of William Shakespeare. By far the most sensible explanation of the dedication – the difficulty of whose interpretation is compounded by its full stop after every word – is that it was composed and printed in a hurry, and without the printer's having full confidence in what the author wanted. The dedication, as a result, is the printer's and publisher's own message (the publisher being Mr W. H., whoever he was).

Barbara Everett believes that W. H. might have been Shakespeare's brother-in-law, William Hathaway, who had access to the collection of sonnet manuscripts in Stratford where Shakespeare had the poems in safekeeping. Certainly the text shows no signs of being pirated: perhaps Shakespeare – by no means the first author to do so – was colluding in an event with which he did not wish to be publicly associated, yet privately wanted to happen. That Shakespeare did not approve is inferred only from the fact, or absence of fact, that he did not dedicate them himself.

Everett advances a tentative though ingenious theory about "W. H." and the Trinitarian conceit of the dedication (*see illustration on facing page*). The reality, here also, may have been simpler and more obvious. Shakespeare, in a way that would seem to be consistent with his behaviour both after this and before it, was undecided as to whether the Sonnets should be published or not. He was quite capable of withdrawing them, legislating against them, or withholding the manuscripts, had he so wished (and it is unlikely that anyone but he would have had copies of such a complete collection of

TO.THE.ONLIE.BEGETTER.OF.
THESE.INSVING.SONNETS.
M<sup>r</sup>.W.H. ALL.HAPPINESSE..
AND.THAT.ETERNITIE.
PROMISED.

BY.

OVR.EVER-LIVING.POET.

WISHETH.

THE.WELL-WISHING.
ADVENTVRER.IN.
SETTING.
FORTH.

T. T.

diverse sonnets). When he came to make his will he left the editors of the First Folio of his plays sums of money in recognition of the agreement into which he had entered with them over publication (and with Burbage who died before the Folio was printed). Shakespeare spent part of his later years revising texts which he had himself retained for that first collected or folio edition.

It is reasonable to suspect, then, that Shakespeare himself not only authorized publication of the Sonnets, but that he was expected to supply the dedication as well. He may well have written a dedication to Southampton which was refused, the Earl no longer wishing to be associated with that early, irresponsible period of his life. But Shakespeare must have had some desire or intention to publish the sequence complete, or he would not have written further sonnets to Southampton as late as 1603, such as the one about his release from the Tower. With Southampton's refusal, Shakespeare became worried about the publication. The publisher, Thorpe, independent and determined – as can be seen from his dedication of another work to the Earl of Pembroke – went ahead. If he had some prior agreement with Shakespeare, he would not have been the first, or the last, publisher to proceed after the author changed his mind. He substituted his own hurried and makeshift dedication for the author's own. The printing was so rushed that the printer had not even time to correct the setting. The page as set contains one significant but all too easy misprint for those haphazardly literate times – an "H" instead of an "S".

Such a mistake would have been welcomed by Shakespeare, who became acutely embarrassed by this strange and powerful record of his emotional growth. He could shield himself through partial anonymity, at least, for no one could now impute the publication of the Sonnets to him. He was exposing himself, but a distant self, not an immediate persona. He wanted the poems to live on, for that very stretch towards eternity that he proclaims in the lines: but he wanted them to live on for the sake of the feelings that had impelled him to compose them, not for personal kudos.

Priced at 5d a copy, they were sold by John Wright, dwelling at Christ Church Gate, and they sold badly; the tragedian Edward Alleyn bought a copy on 19 June 1609. For the fashionable public the age of the sonnet was by 1609 well and truly over, and no one was greatly interested in the personal feelings of an author who had done nothing to sell himself – either to inflate his own image or to flatter his readers. There was no second printing.

Most if not all of the Sonnets were first composed for the eyes of one or two persons only, or for Shakespeare himself alone, as one might write a diary. They were intermediary, experimental works, halfway formulations between completely private thoughts and public utterances. Some had been circulated privately by 1598 when Francis Meres published his *Palladis Tamia: Wit's Treasury*, which mentions, among a list of Shakespeare's achievements, his "sugred Sonnets among his private friends".

Alec Guinness describes how Samuel Butler, author of *Erewhon* and *The Way of All Flesh*, carried out a lengthy enquiry as to what was the right order of the Sonnets. He wrote out each on a separate piece of paper, then spread out the sheets over a huge, billiard-style table and shuffled them into an order. Daily he would consult the pile and rearrange the sheets. Guinness provides a clue as to why the Sonnets were published in 1609. Butler "spent years", he says, working out a final arrangement. And what did he arrive at? "Exactly the same order as in the first edition ... except for four sonnets."

We are led, then, inexorably to this conclusion: the original ordering of the Sonnets is highly professional. Only one person was capable of such professionalism: i.e., the author himself. Shakespeare definitely wanted the Sonnets published and he delayed this until 1609 because he, too, was seeking an imaginative unity in the poems through his subtle and careful ordering. As he sought a satisfactory sequence, he re-read them often, which is why ideas and images from them are so often echoed in his plays. The sequence, with its mixture of teasing, revelation and deliberate obscurity, is unmistakably his own. He wanted the mystery: he orchestrated the obscurity, the misleading or revealing puns on names, such as that in Sonnet 20, "A man in hue, all hues in his controlling", who might (or might not) be William Hughes the boy actor; the echoes in Sonnet 26 of the dedication of *Lucrece* to Southampton; and so on. Shakespeare may well have added new lines, or even new sonnets as afterthoughts, *apologia pro vita sua* – some read like this. In a curious way they mirror, in microcosm, the order and development of his plays.

Even so, a final coherence eluded him. And this is not surprising. The Sonnets describe so many disparate aspects of vanity and sexual experience, yet in many of them the very distillation of the thought expressed deprives it of continuity. To try to arrive at the perfect sequence was the final experiment he could conduct with this form: no doubt he found it highly enjoyable.

As the book was about to appear, he may have noticed the misprint on the dedication page and concluded it was only poetic justice. At least he could be satisfied with the ongoing mystery it would create. And in an age of peace, such as James I had ushered in, Shakespeare knew the power of monumental rhyme.

# Dying menstruums

Between 1610 and 1613 Shakespeare had a hand in three plays, if not more. The first, *Henry VIII*, or as it was first called, *All Is True*, was, like its alternative title, a superficial history play, earthy, gauche, to a degree honest but not remarkably so. Shakespeare presented certain events of the King's life in a well-disciplined way, with plenty of tomfooleries, and not a few processions. But he gave it no unifying theme.

The history is Sunday Review Front history, tastefully sensational but completely untrue to the facts as they are known today. The action covers thirteen years of Henrician rule, from the Field of the Cloth of Gold, in 1520, to the christening of Anne Boleyn's child, Princess Elizabeth, in 1533. Bluff and impersonal, Henry VIII is himself hardly characterized, although given one or two real-life documentary touches, such as the way he leans on Wolsey's shoulder on his first entrance. Buckingham's career blazes and fizzles with some dramatic force; Wolsey, with his baleful secular ambition, is a more interesting character study, but he never quite comes to life with individual wit and fire.

Much of *Henry VIII* is attributed to John Fletcher, which suggests, on the part of those who assign it thus, a childish belief that, first, Shakespeare was incapable of writing badly, and, second, he could not write in the style of Fletcher if he wanted to. But when *Henry VIII* was published in the First Folio of 1623 Fletcher was still alive, and, presumably, would have objected if he had been part author of the work.

Apart from expressing, through Henry, a popular hatred of taxation – the King complains about Wolsey's levying a sixth part of everyone's wealth to pay for the French wars – Shakespeare trod carefully, avoiding controversial issues and presenting the ultimate soap-opera Renaissance prince and his hirelings with complete innocuousness and blandness. The highly controversial subject of Henry's divorce from Katherine of Aragon makes little dramatic impact: as a glove-maker's son Shakespeare stretched his art as the Old Lady in the Queen's antechamber advises Anne Boleyn to do, to make her seductive gifts please Henry:

> the capacity
> Of your soft cheveril conscience would receive
> If you might please to stretch it.

Drawing on his usual historical sources, Hall and Holinshed, with additional material from John Stow's *Annals* and John Foxe's *Book of Martyrs*, Shakespeare steered a middle course through the tangled issues of Henry's divorce; restraint in such a thorny matter cools the temperature to tepidity. It becomes hard for the audience really to care if Anne Boleyn was responsible for Henry's divorce, or if Henry was genuinely conscience-stricken over marrying the wife of his brother Arthur, whether or not that marriage had been consummated.

Shakespeare distorted the historical chronology to suit the pageant. His most flagrant invention was the presence of Henry at Elizabeth's christening in Greenwich: from Hall's account it would appear that Elizabeth's birth, because she was a girl, made him furious and he kept away from the christening. Shakespeare, apprehensive of the contentious material that was to come, wisely ended the play at this point – before Henry's excommunication; before Katherine of Aragon's death; and before the cruel execution of Anne Boleyn. He must have felt inhibited by his own proximity in time to the events of the play.

Only with Wolsey did Shakespeare unbuckle his old talent and allow a full deployment of vitality: Wolsey's vexation of mind is lovingly detailed by Norfolk, who stands observing him, noting

> Some strange commotion
> Is in his brain. He bites his lip, and starts,
> Stops on a sudden, looks upon the ground,

> Then lays his finger on his temple, straight
> Springs out into fast gait, then stops again,
> Strikes his breast hard, and anon he casts
> His eye against the moon. In most strange postures
> We have seen him set himself.

Better still, in one of a sequence of majestic speeches of farewell to his greatness Wolsey echoes those other tragic characters who instinctively turn to water images at the crisis of their passion: "I have ventured", he says of his high-blown pride,

> Like little wanton boys that swim on bladders,
> This many summers in a sea of glory,
> But far beyond my depth . . .

During performances at the Globe of *Henry VIII*, which he also directed, Shakespeare enjoyed an Indian summer of popularity. Six other plays, *Much Ado, Henry IV* Parts One and Two, *Othello, The Winter's Tale* and *The Tempest*, were revived during the court nuptials at Whitehall of James's daughter Elizabeth and Prince Frederick, Elector Palatine of the Rhine, in the late winter of 1613. The King's Men received the fee of £93. 6s. and 8d.

At a performance a few months later, at the end of June 1613, during the elaborate masque and dance at Wolsey's house when Henry first encounters Anne, and where the text calls for shrill and reedy "hautboys", the actors set off a piece of ordnance instead, combined with trumpets. The effect was thrilling. Cannon were often safely fired from the thatched theatre roof; but this time was an exception. The wadding released from the barrel landed on the south side roof, where it smouldered and smoked for a while, then leapt into flame. Within two hours the whole structure was razed to the ground. No one was hurt, except – as one nobleman wrote to his nephew – a man "had his breeches set on fire, that would perhaps have broil'd him, if he had not by the benefit of a provident wit put it out with bottle ale".

The fire was spectacular: nothing like it had been seen since St Paul's steeple burned. The very next day several ballads describing the fire were entered in the Stationers' Register.

Shakespeare partly wrote two other later works: *Cardenio*, which was listed as one of six plays presented at court in May 1613, for which payment of £20 to John Heminges was authorized by the Privy Council, and *The Two Noble Kinsmen*. The latter included a morris dance so successful in the previous performance before James that it received an encore. *Cardenio*, a ghost play based on Cervantes' *Don Quixote*, which appeared in English in 1612, was attributed in a later publication to Fletcher and Shakespeare: its text has been lost. Neither of these plays was included in Heminges and Condell's First Folio, and if they acted on his instructions, which is likely, then Shakespeare did not want them in.

*Two Noble Kinsmen* contains the last professional writing of Shakespeare. Evidence of his involvement is clear. Scholars judge that he wrote roughly a third of the text, notably the formal beginning and much of the outstanding last act. The long meandering scenes engendered out of Palamon's escape from Theseus' jail, which make up the somewhat tedious body of *Two Noble Kinsmen*, appear alien to Shakespeare in mood and style, although in part they read like inferior reworkings of the jail scenes from *Measure for Measure*, and the passages from *Hamlet* on Ophelia's madness. He sketched out a scenario based on these earlier plays, and then gave it to Fletcher to write up. From the arrangement of the play, and by his clear seniority in age and experience, Shakespeare apparently acted as story organizer. And as the parts distinctively his are the beginning, the middle (first part of Act III) and the end (apart from a final Jailer's Daughter scene interpolated to tie up the action here), it seems likely that he "edited" *Two Noble Kinsmen*, and had the final say on it.

But the overall conception of *Two Noble Kinsmen*, like that of *Henry VIII*, is weak and linear, showing by default what terrific organizational energy Shakespeare had put into his earlier masterpieces, how coherently they had evolved one from another, and how unified and conscious had been their creation. Here is the same voice, but tired, able to sing an aria or two but without stamina enough for the whole opera.

*Henry VIII* had been a kind of abdication of character before pageant: the play bears roughly the same relationship to Shakespeare's earlier work as R. C. Sherriff's plays written after *Journey's End* bear to that first play, based as it was on sharp observation and raw emotional experience. Character had always driven Shakespeare's plays forward, the adapted selfhood of the author providing the central generative force of action, and the turning-points which roused dramatic suspense and passion. Even *Henry VIII* was still, if only emblematically, rooted in family life.

*Two Noble Kinsmen* had a theoretical, Shavian contest at its centre.

Two cousins, knights of chivalry, Palamon and Arcite, the protagonists of Chaucer's *The Knight's Tale*, love Emilia, the fair sister of Hippolyta, Theseus' Queen, whom Shakespeare had already portrayed with Theseus in *A Midsummer Night's Dream*.

The problem, baldly stated, is how one of the knights can marry Emilia without the other dying: much of the action has the rivals forewarning each other to fight (with many echoes of the *Dream*'s rival lovers). The chivalric love theme was not developed by Shakespeare with any depth or insight, as he might have done in his prime, but with that reliance on writing poetry that characterizes the ill-organized plays executed in times of fatigue, such as *Troilus and Cressida*. In some of these linear utterances Shakespeare rose, as in *Troilus*, to great poetic heights.

Palamon's prayer to Venus expresses a highly personal and coloured view of a man who practises chasteness, yet is disgusted at the deterioration of sexual mores he sees around him. It is the last great, long speech written by Shakespeare, a *cri de cœur* as surely autobiographical as some of the most naked and apparently vulnerable utterances in the Sonnets. "I was not a lecher, or an adulterer," Shakespeare (in disguise) proclaimed; "I was not a sexually aggressive male, nor was I stuffed with vanity. And now I am old, I am quite happy to renounce Venus."

The sixty lines begin with an invocation of the love goddess, praising her over the fierce tyrant, the cripple, the king and even the "polled bachelor":

> Whose youth, like wanton boys through bonfires,
> Have skipped thy flame, at seventy thou canst catch
> And make him to the scorn of his hoarse throat
> Abuse young lays of love . . .

Palamon then proclaims his own virtues, those of the young love poet who bears love's yoke "as 'twere a wreath of roses" (with echoes of Meres's description of *Venus and Adonis* – "the witty soul of Ovid lives in mellifluous and honey-tongued Shakespeare"). Never at great feasts had he "sought to betray a beauty"; he had been "harsh / To large confessors" and hotly asked them if they had mothers; he had not practised upon man's wife, nor read "the libels . . . of liberal wits". Then the horrific image of an old man screwing a young wife is pulled out of the air just to underline the horror of not accepting age.

> I knew a man
> Of eighty winters, this I told them, who
> A lass of fourteen brided – 'twas thy power
> To put life into dust. The agèd cramp
> Had screwed his square foot round,
> The gout had knit his fingers into knots,
> Torturing convulsions from his globy eyes
> Had almost drawn their spheres, that what was life
> In him seemed torture. This anatomy
> Had by his young fair fere a boy . . .

This is in no way the speech of a young, unmarried knight, and confirms again George Rylands' view of Shakespeare jotting long sections of verse down as they came to him, and then adapting them into a dramatic context: "Poetry was Shakespeare's birthright, the stage his profession."

*"Still music of recorders. Enter Emilia in white, her hair about her shoulders, with a wheaten wreath"* – Shakespeare had always tried to regard love like a physician, observing the course of an illness. Dealing with these last victims of Venus he captured the same understanding and detachment towards, in the words of Racine, "Vénus à sa proie attachée" as he had ever had, as the lovers pass through calms and crises, deceptive improvements and relapses, sick fancies and all the other vicissitudes of love. A trained observer, his attitude had always remained professional.

It is Palamon who loses the contest, who is condemned to death, but wins Emilia. In an extraordinary image, adapted from Chaucer, Arcite is crippled in victory by the behaviour of his horse when trotting in the streets of Athens. Its iron hoofs strike a flint in the pavement which frightens the "hot horse, hot as fire", which then falls to "what disorder / His power could give his will". Shakespeare's old alchemy of concentrated metaphor did not desert him here, especially in the monstrous fable of the horse's behaviour. Arcite's

> victor's wreath
> Even then fell off his head; and presently
> Backward the jade comes o'er and his full poise
> Becomes the rider's load. Yet is he living;
> But such a vessel 'tis that floats but for
> The surge that next approaches.

\*     \*     \*

Shakespeare never invented stories, he looked for them: the thinness of this adaptation presaged a decline, with his retirement from the active stage and from playwriting, of the King's Men, who continued to revive old plays of his. Patently they could not add to them much that was new, so that by January 1615 a correspondent at court wrote that the repertoire was of "such poor stuff that instead of delight they send the auditory away with discontent . . . of five new plays there is not one that pleases; and therefore they are driven to publish over their old, which stand them in best stead and bring them most profit". As Shakespeare himself expressed it, unconscious of some, at least, of the layers of meaning, when he wrote Palamon's address to Venus: "Our stars must glister with new fire, or be / Today extinct". His own plays had not yet gone through that strange and unpredictable chemical process of being transmuted into classics.

*The Tempest* still stood as Shakespeare's goodbye to the extraordinarily deep love–hate relationship he had with his audience. It remained immensely popular, and for that reason was printed first in the folio of 1623, with careful stage directions supplied from the prompt book: perhaps that editorial work which even today playwrights are called upon to do for French's acting editions of their plays, was begun by Shakespeare.

From the off-loaded melancholy strain of Palamon's utterances in *Two Noble Kinsmen* one detects that Shakespeare's old age was not a comfortable one, but that like an old and battered craft he himself was barely afloat and awaiting the "surge that next approaches". He had never had a fallow year, never an enforced early rest due to illness. His art consumed him, providing its own contrasts, relaxations and holidays in a different key, but never leaving him alone. He may have hoped, as he had earlier expressed it, to cash in finally:

> The aim of all is but to nurse the life
> With honour, wealth and ease in waning age,
> And in this aim there is such thwarting strife . . .
>                and oft that wealth dost cost
> The death of all, and all together lost.

But the "thwarting strife" came because he had, as with most human events, allowed the fresh savour of the experience to be undermined by imagining it before arriving at it. Palamon talks of men outliving the love of people, fathers outliving the love of children, and the loathsome misery of age, the gout and rheum "that in lag hours attend the grey approaches".

How self-aware was Shakespeare by this late stage in his life? Less, it must be judged, than earlier, when that personal voice of the poet made itself so felt as in *Hamlet* or even in *As You Like It* as Jaques. The age of the diarist, whose recording self watches his or her behaving self, and sets it down, evaluating day-by-day output or conscience in a kind of inner time-and-motion study, had not arrived. Had Shakespeare lived longer, this is the direction his writing might have taken, but there was no time, or quality of medical care, for a second Shakespeare to be born after the whole body of the plays had been completed. One Shakespeare was enough.

There was a tapering off in the man, as there had been already in the work. Even the last facts about him, squeezed like gold dust by meticulous twentieth-century scholars from the margins of public records, diagnose, for instance, in the war over the enclosures in Stratford and his association with his rich landowner friend William Combe, a lack of engagement, an indifference which declared that he was not particularly bothered one way or other.

When challenged by another Combe, a cousin called John, who left Shakespeare five shillings on his death, Shakespeare supposedly composed extempore some lines of a mock epitaph: "Who lies in this tomb? / Ho! quoth the Devil, 'tis my son John-A-Combe".

John Shakespeare's old workshop in Henley Street had been let and converted into the "Swan and Maidenhead": Shakespeare's sister Joan still lived in the Henley Street house with her family. Susanna Shakespeare gave birth only once: fertility does not seem to have been strong in Shakespeare's children, on the female side at least: on the male side there had been no chance to find out. Dr John Hall continued to build his fame and reputation as a leading physician in the neighbourhood: he had no licence from the Royal College of Physicians, but became so skilled and busy that he declined the civic honours offered him. Puritan by inclination, he began after Shakespeare's death a record of his cures: even "such as hated my religion", he stated in the preface, were quick to employ him.

# The great invisible

"The latter Part of his life was spent, as all Men of good Sense may wish theirs may be, in Ease, Retirement, and the Conversation of his Friends," wrote Nicholas Rowe in his 1709 *Life* of Shakespeare. Gossip adds that King James wrote him an "amicable letter' in his own hand, which may have pleased the poet; that Shakespeare planted a mulberry tree in his garden at New Place, that he would sit on a wooden bench outside with an earthen half-pint mug of ale. No doubt he often recalled and reflected on his dead kinfolk, especially his three dead brothers: Gilbert, with whom he had felt great rivalry, a "gay dog" in the old sense, and a bit of a drunkard; Richard and Edmund, the youngest, teased and protected ... There was that little bastard boy of his ... And of course his own Hamnet.

Men were through their own natures the butts of life, he must have sighed, while women wanted to live in the world and nurture it. All the women he had known saw their men down and under: had his own gift of prophecy not yet deserted him, he might have projected himself into the future, and like a Dickensian ghost, seen the decline of the family line which spanieled his own death at heel. Joyce, who had Shakespeare's protean gift of language but not of construction, does this for him in *Ulysses*, listing, like Banquo's vision in *Macbeth*, the women burying their menfolk:

> Mary, her goodman John, Anne, her poor dear Willun, when he went and died on her, raging that he was the first to go, Joan, her four brothers, Judith, her husband and all her sons, Susan, her husband too, while Susan's daughter, Elizabeth, to use granddaddy's words, wed her second, having killed her first.

Shakespeare had now given up regretting: the burning need for justice, which he meted out in the real world of his plays, had been overtaken by the urge to forgive and become reconciled. He had come to terms with professional remorse:

> The guilty goddess of my harmful deeds
> That did not better for my life provide
> Than public means which public manners breed.

He felt comfortable in what was now a dominantly female house-hold, enjoying the ordinary textures of life, to which he had always felt close: "And being lighted, by the light he spies / Lucretia's glove, wherein her needle sticks". He must have reflected that he had won his great life battle; he had reversed that disgrace suffered by his father. He now lived in the house built by Sir John Clopton; he was Stratford's richest and most illustrious citizen. Life in London, life in the theatre, had always been life passed in exile. He no longer had to watch, guard and comment on himself. He could let it go.

Shakespeare's old friend, Richard Quiney, had died from a blow to the head while acting as town bailiff in 1602. In 1615 Quiney's son Thomas, a vintner and tobacco dealer (and later, only two years after marriage, town chamberlain), was engaged to marry Judith Shakespeare, who was by now thirty-one years of age – therefore, like Anne, middle-aged when she married. She was an attractive woman and certainly had potentially a large dowry: she must have been strong and healthy, for she became the longest-lived of Shakespeare's children, dying in her late seventies. But Thomas, four years her junior, committed "carnal copulation" with another young woman, Margaret Wheeler, and had made her pregnant at the same time as his engagement to Judith. Thomas was tried in a "bawdy court" and fined five shillings (a heavier sentence of doing public penance in a white sheet was remitted). Even so the marriage to Judith went ahead in February 1616. Both Margaret Wheeler and her illegitimate child died a month after the wedding.

Shakespeare's idol was Susanna, described on her monument as "witty above her sex, and wise in salvation"; a loyal wife to Hall, even she did not escape scandal, which took the form of cruel as well as unsavoury slander. In early 1613 John Lane, an Alveston gentleman and a cousin of Thomas Nash, given to libel and disorderly conduct, accused her of infidelity to Hall – "the running of the reins and had been naught" with Ralph Smith, a thirty-five-year-old hatter of Stratford, a business friend of her uncle, at the house of John Palmer. ("Running of the reins" was later defined as gonorrhoea, but is now generally believed to mean the shedding of sperm against someone's will – a colourful phrase to accuse her of dipping into another man's seed.) Susanna brought an immediate action against Lane, which she won in Worcester Consistory Court in July 1613. Lane was excommunicated.

Was Shakespeare in his late years upset by these slanders and misdemeanours? Most likely he integrated them in his faltering stride. He is supposed to have responded angrily to Judith by modifying his will, but he may simply have given her gold plate or coin instead: wealth in rapidly disposable goods was greater in those days than today. In spite of Judith's marriage he kept his gift to her, of his best broad plate, in his will: he also knew that good marriages can come from the most inauspicious beginnings.

In his last years Shakespeare was fortunate still to be surrounded by so many of his family. In particular it was most unusual for a man to be married to the same woman for over thirty years, as Shakespeare had been to Anne. In the context of the times Shakespeare's marriage had been successful. Affection between wife and husband was moderate: spouses either became friendly and companionable towards one another, or they remained distant: the middle class and gentry were adept at managing separate households. A family had a much better chance of survival in a small country town like Stratford: even here family relationships were generally cool and unfriendly, although families stuck together. Men, women and children were extremely short-tempered, unceremonious and basic in expression of their physical and emotional needs.

Anne Shakespeare, sixty now, fed on beef and ale, but with a more refined moral diet, had broad shoulders and a well-developed bust, with a boldness and rotundity of speech which well suited her round and ruddy cheeks. She had been as good a wife as she could have been, loyal, travelling little, but also conforming little to the dicta of the time (as set down by W. Whately in *The Bride Bush*, 1617) that "mine husband is my superior, my better, he hath authority and rule over me; nature hath given it to him . . ." Could Shakespeare any longer reproach Anne for being older than him, and for the way she had swept him into early fatherhood? The answer was no. Early marriage had been the making of him.

Shakespeare has been pictured in these last years as sad and melancholic: a self-projection, too often, of those who write about him. Hesketh Pearson's Shakespeare, perhaps the most evolved and characterful portrait we have had, is pictured as moody and morose, stoutish, heavily footed, easily tired: "Long spells of silence might be followed by brief periods of slightly hysterical hilarity . . . Anger might suddenly flare out for no apparent reason . . . kindliness give way to resentment."

Edward Bond, in his play *Bingo*, depicts an even more tetchy and empty man, who complains how he spent so much of his youth, his best energy, to buy New Place: "Somewhere to be sane in". But it was all a mistake. "My stomach pumps it up when I think of myself . . . I could have done so much." Bond's character-assassination of Shakespeare is abstract and brutalistic.

Through all this my own Shakespeare was watching and waiting. He knew, for he was wise, that with the pressure and expenditure of self and soul his life had entailed, he had not much time. He was not a wreck, not at all like Arcite after his fall from the charger. I suspect his eyes hurt much of the time from the strain he had put them under: and those burning eyes themselves had channelled and isolated much of the knotted pain of character he had explored. He may well have looked an old man, but "His richness and costliness of spirit looked through". He still had elements of vitality; fastidious in habit, sensitive to dirt and evil smells, he continued to practise the habits of moderation noted by Aubrey.

He had passed through many crises, aware of the certainty that life was constantly changing, and that in a successful and evolving lifetime the way to growth both as artist and man was through the acceptance of limits, through the facing of pain, through the giving up of impulses and passions which led to sterility and death. Life had been continually painful and difficult, as for anyone who faces the reality of lies, insecurity, conflict, and his or her own inner laziness. But he had been willing to suffer. In play after play Shakespeare had dealt with himself, his own preoccupations and the lives of those close to him, untying psychic or emotional knots which used up energy as well as supplying it, supplying entertainment and fostering growth. It was not just that he had given his feelings an aesthetic outlet; it was something much deeper and more spiritual than anything Freud could touch upon, in what Pierre Rouve calls "the redemption of my minute personality within the even narrower borders of my personal biography". For Shakespeare expressed and relieved suffering by bringing it out into the open, providing through theatre and through poetry a lay equivalent to what Christianity provided directly in its liturgy and church ritual.

Shakespeare knew what André Gide later called one of the great rules: "Do not linger". Life was a succession of stages, each of them a rebirth; not only the seven physical stages described by Jaques, but stages of a spiritual and emotional journey, which could only be undertaken by the abandonment of previously held views of oneself and of the world. Shakespeare had confronted each change as it occurred in himself, in his family, and in a nation which was never at ease. Picking up, exploring, and then discarding the rapid proliferations of his own identity and feelings became the substance of his art: as Gide also wrote, "All the heaven and hell of his characters is in him". Character was pre-eminent, and so he could not linger: in order to be able to write *Othello* he could not allow himself to become Hamlet. He had always moved on.

It has always been tempting to accept the image of Shakespeare created by the Argentinian writer, Jorge–Luis Borges, in his short story:

> History adds that before or after dying he found himself in the presence of God and told Him: I who have been so many men in vain want to become one and myself. The voice of the Lord answered from a whirl-wind: Neither am I anyone; I have dreamt the world as you dreamt your work, my Shakespeare, and among the forms in my dreams are you, who like myself are many and no one.

It does justice to Shakespeare's protean powers; his invisibility, his anonymity, the actor in his make-up. Yet it, too, is an escapist image, it evades the responsibility of facing God, it is made in the slippery, deliberately mystifying image of Borges himself. Shakespeare, like God, had his certainties too. He had a strong character and an indelibly powerful will, he was extremely sure of his own solid identity. But that identity was continually in crisis and therefore he continually grew. When he needed to he withdrew into a cave where he could protect his own vulner-ability: like his image of snails in *Love's Labour's Lost* – "more soft and sensible / Than are the tender horns of cockled snails" – or in *Venus and Adonis*, when those tender horns were hit, he would shrink backwards

> in his shelly cave with pain,
> And there, all smother'd up, in shade doth sit,
> Long after fearing to creep forth again.

Shakespeare's plays are essentially by-products of his identity crisis and his confrontations: although he managed this in art as no one else has done, the work was never a cold-blooded exercise of ambition, but something springing organically from itself and from qualities in the man.

# Life measured by the space

According to a Protestant Archdeacon who lived in Gloucestershire in the late seventeenth century, Shakespeare "died a papist". At such an idea Victorian biographers threw up their hands in horror, especially Sir Sidney Lee, who dismissed this as "idle gossip" and "irresponsible report". Shakespeare, says Lee, who was knighted for his establishment life of Shakespeare, "was to the last a conforming member of the Church of England".

Shakespeare retained strong, instinctive sympathy with the old faith of Catholicism; he was attached imaginatively to relics and other articles of superstition such as ghosts: but he was not really bothered enough to risk offending anyone by insisting on a Catholic priest at his death.

Outwardly he was a conformist; inwardly he had reflected the religious crisis and divide of his age. His paradoxical religious complexion was best expressed in *Measure for Measure*, the work of a lapsed Catholic who is intimating that one day he may return to the fold of the Church. He presented the Roman viewpoint with instinctive sympathy, from the inside; outwardly he conformed to making the right and acceptable gesture of anti-papist propaganda, a "church papist". For some the ambiguity betokens a fault in the man: "If Shakespeare had sat", Graham Greene writes, "where [Francis] Bacon had sat and given the orders for the torture [of arrested priests], one wonders whether into the great plays which present on the inner side so smooth and ambiguous a surface, there would have crept a more profound doubt ... a sense of a love deeper."

He had always remained as much a competitive nationalist as an inwardly persuaded Catholic; he delighted in playing to the chauvinist crowd – which did not itself care much either way in the great religious divide – but in the end he dismissed this in *Coriolanus*, and in *The Tempest* as Caliban. Rooted in Tudor and Renaissance love of tradition and glory, he spent his old age among children who were to send James's second son, Charles, to the scaffold. He had lived his life among the new free-booting aristocracy, those who fought tooth and nail to hold on to their ill-gotten spoils under Henry, whose materialistic zeal and self-interest was the driving force of the Protestant Reformation. Their descendants were to conspire in 1688 to introduce Dutch William to the throne of England and, as the coldly polished and sceptical oligarchs of the eighteenth century, prepare the way for religion without God. Appetite, the universal wolf, had taken religion away from the poor and given it to the manipulative rich. " 'Ud's pity," Emilia says to Desdemona, "who would not make her husband a cuckold to make him a monarch? I should venture purgatory for't".

Shakespeare had registered the ravages inflicted on the English soul by the dissolution of the monasteries; one of his own theatres, Blackfriars, thrived in what had once been consecrated land; he had interiorized those forlorn and derelict sites as old age:

> That time of year thou mayst in me behold
> When yellow leaves, or none, or few, do hang
> Upon those boughs which shake against the cold,
> Bare ruined choirs where late the sweet birds sang.

Most of the new nobility from Henrician days onwards had been enriched with land and wealth from monastic foundations, or, in Elizabeth's and James's reigns, had their wealth topped up by recusancy fines. The informer would be rewarded with the property and land of those on whom he informed. Loyalty to the crown meant not only taking the oath but zealous anti-Catholicism, a willingness to share spoils which often made the receivers, at a subconscious level, feel guilty at dividing the fruits of crime and ruthless exploitation. The nobility and kings of Shakespeare can, for this reason, so easily be identified with and adapted as modern gangsters, tyrants, totalitarians and capitalist exploiters: the world of Jan Kott's *Shakespeare Our Contemporary*.

Through his uncanny assimilation of classical learning, and by an extraordinary feat of imagination, Shakespeare had equated the English ruling families, the Tudors and the Stuarts, with the ancient, blood-stained dynasties of Greece and Rome. By disguising and adapting the history of his own time and that immediately before it to the more distant past of history or legend – knowing his audiences would identify themselves directly with that past, see its impersonations as allegorical – he had explored the terrible crimes which were at the heart of English royal power in the sixteenth and early seventeenth centuries. The heinous judicial murders of Henry VIII, his blood-stained succession, the death and persecution of Mary Queen of Scots, the Jesuit and Catholic persecution, the threat of pious Spain annexing England as a vassal state and massacring Protestant heretics as Mary had done, the endless plots and counter-plots of nobles and foreign spies: all these, and more, were being constantly turned over, exercised as well as exorcised in the rag-and-bone shop of the human heart. In fictional trappings that were accessible, although parallel and at one remove, easily identifiable and yet concealed, Shakespeare's creations instructed their audi-ences in civilized values. He wanted a stable country for the future, for himself, his family and friends. Thus he had identified a national psyche and become its perceptive and reassuring mouthpiece. To do this he had embraced both sides of the religious schism and roundly lambasted the truly destructive element in the English national character, that of the Puritan who wanted to destroy his own means of livelihood, the theatre.

His was a profoundly Renaissant spirit: paradoxically, like Henry, who seized the wealth of the medieval monasteries and as well as squandering it on war, turned some of it, and especially the fabric of the destroyed buildings themselves, into fantastic Tudor palaces, Shakespeare ransacked the whole medieval heritage of miracle and mystery plays, of classical tradition and modern folklore, in order to build his great baroque palaces of dramatic poetry. There is no doubt which have lasted the better.

Shakespeare remained a believer in the sacred quality of life: he saw local gods everywhere and he admitted the omnipotentiality of God the Father. His local gods were carnal and Roman, and he was happy to reactivate these with glee and with a certain mischief. Everything for him possessed spiritual life and vitality, above all his eternal family of characters, related to and derived from, on the one hand, his own family and background, and on the other the developing family of actors with whom he had spent much of his working life.

This time was now so nearly at an end. "Throughout the whole of life one must continue to learn to live," Seneca had written 1,600 years before. "And what will amaze you even more, throughout life one must learn to die." Shakespeare had experienced many births. The final birth may well have been foreshadowed years before: it could well have been a long-term effect of childhood infection. Southampton died of a recurrent fever, probably malaria; Jonson from a prolonged palsy after a debilitating stroke which changed him into a paralytic invalid; John Donne, of repeated and chronic fevers, and exaltation of "damps and flashings". It may be sentimental to believe that Shakespeare was more worn out than anyone else who lived in those hard times: but "our hero may have died," says Henry James lamely, "since he did so soon – of his unnatural effort".

The age faced death realistically: as for most other endeavours, there were manuals instructing men how to face the end; the scholar kept a skull on his desk or carried with him some other *memento mori*; the great nobleman who had tumbled from high place was judged by his demeanour on the scaffold: "Oft death and judgement, heaven and hell / Who often does think, must needs die well."

Raleigh, who had been Elizabeth's most dazzling courtier, the complete Renaissance man, was incarcerated for treason for twelve years in the bloody Tower. He became friendly with his royal jailer's son, Prince Henry, who said derisively, "Only my father could keep such a bird in a cage." Aged only eighteen, popular and fond of the tilt, the Prince himself died suddenly in November 1612 in the midst of his sister's nuptial festivities. Raleigh was beheaded for no strong reason on his return from an ill-fated expedition to South America. His age, well over sixty, did not prompt James I to be merciful.

"Be absolute for death", the Duke prompts Claudio in *Measure for Measure*. When he drew up his will in January 1616, with Francis Collins, a Warwickshire lawyer, Shakespeare professed his own "perfect health", but this was the usual formula. Following legal practice, the document was unpunctuated, and covered three sheets of parchment. Its careful provisions mainly concerned Susanna and Judith, with whom now rested his hopes, since Hamnet's death, of a male heir to continue the family name. Susanna's male issue would inherit first, failing them Judith's.

Shakespeare commended his soul to God, "assuredly believing through the only merits of Jesus Christ my saviour to be made partaker of life everlasting". There is no reason to believe this was less sincere than his recitation, had he ever been overheard, of the

Lord's Prayer. His bequests included a substantial £150 to Judith, £100 for a marriage portion, the other £50 conditional on her surrendering her claim to a cottage Shakespeare owned on the Rowington estate, which was to go to Susanna.

To his sister Joan he leaves all his "wearing apparell" for her sons – in the absence of any other males in the family they will serve best here – the Henley Street house in which he had been raised, and the sum of £20. Susanna receives the body of his estate, apart from the third Anne receives as life interest, the so-called "widow's portion", along with the right to stay in New Place for as long as she lives. The heirs of Susanna's only daughter, Elizabeth, are to be well endowed. He leaves Susanna all his plate except for the broad silver and gilt bowl which goes to Judith. To Anne, specifically, he leaves his "second best bed with the furniture" of the bedroom it furnishes. (Anne had asked for this, which otherwise would have gone to Susanna. A correspondent in *The Times* in 1977 suggests that this is roughly similar to a modern testator who, having disposed of the bulk of his estate, turns to his solicitor and says, "And don't forget to leave Anne the mini".)

The will is considerate and broad; it spreads beneficence as a public figure might through Stratford friends and neighbours: Shakespeare gives his sword to Thomas Combe, a token of his defence of his land-owner friend, money for memorial rings to Hamnet Sadler, a recusant landowner called William Reynolds, and others. He omits mention of his former court friends and associates, such as Southampton. He leaves money for memorial rings to the other survivors remaining of the original Lord Chamberlain's company with whom he had worked for more than twenty years: John Heminges, Richard Burbage, and Henry Condell. He had made arrangements with these three for his plays' publication (Burbage died in 1619).

The nearness of Shakespeare to the "last enemy" may be inferred from the stated timing of the bequests; the will was drawn up hastily and signed two months after it was first drafted. The impersonal tone, the lack of affectionate or flattering phraseology (in contrast to the dedicatory epistles of *Venus and Adonis* and *The Rape of Lucrece*) reveal that he was in no mood to spread himself. No trace is there at all of the man. It is a purely utilitarian document. Other members of the King's Men made wills full of loving protestations. Shakespeare kept his feelings to himself.

Aged nearly fifty-two, Shakespeare signed each of the will's three pages, "By me, William Shakespeare".

# Anon anon sir

Dr Johnson, in 1783, complained that the age was "running mad after innovation", and that Tyburn itself was not safe from the fury of innovation: hangings were now confined to the prison's private yard. The public, he thundered, was "gratified by a procession; the criminal was supported by it". He pointed out the advantages of a public death: "Scarce any man dies in public but without apparent resolution, from that desire of praise which never quits us".

In ordinary, non-criminal lives, death was not hidden away but attended by relatives and friends. Jonson and Drayton joined Shakespeare – probably knowingly for the last time, as recorded by a Stratford schoolmaster, John Ward, some forty-five years or more after the event – in a "merry meeting", although it is unlikely that Shakespeare drank too hard and "died of a fever there contracted". The meeting more likely took place in Whitehall, where Jonson was immersed in masques and revels, than in Stratford, and they toasted the new folio edition of Jonson's works.

> Death should be public, or else why
> Are neighbours called when people die?

The man who had played and written so many notable death scenes was called to present himself, on his own deathbed in New Place, with wife, daughter, granddaughter, sister, nephews and cousins in attendance. William Hart the hatter, his brother-in-law, had died in Henley Street only six days before; now, surrounded by the public rituals of dying, the playwright felt the sting, or pinch, of the immortal bridegroom.

Shakespeare's body was disembowelled and carefully embalmed for display: led by the High Bailiff, Julius Shaw, one of the witnesses to his will, perhaps 500 or more people came through the door of New Place to register their grief and pay their respects. Two days after his death, recorded as 23 April 1616, his body left home in a wooden coffin with a procession only slightly smaller in scale than that accorded a Clopton or Greville. The hastily repaired great bell in the Guild Chapel tolled for his burial. Because he had been a lay rector, the body was interred within the chancel rail of Holy Trinity Church, which from vandalism and neglect was urgently in need of reglazing and repair. Shakespeare had ordered, so wrote William Hall to Edward Thwaites, these verses to be cut upon his gravestone:

> Reader, for Jesus's Sake forbear
> To dig the dust enclosed here:
> Blessed be he that spares these Stones,
> And cursed be he that moves my bones –

so as to discourage clerks and sextons from displacing his remains to the bone repository of the charnel house. It was a touch worthy of the man who had imagined Hamlet with two gravediggers. Interpreted symbolically by Henry James much later, it inspired James to burn all his own manuscripts and letters, to thwart the post-mortem exploiters and biographers.

After the funeral Anne Shakespeare received a formal delegation of mourners, listening to condolences offered by the worthies of Stratford, all in black-gloved mourning for the occasion. The house was hung with black cloth; perhaps Anne received them sitting upright in that second-best bed under a high black canopy, her kinfolk standing in a mute line at the bed's foot. This is our last sight of this "powerfully, even attractively masculine woman", who had been, as Barbara Everett says, "capable of obsessing her young husband for many miserable jealous years ... an ambitious, clever and wilful woman". Anne had surely been, as Helen promises that her court lover in *All's Well* will find her, the epitome of woman:

> A mother, and a mistress, and a friend
> A phoenix, captain and an enemy,
> A guide, a goddess and a sovereign.

When it was her turn, seven years later, aged sixty-seven, to be buried in Stratford church the brass plate on her coffin was inscribed with an affectionate personal message from a daughter, which one is not identified, who mourns her death. Shakespeare's "wife and daughter", wrote John Dowdell in 1693, "did earnestly desire to be laid in the same grave with him".

No less showy and extravagant than the celebrations attending his departure, and no less stiff and properly provincial and burgess, was the monument in the church, executed by Gheerhart Janssen. If he had ever scrutinized the playwright's features closely, Janssen's baroque limestone carving betrays little sign of it. The man he depicted was no longer "handsome and well-shaped", as Aubrey recorded: there is little sign of the "ready and pleasant smooth wit".

Francis Beaumont died a month before Shakespeare: a much lesser light in the theatre, he was buried in Westminster Abbey. No one at court mentioned Shakespeare's death, no influential man of letters or politics, such as Sir Francis Bacon, recorded the fact. Ronsard had died surrounded by nobles and princes of the Church; Shakespeare died without earthly glory.

*De Shakespeare nostrati*: from his notes Ben Jonson collected the remarks for publication in *Timber* or *Discoveries Made upon Men and Matter* that have given warmth to Shakespeare's monument. "I loved the man, and do honour his memory (on this side idolatry) as much as any. He was (indeed) honest, and of an open and free nature: had an excellent fancy; brave notions, and gentle expressions: wherein he flour'd with that facility, that sometimes it was necessary he should be stopp'd."

William Basse, an Oxford graduate and a retainer of Lord Wenman of Thames, found consolation in the Stratford burial. Basse perceived that Shakespeare was not dead, only asleep; that his life had yet to come. In his "unmolested peace", his cave not shared like that of Spenser, Chaucer and Beaumont in the Abbey, Basse felt that he was better off. Lord not tenant of his grave, under his own carved marble, "Sleepe rare Tragedian Shakespeare, sleep alone". Basse was saying that Shakespeare was unique. In time he would create his own dimension, a torch of greater luminosity and power by which others would be reflected. As in life, so in death, he lay apart. How he would become famous and remain so, in every successive age since his own, is another and very different story.

# Postscript:
## Look here upon this portrait, and on this

The specialists say of the Bax portrait of Shakespeare that the high-domed, bald head could originally have been a well-covered head with the hair scraped off. That it could never have been painted by Frans Hals. And so on ...

But as the painting is believed to date from the early to mid-seventeenth century, it is not clear why anyone should want to forge a painting in the style of a master whose death brought him obscurity for over a hundred years. The dark brown and purplish tones could be those of Hals: the living pose, the dramatic vitality of the picture, are characteristic of a great painter. There is something very camp in the tilt of Shakespeare's head, too, turning boldly over its left shoulder to confront the viewer, which is a constant device of Hals, particularly evident in the portraits of Pieter Cornelisz van der Morsch, the Rommel Pot Player, and most of all Verdonck. There is a similar quill, cut down and held by the engraver, Jean de la Chambre, another famous subject of Hals.

In the attempt to identify both sitter and painter, and in the absence of definite proof, what evidence does carry weight? The authenticity of the popular and much copied Chandos portrait of Shakespeare, whose subject wears a gold earring and has a certain *machismo*, hangs precariously on the slender thread of hearsay evidence from Sir William Davenant, who would claim, according to how deep he was in his cups, that he was either Shakespeare's godson – or his illegitimate child. Apparently Davenant gave the Chandos portrait (whose image of the playwright is remote from any I have) to the actor Betterton, who gave it to one Robert Keck. As David Piper says in *The Image of the Poet*, the painting's pedigree is incredibly complicated, "but cannot in any way be considered proven". The Chandos portrait could, then, be a complete fake, but listed as No. 1 on the register, it hangs in London's National Portrait Gallery.

How and when did the Bax portrait arrive in Italy? William Maxwell, Lord Nithsdale, was a celebrated Jacobite. His escape from the Tower of London in late February 1716 is well documented. He had been captured after the battle of Preston. Condemned to death for his part in the uprising, he was brought to London to be executed on Tower Hill. Winifred, his pretty twenty-six-year-old wife, rode through blizzards from Dumfriesshire to petition King George at St James's Palace, but she was brushed aside. Audaciously, with two other young women and a married pair called the Mills, Lady Nithsdale planned her husband's escape from the Lieutenant's lodging of the Tower. In a copious, hooded gown, Mrs Mill's red wig with ringlets planted on his head, his thick eyebrows painted out with chalk, his cheeks rouged, and with a muffler twined round his chin to hide his beard, Nithsdale was spirited past the guards and warders. He found shelter in the Venetian Embassy, and then escaped to Calais in the livery of a Venetian footman. His sister, who served as Mother Superior in a Flemish convent, could have given him the portrait; he might have purchased it later in Rome where he settled with Winifred, lived happily until his death in 1744, "ever a loyal supporter of the Stuart cause".

Is the painting, which is of a real face, a genuine glimpse of Shakespeare? Who knows or can say. Does not proof, as Elias Canetti writes in *The Human Province*, kill "even the truest things"?

# CHRONOLOGY
# ACKNOWLEDGEMENTS
# SELECT BIBLIOGRAPHY

# CHRONOLOGY

NOTE. The tables that follow are based closely on William Poel's *Prominent Points in the Life and Writings of Shakespeare* (Manchester, 1919). The form and layout of Poel's characterful original have as far as possible been preserved; spellings have been modernized; some inaccuracies corrected. Although referring to the 1864 "Globe" edition of the 1623 Folio, Poel's comparative tables are included. They underline the difficulties to be encountered even in the establishment of act and scene divisions in the plays – a relatively simple area compared with that of textual variants and authenticity.

| FACTS | |
|---|---|
| **(a) STRATFORD-ON-AVON** | **(b) LONDON** |

**(a) STRATFORD-ON-AVON**

1564   BAPTISM, 26 April.

> *Father, Bailiff and called "Master", 1568. Players first visit town\*; Father chief Alderman, 1571. Queen visits Kenilworth, 1575.† First visit of Lord Leicester's players, 1576. Second visit of Leicester's players, 1577. Father's money troubles begin. Mother pawns her estate, Asbyes at Wilmcote, and her lands at Snitterfield, 1578. Father fails to redeem her property, 1580.*

1582   MARRIAGE. Bishop's license issued to marry "William Shakespeare and Anne Whateley of Temple Grafton", 27 Nov. Two Stratford men sign bond for Bishop's leave to marry "William Shagspere and Anne Hathwey", 28 Nov.

1583   DAUGHTER's baptism, 26 May.

1585   TWINS' Baptism, 2 Feb.

> *Father's debts increase. A writ served but no goods to distrain, 1585. He forfeits his Alderman's gown, 1586. He is sued for his brother Henry's debts. He is held in custody or put in prison. Third visit of Leicester's players, 1587.*

1585   (About this time Shakespeare may have left Stratford.)

> *Father, fearing arrest, fined for not going to church, 1592. On or before 1595, Anne borrows forty shillings from a shepherd, who in his will (1602) directs that Shakespeare shall repay. Father in debtor's court for last time, 1595; sells "slip of land" in Henley street, 1596.*

1596   SON dies; buried 11 August. First application to Heralds' College for coat of arms.

1597   Buys NEW PLACE and an acre of land for a loan redemption of £60, although the total price may have been more.

**(b) LONDON**

1593–4   Dedicates his poems, VENUS AND ADONIS, and LUCRECE, to Southampton; they are published by Field, formerly of Stratford.

> *Later editions of "Venus" appeared in 1594, 1596, 1599.*

1594   Named as one of the ACTORS paid 15 March for showing before the Queen at Christmas "twoe severall comedies or enterludes".

1596   ASSESSED 13s. 4d. on property valued at £5 in the parish of St. Helens; he was now lodging in Bankside.

1598   Acts in BEN JONSON's comedy, "Every Man in his Humour".

Refers to SPENSER in "A Midsummer Night's Dream".

> *His name appears for the first time on published plays, "Rich. II." "Rich. III." and "Love Labour's Lost". The title-page of the latter states that the play was acted before the Queen. Twelve of his plays had now been written and acted; four others he was part author. Nine had been printed; two ("Rich. II." "Rich. III.") reached second edition. Some unpublished Sonnets had been circulated among private friends.*

1599   GLOBE PLAYHOUSE built between 1 Jan. and May at a cost of £600. The two Burbages held five shares; Shakespeare, Heminges, Phillips, Pope, and Kempe, five shares between them. Highest price paid by actors for a play at this time was £11.

EARL OF ESSEX's popularity mentioned in fifth chorus of "Hen. V."

---

\* For some years these visits were repeated annually. † Reminiscences of Kenilworth appear in "A Midsummer Night's Dream", and of Stratford-upon-Avon in "The Taming of the Shrew", in "Henry IV. Part II." and in "The Merry Wives of Windsor".

# AND TRADITIONS

*Proved about Shakespeare's Life and Writings*

PERIOD, 1564–1603

| TRADITIONS | CONTEMPORARY EVENTS AND ALLUSIONS | UNPROVED |
|---|---|---|
| That his father was a butcher, *Aubrey*, 1680: a wool-dealer, *Rowe*, 1709: that Shakespeare went to the Stratford Free School, *Rowe*, 1709: that he was once a schoolmaster, *Aubrey*, 1680: that he was apprenticed to a butcher, *Dowdall*, 1693: that he poached Sir Thomas Lucy's deer, *William Fulman*, 1688: that he began as a playhouse servitor, *Dowdall*, 1693: that he held horses for theatregoers, *Old Tradition, quoted by Colley Cibber*, c. 1750: that he received £1,000 from Southampton, *Rowe*, 1709: that he got Ben Jonson's first play acted, *Rowe*, 1709: that he held wit combats with Ben Jonson, *Fuller's Worthies*, c. 1650: that he played the Ghost in "Hamlet", *Rowe*, 1709: and Adam in "As You Like It", *Oldys*, c. 1700: that he returned home once a | 1593 Death of MARLOWE, 30 May.<br><br>1594 SPENSER and DRAYTON praise Shakespeare's Muse.<br><br>1597 ESSEX appointed Earl Marshal and head of Heralds' College; CAMDEN, King of Arms.<br><br>1597 BLACKFRIARS HALL bought by Burbage for £600. Dutchman makes a sketch of SWAN THEATRE from description given by a friend. DEATH OF JAMES BURBAGE, "the first builder of playhouses".<br><br>1598 FRANCIS MERES, a University graduate and divine, quotes a line of Falstaff's, and says that Shakespeare's dramatic art among the English is the best in comedy and tragedy. He names six comedies and six tragedies which had been acted.<br><br>GABRIEL HARVEY writes that Shakespeare's "Venus" delights young folk, but "Lucrece" and the tragedy of "Hamlet" please the wiser sort.<br><br>MARSTON, the dramatist, says that "Romeo and Juliet" was acted at the Curtain playhouse and applauded there.<br><br>HENTZNER, a foreigner, writes that tragedy and comedy are acted in London before large audiences nearly every day.<br><br>Death of SPENSER, 16 Jan.<br><br>SOUTHAMPTON spends an interval of leisure in "merrily going to plays every day". | That Shakespeare was the actor attacked by Robert Greene and defended by Henry Chettle, 1592: that Shakespeare wrote the "Talbot Scenes" (Hen. VI. Part I.), which attracted crowds of spectators, (*Nash*) 1592: that the "Errors" play acted at Gray's Inn, 28 Dec., was Shakespeare's "Comedy of Errors", 1594: that Shakespeare was the "W. S." mentioned on the title-page of "Locrine", a tragedy: and also the "W. S." alluded to in an anonymous poem, "Willobie His Advisa", 1595: that Shakespeare's Sonnets, c. 1598, were autobiographical: that they are printed in the order in which they were written: that "The Passionate Pilgrim", by "W. Shakespeare", and "The Phœnix and the Turtle", by "William Shakespeare", were the work of Shakespeare, 1599: that the Queen alluded to Shakespeare's play when she said, "I am Richard II. know ye not that?" (*4 Aug.* 1601): that Shakespeare is to be identified with "the silver-tongued Melicert", who according to Chettle, "did not drop from his |

*continued overleaf*

## FACTS

| (a) STRATFORD-ON-AVON | (b) LONDON |
|---|---|
| 1597   *A lawsuit to recover Mother's estate. The family described as "of small wealth and very few friends."* | 1600   *First mention of name in Stationers' Register ("Hen. IV. Part II.")* |
| 1598   Third largest owner of corn in his ward. Now called GENTLEMAN and Householder in town documents. Corporation wish to sell him tithes. Stratford man wants to borrow £30. | 1601   Allusion in "Hamlet" to the Town favouring CHILD-PLAYERS. |
| *Coat of Arms granted by Heralds' College. Mother's claim to the arms of Arden of Park Hall refused, 1599. Father dies intestate; buried 8 Sept. 1602.* | 1602   "TWELFTH NIGHT" acted in Middle Temple Hall, 2 Feb. |
| 1602   Buys one hundred and seven ACRES OF LAND near Stratford for £320. Also a COTTAGE and a quarter acre of land at back of New Place. | Quotes MARLOWE in "The Merry Wives of Windsor", and in "As You Like It". |
| | 1603   Acts in Ben Jonson's "SEJANUS". |
| | *By this time 21 of his plays had been acted; 14 published, 10 of them under his name; 10 extra editions had appeared, besides 5 of "Venus" and 2 of "Lucrece". Twenty-eight plays, of which probably four or more were Shakespeare's, were acted by Burbage's Players at Court during the Queen's reign.* |

| TRADITIONS | CONTEMPORARY EVENTS AND ALLUSIONS | UNPROVED |
|---|---|---|
| year, *Aubrey*, 1680: that he planted a mulberry tree at New Place, *R. B. Whelen*, 1760: that the Queen wished him to write a play to show Falstaff in love, *Rowe*, 1709. | 1601 ESSEX REBELLION. "Rich. II." acted at the Globe playhouse on Saturday, 7 Feb.<br><br>IMPRISONMENT of Southampton and EXECUTION of Essex (25 Feb.). Globe players act life and death of Cromwell, Earl of Essex; later "Julius Caesar".<br><br>MANNINGHAM, in his Diary, 13 Mar., relates a story of Richard Burbage, Shakespeare and Courtesan.<br><br>Queen's CHAPEL BOYS of the "Black-friars" satirize the plays and players of the "Globe" in Ben Jonson's "Poetaster".<br><br>1602 "Here's our (actor) Shakespeare puts them all down, aye, and Ben Jonson too." (*Kemp, in The Parnassus Play, Part 3*)<br><br>1603 Death of Queen Elizabeth, 24 Mar.<br><br>*Between 1591 and 1603 forty writers quote or parody lines from Shakespeare's poems and plays, occasionally giving his name.*<br><br>———<br><br>*Burbage's Company of Players visited the following provincial towns:*<br><br>*1593 Coventry, Leicester.*<br>*1594 Winchester, Marlborough.*<br>*1596 Faversham.*<br>*1597 Rye, Dover, Marlborough, Bristol, Bath.* | honied Muse one sable tear" for the death of Elizabeth, who "to his lays opened her Royal Ear", 1603: that Ratsey, a highwayman, alluded to Shakespeare when he told actors to save money in London to buy "some place in the country where their money may bring them dignity and reputation". (*Undated Tract, before 1605.*)<br><br>———<br><br>UNKNOWN<br><br>Date of birth: what he did before he was eighteen: whether he saw the Queen at Kenilworth: date and place of marriage: where he lived afterwards: when he left Stratford: which year he reached London: when he first joined a company of players: when he first returned to Stratford. |

| FACTS | |
|---|---|
| *(a) STRATFORD-ON-AVON* | *(b) LONDON* |

<table>
<tr>
<td>1605</td>
<td>Buys for £440 half the unexpired lease of Stratford TITHES.</td>
</tr>
</table>

*Susanna, his elder daughter, age 24, marries John Hall, age 32, physician of Stratford, June, 1607. Elizabeth, his grand-daughter, born Feb. 1608. Mary, his mother, buried in Parish Church, Sept. 1608.*

1608 GODFATHER to William Walker, son of Henry Walker, mercer and alderman.

1609 Wins case against DEBTOR, who then absconds. Sues Hornby, who had gone bail for debtor. Legal difficulties about tithes begin.

1610 Buys 20 ACRES from John Combe.

1611 Signs PETITION for Bill in Parliament to repair Stratford Highways.

1613 Visits London. Buys HOUSE, with shop and yard in Blackfriars, for £140.

*Fine on Players for acting in the town increased from 10s. to £10, 7 Feb. 1612. His youngest brother, Richard, is buried in the Parish Church, 4 Feb. Slander case in the Ecclesiastical Court about Susanna's honour. Defendants, Lane and Smith, fail to appear, July 1613. A preacher entertained at New Place, 1613.*

1614 Mentioned with some neighbouring gentry as a LEGATEE in John Combe's will. Secures from Combe's heir, William, a deed of indemnity against personal loss if COMMON-FIELDS are enclosed. Does not support protest against the enclosure.

1603 SECOND on the list of players licensed by the King to act in Globe playhouse or elsewhere. FIRST on the list of players receiving scarlet cloth as King's Servants. They are paid £30 for acting before the King at WILTON (2 Dec.); and an additional £30 in consideration of losses due to the Plague in London.*

1604 The KING impersonated on the "Globe" stage in a play setting forth the "Gowrie Conspiracy" of 1600. Twelve of the company paid £1. 16s. each for 18 days' attendance at Somerset House during visit of SPANISH ENVOY.

1605 Lodging now, or recently, with Mountjoy, a wig-maker, in SILVER STREET, Cripplegate. Receives 30s. from a fellow player, PHILLIPS, for a memorial ring. Not mentioned in the CAST (printed 1616) of Ben Jonson's "Volpone".

1607 His brother, EDMUND, a player, buried at S. Saviour's, Southwark, the Great Bell being tolled, 31 Dec.

1608 Takes one Seventh Share in BLACKFRIARS' THEATRE, of which Burbage has now purchased the remaining lease. Chapel Royal Children cease acting there, 1609–10. His share in the "GLOBE" now reduced to one Twelfth, and ultimately to one Fourteenth.

1612 Signs affidavit in the *Bellot v. Mountjoy* case. Described as of Stratford-upon-Avon, Gentleman, of the age of 48 or thereabouts.

*He deposes that the defendant authorized him to promise Bellot a marriage-portion with his daughter, Mary: failing this marriage defendant would no longer support her, 7 May.*

* The first time players had received a Royal Gift.

*Proved about Shakespeare's Life and Writings*

PERIOD, 1603–1616

| TRADITIONS | CONTEMPORARY EVENTS AND ALLUSIONS | UNPROVED |
|---|---|---|
| That his father was "a merry-cheeked old man", *Archdeacon Plume*, 1656: that he received an autograph letter from King James, *Lintot*, 1710: that King Charles read his plays more often than the Bible, *James Cooke*, 1649: that he said he had to kill Mercutio in the third act to save his play, *Dryden*, 1672: that "Troilus and Cressida" was maimed by the omission of act and scene divisions, and that this was the fault of the actors, *Dryden*, 1677: that in the writing of his plays he was guilty of "immorality", *Jeremy Collier*, 1698: that he instructed Taylor in the part of Hamlet, and that the impersonation was imitated by Betterton, *Downes*, 1663: that he wrote for gain and not for glory, *Pope*, 1726: that he satirized his friend, John Combe, in an epitaph | 1603 WILLIAM CAMDEN names Shakespeare, among others, as one of the "most pregnant witts of these our times, whom succeeding ages may justly admire". | That he was loved by Ben Jonson during his lifetime, *"Discoveries"*, printed 1641: that he wrote plays without blotting a line, *Heminges and Condell*, 1623: that he wrote "The London Prodigal", "The Yorkshire Tragedy", and "Pericles", all acted at the "Globe", and printed with his name on the title-pages, 1605–9: that he wrote the "Henry VIII." printed in the First Folio, 1623; that he was joint author with Fletcher of "The Two Noble Kinsmen", the title-page of which gives both their names, 1634: that he was the "Mr. Shakespeare" who, with Burbage, was paid for a herald's device designed for the Earl of Rutland, 1613. |
|  | *Queen Elizabeth buried, 28 Apr.* |  |
|  | JOHN DAVIES of Hereford writes that Shakespeare and Burbage have "wit, courage, good shape, good partes, and all good"; elsewhere he mentions Shakespeare personally: "Some say (good *Will*) which I, in sport, do sing, Had'st thou not plaid some kingly parts in sport, Thou hadst bin a companion for a *King*, And beene a king among the meaner sort." |  |
|  | *Hampton Court Conference. The King's threat to the Puritans, Jan.* |  |
|  | 1604 ANTHONY SCOLOKER writes that an Epistle to the Reader should resemble one of "friendly Shakespeare's tragedies"; it should "please all, like Prince Hamlet". Elsewhere he describes the stage antics of the Prince, "Puts off his cloathes, his shirt he only weares, Much like mad *Hamlet*; thus a passion tears." | — |
|  | *Peace with Spain, followed by the Gunpowder Plot, 5 Nov.* | UNKNOWN |
|  | 1605 BURBAGE says the Queen has seen all the NEW PLAYS, and that the revival of "Love's Labour's Lost" at Southampton's House should "please her exceedingly". | Whether all the "Sonnets", published in 1609, were written before 1598: the chronological order of the plays: date of his final retirement to Stratford: whether he survived all his |

*continued overleaf*

## FACTS

| (a) STRATFORD-ON-AVON | (b) LONDON |
|---|---|

**1616**   Receives first draft of his WILL; wife's name not included, nor those of his fellow actors, 25 Jan.

> *Judith, his younger daughter, age 32, marries Thomas Quiney, age 28, in Parish Church during Lent without license. Summoned before Ecclesiastical Court they fail to appear and are "excommunicated", Feb. 1616.*

Revises and SIGNS Will, 25 March. Assets: £350, in cash, personal belongings, and estate bought for £1,200. The mayor and leading townsmen sign as witnesses.

> LEAVES *to his wife, his second best bed with its furniture: to his daughter Judith, £300, and his silver and gilt bowl: to his grand-daughter, Elizabeth, all the rest of his plate: to his sister, Joan Hart, the Henley Street Cottages, during her lifetime, £20, and his wearing apparel: to her three sons, £5 each: to Thomas Combe, his sword: to his god-son, a gold piece: to the poor, £10: to Heminges, Burbage, Condell, and four townsmen, money for memorial rings: to his daughter,* SUSANNA, *all the remainder of his property, including New Place, Stratford lands, tithes, shares in London theatres, and the Blackfriars' house, with reversion to her issue, Elizabeth, in strict entail to the male heirs, and afterwards to his rightful heirs: to her and to her husband, the rest of his furniture and effects.*

Buried in the CHANCEL of the Parish Church in a grave 17 feet deep, which has never been opened. Entry in Parish Register:

> *Burials, 1616*
> *25 April, Will: Shakspeare, Gent.*

Monument gives date of death, 23 Apr., and age, 53.

---

**1613**   Globe playhouse burnt down 29 June. Rebuilt next year at a cost of £1,600.

**1614**   "My cosen, Shakspeare, comyng yesterday to towne, I went to see him how he did." – T. Greene, 17 Nov.

> *Since 1603 ten more plays, not counting "Pericles", had been written, 4 of them being printed: 15 extra editions had been published including 2 more of "Lucrece". With the "Sonnets", was published "A Lover's Complaint". One hundred and thirty plays, of which at least 13 were Shakespeare's, had been acted by the "Globe" players at Court.*

> *The 5 compositions most frequently mentioned, and quoted from, during his life-time were*
>
> *Venus, 42: Hamlet, 33: Lucrece, 25: Romeo, 16: Rich.III., 14: and the character of Falstaff, 15 times.*

| TRADITIONS | CONTEMPORARY EVENTS AND ALLUSIONS | UNPROVED |
|---|---|---|
| "fastened" to his monument, *Norwich Diary*, 1634: that his last years were spent in ease, retirement, and the conversation of his friends, *Rowe*, 1709: that Sir William D'Avenant seemed contented enough to be thought his son, *Aubrey*, 1680: that Susanna was his favourite daughter, *Rowe*, 1709: that he engaged in a drunken bout at Bideford, *British Magazine*, 1762: that he drank too hard at a merry meeting with Drayton and Jonson, and died of a fever, *John Ward, Vicar of Stratford*, 1662: that he died a Papist, *Rev. Rich. Davies*, 1708: that his wife and daughter wished to be buried in his grave, *Dowdall*, 1693. | 1605 *Owing to the Act of Uniformity, fifteen hundred ministers surrender their livings.*<br><br>1606 DRUMMOND, the poet, has read this year "Venus and Adonis", "Lucrece", "A Midsummer Night's Dream", and "Romeo & Juliet".<br><br>*Many Nonconformists take refuge in Holland, 1608.*<br><br>1609 EDWARD ALLEYN notes in his Diary that he paid 6d. for a copy of the "Sonnets". The author of the PREFACE to "Troilus and Cressida" asserts that even those who dislike the theatre are pleased with Shakespeare's comedies.<br><br>1611 DAVIES reproves Shakespeare for his choice of the Venus legend as a subject for his "eternal lines".<br><br>Dr FORMAN notes that he saw "Cymbeline", "Macbeth", and "A Winter's Tale", at the "Globe".<br><br>*Authorized version of the* BIBLE *published.*<br><br>1615 PHILIP HENSLOWE, theatrical manager, buried in the CHANCEL of S. Saviour's Church, with "afternoon knell of the Great Bell".<br><br>*First Congregational Church in England formed 1616.*<br><br>*During this period some seventy or more writers quote or parody lines from Shakespeare's poems and plays, occasionally giving his name.*<br><br>*Burbage's Company of Players visited the following provincial towns:*<br>1605 *Oxford, Barnstaple.*<br>1606 *Marlborough, Oxford, Leicester, Saffron Walden, Dover, Maidstone.*<br>1607 *Barnstaple, Oxford, Cambridge.*<br>1608 *Marlborough, Coventry.*<br>1609 *Ipswich, Hythe, New Romney.*<br>1610 *Oxford, Dover, Shrewsbury.* | three brothers: on what terms he lived with his wife: who paid for his monument in Stratford Church, and who wrote the inscription for it: whether he wrote the verses inscribed on his grave-stone (1616): whether any of his books and MSS. were in his family's possession at the time of his death. |

TABLE III –

| APPROXIMATE ORDER OF SHAKESPEARE'S PLAYS, | | | | |
|---|---|---|---|---|
| The THEATRE<br>Shoreditch | Newington Butts<br>Lambeth | The ROSE<br>Bankside | Place of<br>Representation not<br>known | The CURTAIN<br>Shoreditch |
| 1587–1597 | | 1592–1594. | 1590–1597. | 1595–1598. |
| | | 11 Apr. 1592.<br>Titus Andronicus. | Two Gentlemen of<br>Verona. | Romeo and Juliet. |
| | | | Richard III. | Ben Jonson's Comedy,<br>"Every Man in his<br>Humour" was acted in<br>this theatre by Burbage's<br>players, 1597–8. |
| | | | Comedy of Errors. | |
| 1587–1589 ?<br>Thos. Kyd's (?) Old<br>Play of Hamlet<br>and<br>Marlowe's<br>Doctor Faustus<br>are mentioned as<br>having been acted<br>here some time<br>previous to 1596. | 26 Feb. 1591.<br>Marlowe's<br>Jew of Malta.<br><br>3 Mar. 1592.<br>Hen. VI. Part I. | Edward III.<br>(Countess Episode)<br><br>25 Sept. 1602.<br>Kyd's<br>Spanish Tragedy,<br>with additions by<br>Ben Jonson. | Love's Labour's Lost.<br><br>The Taming of the<br>Shrew.<br><br>Midsummer-Night's<br>Dream.<br><br>Merchant of Venice. | Much Ado About<br>Nothing.<br><br>Hamlet (rewritten by<br>Shakespeare, printed<br>1604?)<br><br>Hen. IV. Part I. |
| Hen. VI. Part II.<br>Hen. VI. Part III. | 9 June 1594.<br>Old Play of<br>Hamlet.<br>(revised) | | King John.<br><br>Richard II. | Hen. IV. Part II.<br><br>Merry Wives of<br>Windsor.<br>(Windsor) |
| | | | Most of these plays may<br>have been acted at the<br>Theatre. | |
| | | The Cross Keys,<br>Inn Yard,<br>Gracechurch Street. | | |
| | | 1594.<br>Burbage, with his<br>players, and<br>Shakespeare acted<br>here some part of this<br>year. | | |

# INDICATING WHERE THEY WERE ACTED IN LONDON, 1591–1642

| The GLOBE Bankside | The GLOBE Bankside | Blackfriars' Playhouse | At Court | At Court |
|---|---|---|---|---|
| 1599–1613. | 1599–1613. | 1597–1609. | *For Queen Elizabeth.* | *For King Charles.* |
| ——— | ——— | *Rented by the Children of the Chapel Royal who appeared, 1601, in Ben Jonson's Comedy, "The Poetaster".* | 1594 Comedy of Errors. | 1633 Richard III. |
| *New Plays* | *Revivals* | | 1598 Love's Labour's Lost. | — Taming of Shrew. |
| | | ——— | 1599 Merry Wives (?) | 1634 Cymbeline. |
| Henry V. | | | 1603 Midsummer-Night's Dream (?) | — Winter's Tale. |
| | Romeo and Juliet. | | | 1636 Othello. |
| As You Like It. | Richard II. | 1610–1642. | | 1637 Julius Caesar. |
| Julius Caesar. | Richard III. | Burbage's players were now acting at the "Globe" and at the "Blackfriars". | ——— | |
| Hamlet (*final version, printed 1623?*) | Henry IV. Part I. | | *For King James.* | |
| Twelfth Night. | Henry IV. Part II. | | 1604. Othello. | |
| All's Well That Ends Well. | Merry Wives. | ——— | — Merry Wives. | |
| | Troilus & Cressida. | *Revivals.* | — Measure for Measure. | |
| Measure for Measure. | | Merchant of Venice. | — Comedy of Errors. | |
| | ——— | | 1605 Love's Labour's Lost. | |
| Othello. | 1614–1642. | Othello. | — Henry V. | |
| Macbeth. | Romeo and Juliet. | Taming of Shrew. | — Merchant of Venice. (*twice*) | |
| King Lear. | Richard II. | | 1606 Lear. | |
| | Richard III. | | 1611 Tempest. | |
| Timon of Athens. | Merchant of Venice. | | — Winter's Tale. | |
| | | | 1612 Much Ado. | At the Inns of Court |
| Antony & Cleopatra. | Merry Wives. | | — Tempest. | |
| | Henry V. | | — Winter's Tale. | 1594. |
| Pericles. | Hamlet. | | — Merry Wives. | |
| | | | — Othello. | Comedy of Errors (*in Gray's Inn Hall*) |
| Coriolanus. | Taming of Shrew. | | — Julius Caesar. | |
| | | | 1613 Hen. IV. Pt. I. | |
| Cymbeline. | Othello. | | — Much Ado. | |
| | King Lear. | | 1618 Twelfth Night. | 1602. |
| Winter's Tale. | Pericles. | | — Winter's Tale. | |
| | | | 1619 Two Noble Kinsmen. | Twelfth Night (*in Middle Temple Hall*). |
| Tempest. | | | 1622 Twelfth Night. | |
| | | | 1624 Winter's Tale. | |
| Henry VIII. | | | | |

TABLE IV – PLAYS

## A TABLE GIVING AN ANALYSIS OF ACT AND SCENE DIVISIONS, IN THE

The titles of the plays follow the same order as in the folio. Column 1 shows the number of lines in each play as given in the Globe edition: column 2 shows the order according to the length, beginning with the shortest play.

| TOTAL LINES | LENGTH ORDER | COMEDIES | ACT I | ACT II | ACT III | ACT IV | ACT V |
|---|---|---|---|---|---|---|---|
| 2042 | 3 | §**Tempest | 572 | 519 | 366 | 267 | 318 |
| 2386 | 8 | §**Two Gentlemen of Verona | 392 | 782 | 493 | 475 | 244 |
| 3022 | 24 | **Merry Wives of Windsor | 633 | 677 | 759 | 614 | 339 |
| 2812 | 19 | §*†Measure for Measure | 426 | 707 | 577 | 557 | 545 |
| 1756 | 1 | *Comedy of Errors | 263 | 317 | 313 | 438 | 425 |
| 2668 | 14 | *Much Ado About Nothing | 435 | 734 | 459 | 430 | 610 |
| 2785 | 17 | *Love's Labour's Lost | 506 | 259 | 207 | 709 | 1104 |
| 2205 | 5 | *Midsummer-Night's Dream | 364 | 464 | 669 | 263 | 445 |
| 2614 | 12 | *Merchant of Venice | 517 | 633 | 680 | 477 | 307 |
| 2851 | 20 | **As You Like It | 621 | 532 | 724 | 525 | 449 |
| 2373 | 7 | †The Taming of the Shrew | 541 | 413 | 346 | 729 | 344 |
| 2950 | 22 | *All's Well that Ends Well | 582 | 758 | 474 | 704 | 432 |
| 2690 | 15 | **Twelfth Night | 628 | 651 | 747 | 247 | 417 |
| 3074 | 27 | §**Winter's Tale | 515 | 472 | 409 | 1102 | 576 |
| | | **HISTORIES** | | | | | |
| 2572 | 11 | ††King John | 276 | 598 | 615 | 562 | 521 |
| 2752 | 16 | **Richard II | 648 | 644 | 579 | 334 | 547 |
| 3027 | 25 | **1 King Henry IV | 651 | 945 | 683 | 291 | 457 |
| 3365 | 34 | *†2 King Henry IV | 603 | 893 | 466 | 867 | 536 |
| 3146 | 28 | *King Henry V | 408 | 438 | 718 | 986 | 596 |
| 2638 | 13 | †††1 King Henry VI | 560 | 486 | 474 | 557 | 561 |
| 3160 | 29 | ‡2 King Henry VI | 675 | 504 | 829 | 813 | 339 |
| 2889 | 21 | ‡3 King Henry VI | 580 | 692 | 561 | 560 | 496 |
| 3621 | 36 | *†Richard III | 1073 | 414 | 829 | 847 | 458 |
| 2796 | 18 | **Henry VIII | 615 | 661 | 644 | 310 | 566 |
| 3464 | 35 | ‡Troilus and Cressida | 832 | 632 | 707 | 649 | 644 |
| | | **TRAGEDIES** | | | | | |
| 3313 | 30 | *Coriolanus | 773 | 721 | 624 | 668 | 527 |
| 2523 | 10 | *Titus Andronicus | 495 | 324 | 386 | 543 | 575 |
| 3017 | 23 | ‡Romeo and Juliet | 715 | 674 | 797 | 406 | 425 |
| 1946 | 2 | §‡Timon of Athens | 257 | 243 | 469 | 634 | 343 |
| 2477 | 9 | *Julius Caesar | 570 | 525 | 615 | 412 | 355 |
| 2080 | 4 | **Macbeth | 449 | 331 | 450 | 483 | 367 |
| 3930 | 37 | ††Hamlet | 851 | 751 | 928 | 662 | 738 |
| 3328 | 32 | *†King Lear | 964 | 644 | 618 | 696 | 406 |
| 3316 | 31 | **Othello | 692 | 728 | 745 | 651 | 500 |
| 3063 | 26 | ‡Antony and Cleopatra | 532 | 761 | 755 | 570 | 445 |
| 3340 | 33 | **Cymbeline | 742 | 469 | 755 | 530 | 844 |
| 2215 | 6 | *Pericles* | 443 | 496 | 252 | 590 | 434 |

\* Divided into Acts but not into Scenes.     \*\* Divided into Acts and Scenes.     \*† Some irregularities in the Scene Divisions.     † Some irregularities in the Act Divisions.     †† Irregular Divisions both in Acts and Scenes.
‡ Not divided into Acts or Scenes.     § A list of the characters is printed for this play.

## REMARKS

robably the only play in the volume written in acts and scenes by Shakespeare. Note the pause after Act 4 where Prospero finishes the act with a speech and opens the next act with soliloquy.

Scene 2, Scene 3, of Act 1 no change of scene is needed. During Scene 1 of Act 3 the action changes from the prison cell to the street. These division errors are corrected in the Globe edition.

nce there are no scene-divisions in this comedy, the words *Scena Prima* are not wanted after *Actus Primus*. They are omitted from Act 2, and reappear after the names of the subsequent acts.

this play the words *Scena Prima* occur only after Act 1.

cts 4 and 5 are both named *Actus Quartus*. Note that Act 5 is more than four times the length of Act 2. As a rule the last act is the shortest.

ote that five consecutive plays are divided into acts but not into scenes. The Globe edition divides Act 2 of this play into nine scenes.

he *Induction* is not separated from the rest of the play; Act 1 is followed by Act 3. The Globe edition corrects these errors and alters the positions of the remaining act divisions.

ena Prima* is only added to Act 1. In Act 4 a ruled line is drawn across the column of the page where a scene ends.

nis Actus* is printed at the close of each act except the third act, where there is no pause in the action, and no division should have been made.

ene 2 of Act 4, where the characters enter, should be Scene 1. The Globe edition does not correct this error. Note the length of this act.

cts 4 and 5 are both named *Actus Quartus*. The length of Act 2 is only 74 lines; the Globe edition throws back the act to the position of Scene 2, Act 1, then turns Act 2 into Act 3, omits the words Act 3, adding a new scene-division.

ne Globe edition divides Scene 3 of Act 5 into two scenes, a needless addition.

he Globe edition divides Scene 2 of Act 5 into two scenes, which is again unnecessary.

ene 1 of Act 1 should begin after the *Induction*. The Globe edition corrects the error; it also divides Scene 1 of Act 4 into three scenes, and Scene 2 of the same act into two scenes.

ene 1 of Act 1 is here correctly placed after the prologue. The second speech of the Chorus comes in the middle of Act 1, and again at the opening of Acts 2, 3 and 5. But there is no Chorus to open Act 4. The Globe edition rearranges the act-divisions, so that a Chorus opens each act, and adds scene-divisions to the five acts.

cts 1 and 2 are not divided into scenes. Act 3 is divided into four scenes, the same divisions appearing in the Globe edition. Act 4 is divided into three scenes and Act 5 is in a scene of 108 lines. The Globe edition turns the second scene of Act 4 into Act 5, and rearranges the last two acts into seven and five scenes respectively.

though there are neither act nor scene-divisions in this play, the words *Actus Primus, Scena Prima*, are printed under the title.

gain the words *Actus Primus, Scena Prima*, appear under the title.

Act 3 the Globe edition adds three more scene-divisions, and makes an additional division in Scene 2, Act 4. After Scene 2 there are no more scene-divisions in Act 5, but the Globe edition adds another three scenes.

is play was probably written in acts and scenes, but not by Shakespeare. In Act 5 the Globe edition adds a third scene.

is play, while in the printers' hands, was removed from its position in the "Tragedies" and inserted after the "Histories"; it is not among the list of plays, and is not paged.

e words *Scena Prima* occur only after Act 1. The Globe edition divides the first act into ten scenes.

ena Prima* is added to the words *Actus Primus*. Act 2 is spelt "Actus Secunda".

e words *Actus Primus, Scena Prima*, are printed under the title of the play.

e words *Actus Primus, Scena Prima*, are printed under the title of the play.

e words *Scena Prima* appear after Act 1.

e Globe edition adds an eighth scene to the last act.

this play there are no divisions of acts or scenes after Act 2, Scene 2, and to *Actus Secundus* are not added the words *Scena Prima*.

Act 2 the Globe edition adds two more scene-divisions. In Act 4 the text of a whole scene is omitted which in the Globe edition is named Scene 3, and the last four scenes of the act are numbered 3, 4, 5, 7.

Act 2 the Globe edition adds a scene-division which is numbered 3.

usual *Actus Primus, Scena Prima*, is printed below the title of the play, there being no act or scene-divisions in the play.

Act 1 the Globe edition marks Scene 1 and 2 as one scene. In Act 2 it adds a scene-division to Scene 4, and in Act 3 it omits one of the scene-divisions.

is play is not in the folio.

te: According to Marvin Spevack's *Concordance* (1968–70), the complete plays contain 31,959 speeches, 21,726 in verse, 062 in prose and 171 in verse and prose. There are 118,406 lines, 91,464 in verse, 26,942 in prose; 5,572 are split. akespeare wrote a total of 884,647 words, 680,755 verse, 203,892 prose, and employed 29,066 different words.

# Acknowledgments

I must thank the many London and Paris newspapers and magazines who sent me to review or write about Shakespeare. These include *The Sunday Times, The Times, The Financial Times, Times Literary Supplement, The International Herald Tribune, The Guardian, The Daily Mail, Vogue Magazine, Harpers and Queen, Plays and Players.*

I thank the following for their help and support, and in particular for being interviewed, or for contributing in other ways. John Arlott, the late Dame Peggy Ashcroft, John Barton, John Bayley, Jean-Louis Barrault, the late Sir Isaiah Berlin, Peter Brook, Jean-Claude Carrière, Simon Callow, Edward Chaney, Dame Judi Dench, Margaret Drabble, Barbara Everett, Sir Richard Eyre, Angela Fox, the late Jonathan Griffin, Sir Alec Guinness, Sir Peter Hall, Michael Holroyd, Richard Holmes, Emrys Hughes, Sir Derek Jacobi, Barbara Jefford, Christine Kelly, Christopher Lloyd, Shaun MacLoughlin, Roger Michel, Jonathan Miller, Fr Thomas More, Dame Iris Murdoch, Trevor Nunn, Terry Palmer, John Peter, Pierre Rouve, Hilary Rubinstein, George Rylands, Anthony Sher, Ned Sherrin, Anthony Storr, the late J. C. Trewin, John Tydeman, Guy Woolfenden.

I have also consulted the unfinished research of the late Edward Tangye Lean, a collection of files, notes and xeroxes, which now resides in the Shakespeare Birthplace Trust Record Office: to Mrs Tangye Lean I extend my gratitude for drawing on some of this material.

For quotation from the plays and poems I have used the Oxford Compact Edition of *William Shakespeare: The Complete Works* (1988), edited by Stanley Wells and Gary Taylor. Sometimes I have retained the character spelling of more traditional editions (for example, with Imogen); occasionally, I quote snatches of text I could not find in the Oxford

Edition (for example, a passage about Quinapalus in *Twelfth Night*).

I warmly thank Ion Trewin, for many forms of help during the preparation of this book, not least for his detailed and searching comments on the finished work. The shape of the book did not by any means evolve in a straightforward way, and to the late Catharine Carver I am especially grateful for suggestions at all stages. I also thank Deborah Rogers for her valuable participation.

I am grateful to the editors of and contributors to the following newspapers and magazines in which articles, reviews, or items of information, etc. I have consulted, appeared: *Daily Mail, Daily Telegraph, Encore, Evening Standard, Financial Times, The Independent, Irish Times, London Review of Books, New York Times, Observer, Plays and Players, Spectator, Sunday Times, Times Literary Supplement, Theatre Quarterly, The Times, Vogue.* I thank them for the pieces on which I have drawn on in preparation for this book. I also thank my publisher, Glenn Young, for his constructive comments.

G. O'C
*Oxford*
*June 1999*

# Select Bibliography

Following are the principal published sources which I have consulted. The place of publication is London, unless otherwise indicated.

John Cranford Adams, *The Globe Playhouse* (Cambridge, Mass., 1942)

G. Abbott, *Great Escapes from the Tower of London* (1982)

Joseph Quincy Adams, *Shakespearean Playhouses* (Boston, 1917)

Peter Alexander, *Shakespeare's Life and Art* (1939)

—— *Shakespeare* (1964)

Maurice Ashley, *England in the Seventeenth Century* (1952)

Erich Auerbach, *Mimesis* (1957)

R. C. Bald, *John Donne: A Life* (1970)

T. W. Baldwin, *William Shakspere's Small Latine & Lesse Greeke* (Urbana, Ill., 1944)

Clifford Bax, *Rosemary for Remembrance* (1948)

John Bayley, *The Uses of Division* (1976)

J. B. Black, *The Reign of Elizabeth* (1959)

Frederick S. Boas, *Christopher Marlowe* (1940)

—— *Shakespeare and the Universities* (1923)

M. C. Bradbrook, *Elizabethan Stage Conditions* (Cambridge, 1932)

A. C. Bradley, *Shakespearian Tragedy* (1952)

Ivor Brown, *Shakespeare* (1949)

Peter Brook, *The Shifting Point* (1988)

Anthony Burgess, *Shakespeare* (1970)

—— *Nothing Like the Sun* (1964)

Simon Callow, *On Being an Actor* (1984)

Jerome Carcopino, *Daily Life in Ancient Rome* (1956)

John Carey, *John Donne: Life, Mind and Art* (1983)

Stanley Cavell, *Disowning Knowledge* (Cambridge, 1987)

E. K. Chambers, *The Elizabethan Stage* (1923)

—— *William Shakespeare; A Study of Facts and Problems* (1930)

Marchette Chute, *Shakespeare of London* (New York, 1949)

—— *Ben Jonson of Westminster* (New York, 1953)

Wolfgang Clemen, *The Development of Shakespeare's Imagery* (1977)

Roland Connelly, *No Greater Love* (Great Wakering, 1987)

John W. Cunliffe, *The Influence of Seneca on Elizabethan Tragedy* (1925)

W. Robertson Davies, *Shakespeare's Boy Actors* (1939)

Daphne du Maurier, *Golden Lads: A Study of Anthony Bacon, Francis and their Friends* (1975)

Richard Ellmann, *Yeats, The Man and the Masks* (1971)

Barbara Everett, *Young Hamlet: Essays on Shakespeare's Tragedies* (1989)

Leslie A. Fiedler, *The Stranger in Shakespeare* (1973)

Antonia Fraser, *Mary Queen of Scots* (1969)

Edgar I. Fripp, *Master Richard Quyny* (1924)

—— *Shakespeare, Man and Artist* (1938)

—— *Shakespeare's Stratford* (1928)

Joseph William Gray, *Shakespeare's Marriage* (1905)

Graham Greene, *The Power and the Glory* (1946)

—— *Collected Essays* (1969)

Germaine Greer, *Shakespeare* (1986)

F. E. Halliday, *A Shakespeare Companion* (1969)

—— *Shakespeare: A Pictorial Record* (1956)

J. O. Halliwell-Phillipps, *Outlines of the Life of Shakespeare* (1886)

Martin Holmes, *Shakespeare and his Players* (1972)

E. A. J. Honigmann, *Shakespeare, the 'lost years'* (Manchester, 1985)

J. Leslie Hotson, *Shakespeare versus Shallow* (1931)

—— *The First Night of Twelfth Night* (1954)

—— *Mr W.H.* (1964)

R. Houlbrooke, *The English Family 1450–1700* (1984)

Ted Hughes, ed., *A Choice of Shakespeare's Verse* (1971)

Aldous Huxley, *The Art of Seeing* (1943)

Elizabeth Jenkins, *Elizabeth the Great* (1958)

Emrys Jones, *The Origins of Shakespeare* (1977)

—— *Scenic Form in Shakespeare* (1971)

Hugh Kingsmill, *The Return of William Shakespeare* (1929)

Jan Kott, *Shakespeare Our Contemporary* (1964)

D. W. Lucas, *The Greek Tragic Poets* (1950)

Edmund Malone, *The Life of William Shakespeare* (1821)

John Mortimer, *Will Shakespeare* (1975)

Kenneth Muir and Sean O'Loughlin, *Voyage to Illyria* (1937)

J. E. Neale, *Queen Elizabeth* (1934)

George Parfitt, *John Donne, A Literary Life* (1989)

Eric Partridge, *Shakespeare's Bawdy* (1947)

Hesketh Pearson, *A Life of Shakespeare* (1949)

David Riggs, *Ben Jonson: A Life* (Cambridge, Mass., 1989)

A. L. Rowse, *The England of Elizabeth* (1950)

—— *Shakespeare's Southampton: Patron of Virginia* (1965)

—— *Shakespeare the Man* (1973)

George Rylands, *Rylands* (ed. Lord Rothschild) (1988)

Andrew St George, *Brothers in Shakespeare's Plays* (1983)

J. J. Scarisbrick, *Henry VIII* (1968)

S. Schoenbaum, *Shakespeare's Lives* (Oxford, 1970)

—— *William Shakespeare: A Compact Documentary Life* (1987)

Naseeb Shaheen, *Biblical References in Shakespeare's Tragedies* (Newark, Del., 1982)

*Shakespeare's England* (Oxford, 1932)

Seymour Slive, *Frans Hals* (1989)

J. S. Smart, *Shakespeare, Truth and Tradition* (1928)

Lacey Baldwin Smith, *Treason in Tudor England* (1986)

Caroline F. E. Spurgeon, *Shakespeare's Imagery* (Cambridge, 1935)

Lawrence Stone, *The Family, Sex and Marriage in England 1500–1800* (1977)

Charlotte C. Stopes, *Burbage and Shakespeare's Stage* (1913)

—— *Shakespeare's Environment* (1914)

Marvin Spevack, *A Complete and Systematic Concordance to the Works of Shakespeare* (Hildesheim, 1968–70)

Lytton Strachey, *Elizabeth & Essex* (Oxford, 1981)

Keith Thomas, *Religion and the Decline of Magic* (1971)

E. M. W. Tillyard, *The Elizabethan World Picture* (1943)

——*Shakespeare's History Plays* (1946)

J. C. Trewin, *Five & Eighty Hamlets* (1988)

Enid Welsford, *Fool: His Social and Literary History* (1935)

Emlyn Williams, *Spring 1600* (1946)

F. P. Wilson, *The Plague in Shakespeare's London* (Oxford, 1927)

John Dover Wilson, *Life in Shakespeare's England* (1911)

Stanley Wells, *Shakespeare* (1978)

Frances A. Yates, *Shakespeare's Last Plays* (1975)

# NOTES AND REFERENCES

# INDEX

This book was planned to be read without footnotes and without the sometimes off-putting clutter of scholarly references and citations. Should any reader wish to explore further the sources on which I have based my account, including the "mundane" documentary evidence, I have grouped together under the headings for each chapter a guide to these origins.

Judged by the number of books, editions of works and amount of critical attention, knowledge about Shakespeare would appear in recent years to have multiplied from the reliable repositories of primary source material. But this is not the case. Very little that is genuinely new has been uncovered in the last twenty years, although minor finds have been trumpeted in importance out of all proportion to their value.

The notes, I hope, will both serve to add some landscape to, and signpost the path I have chosen through literally hundreds of these repositories or different approaches. My own method, of using a colloquium of contemporary voices to give a new and sometimes unexpected perspective on Shakespeare, is as far as I know original.

For each chapter I have also added some further observations which would have disrupted the flow of narrative, and which may or may not prove of interest. Nearly all the material I refer to is excellently indexed and is so easily accessible that I have kept citations to the minimum. I have tended not to repeat sources when from the continuity of similar material they can be inferred from the text. Anyone bold enough to track down chapter and verse should not find it difficult.

Before researching and writing this book my previous experience of Shakespeare was both practical and literary. I have acted in several plays, and my largest Shakespearian role was that of Oberon in *A Midsummer Night's Dream*. I have directed or been involved in numerous Shakespeare productions, with the Royal Shakespeare Company and elsewhere (one early production of *Hamlet*, which I directed and in which I played

Fortinbras, had Derek Jacobi in the title role). I have reviewed all the plays, most of them many times, for the *Financial Times* or other journals.

On the literary front my work on biographies of Ralph Richardson, Laurence Olivier, Vivien Leigh, Peggy Ashcroft and Alec Guinness has provided many valuable insights into the nature of the actor which I believe Shakespeare was at heart. In particular, close study of Sean O'Casey's life, for which I was fortunate enough to be provided with a wealth of original documentary evidence and a rich period background, proved an invaluable preparation.

It was my complete immersion in Peter Brook's production of *The Mahabharata* as its chronicler that I found Shakespeare first identifying his shadowy self as a tangible proposition for a life.

*The Mahabharata*, as well as being the Hindu epic, was in Brook's production a giant distillation of Shakespeare's history plays, containing resonances of the tragedies and comedies, perfected through Brook's other work, moulded in Shakespearian complexity, and dipped in universal ink. It was the influence of Brook which prompted me to begin.

When Ted Hughes worked with Brook on *Orghast* he acknowledged that for both of them the true ideal for a "theatre simultaneously sacred and profane, simultaneously a revelation of spiritual being and an explosive image of life's infinite animal power and psychological abundance" was Shakespeare (*Shakespeare and the Goddess of Complete Being*, 1992).

# ABBREVIATIONS

In the notes I have used the following abbreviations: the place of publication is London unless otherwise stated.

| | |
|---|---|
| Eric Auerbach, *Mimesis* (Princetown, 1968) | **Auerbach** |
| Frederick S. Boas, *Christopher Marlowe* (1940) | **Boas** |
| Stanley Cavell, *Disowning Knowledge* (Cambridge, 1987) | **Cavell** |
| E. K. Chambers, *The Elizabethan Stage* (1923) | **ES** |
| *William Shakespeare; A Study of Facts and Problems* (1930) | **EKC** |
| Marchette Chute, *Shakespeare of London* (New York, 1949) | **Chute** |
| F. E. Halliday, *A Shakespeare Companion* (1969) | **Halliday** |
| Martin Holmes, *Shakespeare and his Players* (1972) | **Holmes** |
| E. A. J. Honigmann, *Shakespeare, the 'lost years'* (Manchester, 1985) | **Honigmann** |
| R. Houlbrooke, *The English Family 1450-1700* (1984) | **Houlbrooke** |
| Eric Partridge, *Shakespeare's Bawdy* (1947) | **Partridge** |
| S. Schoenbaum, *Shakespeare's Lives* (Oxford, 1970) | **SS Lives** |
| *William Shakespeare: A Compact Documentary Life* (1987) | **SSC DOC** |
| Lacey Baldwin Smith, *Treason in Tudor England* (1986) | **Smith** |
| Caroline F. E. Spurgeon, *Shakespeare's Imagery* (Cambridge, 1935) | **Spurgeon** |
| Lawrence Stone, *The Family, Sex and Marriage in England 1500-1800* (1977) | **Stone** |
| Keith Thomas, *Religion and the Decline of Magic* (1971) | **Thomas** |
| F.P. Wilson, *The Plague in Shakespeare's London* (Oxford, 1927) | **Wilson** |

# NOTES

## INTRODUCTION (pp 1-2)

Peter Brook refers to the existence of the "secret play" in an essay written in French as introduction to his French production of *The Tempest* (1990). See also Flaubert (Correspondence, 1852 vol. II, p. 155) "L'auteur dans son oevre doit être comme dieu dans l'univers, présent partout, et visible nulle part."

## BLESSED IS THE WOMB (pp 5-10)

The concentrated recreation of Shakespeare's early manhood has multiple sources; main among them are Cavell, chapters 3-6, his "Recounting Gains Showing Losses" in *The Winter's Tale* and René Girard, *A Theatre of Envy* (New York, 1991), whose discussion of families and heredity in relation to "mimetic desire" breaks new ground. The importance of twins is acutely unravelled in Andrew St. George's *Brothers in Shakespeare's Plays* (1983); Smith supplies the treason image of Mary Queen of Scots; Partridge documents the Shakespeare obsession with woman's procreative equipment.

The factual documentary basis of the chapter may be checked in the tables of facts and traditions (pages 310 to 321). The accounts of Shakespeare's home, family are drawn from the conventional and most cited modern sources (SSC DOC and EKC) which in turn go back to J.S. Smart, *Shakespeare: Truth and Tradition* (1928), Sidney Lee, *Life of Shakespeare* (1898), J.O. Halliwell-Phillipps, *Outlines of the Life of Shakespeare* (1886), and even Edmund Malone, *The Life of William Shakespeare* (1821).

Recent academic biographies, Dennis Kay, *Shakespeare: His Life, Work and Era* (1992), Park Honan's *Shakespeare A Life* (1998), draw mainly on the same sources. It is fascinating to note how scholars instinctively shy away from procreative images (there is no entry under "pregnancy" in Spurgeon), although Spurgeon's work has clues as to how Shakespeare thought and felt. The actor Terry Palmer proved especially valuable in the explanation of "teeming" metaphors (see also pp. 99-102).

For Shakespeare as director: see *No Bed for Bacon*, Caryl Brahms and S.J. Simon, from *A Mutual Pair* (1976). There are strong similarities between the highly entertaining film *Shakespeare in Love* (1998), directed by John Madden, and this skit, with its warning to scholars, "This book is fundamentally unsound." The reader is challenged to see how many can be found: not least is the opening scene where Shakespeare, a melancholy figure, sits tracing his signature on a pad

Shakesper
Shakspere
Shakspar

– "He always practised tracing his signature when he was bored." Then there is the Walter Raleigh joke with the cloak; the rivalry between the Henslowe and Burbage theatre companies; the role of the Master of the Revels; the orphaned lady of honour at court whose name is Lady Viola, and who cross-dresses and pursues the actor by enrolling in his company, then is discovered. He writes to her, "Shall I compare thee to a summer's day?" The main difference between *No Bed for Bacon* and *Shakespeare in Love* is that in the film "Will" is "dumbed down" as a "jobbing playwright", while Lady Viola subjugates him, and (as the empowered female) rescues him from his debts before her departure. The book has Shakespeare leaving her.

## RAGE AND SWELL (pp 11-19)

All the contemporary figures in this and subsequent chapters are quoted direct from interviews with the author.

The idea that Shakespeare interiorised the violence of his age is based on reading J. Piaget: "In order to know objects, the subject must act upon them, and therefore transform them: he must displace, connect, combine, take apart, and reassemble them. From the most elementary sensorimotor actions (such as pulling and pushing) to the most sophisticated intellectual operations, which are interiorised actions, carried out mentally (e.g. joining together, putting in order, putting into one-to-one correspondence), knowledge is constantly linked with actions or operations, that is, with transformations." (*The Construction of Reality in the Child*, New York, 1954). See also Gil Bailie, *Violence Unveiled* (New York, 1997).

Sources of the narrative of the family, Stratford and the local inhabitants are the same as those cited above, but also material comes from the Shakespeare Birthplace Trust Record Office (Mrs Tangye Lean's collection), the Folger Library, Washington, the Public Records Office, Kew, the Bodleian Library, Oxford, and the British Library etc..

John Dover Wilson's *Shakespeare's England* is a valuable background source, as is F.E. Halliday's *A Shakespeare Companion* (1964); beggars are a particular preoccupation in Thomas.

I have drawn on Peter Ackroyd's *Life of Dickens* (1990) for comparison of Shakespeare with the novelist: also letters from George Rylands have supplied valuable notions.

Taking one product (p. 17) and turning it into another (as in the glove-maker image) has became a concern of more recent Shakespeare criticism, with the widely propagated idea that there is no such thing as authorship and character. "The areas on which academic expertise can be shown grow smaller as the competitive field expands, and they take on more Shakespeare – excluding theoretical lineaments as another form of self-identification". Barbara Everett, *Essay in Shakespeare and the Twentieth Century* (Los Angeles, 1996, pp. 215-229).

## THE KINGDOM OF CHILDHOOD (pp 19-25)

Sources for this chapter: George A. Plimpton, *The Education of Shakespeare* (1933); T.W. Baldwin, *William Shakespeare's Small Latin & Lesse Greek* (1944); see also E.A.J. Honigmann, *Shakespeare; the 'lost years'* (1985). No specialised account of Shakespeare's early years and Stratford background rivals that of S. Schoenbaum's *A Compact Documentary Life* (1987) for its concise summation and its factual authority. But he, in his own fashion, speculates as does every other biographer of Shakespeare. Here are some examples. "Surely his imagination did not stand aloof from the vessels and vestments of Catholicism. Nor was he unmoved by the abandoned abbeys and monasteries left crumbling in the wake of the Reformation; in his 73rd Sonnet these are evoked by the poignant metaphor of the bare ruined choirs." (p.60) "Shakespeare does not seem to have cherished especially tender memories of these [school] days." (p.64) "...William would have found himself, at the age of fifteen or thereabouts, confronted with the necessity of earning his living." As in his *Shakespeare's Lives* Shoenbaum sifts other biographers admirably, drawing on and citing other biographers, for example Chute and A.L. Rowse, but remaining aloof. As an accessible guide to all Shakespeare biographical resources SS Lives is incomparable. The recent biography (1998) by Park Honan, claims new evidence of Shakespeare's mother's quick intelligence "and familiarity with a quill pen," and "fresh details about his youth [that] show that he did not leave home unprepared for his career."

J. Bronowski is quoted from Shakespeare *The Comprehensive Soul* (BBC Talks 1965). The romantic poets, their letters and poetic theories, are highlighted in Jonathan Bates, *Shakespeare and the English Romantic Imagination* (1986) and Herbert Read's *The Pure Voice of Feeling* (1954); the author's reading of Coleridge's *Biographia Literaria* also is a source for the account of Shakespeare's developing imagination. Anthony

Storr, *The School of Genius* (1988) investigates how solitude can be crucial to genius. My interview with Richard Holmes, Coleridge's biographer, proved especially helpful.

Vivid descriptive sources of London and its life are found in John Stow, *A Survey of London* (originally 1603, Oxford 1971) and Norman Lloyd Williams, *Tudor London Visited* (1991).

## A FATHER FORGOTTEN (pp 25-35)

I have drawn for this chapter on the many references in Shakespeare's age to literary and dramatic works as children. Gabriel Harvey was a barrister and a friend of Edmund Spenser, author of *Pierce's Superogation* (1593). Other savage metaphors of generation are found in John Lyly's *Emblems and His England* (1582), Thomas Dekker's *News From Hell* (1606) and *The Whore of Babylon* (1606). I have continually consulted Smith for the devastating effect of Protestantism on the Tudor mind: he writes, "Paranoia was a disease of the spirit, a 'subtle humour' that, in the opinion of Cardinal Allen, was crucifying the soul of Tudor England." See also Cardinal William Allen, *A True, Sincere, and Modest Defense of English Catholics* (1588) (New York, 1965). Also valuable has been J.J. Scarisbrick, *Henry VIII* (1968). Stephen Greenblatt wrote of Tudor politics in *Renaissance Self-fashioning* (Chicago 1980), that it was "fundamentally insane, its practitioners in the grip of 'frenzies'." The quotation from Aubrey Lewis is from *Shakespeare, The Comprehensive Soul* (BBC Talks, 1965); how close Shakespeare was to biblical orthodoxy can be followed in Naseeb Shaheen's two books on the Tragedies and the History Plays. But A.C. Bradley's *Shakespearian Tragedy* (1952) must not be forgotten: Bradley also wrote an essay which maintained that Shakespeare in his plays and poems betrayed his identity (*Oxford Lectures on Poetry*, 1909).

For Shakespeare's discovery of literature George Rylands was especially helpful in his interview with the author. So also were Emrys Jones and John Bayley. I have also consulted Jonathan Bates and, on the "lost years," I have drawn on P. Millward's *Shakespeare's Religious Background* (1973) as well as Honigmann. This last book, although convincingly documented and having a considerable influence on recent Shakespeare studies, is still a speculative endeavour. The account of Edmund Campion is based on Evelyn Waugh's *Edmund Campion* (1935); see also Garry O'Connor, *Campion's Ghost* (1992).

See Auerbach for a masterly assessment of the new self-definition found in Montaigne's essays. I have again drawn on Smith's graphic description of the Tudor battle between good and evil (Ch. 1). As a study of Shakespeare's alienation, Leslie A. Fiedler, *The Stranger in Shakespeare* (1993) is helpful.

## FIRE IN THE BLOOD (pp 35-40)

For the sources of this chapter, on the documentary side, see EKC and SSC DOC; for more general discussion Joseph William Gray, *Shakespeare's Marriage* (1905); Hesketh Pearson, *A Life of Shakespeare* (1949). See the account of Shakespeare's marriage in Hugh Kingsmill's *The Return of William Shakespeare* (1929): "Shakespeare sighed: it is just this reluctance of other people to think and feel exactly as one does oneself – or, I suppose it would be fairer to say, it is the reluctance or, rather, the inability of anyone individual to identify himself with any other individual – which constitutes the true tragedy of life." (p. 174). Kingsmill's verbal portrait, written in 1929, uncannily resembles the Bax portrait. As to his political character Kingsmill writes, "My own idea about Shakespeare is that he'd control labour with a machine-gun, if he got half the chance."

Trevor Nunn also told the author, "His career in London is the career of an exile. Somebody who has already forfeited the notion of being acceptable in all parts of society... I don't at all have the sense of a man who could ever look in a mirror – except to find out about his own nature... I am sure to be in his presence could be uncomfortable, dangerous *and* unsettling.." E.A. J. Honigmann supports the idea that Shakespeare treated Anne with the "sustained rage" of the "solitary inner man". ("The Second-Best Bed," *The New York Review of Books,* 7 Nov 1991).

I have drawn on Richard Ellmann's *Yeats, The Man and the Masks* (1971) for comparisons of Yeats with Shakespeare. See also W.B. Yeats *Collected Poems* (1952); Ivor Brown's *Shakespeare* (1949) and Kenneth Muir and Sean O'Loughlin *The Voyage to Illyria* (1937). On the subject of Shakespeare's biography, Muir and O'Loughlin quote R.W. Emerson: "Shakespeare is the only biographer of Shakespeare... So far from Shakespeare's being the least known, he is the one person in all modern history fully known to us." (p.1)

Ivor Brown quotes Bernard Shaw: "With the plays and sonnets in our hands we know more about Shakespeare than we know about Dickens or Thackeray." This last, however, may be reckoned provocative.

Other sources for this chapter are *The Rape of Lucrece, Venus and Adonis* and René Girard's study of envy in Shakespeare ("envy the aphrodisiac par excellence"). Wider social sources are A. McFarlane, *Marriage and Love in England: Modes of Reproduction 1300-1840* (1986); R. Houlbrooke, *The English Family 1450-1700* (1984) and L. Stone *The Family: Sex and Marriage in England 1500-1800* (1977).

## A GREAT PROFESSION (pp 43-48)

See Duff Cooper: *Sergeant Shakespeare* for fuller discussion of Shakespeare's possible military involvement. Also helpful were Richard Eyre, John Barton and George Rylands, interviewed by the author. There are elaborate military metaphors in *Romeo and Juliet* and *The Rape of Lucrece* (see Spurgeon). Source of John

Donne's Cadiz expedition is R.C. Bald's *John Donne: A Life* (1970); Walter Scott, *Woodstock* (1969), Lytton Strachey *Elizabeth and Essex* (Oxford, 1987) contain also vivid descriptions of campaigns. The best account of Sidney's life is Katherine Duncan-Jones, *The Life of Sir Philip Sydney* (1990). Main sources for material about the life of Ben Jonson are Marchette Chute's *Ben Jonson of Westminster* (New York, 1953) and David Riggs, *Ben Jonson* (1989).

## FACTIONS AND FICTIONS (pp 48-55)

There is a curious tradition that Shakespeare wrote the English translation of the 46th Psalm of the 1611 Authorised version of the Bible. According to Bishop Mark Hodson (London *Times*, 23 April 1976) "How the Bard found his way into the scriptures through a piece of secret writing," Shakespeare signed "the 46th Psalm because the 46th word from the beginning is 'Shake' ('though the mountains shake with the swelling thereof'), while the 46th word from the end is 'spear' ('He breaketh the bow, and cutteth the spear in sunder.')" Anthony Burgess also referred to this in his 1970 biography: "the greatest prose-work of all time has the name of the greatest poet set cunningly in it." However, the words "shake" and "spear" occur in roughly the same place in Shakespeare's favourite 1560 edition of the Bible, which prepared by the Protestant Marian exiles in Geneva, outsold all other versions, and contributed to the language such striking phrases as "through a glass darkly". So much for what many have described as an "astonishing" cryptogram.

The Folger Library has a Geneva Bible originally purchased in 1570. It contains hundred of marked verses and underlined passages apparently in the original owner's hand, which correspond with Shakespeare's use of the Bible. See also Naseeb Shaheen, *Biblical References in Shakespeare's Tragedies* (1987). Introduction and Ch. 1, "The English Bible in Shakespeare's Day."

I have drawn on John Gerard's *The Autobiography of an Elizabethan* (trans. from Latin by Philip Caramon, with an introduction by Grahame Greene (See quotation on p. 297). This is one of the best (and most overlooked) of contemporary sources.

The theme of the puritan suppression of laughter figures prominently in Umberto Eco, *The Name of the Rose* (1983).

A main source for the influence of the classical literary world is Emrys Jones, *The Origin's of Shakespeare* (1977). For the effects of news on social life see also Thomas.

Shakespeare's view of soldiery from "below", so to speak, is one of the keys to his popular success. It is highly unlikely that any social equal to those he describes could have pictured these figures in such racy and vivid detail. Again the motivation of mimetic desire (Girard) is convincing.

## THE WONDER OF OUR STAGE (pp 55-62)

I am indebted to many sources for the account of how Shakespeare became an actor. All those I interviewed had much to contribute. John Barton was illuminating on character, "self" and motivation. The documentary sources are ES, SSC DOC and EKC. In addition to main documentary sources already cited I must mention John Quincy Adams, *Shakespearian Playhouses* (Boston, 1917).

Enid Welsford, *Fool: His Social and Literary History* (1935) and especially Martin Holmes, *Shakespeare and his Players* (1972) relate the players to the plays and their author; Halliday is always helpful in its brief summaries of matters relevant to the life sources of Shakespeare and his works. Greenblatt's *Shakespearian Negotiations* (Oxford, 1988) has a valuable section on the slippery self-hood of an age remarkably similar to our own.  Germaine Greer, *Shakespeare* (1986) also discusses identity in relation to soul and art: "His personages are not involved in a search for identity but search for ways to transcend that identity, which is transitory, and free the spirit, which is made in God's likeness, eternal and immutable." (Ch. 3).  Wolfgang Clemen, *Shakespeare's Dramatic Art* (1972) has a valuable chapter on Shakespeare and Montaigne: Clemen summarises the essayist's view.  "In the case of man we cannot simply conclude from the outside what is inside, because either consciously or unconsciously he would put on a mask; but on the inside it is just as difficult, because he is controlled by changing contradictory traits of character.  Montaigne avows: "We are all framed of flaps and patches and of so shapelesse and diverse a contexture, that every peece and every moment playeth his part.  And there is as much difference found between us and our selves, as there is between our selves and others" (11.1).  Man is in himself an inconsistent, enigmatic, variegated being 'but a botching and party-coloured worke' as Montaigne avows.  When we have penetrated through the deceptive exterior of appearance and imagine we have come to the real man, a new uncertainty arises.  For what is the real man?" (pp.185-8):

Other chapter sources:  Emrys Jones, *Scenic Form in Shakespeare* (1970), *Henslowe's Diary* (ed. R.A. Foakes and R.T. Richert (1961); *Documents of the Rose Playhouse* (ed. C.C. Rutter (1984); A. Gurr, *The Shakespearian Stage, 1574-1642* (1980), Peter Alexander, *Shakespeare* (1964), M.C. Bradbrook, *Elizabethan Stage Conditions* (1932), W. Robertson Davis, *Shakespeare's Boy Actor* (1939), Allardyce Nicoll, *Shakespeare Survey* (1948-1965).

## OUTER AND INNER WORLDS (pages 62-69)

Thomas Heywood also wrote the *Apology for Actors* (1612), a reply to puritan attacks on the theatre, valuable as a source of theatrical material. Many of the same sources of the previous chapter are applicable here. I am beholden also to Jean-Louis Barrault, whom I interviewed and to his memoir, *Memories For Tomorrow* (1974). For more clues to Shakespeare's developing character I am indebted to Chute, A.L. Rowse, and Hesketh Pearson. As literary and biographical scholarship has, in the opinion of some, declined into historicism and post-modernist deconstruction the critic, the reader (presumably also the specta-tor) have come to assume greater importance. The receiver becomes empowered and controlling, the genius of the artist is demoted, while the sense, in literary studies, that man has a soul, has virtually disappeared. Here, for example, is Terry Eagleton writing of Shakespeare's biography (*The Independent on Sunday* 17 Nov 1991): "There is no mystery to the man Shakespeare, no secret life, no elusive depth... To write... of the man Shakespeare "wanting", "recognising", "recalling" and so forth is like ascribing a spiritual life to a slug." Eagleton is the Oxford University Warton Professor of English.

The contemporary conclusion would seem to be that Shakespeare can be tailored and coloured to fit any subjective notion where the writer's critical ego is as important as and equal to that of the playwright (see also Gary Taylor, *Re-inventing Shakespeare* (1989), for changing cultural attitudes to Shakespeare).

## THE GROUND PLAN OF IMAGINATION (pp 69-73)

John Tydeman further told the author: "The older school of actors feel they possess him... He unites people under the cloak of his warmth." He made the valuable point that "Everyone [the actors] in a Chekhov play is always happy. They're usually happy in a Shakespeare play." Can the same be said of actors in Beckett or Pinter?

Barbara Jefford told the author that Rosalind was the best woman's part. "I am sure he was aware what he was doing in terms of people's personalities and characters… the fact they can be done in so many different ways."

My sources for material about Queen Elizabeth are J.E. Neale, *Queen Elizabeth* (1934), Elizabeth Jenkins, *Elizabeth the Great* (1958), J.B. Black, *The Reign of Elizabeth* (1959), John Stow, E.M.W. Tillyard, *The Elizabethan World Picture* (1972), Lacey Baldwin Smith, *Elizabeth Tudor: Portrait of a Queen* (1976). The structure of allegory in Spenser is explained in C.S. Lewis, *The Allegory of Love* (1936) which contains a seminal study of Spenser's meanings and how he conveys them. See also *Edmund Spenser: A Critical Anthology* (ed Paul J. Albers, 1969). The Coleridge quotation is from *Coleridge's Shakespearian Criticism* (ed T.M. Taysor) (1930). Holmes is especially vivid from the playgoer's point of view on *Titus Andronicus* (pp. 9-13).

## HALF A GOD (pp 73-81)

In one of many publications in 1993, the 400th anniversary of Marlowe's murder, the playwright was shown as an undersized, rabid homosexual clacking around on high heels and meeting death by having his penis cut off. A.D. Wraight claims, in the *Story that the Sonnets Tell,* that the Canterbury-born scholar was also the unlettered Stratford hack Shakespeare. His killing was faked by Thomas Walsingham and backed by Queen Elizabeth to free Marlowe from charges of being a spy and an atheist. He wrote the Sonnets in gratitude to Walsingham for saving him. He then went off to Italy to research the background for *Romeo and Juliet.* As with the "tissue of twaddle" advanced by Baconians, Shakespeare was his *nom-de-plume.* Wraight, like most supporters of the 64 alternative candidates proposed for Shakespeare, assaults the bastions of common sense with cryptograms and abstruse knowledge. Most of the "disbelievers", who tend to be snobs and elitists, cannot bear the idea that Shakespeare led a dull life: Wraight cannot stomach him being, as she says, "a monumental bore." She gives not only herself away, but the whole breed of like-minded fanatics who recycle their theories endlessly (hers, notably, are similar to Calvin Hoffman's in *The Murder of the Man who was Shakespeare* (1956) and the novel *It Was Marlowe: A Story of the Secret of Three Centuries*), when she writes, "There is no man of genius around whom such an accretion of hypotheses and myths has bred, protecting and encapsulating his person from its historic, dim obscurity which, when placed in the context of factual documentation breathes *only* [my italics] an air of mediocrity." For a complete survey of the "Deviations" see SS Lives pp. 530-629.

Peter Brook was once asked in Russia by a Tadjik if he didn't agree that Shakespeare came from the Middle East, because of the Persian words sheikh and pir (a venerable sage). Brook replied that on that basis Chekhov would be Czech and the Tadjik left, disappointed (Peter Brook, *Threads of Time*, 1999). Brook believed that Shakespeare was unique precisely because of his "refusal to put himself in the foreground. There are few such authors with such a need to conceal themselves completely. Shakespeare used all his art to prevent his personal life, his foibles, his opinions, what we call his universe becoming visible" (Brook to author, 1990).

"...The playwright and pamphleteer Thomas Nashe wrote..." in *Pierce Penilesse* (1592): this was apparently the first certain reference to a work by Shakespeare. The best accounts of Marlowe's death are in Frederick S. Boas's *Christopher Marlowe* (1940) and J. Leslie Hotson's *The Death of Christopher Marlowe (1925)*. Jonathan Bate deals with Marlowe's influence in a discussion of Harold Bloom's proposition in *The Anxiety of Influence* (1973) that literary creation is a form of misinterpretation. "Shakespeare, I suggest, only became Shakespeare because of the death of Marlowe. And he remained peculiarly haunted by that death" (p. 105).

Apropos the adaptation of *Henry VI* Peter Hall the director objected to one passage he was sure Barton had written in parody of Shakespeare: on returning to the text they found it was original Shakespeare. The author attended rehearsals at Stratford-upon-Avon of *The Wars of the Roses*: see also Garry O'Connor, *The Secret Woman: A Life of Peggy Ashcroft* (1998).

Shakespeare may not have been too worried about historical accuracy in his history plays, but the distinguished Victorian historian J.H. Froude commented, "The most perfect history of England is to be found, in my opinion, in Shakespeare's historical plays." Froude was the first English historian to make a thorough and systematic use of archive material.

## THE BODY IS HIS BOOK (pp 81-87)

Shakespeare travelled more than we like to imagine. A man or woman could ride 50 miles a day (30 miles for a leisured gentleman). Saddles were small, hard and uncomfortable, especially for bony riders. Well-born students walked long distances to universities. Richard Hooker, later Archbishop, walked from Oxford to Exeter in 1570. Actors "strolled" with baggage piled on a wagon. An average was 25 miles a day. Less than 2 weeks would get you from end to end of England (Holmes).

The William Reynolds incident is recounted fully in J. Leslie Hotson, *Shakespeare's Sonnets Dated* (1964, p. 141). The main portraits of Queen Elizabeth can be viewed in the National Portrait Gallery, London and Lytton Strachey, *Elizabeth and Essex* (Oxford 1981) is worth reading for vivid faction. For the Queen's biographies see above. The quotation (p.86) is from Elizabeth Jenkins, *Elizabeth the Great* (1958). Jenkins is revealing about the Queen's self-presentation, her virginity and her virtual absence of periods.

## DROPS OF WATER (pp 87-91)

That Shakespeare lets us know everything there is to be known about himself is largely a matter of interpretation. René Girard, *A Theatre of Envy* (New York, 1991) is highly relevant here, for it describes brilliantly his repeated habits of mind. See also Auerbach Ch. 13, "The Weary Prince," on how Shakespeare both embraces and transcends reality. See also Goethe's *Wilhelm Meister's Lehrfahre* (book 4, chapters 3 and 13). But caution is advised: "The road to Xanadu could not be more phantonthronged than the voyage to Illyria," (A.L. Attwater quoted in Muir and O'Loughlin).

I owe much of my understanding of Coleridge's poetic process to Herbert Read, *The Time Voice of Feeling* (1954). Coleridge said, "So he *is* : so he *writes*."

## QUEINT MISTERY OF OVID (pp 91-99)

Ted Hughes, whose penultimate published work was a translation of Ovid, wrote also of Shakespeare, "The Shakespearian Fable... is really the account of how, in the religious struggle that lasted from the middle of the sixteenth century to the middle of the seventeenth, England lost her soul... our national poems are tragedies for a good reason." (*A Choice of Shakespeare's Verse*, 1971). Jonathan Bate, *The Genius of Shakespeare* (1997) in a valuable chapter on the authorship controversy attacks the contention of anti-Stratfordians that no letters of Shakespeare survive. Bate suggests the two dedications to Southampton are two such letters which do, "couched in the servile language which low-born writers had no choice but to use if they aspired to the patronage of aristocrats." Bate's book is worth reading as a biography of Shakespeare's talent and reputation beyond the limits of his actual life, and covers much of the same ground as Gary Taylor, *Reinventing Shakespeare*.

I have also drawn on Rowse's Shakespeare's *Southampton* (1965) and J. Leslie Hotson, *Mr W.H.* (1964), on A.L. Rowse, *Shakespeare The Man* (1973) and W.H. Auden's introduction to The Sonnets (New York, 1964) pp. 98-99. See also Richard Burton, *The Anatomy of Melancholy*, (1932).

## THE LURE OF FOREIGN PARTS (pp 99-105)

F.P. Wilson, *The Plague in Shakespeare's London* (Oxford 1927) puts a case for Shakespeare visiting Tichfield in 1593. In Daphne du Maurier's *Golden Lads* (1975) Anthony Bacon's escape from the death sentence in Navarre for committing sodomy is narrated with detailed documentation. She writes (p. 120) that Shakespeare was lodging in Bishopsgate when Bacon came to live next door at the Bull Inn. "It is not unreasonable to suppose that the young actor-playwright, patronised as he was by Essex's friend the Earl of Southampton, became acquainted with the Earl of Essex's director of intelligence, Anthony Bacon."

The Harley Granville-Barker *Prefaces to Shakespeare* (1927) are lively reading from the viewpoint of director and playwright. Granville-Barker had the distinction of acting Shakespeare (in Bernard Shaw's *The Dark Lady of the Sonnets*, (Haymarket Theatre 1910). For another theatrical version of the man see Emlyn Williams, *Spring 1600* (1946).

(Pages 104-118)

Few biographers or critics portray or acknowledge Shakespeare as a man who made decisions and choices. Most show him a blurred mosaic or composite of proven or unproven documentary material much of which renders him flat and two-dimensional. He thus appears passive to the known facts. Thus the biographer is presented with difficult choices over whether to promote Shakespeare into a system of thoughts, actions, beliefs which are consistent; or to "deconstruct" him from what is known and from his works; or to abandon any attempt at all at making an intelligible system of him; or to walk around him putting him in a frame, as some of the impressionist painters did with their subjects. I believe the best criterion is the same as that for judging the quality of a portrait: namely, is it a picture that both resembles its subject *and* displays an artistic transference of personality from its executor?

## A FRIEND'S INFIRMITIES (pp 109-118)

For Southampton travelling to Italy see Rowse, *Shakespeare's Southampton (p 108)*. For Southampton as a subject for envy see René Girard, *A Theatre of Envy*, in which mimetic desire is described as an energising motivative force in all Shakespeare's plays. See further W.H. Auden's admirable introduction to Sylvan Barnet's edition of The Sonnets (New York, 1964). Auden writes that the Sonnets are "the best touchstone I know of distinguishing the sheep from the goats" among those who write about Shakespeare. Auden deals fully and convincingly with the homosexual versus heterosexual controversy which centres on these poems. See also Oscar Wilde, *The Portrait of Mr W.H.* (1889), Samual Butler, *Shakespeare's Sonnets Reconsidered* (1899). Sydney Lee's treatment of the Sonnets in *a Life of William Shakespeare* (1898) is the most original section concerned. His self-satisfaction is typically Victorian "Chaucer and Sir Walter Scott among writers of exalted genius, vie with Shakespeare in the sobriety of their persual aims and the sanity of their mental attitides towards life's ordinary incidents." See also Logan Pearsall Smith *On Reading Shakespeare* (1993).

## INVESTIGATION OF MARRIAGE (pp 118-122)

I have consulted Houlbrooke and Stone for this discussion of Shakespeare's marriage in order to see it in a wider contemporary context. Re *Perestroika*, curiously enough *Romeo and Juliet* was much revived in Soviet Russia just after the Second World War, in a campaign for better family life. A British journalist wrote

> The Soviet state could now maintain
> That Blackguard British Bourgeois Bard
> Had not lived utterly in vain.

See also Barbara Everett, *Mrs Shakespeare* (*London Review of Books*, 18 Dec 1986); Denis de Rougemont *Passion and Society* (1952) investigates the basic dilemma of marriage and adulterous love at the heart of Western European culture.

## LA PASSIONATA (pages 123-133)

Edward Chaney, *Quo Vadis? Travel as Education And The Impact Of Italy In The Sixteenth Century* (1988) contains excellent descriptions of the impact of Italian travel on Shakespeare and his contemporaries. Fear and proscription of Italianate papism was unable to halve the travel boom: "If Shakespeare filled part of his 'lost years' with a journey to Italy – 'a harmless fantasy' allowed us even by Samuel Schoenbaum – he would have been careful not to leave any evidence of having done so" (p.13).

Spurgeon remains the unequalled source of how Shakespeare communicated his temperament through images. She quotes Virginia Woolf, *Orlando* (1928): "Every secret of a writer's soul, every experience of his life, every quality of his mind, is written large in his work, yet we require critics to explain the one and biographers to expound the other" (pp. 189-90). Spurgeon also quotes Vernon Lee, *The Handling of Words* (1920) "The real revelation of the writer (as of the artist) comes in a far subtler way than by... autobiography; and comes despite all effort to elude it. For what the writer does communicate is his temperament, his organic personality, with its preferences and aversions, its pace and rhythm and impact and balance, its swiftness or languor... and this he does equally whether he be rehearsing veraciously his own concerns or inventing someone else's." Spurgeon, from the imagery, differentiates convincingly between Bacon and Shakespeare: Bacon's "emotions were stimulated almost exclusively by *thought* whereas Shakespeare's were stimulated by *feeling*" (p.15).

For further discussion of European passion see Denis de Rougemont's *Passion and Society* (1952).


## LAWFUL MAGIC (pp 133-140)

Intricate technicalities (p. 139)... in *Playing Shakespeare* (1975), John Barton usefully explores with leading actors the technicalities of verse, vocabulary, punctuation etc.... Richard Pasco is quoted on Richard II's tragedy: "He never really discovered himself... He's in a state of almost perpetual bewilderment... there are glimpses of his search for himself and his internal reality." (p.122)

Derek Jacobi also said to author, "He related great events to the man in the street: he brought great kings and princes down to that level... he had a lot of romance in his soul."

The occasion of the staging of *A Midsummer Night's Dream* is described in EKC and Andrew Gurr *The Shakespearian Playing Companies* (1996).

## THE SHAPE OF GRIEF (pages 140-149)

John Mortimer, *Will Shakespeare* (1975) entertainingly recon-
structs Shakespeare in London being visited by Hamnet who is
brain-damaged and a mute. Having confronted his father's dark
Lady Hamnet dies of a cold. Mortimer's Dark Lady is a judge's
wife who cross-dresses like Viola in order to watch plays (echoed
in *Shakespeare In Love*).

The question of Shakespeare's homosexuality has
become a lucrative growth area recently in Shakespeare studies.
Just as Shakespeare's authorship was never in doubt for two hundred years until he had been hailed as a genius, even a god, so his
orthodox sexuality was never questioned until elevated to a faith,
and heretics emerged. Oscar Wilde's idea (*The Portrait of Mr
W.H.*) that Shakespeare loved a boy actor was enthusiastically
embraced by André Gide, then Samuel Butler, *Shakespeare's
Sonnets reconsidered* (1899). Recently there are Joseph
Péquigney's *Such is My Love* and Bruce R. Smith's *Homosexual
Desire in Shakespeare's England* (Chicago, 1997). Rowse thought
Shakespeare was "in imagination and appetite wholly heterosexual;" Schoenbaum attacks the homosexual dissidents as "pseudo-
scholarly," Wilde's boy actor as the "epicene figment of an
invert's imagination." In this author's view Shakespeare's attachment to Southampton had more to do with money, with self-
advancement and ambition, than with sex.

Edward A. Armstrong's *Shakespeare's Imagination* (1946)
detects a peculiar obsessiveness in Shakespeare's make-up.

For A.L. Rowse's theories about the Dark Lady see
*Shakespeare The Man,* and John Bayley, *The Uses of Vision*
(1976). See also John Bayley, "Who was the 'man right fair' of
the Sonnets?" (*Times Literary Supplement,* 4 Jan 1974). For fur-
ther discussion of "the hothouse of sex in his head," see Stephen
Greenblatt's chapter of "Fiction and Friction" in *Shakespearian
Negotiations.* "More than any of his contemporaries,
Shakespeare discovered how to use the erotic power that the the-

atre could appropriate... [it] entailed above all the representation of the emergence of identity through the experience of erotic heat... sexual heat, we recall, is not different in kind from all other heat, including that produced by the imagination. Shakespeare realised that if sexual chafing could not be presented literally on stage, it could be represented figuratively: friction could be fictionalised, chafing chastened into... witty, erotically charged sparring." (pp 88-9).

## THE ABSENCE OF MOTHERS (pp 149-159)

*Sir John Oldcastle,* the play attributed for a while to Shakespeare was the Admiral's reply to the success of Falstaff. It was acted at Hunsden House, Blackfriars, in March 1600.

Barbara Everett (*London Review of Books,* 16 Aug 1990) analyses the new and sterile contemporary disbelief in "character in general and Falstaff in particular. The time span of this disbelief can probably be synchronised with the full professionalising of literary studies into the academic."

One has to sympathise, to some degree, with the problem of Shakespeare critics and academic commentators: the pressure is on them to find and publish contributions to the Shakespeare study industry as a means of asserting their credentials. Yet over the centuries the works themselves have stimulated such lively response from everyone who has set pen to paper that there is little to be said which is not a repetition of earlier minds. Many of the critics of the earlier part of this century who are at present ignored or forgotten have simply had their ideas appropriated, if slightly adapted by more recent scholars. I am struck by those who have hardly published a word, such as George Rylands, an outstanding theatrical academic whose intuitions blazed with convincing illumination. It goes without saying that the aperçues of those directors and actors who work continually with the plays far exceeds the theories of text-bound scholars.

Peter Hall, who directed Dustin Hoffman as Shylock, told the author "Shakespeare wrote *The Merchant* for an avowedly anti-semitic audience yet... how anyone can ever see it as anti-semitic is beyond me. Shylock is not a hypocrite... He's not a hidden character."

Hazlitt's formulation of the romantic process is to be found in his *Lectures on the English Poets* (1818).

## GREEN FIELDS (pp 159-167)

For material relating to the theatres, London and Stratford I return to the basic sources of EC, EKC, Stow and SSC DOC. Chute also places Shakespeare successfully at the centre of authentically realized circumstances of his age. For the discussion of classical sources see T.W. Baldwin, *William Shakespeare's Small Latine of Lesse Greek* (Urbana, 111, 1944)

The facts of John Shakespeare's life:

1556-76 The twenty years are years of prosperity:

1556. Buys two houses; the 'Woolshop' in Henley Street and another in Greenhill Street.

1557. Marries Mary Arden, daughter of his father's landlord at Snitterfield.

1558. Birth of his first child, Joan. (Six other children were born 1562-74, and Edmund in 1580.)

1557-62. Successively borough constable, affeeror (assessor of fines), and chamberlain.

1561. Administers his father's estate.

1564. Birth of William Shakespeare.

1565. Alderman; 1568. Bailiff (Mayor).; 1571. Chief alderman and J.P.

1575. Buys two more houses; sites unknown, but probably the Birthplace, and an adjoining house to the west, destroyed in the fire of 1594. The twenty years 1576-96 appear to be years of adversity.

1577. He ceases to attend council meetings.

1578-9. Mortgages his wife's Wilmcote property, lets Asbies, and sells her share in the Snitterfield estate.

1580. Fined £40 for failing to appear before the court of Queen's Bench to give security that he would keep the peace.

1586. Replaced by another alderman because 'Mr Shaxpere dothe not come to the halles when the be warned, nor hathe not done of longe tyme."

1587. Sued for part of the debt of his brother Henry.

1592. Included in a list of recusants 'for not comminge monethlie to the churche... It is sayd... for feare of process for debtte'.
His fortunes are restored 1596-1601, probably by the poet:

1596. The Grant of Arms.

1597.   His son William buys New Place. Attempts to recover the mortgaged estate from John Lambert.

1599. Applies for leave to impale the arms of Arden.

1601.   Again appears as a member of the borough council.   On 8 September, 'Mr Johannes Shakspeare was buried in Stratford churchyard. (Halliwell, pp. 441-2)

## LIFE MEASURED BY THE ACT (pp 167-176)

See Halliday (pp 90-95) for his documentary summary of the Lord Chamberlain's Men. Holmes is also helpful: that a much padded Kempe played Falstaff is suggested in Mark Honan, *Shakespeare: A Life* (1998);  it seems unlikely. I have drawn also on Enid Welsford, *Fool: His Social and Literary History* (1935). William Oldys (1696-1761) wrote a *Life of Shakespeare*, now lost, but anecdotes from it were printed in George Steevens in his edition of Shakespeare 1778.    John Masefield, *William Shakespeare*, appeared in 1911, containing short appreciations of the poems and plays.   The standard Ben Jonson biography is David Riggs, *Ben Jonson: A Life* (Cambridge, Mass. 1989); but Marchette Chute: *Ben Jonson of Westminster* (New York, 1953) is a valuable source.

## THE COCKLE OF REBELLION (pp 176-183)

Essex was an old-style Catholic aristocrat.   Burghley was an *arriviste* fat on church lands, about which he was extremely superstitions (Thomas pp 90-132); from the highest to the low it was a quarrelsome age; the bad meat diet, constant drinking, continuous pain from small and large ailments put tempers continually on edge. Southampton quarrelled with Montgomery at court over a game of tennis. Raleigh and Essex quarrelled, so did Sidney and Oxford.

Smith makes the point that secrets in Tudor England were extremely difficult to keep, which is why treason so rarely prospered. Stone and Thomas also show at length how privacy was non-existent, spying, prying and questioning were universal, while general curiosity left no sexual indiscretion hidden. If Shakespeare had not been Shakespeare we would certainly have known about it.

The best account of the Poetomachia is to be found in Gurr, *Shakespearian Stage and Playgoing in Shakespeare's London.* Dekker's *Satiromastix* is available in *The Dramatic Works of Thomas Dekker* (ed. F. Bowers, 1953-61). Dekker was the most attractive of Shakespeare's contemporaries, and with his kindliness and charm, a contrast to the arrogance of Ben Jonson. *The Three Parnassus Plays* (ed. J.B. Leishman, 1949) also contain important references to Shakespeare, Jonson, actors, etc..., Will Kempe in *3 Parnassus* refers to Shakespeare having given the "pestilent" fellow Jonson a "purge" in return for his "pill"; Shakespeare refers to the Poetomachia in *Hamlet,* II, ii.

## I AM THAT I AM (pages 183-195)

The Kingsley Amis comment on Hamlet being "nice" like a woman rather than a man should be contrasted with the same author's generally more cynical line on women: (*Jakes Thing,* 1989, pp. 316). I have drawn on J.C. Trewin's *Five & Eighty Hamlets* (1988); also on Auerbach Ch. 12 "Montaigne L'Humaine Condition" in René Girard's analysis of Hamlet's envy, schizophrenia, and especially revenge is masterly (*A Theatre of Envy,* 1991, pp. 279-289): "What Hamlet resents in Ophelia is what any human being always resents in another human being, the visible signs of his own weakness."

Hamlet and Hamnet: Barbara Everett (*London Review of Books*, 31 Mar 1988): "Biographers sometimes speculate on the relevance to the tragedy of the death... of Hamnet. What does-n't however, seem to be noticed is that in the very year of the boy's death Shakespeare's father – or the writer on his behalf – successfully applied for a coat of arms, thus ambitiously attaining the status of Gentleman. It may be that these two events became one in Shakespeare's mind: the seed from which his tragedy of a son began growing."

Kyd's torture is described in Boas (pp. 241-4, 307-311). Kyd brought against Marlowe a political charge of a treasonable nature, and called him "intemperate and of a cruel heart."

In my treatment of *Hamlet* as the study of genius in crisis I am indebted to Anthony Storr, *The School of Genius*. See also L.C. Knights, *An Approach to Hamlet* (1961). Harold Bloom's portentiously titled *Shakespeare: The Invention of the Human* (1999) advances the theory that the Oedipus complex of psychoanalyses should more accurately have been identified as originating in *Hamlet* instead of in the Sophocles play.

## WHOLE MEN SICK (pp 199-204)

The most celebrated account of the flawed quality of *Hamlet* as a play is T.S. Eliot's *Selected Essays* (1952): "So far from being Shakespeare's masterpiece, the play is most certainly an artistic failure." Bradley's essay in *Shakespearian Tragedy* is biographically revealing, as well as still masterly criticism.

I have used Simon Trussler's edition of *The New Inn* (1987). For an early study of Hamlet's character W.W. Goethe's *Wilhelm Meister* (1795) (pp 141-148). For psychoanalytical investigation see Ernest Jones's *Hamlet and Oedipus* (1944). H.G. McCurdy, *The Personality of Shakespeare* (1953) defines personality types of characters and explains the poet's paranoid suspiciousness by virtue of the suppression by Shakespeare of his feminine traits and a homosexual tendency. The dramatist emerges as a bisexual personality, aggressive with wildly fluctuating moods. For J. Bronowski's study of Shakespeare's view of nature see *Shakespeare, the Comprehensive Soul* (BBC Talks 1965). Aubrey Lewis contributes to this collection, so does F. Dessetor on "Religion in Shakespeare". Norman Holland, *Psychoanalysis and Shakespeare* (1966) has a useful chapter. See also Bloom's *The Invention of the Human* (1999). Simon Callow quoted from interview with the author. I have also drawn from Callow's *On Being an Actor* (1984): the "incompleteness of being" is investigated in its wider applications in René Girard's theory of mimetic desire. See also Callow's *Shakespeare, Sex and a Dark Secret* (*Evening Standard*, 8 Oct 1992).

## DOUBLE BLESSING (pp 204-210)

Francis Bacon's Latin works are but one of many indications that Bacon could not have written Shakespeare. Dispute over whether Shakespeare was really Shakespeare continues and intensifies. 20th Century "Authorities" begin with Sigmund Freud, with various claims why a glove-maker's son from Stratford, with only a grammar-school education, could never have written the plays and poems attributed to William Shakespeare. Mass media speculation about this so-called "disputed" authorship has become widespread, reflecting an age which is rife with a need to reconstruct, or re-invent Shakespeare as someone else; *Time Magazine* (15 Feb 1999) – "What if we've actually been tracking the wrong Englishman?" – *The Washington Post* (24 Jan, 1999) "Shakespeare in trouble". There is a monthly broadsheet produced by a Hove-based editor who collects endless "evidence" to demolish the credibility of William Shakespeare. "Why are the spokesmen for Shakespeare so silent?" he asks.

I do not think Shakespeare would have cared either way: his concern was not the same as those who try to prove Shakespeare was not the author of the plays and poems. As G.K. Chesterton expressed it (in his essay "On Shakespeare"), "My greatest proof that Shakespeare *was* Shakespeare was that Shakespeare would not have cared either way or been particularly bothered had the work been attributed to someone else. The great and eternal works of the mediaeval period are the cathedrals; their exquisite alabaster images might have been smashed by the puritans, their colour and glory scratched out, but essentially they remain. Shakespeare's work has a cathedral dimension: anonymous; there not for the glory of its creators, but for its creator's maker. The sane man who is sane enough to see that Shakespeare wrote Shakespeare is the man who is sane enough not to worry whether he did or not." Andrew St. George, *Brothers in Shakespeare's Plays: No Common Tie* (1983) gives an excellent account of the primordial sanctity of family relationships in the works of Shakespeare.

## A SENSE OF LIMIT (pp 210-221)

The very short poems proliferate as new finds for Shakespeare scholars. Gary Taylor (1985) found "Shall I die? Shall I fly..." which John Carey described as feeble. Peter Levi, in his life of Shakespeare, tried again in 1988. As Philip Howard (*The Times*, 21 Sept 1984) wrote, "Shakespeare is a lake in which elephants can swim and lambs can paddle."

Michael Holroyd's observation about critics deserves to be expanded. The portrait of Southampton is in the National Portrait Gallery London; the biographer is A.L. Rowse.

John Donne's sermons, from *John Donne Collected Poetry and Selected Prose* (ed. John Hayward, 1990). On the Shakespeare epitaphs, see Honigmann: *Shakespeare, the Lost Years*, Ch 7 and Ch 9 for *The Phoenix and Turtle*.

## THE GATHERED SELF (pp 221-229)

"Peace proclaims olives," Sonnet 107: for Ben Jonson's relationship with the court of King James see David Rigg, *Ben Jonson* (Ch 6). In the new reign of James I the Chamberlain's men were taken into his service as the King's Servants and Grooms of the Chamber:

> Knowe yee that Wee ... do licence and auctho-
> rize theise our Servauntes Lawrence Fletcher,
> William Shakespeare, Richard Burbage,
> Augustyne Phillippes, Iohn Heninges, Henrie
> Condell, William Sly, Robert Armyn, Richard
> Cowly, and the rest of their Assosiates freely to
> vse and exercise the Arte and faculty of playinge
> ... when the infection of the plague shall
> decrease, as well within theire nowe vsual howse
> called the Globe within our County of Surrey, as
> alsoe within anie towne halls or Moute halls or
> other conveniente places within the liberties and
> freedome of ani other Cittie, vniversitie, towne,
> or Boroughe whatsoever within our said Realmes
> and domynions.   (Letters patent of 19 May
> 1603, Halliwell p.93).

On *Measure for Measure* see Francis Fergusson's 1951 Harvard Lecture (printed in *The Human Image in Dramatic Literature* (New York, 1957).

## DEEDS OF DARKNESS (pp 229-247)

James I was so frightened of being stabbed he wore many doublets as a protective layer, and thus he sweated terribly. I am indebted as source material for this chapter to Stanley Cavell, *Disowning Knowledge*, Ch 3; to Emrys Jones, *Scenic Form in Shakespeare* (1971), and Barbara Everett.  Laurence Olivier's statement comes from Melvyn Bragg, *Laurence Olivier (1989)*. For the biblical and liturgical references see Naseeb Shaheen, *Biblical References in Shakespeare's Tragedies* (1984). No account of *Macbeth* equals that of A.C. Bradley, *Shakespearian Tragedy* (1952). Fr. Henry Garnett, the Jesuit, was tried for high treason on 28 March 1606, but his defence by equivocation did not save him from being hanged on 3 May. Yeats on Shakespeare, see Richard Ellmann, *The Man and the Masks* (1971); also Garry O'Connor *Sean O'Casey, A Life* (1988).

James Joyce *Ulysses* (1957) has illuminating material on the tragedies and the family of Shakespeare (pp. 179-200): "In his trinity of black Wills, the villain Shakebags, Iago, Richard Crookback, Edmund in *King Lear*, two bear the wicked uncles' names. Nay, that last play was written or being written while his brother lay dying in Southwark." See also Leo Tolstoy, *Shakespeare and the Drama* (1906) which finds Shakespeare's view of life immoral, and his works, *King Lear* especially, detestable. See Cavell's reading of *King Lear*, "The Avoidance of Love" Ch. 2 (pp 39-125). For material in this chapter I am also indebted to John Bayley, Trevor Nunn, Jonathan Miller, Derek Jacobi.

## VIOLENT VANITIES (pp 247-255)

The full text of Augustine Phillips's will:

> Item, I geve and bequeathe unto and amongste the hyred men of the Company which I am of, which shalbe at the tyme of my decease, the some of fyve pounds of lawfull money of England to be equally distributed amongeste them, Item, I geve and bequeathe to my Fellowe William Shakespeare a thirty shillings peece in gould, To my Fellowe Henry Condell one other thirty shillinge peece in gould, To my Servaunte Christopher Beeston thirty shillings in gould, To

my Fellowe Lawrence Fletcher twenty shillings in gould [and 'twenty shillings in gould' to his other fellows, Robert Armyne, Richard Coweley, Alexander Cook, Nicholas Tooley]. Item, I geve to Samuell Gilborne my late apprentice, the some of fortye shillings, and my mouse colloured velvit hose, and a white taffety dublet, a blacke taffety suite, my purple cloke, sword and dagger, and my base viall. Item, I geve to James Sands my Apprentice the some of fortye shillings and a citterne a bandore and a lute, to be paid and delivered unto him at the expiracion of his terme of yeres in his indenture of apprenticehood. (Halliwell p. 367)

See also Thomas Heywood, *Apology for Actors* (1612). For this chapter I have drawn again on Coleridge's *Shakespeare Criticism* (1930), on Cavell, and Naseeb Shaheen's *Biblical References in Shakespeare's Tragedies* (pp 175-186); see also G. Wilson Knight, *The Wheel of Fire* (1930); William Empson, *Seven Types of Ambiguity* (1961).

## THE RESTORATION OF MOTHERS (pp 255-261)

On Shakespeare's mother's death, see Georg Brandes *William Shakespeare: A Critical Study* (1898). It influenced the celebrated Shakespeare passage in Joyce's *Ulysses*.

For sources of *Pericles* and of other later plays where some doubts over Shakespeare's authorship persist sees the Oxford *Works*. Also Kenneth Muir, *Shakespeare's Sources* (1977). Barbara Jefford and Peggy Ashcroft to the author.

## FLYING THE COURTS OF PRINCES (pp 261-265)

For this chapter I have drawn on Frances A. Yates, *Shakespeare's Last Plays* (1975). I am especially indebted to the late Iris Murdoch for her several interviews; also to her husband John Bayley. Elias Canetti has supplied a variety of formative perceptions in *Crowds and Power* (1952) and *The Conscience of Words* (1986). This British Nobel-Prize-winning-author influenced Peter Hall in his productions of the history plays at Stratford-upon-Avon. I am grateful to Michael Holroyd for outlining his obsession with *The Tempest*. See also Jean-Paul Sartre *L'Imagination* (Paris, 1965) and C.G. Jung, *Memories, Dreams, Reflections* (1983).

## SICK MEN WHOLE (pp 265-269)

See Lytton Strachey *Elizabeth and Essex* Ch's VIII-XI. An especially striking passage: "Human beings no doubt would cease to be human beings unless they were inconsistent; but the inconsistency of the Elizabethans exceeds the limits permitted to man. Their elements fly off from one another wildly; we seize them; we struggle hard to shake them together into a single compound, and the retort bursts. How is it possible to give a coherent account of their subtlety and their *naiveté*, their delicacy and their brutality, their piety and their lust?" The French Ambassador, De Maisse, commented, "The Court is a prey of two evils – delay and inconstancy; and the cause is the sex of the sovereign."

Simon Forman's comments on performances of Shakespeare's plays are to be found in EKC, II, 337-41; also in *The Case Books of Simon Forman* (ed. H.L. Rowse) (1974).

## WHAT'S IN A FACE? (pp 273-278)

Clifford Bax, *Rosemary for Remembrance* (1948). David Piper in *The Image of the Poet* (Oxford, 1982) has a valuable chapter on Shakespeare images; "Shakespeare, A Wretched Picture and Worse Bust," pp. 11-22. For Piper only the engraving and the bust are authentic images: both are vouched for implicitly in the First Folio (1623). The engraving is the frontispiece, the bust in the church referred to in the celebratory poem by Leonard Digges, among those that preface the plays. They were "vouched for, passed for publication as likenesses of Shakespeare by those who knew him – accepted or, at least not rejected by them."

Piper, however, does not accept the Chandos portrait was proven to be of Shakespeare (as were the other two, however badly executed they were). He writes, "the problem that remains, and is likely to remain ever unproven, is whether its subject is Shakespeare or some other contemporary who shared some physical features with him."


## IN ONE PERSON MANY PEOPLE (pp 278-284)

See Henry James' preface to *The Tempest* (1907, ed. Sir Sidney Lee). Morris Gedge, the keeper in James's story *The Birthplace*, which does not mention either Shakespeare or Stratford, confides to the visiting American couple (and supports the idea of the anonymity of Shakespeare. "There is no author ... There are all the immortal people – *in* the work; but there's nobody else". But then, fearing to lose his job he makes an effort to embroider the legend with delicate improvisations, and yields to his reconstructing imagination. The remarkable discovery of the Belott-Mountjoy lawsuit was made in 1909 by the American scholar Charles William Wallace and his wife Hulda Alfreda (see SS Lives, pp. 645-657). Edmund Shakespeare's death in Southwark: see Chute (p. 239).

## DYING MENSTRUUMS (pp 284-292)

The view of love as an illness is explored in Denis de Rougement's *Passion and Society*, the "tapering off in the man" Shakespeare is illustrated in various legends, admirably summarised in SS Lives (pp. 114-124).

The New Cambridge *Henry VIII* (1990) provides further information on a recent discovery (1981) of a further Globe fire account.

## THE GREAT INVISIBLE (pp 292-297)

Jorge-Luis Borges wrote another short story, *Shakespeare's Memory* (*The Times*, 31 Dec 1985), in which the scholarly protagonist is offered, at a congress, Shakespeare's memory from his youngest days to early April 1616. He asks the man who offers it, "What have you done with Shakespeare's memory?... There was silence, and then he said: "I have written a fictionalised biography which earned the critic's scorn and some commercial success in the United States and in the colonies." The scholar accepts the gift. "A man's memory is not a sum: it is a disorder of undefined possibilities," writes Borges. At first the scholar feels the happiness of being Shakespeare, "in the last the oppression and terror." Finally he passes the gift on to someone else. "Shakespeare's memory was unable to reveal anything other than the facts."

"In my end is my beginning:" for sources of these later chapters we return to those of the early chapters, notably EKC and SSC DOC. For discussion of marriage again see Stone; also André Gide, *The Correspondence between Paul Claude and André Gide* (trans. John Russell, 1952). Pierre Rouve in conversation with the author pointed out the similarities with recent events in Russia.

## LIFE MEASURED BY THE SPACE (pp 297-302)

Shakespeare's will is preserved at Somerset House; a copy was discovered in 1749 by Joseph Greene, Master of Stratford Grammar School. See also EKC; II, SSC DOC for the text; Edgar I. Fripp, *Master Richard Quyny* (1924). T.S. Eliot also observes in *Collected Essays,* that Shakespeare had not a profound view of life as Dante: his vision was expansive rather than intensive (pp. 237-277).

## ANON ANON SIR (pp 302-306)

For accounts of how a gentleman of Shakespeare's wealth and rank would be attended at death and interred see Houlbrooke, also Thomas.

John Dowdell's letter, 10 April 1693, is in the Folger Shakespeare Library: Dowdell accurately quotes Shakespeare's epitaph and the curse, and corroborates John Aubrey's story in his brief life that Shakespeare was a butcher's apprentice.

See notes above on Shakespeare portraiture (David Piper, *The Image of the Poet*): on proof and facts one might consider the famous observation of the French statesman C. M. de Tallyrand-Perigord, *Memoirs* (1891-2) "There is nothing which can so easily be arranged as facts."

# Index

*Note*: WS in the index stands for William Shakespeare; his works are indexed under his name.

publication: pirate, 169, 181; Jonson
and copyright, 181; of WS's plays,
279, 301: *Much Ado About Nothing*,
169; *Othello*, 235; Sonnets, 115–16,
278–82; *see also* Folio, First
Puritanism, 2, 79, 96–7; in Stratford,
18, 25, 291; opposition to theatre,
160, 299; and *Venus and Adonis*,
92–3; and *Measure for Measure*,
224–5; under James I, 241

Quiney, Richard (actor), 293
Quiney, Thomas (son-in-law of WS),
293

Raleigh, Sir Walter, 193, 254, 258;
death, 300
Reformation, 298, 299
religion, *see* Catholicism;
Protestantism; Puritanism
Renolds, William, 84
reputation, 25–7, 33
revenge plays, 230
Reynolds, William (landowner), 301
rhetoric, 23, 100
Richardson, Sir Ralph, 132, 155, 274
Richmond, 212–13
Rochester, John Wilmot, Earl of, 144
Roe, Sir John, 247
Rogers, Paul, 3
Roman heritage, 261
Romney, George: portrait of WS, 273
Ronsard, Pierre de, 304
Rookwood, Ambrose, 240
Rose theatre, Southwark, 58, 73, 104,
161
Rouve, Pierre, 120, 295
Rowe, Nicholas, 14, 93, 274, 292
Rowse, A. L., 143–4, 274
Royal Courts, 25
Royal Shakespeare Company,
Stratford, 3–4
Rutland, Francis Manners, 6th Earl of,
191, 279
Rylands, George, 28, 62, 134, 289

Sadler, Hamnet, 38, 146, 241; in WS's
will, 301
Sadler, Judith, 38, 146, 241

Salusbury, Sir John, 210–11
Salusbury, Thomas, 210–11
Savary, Jérôme, 72
Schoenbaum, Samuel: *Shakespeare's
Lives*, 2
Scofield, Paul, 3
Scott, Sir Walter: *Kenilworth*, 110–11
Seneca, 299
sexuality, 48, 91–2, 95–7, 142–5;
homosexuality, 95–7, 143, 192
Shakespeare, Anne (sister of WS), 15
Shakespeare, Anne (*née* Hathaway;
wife of WS): family, 9, 35;
character, 36, 39, 303; first
pregnancy, 9, 10, 35–6; married life,
9, 11, 12–13, 36–40, 81–3, 120–1,
146, 253–4, 265, 294; in WS's will,
301; widowhood, 303; death, 303;
portrayed in *Venus and Adonis*, 81–2;
in *The Taming of the Shrew*, 121; in
*Antony and Cleopatra*, 253–4
Shakespeare, Edmund (brother of
WS), 15, 38, 292; son, 279, 292;
death, 279
Shakespeare, Gilbert (brother of WS),
15, 20, 38, 246, 292; death, 279
Shakespeare, Hamnet (son of WS), 38,
40; death, 145–8, 185, 201, 204,
263–4
Shakespeare, Joan (first sister of WS),
14
Shakespeare, Joan (sister of WS, born
1559; later wife of William Hart), 15,
20, 38, 279, 291; in WS's will, 301
Shakespeare, John (father of WS):
character, 17–19; career, 14, 17–19;
children, 9–10; relations with WS,
10, 27, 163, 184, 201–2, 220;
disgrace, 25–8, 30–1, 33–4, 184,
241–2, 246; coat of arms, 153;
portrayed as Falstaff, 156; as Lear,
245–6; later life, 163, 216; death,
216, 220; will, 279
Shakespeare, Judith (daughter of WS),
38, 39, 147; loss of twin, 204–5;
marriage, 293, 294; in WS's will,
294, 300
Shakespeare, Margaret (sister of WS),
15

# SHAKESCENES:
## SHAKESPEARE
## FOR TWO
### The Shakespeare Scenebook

## EDITED AND WITH AN INTRODUCTION
## BY JOHN RUSSELL BROWN

Shakespeare's plays are not the preserve of "Shakespearean Actors" who specialize in a remote species of dramatic life. Shakespeare asks to be performed by all good actors. Here in the introduction, "Advice to Actors," and in the notes to each of thirty–five scenes, John Russell Brown offers sensible guidance for those who have little or no experience with the formidable Bard. Thirty-five scenes are presented in newly edited texts, with notes which clarify meanings, topical references, puns, ambiguities, etc. Each scene has been chosen for its independent life requiring only the simplest of stage properties and the barest of spaces. A brief description of characters and situation prefaces each scene and is followed by a commentary which discusses its major acting challenges and opportunities.

**paper • ISBN 1-55783-049-5**

# THE ACTOR AND THE TEXT
## by Cicely Berry

As voice director of the Royal Shakespeare Company, Cicely Berry has worked with actors such as Jeremy Irons, Derek Jacobi, Jonathan Pryce, Sinead Cusack and Antony Sher. *The Actor and The Text* brings Ms. Berry's methods of applying vocal production skills within a text to the general public.

While this book focuses primarily on speaking Shakespeare, Ms. Berry also includes the speaking of some modern playwrights, such as Edward Bond.

As Ms. Berry describes her own volume in the introduction:

" … this book is not simply about making the voice sound more interesting. It is about getting inside the words we use …It is about making the language organic, so that the words act as a spur to the sound …"

**paper•ISBN 1-155783-138-6**

# RECYCLING SHAKESPEARE
## by Charles Marowitz

Marowitz' irreverent approach to the bard is destined to outrage Shakespearean scholars across the globe. Marowitz rejects the notion that a "classic" is a sacrosanct entity fixed in time and bounded by its text. A living classic, according to Marowitz, should provoke lively response—even indignation!

In the same way that Shakespeare himself continued to meditate and transform his own ideas and the shape they took, Marowitz gives us license to continue that meditation in productions extrapolated from Shakespeare's work. Shakespeare becomes the greatest of all catalysts who stimulates a constant re-formulation of the fundamental questions of philosophy, history and meaning. Marowitz introduces us to Shakespeare as an active contemporary collaborator who strives with us to yield a vibrant contemporary theatre.

**paper • ISBN: 1-55783-094-0**

# THE REDUCED SHAKESPEARE COMPANY'S

# COMPLEAT WORKS OF WLLM SHKSPR (abridged)

## by JESS BORGESON, ADAM LONG, and DANIEL SINGER

"ABSL HLRS." —*The Independent* (London)

"Shakespeare writ small, as you might like it! . . . Pithier-than-Python parodies . . . not to be confused with that august English company with the same initials. This iconoclastic American Troupe does more with less."

— *The New York Times*

"Shakespeare as written by *Reader's Digest*, acted by Monty Python, and performed at the speed of the Minute Waltz. So Forsooth! Get thee to the RSC's delightfully fractured *Compleat Works*."

— *Los Angeles Herald*

ISBN 1-55783-157-2 • $8.95 • PAPER

# SHAKESPEARE'S PLAYS IN PERFORMANCE by John Russell Brown

In this volume, John Russell Brown snatches Shakespeare from the clutches of dusty academics and thrusts him centerstage where he belongs—in performance.

Brown's thorough analysis of the theatrical experience of Shakespeare forcibly demonstrates how the text is brought to life: awakened, colored, emphasized, and extended by actors and audiences, designers and directors.

"A knowledge of what precisely can and should happen when a play is performed is, for me, the essential first step towards an understanding of Shakespeare."
—*from the Introduction by John Russell Brown*

**paper•ISBN 1-55783-136-X•**